Selected Prais

Young Woman and the Sea

A *WALL STREET JOURNAL* BEST SUMMER READ

"A revelation [and] much more than a biography. The author uses swimming to explore American society's changing attitudes toward women and sports . . . and nineteen-year-old Trudy Ederle surged on this wave of confidence and emancipation." —*Parade*

"A great summer read. . . . The book swishes around like the tide, from the history of swimming (especially women's swimming and the development of the American crawl) to the conditions that created the English Channel—'some of the roughest and most unpredictable waters in the world'—and its legendary conquerors." —*The New Yorker*

"Stout's moving book recovers the exhilarating story of a young girl who found her true self out in the water and paved the way for women in sports today." —*Publishers Weekly* **(starred review)**

"Glenn Stout brings the women's sports pioneer back to life with an engaging, deeply researched account." —*Sports Illustrated*

"Poignant. . . . Stout's biography does a good job of fishing Ederle out of the deep waters of historical forgetfulness and setting her in the context of her times." —**Maureen Corrigan,** *Fresh Air*

"Masterly." —*Christian Science Monitor*

Selected Books by Glenn Stout

Tiger Girl and the Candy Kid
The Pats
The Selling of the Babe
Fenway 1912
The Cubs
Nine Months at Ground Zero
Red Sox Century
Yankees Century

Young Woman and the Sea

How Trudy Ederle
Conquered the English Channel
and Inspired the World

Glenn Stout

Mariner Books
New York   Boston

To my daughter, Saorla,
granddaughter Claire Anne,
and young women everywhere
who might someday ask
"What for?"

HarperCollins books may be purchased for educational, business,
or sales promotional use. For information, please email the Special Markets
Department at SPsales@harpercollins.com.

A hardcover edition of this book was published in 2009
by Houghton Mifflin Harcourt.

FIRST MARINER BOOKS PAPERBACK EDITION PUBLISHED 2022.

Designed by Brian Moore

The Library of Congress has catalogued a previous edition of this title as follows:
Stout, Glenn, 2009.
Young woman and the sea: how Trudy Ederle conquered
the English Channel and inspired the world / Glenn Stout.
p. cm.
Includes bibliographical references and index.
ISBN 978-0-618-85868-2 (hardcover)
1. Ederle, Gertrude, 1906–2003. 2. Swimmers — United States — Biography.
3. Women swimmers — United States — Biography. I. Title.
GV838.E34S76 2009
797.2'1092 — dc22 [B] 2008053370

ISBN 978-0-06-330539-7 (pbk.)

24 25 26   CPI   10 9 8 7 6 5

Contents

The Channel swim, being within possibility but never easy, is as satisfying a feat as can be imagined in any field of physical enterprise. None but first class athletes can presume to essay it; but they can enter the lists from all parts of the world and the waters thereof, just as they are, without implements and without artifice, men and women against wind and tide.

—*Times* of London, August 7, 1926

Prologue

The English Channel, 51°09' N, 1°26' E, approximately 2.5 miles SSE of Kingsdown Beach, Great Britain. 17:30 French Summer Time, August 6, 1926.

She has been in the water for nearly twelve hours, tossed up and down, forward and back, upside down and sideways in the froth and spray of the channel between France and England. The white cliffs of Dover loom over the horizon in the fading light only a few miles ahead, and Cape Gris-Nez, the headland where she entered the water in France, is now nearly twenty miles and half a day behind her. The water temperature hovers just above sixty degrees, cold, no warmer than the surrounding air. It is raining and the white-capped waves are running nearly six feet, tossing her up and down and up again with each surge. A stiff wind blows the spray from atop the waves back into her face.

But Trudy Ederle doesn't really notice, not anymore. Every moment, every breath, every stroke of her arms and kick of her legs is the same. The young woman swimming in the sea is wearing a nearly scandalous two-piece, silk swimming suit. She is covered in sheep grease and petroleum jelly and wears a tight rubber bathing cap over her close-cropped auburn hair. Amber-tinted goggles shield her eyes from the salt water. To her, the sea is not the slate gray it appears from above, or blue, or green. Through the goggles it is a delicious golden ochre.

She has been swimming since dawn, first at twenty-eight strokes per minute, and now, after almost twelve hours, a slightly slower twenty-two or twenty-four, swimming a new stroke known as the American crawl, a stroke no one has ever used to cross the English Channel.

In all of human history, only five men have ever made such a crossing. No woman has ever swum the Channel before, and only a handful have ever tried. For more than a year, however, the world has followed Trudy's quest, first tracking her failure and now, on this day, hoping for her success. If she makes it across she will be the most recognized and famous woman in the world. Everywhere, from the Ederles' summer home in Highlands, New Jersey, to the White House in Washington, D.C., and Lloyd's of London, where oddsmakers give her only a slim chance of succeeding, everyone is listening to the radio and reading newspaper bulletins and rooting for her to succeed. She has captured their imaginations. And if she succeeds, she will win their hearts as well.

Trudy does not think of this, any of it, for such thoughts left her consciousness hours ago, and now there is only this moment, broken into breaths. Every fourth stroke she tilts her head, takes a mouthful of air, then slowly exhales from her nose, watching the bubbles dance before her face as if they belong to some other creature swimming below her, just out sight, and she is somehow riding on its crest.

It is quiet but it is not completely silent. The sea makes its own muffled sound, and she cannot discern the splash that comes from her arms pinwheeling into the water from the slap of the sea itself against her body, or that of the waves colliding and collapsing and rising again. She is half in, half out of the water, testing the surface beneath the stray gull that sounds overhead, pulling herself and being pulled by the tides and the currents at the same time.

There are two boats, motorized tugs, one several yards behind her to the starboard side, and another, farther off to the stern, both straining to keep her in sight as she lifts and falls and slips between the waves. The faint hum of the engines spreads like velvet in the water, as natural and soundless as the beating of her own heart.

One boat holds her father, her sister Meg, her ghostwriter, Julia, and her trainer and coach, Bill Burgess, one of those five men who have swum the Channel before. The second boat holds the press, reporters wrapped in rain gear scratching notes on pads of paper and typing out dispatches in the pilothouse to be sent ashore by wireless. They are waiting for the final moment: the instant she makes it across, is pulled from the water short of her goal, or, as some fear, slips from consciousness and disappears forever beneath the waves. Whatever happens—success, failure, or tragedy—will be a headline the next morning. Trudy Ederle will be either a heroine or a figure of pity known to nearly every man, woman, and child who can read a newspaper.

She does not think of this. Her thoughts have slowed, and she is all sense—touch and taste, sight and sound.

She feels these things from afar, notes the sensations, and continues as if she is a kind of artist taking stock of the features of a model, working on a still life, oblivious to time. She does not, really, feel them herself, for her consciousness has closed her off from her own body. She is only a spectator peering out from far inside, focused only on this next stroke, this next breath.

She is exhausted but not tired. She is cold but does not feel cold. How strange is that? Her lips are chapped and cracking, her thighs and armpits chaffed and stinging, her ears inflamed, her tongue swollen by salt water. Her limbs are numb, and her feet and legs kick on of their own accord. But her center is warm, even glowing, the embers protected deep within.

And there is no place in the world she would rather be. She has hours still to go, and she is deliriously, hopelessly happy.

On the rare clear day when fog and clouds do not obscure the view, at the English Channel's narrowest point, when one gazes toward England from Cape Gris-Nez in France, the English coastline looks tantalizingly close. The gleaming cliffs of Dover stretch along the horizon in a horizontal stream like a landscape in an oil painting, a smear of titanium white touched with cadmium yellow, daubed above an azure sea. From the heights at Cape Gris-Nez, where wildflowers dance in the offshore breezes, the waters in mid-Channel, filled with boats of all shapes and sizes, can look deceptively calm, even placid. Swimming from one coast to the other seems more a matter of willpower and stamina than anything else, a difficult task, to be sure, and one that requires significant discipline and great athletic ability, but not an impossible one.

Yet those clear days that make the Channel swim seem so feasible are not just uncommon, but, in fact, a cruel illusion. There are reasons far, far fewer human beings have swum the English Channel than have climbed Mount Everest. More than three thousand people have stood on top of the world since Tensing Norgay and Sir

Edmund Hillary first accomplished the feat in 1953, yet only nine hundred or so solo swimmers—one out of every ten who make the attempt—have succeeded in swimming the English Channel. The fine weather that makes the journey appear so attainable rarely lasts for long. Conditions in the English Channel can and do change in minutes. A day that begins with gentle breezes and bright sunshine can end in a full-blown gale that even today regularly drives huge ships up onto the shore and sends even the most experienced sailors to their deaths. The waters of the Channel, even in midsummer, in bright sunshine, are bone-chillingly cold, rarely warming much above sixty degrees. Bad weather, not good, is the norm. On most days both the French and the English coasts are obscured behind banks of fog and thick clouds. Each shore is invisible not only from the other, but also to most ships that ply the passage in between. The proximity of either shore provides little comfort.

The waters of the Channel are rarely quiet. The surf claws at each coast with ferocity, relentlessly wearing it down and occasionally and inexorably causing portions of the cliffs and headlands along the shore to collapse and slip into the sea. In this way the Channel grows ever wider each day as the tides and currents funneled through the narrow passage between the northern Atlantic and the North Sea cause the waters of the Channel to lift and heave as if trying to rip the fabric of what the French refer to as *La Manche*, "the sleeve."

To fully understand the achievement of Trudy Ederle, one must also understand the Channel itself, which is unlike any other body of water on the planet. The waters of the North Sea and those of the Atlantic, brought together in a vicious collision that first created the Channel, have yet to rest. They grasp and pull at everyone and everything that breach their waters. One does not cross the Channel as much as one learns its intricacies and then tries to sneak across before they turn violent and deadly.

Today, those swimmers who choose to test the waters of the Channel do so for the same reasons that Sir Edmund Hillary chose to climb Mount Everest—because "it is there," a well-defined challenge and a way to test oneself. If the weather cooperates and the swimmer is in adequate physical condition, psychologically prepared to swim for upward of half a day, and can avoid hypothermia, the path across the Channel is well known. Over time the captains of escort boats and swimmers have managed to decode the complicated tides and currents, and modern sports medicine is adept at preparing swimmers for the challenge through healthy nutrition and exercise and assisting them along the way with proper sustenance and fluids.

None of this was the case in 1926. A true pioneer, Trudy Ederle enjoyed none of these advantages. She did not choose to swim the Channel as some kind of complicated existential test, but for reasons that were both larger than herself and intensely personal. She wanted to swim the Channel, but—at least at the beginning—she did not need to do so.

She knew, of course, that no woman had ever swum the Channel before. From 1922 through 1925 she had been the greatest female swimmer the world had ever seen, winning Olympic medals and setting more than a dozen world records, leaving the English Channel as her only remaining challenge. While she wanted to prove to those who believed a woman could not swim the Channel that, in fact, a woman could, and that she was that woman, Trudy Ederle was no feminist swimming for a cause. Although she was fully aware of the significance of doing what no woman had ever done before, she first decided to try to swim the Channel in 1925 simply because she had nothing left to accomplish in her sport and because others—her coaches and her family—believed she could.

She failed in that attempt, pulled from the water only halfway across, and afterward members of the crowd nodded knowingly, certain that if Trudy Ederle could not swim the English Channel, then in all likelihood no woman could. And even if a woman ever did swim the Channel, she would not do so using the American crawl. And, most assuredly, her name would not be Trudy Ederle.

The only way for Trudy to prove everyone wrong was to try again—and succeed. Swimming the English Channel became a challenge to her imagination. Crossing that divide would prove to be the ultimate test of man's—and a woman's—endurance.

1

Overboard

IT WAS A PERFECT EARLY summer morning, the kind that remains etched in the memory forever, the sky a brilliant blue and the air cool and crisp as a white linen sheet hung out to dry. In the Lower East Side neighborhood known as Kleindeutschland, or, to outsiders, as Little Germany, the morning of June 15, 1904, made it possible for residents to forget their twelve-hour workdays and harsh living conditions in darkened tenements. The day had finally come.

In their tenement at 404 East Fifth Street, thirty-one-year-old Anna Weber, her husband, Frank, and their two children, Emma, ten, and Frank Jr., seven, were up early. While Anna made lunch and carefully packed it in a basket, the children danced around the apartment, periodically sticking their heads out the window, hardly able to contain themselves. Feeling the breeze and seeing the clear sky overhead, they squealed with delight and jabbered excitedly about the adventure soon to come.

For weeks the young family had looked forward to the annual excursion sponsored by St. Mark's Lutheran Church, where most residents of Kleindeutschland worshipped. The outing had come to mark the beginning of summer, and this year Reverend Haas of St. Mark's had rented an enormous steamship, the *General Slocum*, capable of carrying as many as three thousand passengers, to ferry church members up the East River and into Long Island Sound to a park. There, at a place called Locust Grove, they planned to spend the day playing games, listening to music, picnicking, and splashing and playing in the cool waters of the sound. For one day, anyway, they would all be able to forget the smell of rotting garbage and offal hanging in the air, the constant noise and clatter of the streets, and the struggle to adapt to a new country. For one day they would live the life they aspired to, one of leisure and joy. In the Webers' apartment Emma and Frank gulped down their breakfast then dressed quickly in their best summer clothes, urging their parents to hurry up.

The family made their way to the Third Street pier, just north of Houston Street, arriving early so they could meet up with Anna's sister, Martha, and her brother Paul and his wife and three young children. As the youngsters played together on the pier, anticipation grew, and when the *Slocum* finally appeared steaming upriver just before 8:00 A.M., a few cheers and squeals of delight sounded along the pier. Even though no one would be allowed to board the vessel until 8:45 A.M. and it was not scheduled to depart until 9:30, the Weber family got into line, anxious to get a good spot on deck from which to enjoy the journey up the East River.

Although the crowd on the pier included many men, Anna's husband was one of only a few dozen fortunate enough to be among the thirteen hundred people waiting to board the steamship. It was a Wednesday, a workday, and most fathers could not dare risk taking a day off, not even for this. Most simply walked their families to the pier, said their goodbyes, and headed off to work, leaving their wives and children to enjoy the rare holiday from city living.

One of New York's largest wheel-driven passenger steamships, the *General Slocum*, made primarily of oak and pine, was 235 feet long and 37 feet wide, weighed 1,300 tons, and boasted of three decks. A side-wheeler, on each side of the boat at midships was an enormous paddle wheel thirty-one feet across and sporting twenty-six paddles.

As the crowd grew, the twenty-two-man crew busied itself on board, cleaning the decks, polishing the brass, and loading up the last supplies needed for the trip—ice, refreshments, and glassware. In the morning light the *Slocum*, covered in coat after coat of thick white paint, gleamed beneath the sun, making the ship, which had first launched in 1891, appear almost new.

At 8:45 A.M. a member of the crew unceremoniously unhooked the chain that ran across the gangplank. Reverend Haas stood at the end of the gangway and greeted the passengers personally as they arrived on board. Anna and her extended family made their way to the middle deck toward the prow of the boat. As the children went exploring the adults warned them to stay within earshot, then chatted and laughed and leaned on the rails, watching the river traffic and seeing Manhattan come to life. Finally, just after 9:30 A.M., as a few final stragglers raced down the pier and crossed the gangplank, the engines churned, and the *Slocum* pulled away from the pier and into the East River, black coal smoke pouring from each of the two stacks that towered over the deck.

There was no rush. The *Slocum* leisurely moved up the East River, slowly gaining speed. The water was like glass, and those aboard the vessel could barely tell the ship was moving, yet at full steam she elegantly and sleekly ripped through the water at sixteen knots. On one of the decks a German band played familiar songs—American tunes, like "Swanee River," as well as "On the Beautiful Rhine" and other German songs, giving the journey the feel of something like a moving carnival. It was a perfect day—everyone kept saying so.

But just after 10:00 A.M., as the boat steamed up the East River toward Long Island Sound, a young boy exploring the lower deck at amidships, just in front of the pilothouse, sniffed the air. Woodsmoke. Living in the tenements, where even the smallest fire could spread rapidly and endanger dozens, if not hundreds of residents, even young children were attuned to the fear of fire. The boy sensed that there was something not right with the smell of woodsmoke below decks. Glancing around he noticed a small puff of smoke rising slowly up a narrow stairway.

Turning on his heels, the boy found a deckhand, told the young man that he smelled smoke, and led the crewman back to the top of the stairs. The sailor then followed his nose down the stairs to the doorway to a storage room. At the bottom of the steps, barely visible, he saw a few faint wisps of white smoke escaping from beneath the door, then rising up the stairs and rapidly dissipating.

Inside a small fire was smoldering. The floor was littered with straw and excelsior that had been used as packing material, and sometime earlier that morning, somehow, an ember had fallen to the floor, likely from a discarded match used to light a lamp or from the ash of a cigarette or cigar. There it had smoldered and perhaps even briefly turned to flame, but behind the closed door and virtually starved of oxygen, the fire barely stayed lit. Had the door remained closed for the rest of the day, it may well have gone out on its own.

But the deckhand, poorly trained and inexperienced, made a terrible mistake. Instead of calling one of his superiors for assistance and then preparing to fight the fire, he impulsively opened the door.

After a moment of hesitation, as if taking in a big breath, the fire inhaled the precious oxygen the open door now provided and roared to life. The flames licked upward and the excelsior burst into flame, nearly filling the room and sending a blast of heat toward the doorway. The crewman suddenly realized his mistake and panicked yet again. Instead of slamming the door shut and retreating, calling an alarm, he left the door open and tried to smother the flames with the only item within reach—a bag of charcoal. He threw the heavy bag on the source of the fire, which momentarily squashed flames, leaving only smoke. The deckhand raced away to get help, but instead of closing the door, he left it wide open.

With each step he took, oxygen and flame combined to kill. The fires roared back to life, and within minutes the flames raced out the open door and up the stairs. The blaze began to spread quickly as the wooden vessel, covered by layer upon layer of highly flammable paint, proved to be near-perfect fuel.

By the time the deckhand and other crew members made their way to the lower deck, the fire was serious, but not out of control. Yet they did not panic, not yet. The boat was equipped with standpipes and water hoses, and if the crew could get water to the fire quickly, there was still time to quench the flames.

As rapidly as possible the crew pulled the hoses from the reels on which they hung and twisted the valves to open the flow of water. The water came, but instead of flowing through the hoses to the nozzle, as soon as the hoses became pressurized, they split, and instead of a stream of water being directed at the fire, the water simply spilled harmlessly—and ineffectively—over the deck.

Although the *General Slocum* had been launched in 1891, the canvas hoses had never been tested or even adequately inspected since. Fourteen years of exposure to the elements left them brittle and rotten.

The crewmen quickly processed the meaning of that failure and quickly abandoned their duties, racing toward the upper decks where more than thirteen hundred passengers were still oblivious to the danger spreading below.

Anna Weber and her party were chatting happily, unaware of

the growing alarm down below, when all of a sudden a large puff of smoke belched out of a stairwell. Everyone stopped talking for a moment, and then someone quipped, "Don't mind that, it's just the chowder cooking." Anna let loose a nervous laugh, but within seconds flame followed smoke, and then the passengers heard the crew racing through the ship, yelling "fire" and spreading panic as fast as the flames.

In a heartbeat everyone on deck leapt into action. Anna, like nearly every other mother aboard the vessel, began screaming and calling for her children. Anna's husband raced into the crowd to find them and disappeared almost instantly.

It was a perilous situation, but not yet a very deadly one, for dozens of piers lined the river's edge. The captain of the *Slocum*, Edward Van Schaik, was now aware that his boat was on fire. All he needed to do was throttle back on the engines and pull alongside the nearest pier, an act that would have taken only a minute or two and would have given most of his passengers a chance to disembark.

But like the crewman who had first discovered the blaze, Van Schaik also made a fateful error. Looking down to either side from his vantage point in the pilothouse, although he saw smoke, he thought the fire was smaller and somewhat more contained than it was. He misjudged the seriousness of the situation, and, instead of fearing for the safety of his passengers, his first concern was that if he pulled up to a dock the fire might spread from his vessel, cause the pier to catch on fire, and then, perhaps, cause a larger fire onshore. Van Schaik decided instead to keep steaming upriver at full speed. He knew the East River well and planned to run the ship aground on North Brother Island, a twenty-acre islet in the entrance to Long Island Sound.

Although North Brother Island was less than five minutes away, to those on board the vessel each subsequent second was an eternity. No one knew Van Schaik's plans—all they knew was that flames and smoke were rapidly approaching. Anna Weber heard a man calling to "get the life preservers," and like dozens of other passengers, Anna climbed atop chairs and tables to reach the deck ceiling where the preservers were stored overhead. Some were wired fast, and others crumbled to the touch, but some passengers managed to pull some loose then strap them on each other and their children.

In a sense, Anna was lucky. She was unable to find a preserver. Those who did leapt overboard, where they bobbed to the surface for a moment, thinking they were safe, but then, after only a few seconds, most began to sink. Like the fire hoses, the life preservers on board the *Slocum* also dated from 1891. Their canvas covers had rotted, and the cork used to provide flotation had degraded into dust, losing all buoyancy. Instead of saving lives, as the cork dust became waterlogged the life preservers became dead weight. One might as well have strapped on a concrete block.

Some passengers and crew members then turned their attention to the vessel's lifeboats, which, like the preservers, were plentiful, more than enough to save everyone. But they too were useless. At some time in the past they had been wired fast where they hung and were now impossible to lower into the water.

By now portions of the middle deck were ablaze, and flames ran horizontally across the ceiling. Anna Weber felt the heat on her face and her hair caught fire. Each breath was like the blast from a furnace, and every surface she touched with her hands blistered her flesh. The crowd surged and carried Anna, still screaming for her children and husband, toward the side of the boat.

As the fire grew it created a terrible dilemma for some. Mothers had to choose between the prospect of burning to death with their children or jumping overboard with them into the waters of the East River. For most, the fear of fire proved more powerful than the fear of drowning. As the boat steamed toward North Brother Island, hundreds of passengers, one after the other, from all sides and all decks, leapt or were pushed into the water.

Most didn't have a chance. Only a handful of the passengers knew how to swim. It seems unbelievable today, but one hundred or so years ago the ability to swim was almost entirely unknown, a skill practiced by only a few men and virtually no women, for in the Victorian era swimming, for a woman, was considered immoral. Learning to swim was taboo.

By the time the boat lurched to a halt in the shallows of North Brother Island, hundreds had jumped overboard and already drowned, while hundreds more had burned to death as the decks began collapsing on one another. Yet hundreds more still remained aboard the vessel, and now the bow of the boat was buried in the sandy bottom only twenty feet offshore in seven feet of water, while the stern lay only fifty feet from shore in thirty feet of water. For those still huddling along the railing, safety was only a few strong swim strokes away.

For most, however, making it to land was as daunting and as likely as making it across the English Channel. Even those few who could swim were burdened by layer upon layer of heavy woolen clothing that acted like a straitjacket.

Still, they tried, mothers and sons and daughters alike. Human beings poured from the vessel, leaping and diving and even being thrown, and for a few moments the water around the boat was alive with people. Anna Weber, like most of the women, could not swim but neither could she convince herself to jump. She somehow found a rope dangling over the side and lowered herself into the water, but since she could not swim, even as the boat kept burning and she felt the flames begin to scorch her hair again, she held fast. She watched as everyone struggled to stay afloat, children grabbing onto their mothers in terror, but with each passing second one head after another slipped beneath the surface. The few who could swim and somehow managed to stay afloat despite their heavy garments had to fight off the desperate grips of those who did not.

Anna was one of the few lucky ones. A man who could swim— she never learned who—grabbed her and convinced her to let go of the rope and somehow pulled her to shore. But hundreds drowned within only a few yards of the beach, some in water so shallow that had they only thought to stand, they would have survived. Yet these nonswimmers were in such fear of the water that as soon as they hit the surface they immediately panicked, breathed in water, and drowned.

Soon screams of panic turned first to soft moans and then to silence, replaced by the crackling roar of the huge vessel fully engulfed in flame. In only fifteen minutes the *Slocum* burned to the waterline and then bobbed on the surface, steam and smoke rising in the air.

The scene on the beach at North Brother Island was horrific. Each wave delivered more and more bodies to the beach, while hundreds of bodies bobbed face down in the water. Most survivors did not scream or wail or cry, not yet, but stood or sat on the beach in stunned silence, in shock. Anna found her husband on the beach, alive, but nearly naked, his clothes burned off. But their two children were gone, as was her sister, brother, sister-in-law, and, save for the youngest, an infant who miraculously survived, her children as well.

With the carcass of the boat sitting so close to shore, it did not seem possible that so many had died. Captain Van Schaik, who managed to make his way to shore after running the boat aground, was incredulous at the carnage. "I do not understand," he said a short time later, "how so many were lost." While approximately 300 passengers survived, a total of 1,021 victims were eventually recovered from both the boat itself, trapped under collapsing decks, and from the waters of the East River. Many of the drowned were found still clutching one another.

The disaster was the biggest single loss of life in the history of New York City at the time and remained so until the terrorist attacks of September 11, 2001. Although the vast majority of those who died were residents of Kleindeutschland, all New York mourned. The newspaper descriptions of the panic on board the vessel and the photographs of the bodies of so many women and children laid out on the gravel beach at North Brother Island were almost unbearable.

Women, in particular, were affected, for in the body of each mother and each son or daughter they saw themselves and saw just how random and pointless and unnecessary each death had been. While the government quickly reacted to the tragedy and concluded that the dead were victims not only of the greed of the company that operated the vessel, Van Schaik's poor decision, the cowardice of many crew members, and the corruption of Tammany Hall officials whose safety inspections of the vessel had taken place on paper only, the women of New York City and some other enlightened members of the public arrived at an even broader conclusion. While greed and corruption had certainly played a role in the tragedy, so too did an outdated and oppressive set of social mores that discouraged women from learning how to swim and take control of their own destiny. Most of those who had known how to swim—mostly male crew members and young men and boys—had survived. Those who did not know how to swim—mothers and young women and girls—had not.

It was murder, pure and simple—death by repression. They had been murdered as surely as if they had been tied to one another, ferried far offshore, weighed down with stones, and dropped into the depths. The broken hoses, tattered life jackets, and inaccessible life-boats did not, in the end, matter as much as the oppressive moral climate that prevented women from learning one of the most basic skills of survival. They never had a chance.

That realization, like a pebble dropped in the water that sends out a single small ripple, would, over time, grow into a mighty wave that would lift all women, sending one, Trudy Ederle, across the English Channel.

2

The Challenge

MARKED BY LAND'S END on the southwest coast of England and
the Strait of Dover to the east, the English Channel stretches some
350 miles in length, an arm of the Atlantic Ocean that joins the Atlantic to the North Sea. Relatively shallow, with a depth that generally varies between 500 and 150 feet in mid-Channel, at its widest
point the Channel is more than 150 miles across. Yet at its narrowest,
the Strait of Dover between the English city of Dover and the French
city of Calais, the Channel is only twenty-one miles wide. In good
weather, one can stand on either shore and see across to the other
side, making the crossing of the Channel a tantalizing prospect.

There are no witnesses to the first human crossing of the English
Channel, no ancient account of daring celebrated in poetry or some
other epic. Yet for as long as human beings have gazed across the English Channel toward the thin strip of land on the opposite horizon,
they have dreamed of crossing it. Sometime after the last ice age ended
nearly ten thousand years ago, the first boat crossing was made in a
boat carved by means of stone tools from a great earthen log. This first
trip was likely an accidental excursion that began in coastal marshes
and pools in pursuit of game and fish before a rising tide and too-
strong current pulled the boat and its occupants into the sea. After a
number of hours or days adrift, they came to rest across the Channel
on the opposite shore, where they were likely greeted with hostility by
local residents, if not attacked and killed on the spot.

Over time, as boatbuilding and navigational skills increased, human beings learned to make this journey on purpose, and scholars
agree that by 2000 B.C. cross-Channel human contact was a more

or less regular occurrence. Yet even as these crossings became commonplace, they were never without danger.

If one of these intrepid early travelers were knocked or swept overboard, unless he or she was able to grasp onto something that floated and reboard the vessel, death in the cold Channel waters was only a few moments away. If the entire ship was swamped and sunk, unless the vessel was very close to shore, exposure to the water meant certain death. That is because in all likelihood these early travelers shared the same deficit as the passengers on the *Slocum*—they could not swim. That ability was as lost and unavailable to them as the ability to breathe underwater or fly through the air like a bird.

Unlike many of our relatives in the animal kingdom, human beings, like other primates, cannot swim by instinct. Although a human baby will instinctively hold its breath when submerged and move about as if still immersed in amniotic fluid, the infant will make no attempt to surface and breathe. By the time children are only a year or two old, most have lost the instinct to hold their breath, which is why there are labels on buckets and pails that warn parents against leaving young children alone in proximity to anything that can hold even a few inches of water. Even a few moments under water can be enough to cause drowning.

Nevertheless, in some other, mostly warmer parts of the globe, human beings have been swimming for thousands of years, a skill they probably learned while looking for food along the shore and in the shallows. The earliest visual depiction of swimmers dates from the Stone Age, and swimmers are depicted on clay seals and bas-reliefs that date back to the beginning of civilization itself, as the Egyptians, Minoans, Assyrians, Greeks, and many other ancient cultures were known to swim, some apparently even using a version of the now familiar overarm stroke known as the "crawl" or, more commonly today, the "freestyle" stroke. In ancient Greece, surrounded by the warm waters of the Mediterranean, the swimming tradition was such a central part of Greek lifestyle and culture that one could not hold public office unless one knew how to swim.

After the fall of Greece, swimming remained popular under Roman rule, and, as the Roman Empire spread to Europe, the knowledge of how to swim, like that of sailing, was one of many cultural improvements exported to the nether reaches of the empire. In fact, a

Marseilles-based Greek named Pitheas made the first known voyage by sail into the English Channel, and for the next two thousand years the boat remained the only way possible to cross the Channel.

Yet even as the Romans conquered most of western Europe, they did not pass on their knowledge of how to swim to the local population, and after Rome fell in the fourth century and the empire fractured and split apart, the ability to swim became an ever more elusive skill known to only a select few. To most Europeans, particularly of the peasant class, large bodies of water came to be objects of fear, the domain of monsters and other beasts real and imagined. Even smaller bodies of water such as rivers, streams, and swamps were viewed warily, the domain of unhealthy vapors and the cause of mysterious fevers, illnesses, and unexplained disappearances.

The ability to swim became a rare skill that was practiced in secret, if at all, and so charged with mystical significance that most people began to connect it with the supernatural. Trial by water—*indicium aquae*—was believed to be an infallible test to ferret out witches and others suspected of practicing the black arts. Suspected witches and wizards were thrown into the water, often while bound. If the accused sank and drowned, he or she was presumed to be innocent, while those who fought against their fate and kicked until they floated—in effect, until they swam—were instantly judged guilty and often executed. First performed in the ninth century, the practice was used throughout most of western Europe. Although it ceased to be an official English law under Henry III in 1219, for the next six centuries the ritual, also known as "swimming a witch," was still widely practiced in England and elsewhere.

Although swimming was a lost art among most Europeans, the skill did not entirely disappear—swimming was one of the seven skills required of knights. Yet most western Europeans were probably not even aware that human beings *could* swim without supernatural assistance.

By the fourteenth and fifteenth centuries swimming had, in fact, all but disappeared in the western world. In the wake of the Protestant reformation, increasingly conservative moral values combined with simple superstition to make the act of swimming a virtual sin. To swim, one had to remove most, if not all, clothing, which was thought to lead inevitably to impure thoughts in regard to sex. Nakedness was so discouraged by both the Catholic and Protestant churches that even simple bathing was taboo. At Cambridge University any student caught swimming risked a public flogging, a fine, and a day in the stocks. People didn't learn to swim because there was no one to teach them.

It took the written word—and books—to begin to effect a change. The first book on swimming was published in 1538 by Nicolas Wynman, a German professor of languages, and entitled *A Dialogue on the Art of Swimming*. The volume provided rudimentary instruction in the breaststroke and presented swimming not as some mystery, but as a simple skill that could be acquired and learned. A second book, *L'Art de Nager* (*The Art of Swimming*) by the French author Melchisedech Thevenot, published in 1696, described the breaststroke in more detail, and after the book was translated into English it received wide distribution and became the standard swimming manual. In 1754 the physician Richard Russell further demystified swimming when he began prescribing seawater baths to patients and members of the nobility. Over the next hundred years or so swimming became more commonplace and more acceptable, although the practice of "swimming a witch" was still used by the ignorant in rural areas of England well into the nineteenth century.

In Europe, the breaststroke became, for all intents and purposes, swimming. Over time more and more people learned the stroke. Because one could swim the stroke while still clothed, and even then the bulk of the body remained underwater, hidden from view, with only the head above the surface, the breaststroke did not offend moral sensibilities. Although the stroke was easy to learn and required relatively little effort to stay afloat, it was not particularly efficient or fast, as one soon tired of keeping the head unnaturally raised above the water. Its use was almost exclusive to calmer waters—protected bays, sleepy rivers, ponds, and private baths.

No one purposely swam in the open ocean, far from shore where waves could make keeping the head out of water difficult and exhaustion caused by swimming while clothed was dangerous. That was considered madness. The notion that anyone might one day swim a distance as great as that of the English Channel seemed as likely as man one day reaching the moon.

For almost as long as men and women have gazed across the Channel they have also schemed and dreamed about various ways to cross

it. For centuries dreamers had imagined one day digging a tunnel beneath the Channel, while others prophesied that humans would one
day cross the Channel in the air, like the birds that flew over its waters so effortlessly. Yet despite these dreams, until the late eighteenth
century, passage by boat remained the only possible way of crossing
the Channel. Then, in 1782, two French brothers, Joseph and Jacques
Montgolfier, heralded a new mode of travel.

The brothers, who operated a paper mill, noticed that not only did
the smoke from their operation rise into the air, but when one brother
filled a paper bag with smoke, it too rose in the sky. Inspired, the two
brothers concluded that if they could build a bag large enough and
fill it with heated air, it might be possible to lift a man into the sky.

After nearly a year of experimentation, on June 4, 1783, they succeeded in building an unmanned balloon that rose more than a mile
into the air, and within a few months they succeeded in lifting a man
off the ground.

The accomplishment spawned a period of something approaching
balloon-mania among the public, and soon dozens of other French-
men were not only copying the brothers, but trying to improve upon
their design. These early balloonists soon discovered that not only
could they rise in the air, but once aloft the balloon could be driven
by the winds and provide an utterly new way to travel. After a series
of successful flights on land, for these early balloonists a trip across
the English Channel became the obvious and undeniable goal.

Jean Pierre Francois Blanchard succeeded in doing just that. After
building his own balloon and making a series of land-based flights,
he traveled to England to make his attempt. On January 7, 1785,
with another balloonist on the French side of the Channel waiting
for favorable weather to launch his own balloon and make his own
crossing, Blanchard and an American doctor, John Jeffries, who had
served as a British Army surgeon during the Revolutionary War,
took to the air at Dover Castle.

Catching the prevailing wind, the balloon floated eastward and
success seemed certain. Then the balloon suddenly began losing air
and plummeted toward the sea. For a time the two men feared that
they would land in the Channel and drown, for neither could swim,
and the cold Channel waters promised a quick death.

They saved themselves. The two had filled the passenger basket with ballast and all sorts of memorial cargo, including a packet of mail to be delivered from England to France. As the balloon dropped they started tossing items overboard as quickly as possible, including most of their own heavy clothing, which they had needed to stay warm on the long crossing. Not until the two men were stripped down to street clothes did the balloon stop dropping and begin a slow but steady rise into the air. Everything else, save the packet of mail, had been thrown overboard.

Two and a half hours after they first took to the air the balloon finally came back to earth in France, landing roughly in the Fellmores Forest. The Channel had not only been crossed, but crossing the Channel—by any means—now became the world standard of adventure, an accomplishment that all but guaranteed fame and fortune.

Balloonists on each side of the Channel scrambled first to match Blanchard's achievement, then better it by building bigger balloons that could rise higher and drift both farther and more quickly, or carry more cargo and more and more passengers. In only a few decades crossing the Channel by balloon became nearly as safe and commonplace as crossing the waters by boat.

Adventurers on both coasts looked across the Channel and soon began to dream of yet another challenge.

3

Highlands

TRUDY DID NOT like it, not one little bit.

Standing in the sand looking at her sisters, Helen and Meg, laugh and splash about and swim in the warm waters and gentle surf of the Shrewsbury River estuary in Atlantic Highlands, New Jersey, Trudy's face was fixed in a deep pout, a frown upon her lips.

Just a few months before, her father, Heiner Ederle, a successful Manhattan butcher, had purchased a small summer cottage in Atlantic Highlands. The Highlands was virtually surrounded by water, hemmed in by the ocean on one side and the Navesink River and Shrewsbury River estuary on the other, with Sandy Hook, a barrier beach, protecting the Highlands from the turbid waters of the open ocean. From the front porch of the Ederles' small cottage, which was only a few dozen yards from the water, one could not help but see the ocean, and the beach was only a few steps away.

Yet for Trudy Ederle, at age nine the youngest of Ederle's three young daughters, the view was nothing but a tease. She could not swim, and because she could not swim she was not allowed to go alone with her two older sisters to the beach, to play and splash in the water with other children. While her sisters frolicked with other kids in water and let the waves toss them about, Trudy had to either stay home or wade in water below her knees. Margaret—Trudy always called her Meg—and Helen were allowed to go farther out where they could dive under the water and bob around like corks. During a recent visit to Germany, where each spent hours with their many cousins and other relatives at a familiar swimming hole, both Meg and Helen had learned to swim, mastering the dog paddle and the breaststroke. Trudy had gone to the swimming hole, too, but once, when she was playing in the water and everyone was turned around and looking the other direction, she had slipped in just over her head and had to be pulled out, sputtering, to shore. She hadn't come close to drowning, not really, but it had given her father and mother a start, and now they were protective, maybe even overprotective, of their youngest daughter.

Trudy didn't think it was fair that Meg and Helen could go to the beach and that she could not unless either her father or mother or one of her many aunts and uncles was with her. She particularly didn't think it was fair that she couldn't go with Meg. She worshipped her older sister, who had doted on her as she was growing up as if she were a special doll all her own, and now Trudy followed Meg everywhere and tried to do everything Meg did.

Now she sat roughly in the sand and began taking out her disappointment by digging into it with a stick—well, it just wasn't *fair*. Why, she must have wondered, did they even bother coming to the Highlands instead of staying home in New York, when she wasn't allowed to go to the beach and go swimming?

The fact that Heiner Ederle owned a summer home in the Highlands was a measure of just how successful he had become since immigrating to America more than two decades before. He had arrived in 1892 as a sixteen-year-old after a one-week journey on the steamship *Havel* of the North German Lloyd Line. One of twenty children, for twenty hard-earned dollars he had left his family behind and booked passage in steerage for the trip from Bremen to New York, spending most of the voyage crammed on a noisy lower deck with little sanitation, poor food, and no privacy. When the ship approached New York Harbor on the morning of May 25, 1892, Ederle's first glimpse of America was likely the hills that gave Highlands its name, for the first sight most immigrants from Europe gained of the United States was not the Statue of Liberty or the skyline of Manhattan, but the dark silhouette of what geologists know as the Atlantic Highlands in New Jersey. The most prominent headland along the Atlantic coast south of the state of Maine, the Highlands rise more than two hundred feet above sea level, topped by the massive, brownstone lighthouse known as Twin Lights, then the brightest lighthouse in North America. Ocean travelers could detect Twin Lights' glow while still seventy miles from shore. At twenty miles the lights themselves became visible, and soon after one could see land. If Heiner Ederle, who soon after arriving at Ellis Island would anglicize his name to Henry, was looking for a sign that his journey to America would prove to be both wise and profitable, the Highlands would be that sign. His first view of the United States would point him toward his family's destiny.

When he arrived in New York, Ederle found a welcoming environment. There was already a large, vibrant, and supportive German-American community, and unlike among other immigrant groups, such as the Irish, most German immigrants were craftsmen or semiskilled workers. Although Henry Ederle listed his occupation as "laborer" on the manifest of the *Havel*, in Bissingen, Germany, he had worked on the Ederle family farm and inn, gaining both a wide variety of work experience and a strong work ethic.

Soon after he arrived in New York, Ederle, who had always helped butcher the family livestock, found work as a delivery boy and apprentice butcher in a small butcher shop at 110 Amsterdam Avenue, between Sixty-fifth and Sixty-sixth streets on the Upper West Side, near the piers that delivered livestock to Manhattan. Instead of living in a German enclave like Kleindeutschland, Henry Ederle took a room nearby. In only a few years he was able to buy out the proprietor and open the store under his own name. After he sent letters back home describing the opportunity that awaited those who immigrated to America, a number of cousins, siblings, and other relatives joined him in New York, many on prepaid tickets purchased either by Ederle or by the growing Ederle clan in America, and went to work for him at the butcher shop.

By the early 1900s Ederle was in business with his brother Johann, or John. Although the business began as a simple butcher shop, before long Ederle Brothers Meats was producing its own sausages and other specialty meats craved by new immigrants hungry for a taste of the old country.

In 1901 Henry Ederle married twenty-year-old German immigrant Gertrud Haverstroh, from Königsberg, East Prussia, which is now a part of Russia. A short time later their first child, Helen, was born. Another daughter, Margaret, soon followed, and on October 23, 1905, a third daughter, Gertrude Caroline, was born.

There was nothing remarkable about the young child, who almost everyone called Trudy, apart from the robust health that characterized most of the Ederles, many of whom traditionally lived into their eighties or nineties. But in 1910 when Trudy was only five years old, that all changed.

An outbreak of measles swept the city and, in a crowded urban environment like New York, nearly reached epidemic stage, a problem local health officials blamed, in all likelihood erroneously, on the constant influx of new immigrants. No vaccines yet existed to control such ailments, and the mechanisms of viral diseases such as polio and measles were poorly understood. Trudy Ederle was one of the thousands of New York youngsters to contract the disease.

At first, she didn't feel bad at all, for the measles virus strikes with little warning. But over the course of only a few hours Trudy was seized by a high fever accompanied by congestion, watery eyes, and a rash that began on her cheeks and spread over her entire body, causing her mother to put her to bed and try to keep her other children from getting the disease.

Then, as now, once measles sets in there is little to be done. Trudy was feverish, and her mother placed cool towels on her forehead and wiped her arms and legs with cool water, praying for the fever to break. For most children afflicted with measles, the fever is by far the most hazardous symptom, as it can sometimes rise to dangerous levels. If a fever is not controlled, temperatures above 105 degrees for an extended period of time can cause irrevocable brain damage.

After her mother spent a few sleepless nights caring for her, Trudy's fever broke and she appeared to recover, apparently none the worse. But over the next few weeks her family realized that Trudy had not emerged unscathed.

They began to notice subtle changes in the way she reacted and behaved. Street noise and the clatter of city life seemed to distract her. She sometimes misheard what was said and began to speak louder than she had before. When everyone was talking at once—a common occurrence at family get-togethers when German and heavily accented English flew back and forth across the dinner table in overlapping conversations, Trudy seemed confused. It soon became apparent that she simply didn't hear very well anymore.

As soon as her parents realized what was happening, they rushed their daughter to a doctor. She had an ear infection and hearing loss caused by her bout with measles. Although doctors at the time knew there was some connection between the two events, they didn't really understand how the illness affects hearing. The disease had caused a blockage in her Eustachian tubes, which allow fluid and mucous to drain, and regulate pressure between the middle ear and the outside atmosphere. When Trudy's tubes became blocked, bacteria became trapped in the middle ear, causing an infection, known as otitis media, leading to a buildup of fluid that dampens the efficient transfer of sound energy, first resulting in a temporary hearing loss. While such infections are common in children, today they can usually be successfully treated with antibiotics. When that fails, minor surgery to provide ventilation to the middle ear usually solves the problem, and when the infection clears, hearing returns to its prior state.

Unfortunately, none of these options were yet available to Trudy Ederle. Her ear infection lingered, turning a small problem into a much more serious and permanent condition. The infection spread to surround the three bones of the inner ear and further suppressed her ability to hear. Within only a few weeks the chronic infection caused permanent damage to her eardrum, the bones of the ear, and even the nerves, resulting in a significant and permanent loss of hearing.

Although Trudy's doctors were able to diagnose the condition, they were powerless to reverse the damage. Her hearing loss was significant and more profound in her right ear, but she was fortunate that she could already speak and she retained enough hearing that she was not yet significantly disabled. She was still able to live a fulfilling life.

Trudy resumed her usual activities, but now she and Meg grew even closer. Meg understood that Trudy sometimes had difficulty hearing, and she became adept at helping her sister without making it obvious, for example, by repeating others' statements back to Trudy and asking if she agreed or not, rather than simply repeating the statements and drawing attention to her sister's malady.

Meanwhile, Ederle Brothers Meats was a resounding success. By 1910 the family could employ a young woman to help with chores and look after the children, which after the birth of a son, George, in 1911, and another daughter, Emma, two years later, now numbered five and would eventually grow to include seven. Gertrud, who had helped out behind the counter in the butcher shop, was able to give up that task and become a full-time homemaker. Although the butcher shop maintained a retail storefront, Ederle Brothers Meats was also supplying sausages and other items to other retailers, something that was becoming an ever more important part of the business.

Henry Ederle had built the kind of life that made America so attractive to immigrants in the first place. Not yet forty years old, by 1914 Henry was in virtual semiretirement. Surrounded by his loving family, Ederle was well respected in his community and financially secure enough to dabble in other businesses and invest his extra cash in real estate. That year he took the entire family on an extended trip back to Bissingen, Germany, to visit his mother and other family members, leaving the business in the custody of relatives. Upon his return, he began looking for a place outside the city to spend the summer, and, perhaps remembering that the Highlands had been his first glimpse of his new country, he finally decided on a cozy, two-room red wood bungalow fronted by a picket fence only a short walk from the water.

Early in the summer of 1915, only a short time after buying the cottage, Henry Ederle roused his three young daughters from sleep, and after a hearty breakfast, he led them out the door toward the beach. Trudy was ecstatic. Since her father was coming along this time, she'd get to go in the water.

The brief walk to the beach was a joy to the young family. Although the Highlands had once been a simple, sleepy fishing village, home to lobster fishermen and clammers who worked the flats at Sandy Hook, after the railroad came to Highlands in 1892 the nature of the community began to change. It was suddenly within reach of New York, and soon New Yorkers eager to escape the heat of the city for Highlands' cool offshore breezes and relaxed pace began making regular visits, turning the town into a popular summer resort. Steamships began to make regular stops at the Highlands, enabling people like George McClellan Jr., the son of the Civil War general and mayor of New York at the time of the *General Slocum* disaster, to spend the summer in the Highlands and commute to New York. By 1910, each summer the population swelled to three or four times its year-round total of around a thousand people. Many of these summer residents were German, Swedish, and Norwegian, for the Highlands were easily reached from ethnic neighborhoods in lower Manhattan and Brooklyn.

As Henry Ederle walked with his daughters down to the beach that morning, the scene was still sleepy, yet by the afternoon the atmosphere near the water would begin to resemble a small-town carnival. Although Bay Avenue, the main thoroughfare, was still unpaved, it was lined with tourist hotels surrounded by large covered porches, like the Johnson, the Twilight, the Highlander, and the Overlook. With the hotels and other businesses connected to each other by wood plank sidewalks, Highlands reminded many first visitors of a frontier town. All day long small restaurants, luncheonettes, candy shops, soda fountains, clam shacks, and pool parlors bustled with activity as passengers disembarked from either the railroad station or the Patten Line Pier. Visitors strolled Bay Avenue in droves, filling the sidewalks, and young men in straw hats and women carrying parasols flirted as they strolled along.

On hot afternoons when the sun burned through the morning fog and haze, the beaches filled rapidly. Since the time of the *Slocum* disaster, swimming, or at least wading in the shallows, was becoming more and more acceptable, particularly for children and younger people. As a print advertisement for a popular cereal stated, "Grandmother went bathing—girls like Molly go in for a swim." Although Victorian standards of dress and behavior were still in place, that was beginning to change. For the young the pursuit of fun was a goal in and of itself. At night the dance halls opened, and jazz and other music filled the air. Some halls and hotels sponsored special nights featuring German or Swedish music, attracting the new immigrants. Near the waterfront were arcades, carousels, and various games of chance. Visitors who could not afford a room at a hotel often pitched tents on the beach and made small fires from driftwood. Lights twinkled from boats offshore, and to the north the glow from the lights of Manhattan lit the sky.

The Ederle children—except for Trudy—had loved the Highlands instantly. There were other children everywhere, and there were always places to explore. A drawbridge crossing the estuary was an ongoing attraction, as neighborhood children goaded and dared one another into catching a ride on the structure. At the foot of nearly every street was a pier and a small beach, and there were larger beaches on Sandy Hook.

That was, however, the cause of some concern in regard to Trudy. Even though the surf was usually relatively gentle in Highlands proper, Sandy Hook was completely exposed, and in the estuary the tides ran strong. It was easy for nonswimmers to lose their footing and slip beneath the waters, and summers were often marred by accidental drownings.

There was, of course, no formal swimming program for children in Highlands, because there were virtually no formal swimming programs for children anywhere. Most youngsters learned to swim from one another, in secret, and often at risk, or by the tried, true, and incredibly dangerous "sink or swim" method, in which every success was counterbalanced by a terrifying failure that often left the child sputtering and in dread fear of the water for the rest of their life.

That is why, hand in hand, Henry was leading Trudy and his two older daughters to the Patten Line Pier at the base of Bay Avenue. There would be no relaxing in the summer cottage until the Ederles knew all their children could be trusted in the water, and now it was time for Trudy to learn how to swim. When they arrived they found a gaggle of children playing on the beach, picking through the seaweed washed up onshore by the gentle surf, throwing clamshells into the water, and splashing one another in the shallows. Farther out, older boys and young men thrashed through the water, trying to impress one another with their fancy overarm strokes. On the pier itself a few tourists simply gazed out over the water, taking in the view and the salt air of the fine summer morning, and a few fishermen sat on buckets leisurely casting their lines into the water.

Henry Ederle, too, carried a line to the pier, but not the fine filament used for fishing. Instead he held a twisted skein of clothesline. At the water's edge he stood his youngest daughter before him and, as her sisters looked on, he trussed the length of clothesline around his daughter's waist and torso with the practiced hand of a butcher who had spent years behind the counter wrapping meat, tying her securely, but not too tightly. Leaving her older sisters at Trudy's side, he then walked back up the beach and then out upon the pier, uncoiling and playing out the line with each step, until he stood above his daughter and could look down on her from atop the pier.

He called down and encouraged Trudy to slowly walk into the water. She needed little prodding. Accompanied by Helen and Margaret, Trudy waded confidently into the waters as Henry Ederle walked a parallel path on the pier itself, taking in slack on the line as if his daughter were a fish he had hooked but was not quite ready to reel in.

Holding the rope securely in his hands, he urged his daughter into deeper water, all the while keeping a tight grip on the line. As she waded more cautiously out into the sound, the water rose up her body, first covering her knees, then her waist, then reaching up to her neck. With her sisters and her father offering words of encouragement, Trudy then took another few short steps, bouncing on her tiptoes on the bottom until, suddenly, her feet no longer touched.

She was floating, a strange sensation that was at once utterly new yet strangely familiar, a sensation that caused her first to gasp and then squeal, delighted to be suspended in the water, her arms and legs free to move about. Then, as she breathed out and lost buoyancy, she started to slip beneath the water and looked to her father with panic-stricken eyes, thrashing her arms and sputtering. He deftly pulled the rope taut and pulled his daughter to the surface, bobbing alongside the pier, where she grasped at a piling as she caught her breath and calmed down. Then, with Helen and Margaret often paddling along nearby, and giving their younger sister advice and encouragement, she slipped away from the piling and into the deeper water, paddling with her hands like they did, lifting her head up and kicking madly with her feet, trying to stay afloat.

With each breath more of her fear and anxiety gave way and in their place came peace and joy. Helen and Meg gently teased their younger sister farther out, periodically allowing her to reach out and hang on and catch her breath, wrapping their arms around her, laughing and smiling as she beamed back at them. Trudy was equal now, just like them, exactly the same, able to do what they did.

In a few short minutes Trudy completely forgot about the line tied around her waist, which her father now allowed to go slack. Then, as her sisters let go and dove beneath the water to pop up again and surprise her, for a moment she forgot everything and simply floated in the water, feeling the buoyancy of her own body and the gentle ocean swells that lifted her up and down but always held her, embracing her on all sides.

She could swim. And then her sisters popped back out of the water and reached out for her again, and she followed them into the waves, grinning and giggling as the three girls all floated together.

Trudy loved this feeling—nothing would ever be the same—and the ocean, which had always been a barrier before, now opened to her like another world, a place where there was nothing to block her view or stop her but herself.

4

The Painter

TRUDY WAS NOT the first person to fall in love with the embrace of the sea and swimming.

In the spring of 1832, George Catlin, a slightly built, thirty-seven-year-old former attorney, paddled up the Missouri River from St. Louis in search of subjects for painting. He stopped some eighteen hundred miles later, just north of what is now Bismarck, North Dakota, where the Knife River, after winding several hundred miles through the lush grassland prairies, intersects with the Missouri. There Catlin made contact with two little-known bands of Native Americans, the two-thousand-member Mandan tribe, who lived in two adjacent villages at the confluence of the rivers, and their allies, the Hidatsa, a smaller band of about five hundred whose village bordered those of the Mandan.

They were not entirely unknown, having first been "discovered" by white explorers in 1738, and in 1804 Lewis and Clark spent time with the tribes. But where others had simply met them, traded for or simply taken what they needed, and moved on, in 1832 Catlin stayed and studied them, making sketches that he later planned on turning into paintings and taking detailed, written notes on all aspects of their culture.

Catlin felt far more comfortable among the Mandan and Hidatsa than he had been in either the courtroom or the drawing room where he had sketched many of the subjects of his portraits. They had looked down on him as if he were some kind of craftsman, like a boot maker, uninterested in the process of his art, solely concerned with whether the final product was flattering.

Then there were the critics, the swells with classical backgrounds who had journeyed to Europe and, even though they were American themselves, looked with disdain toward artists of their own nationality. They found fault with almost every painting Catlin had ever made, particularly taking him to task for his inability to render perspective. Anytime he was called upon to paint more than one or two figures, as in a group meeting, Catlin had struggled mightily, unable to capture the relative changes in size that denote distance.

The Mandan and Hidatsa people gave him no such criticism. To them, Catlin was a curiosity, but one upon which they cast no judgment. They soon grew accustomed to watching him sitting quietly and sketching upon a pad of paper, and gave him great latitude to move among them. He was no threat, made no demands, and was welcome to observe them as he wished.

Although Catlin convinced some of his Native hosts to sit for portraits and spent hours observing both rituals and more mundane daily tasks, at other times he went off on his own, roaming the bluffs surrounding the villages, where he could view the Mandan and Hidatsa from afar. Nearly every day he witnessed them gathering along the shores of the Knife River, both for the purposes of bathing and for pure pleasure.

For years, westerners had noted that Indigenous peoples in the Americas, Polynesia, and the Far East could not only swim, but that they swam better than anyone in the West. As one Virginia colonist noted, "They strike not out both hands together, but alternately one after another, whereby they are able to swim both farther and faster than we do." It was a curiosity, but despite the fact that some members of the upper crust were gingerly stepping into the water and testing their skill and bravery with the breaststroke, making daring long-distance swims either down rivers or between towns along the seacoast, hugging close to the shore as they plodded along, no one in the West thought about emulating the savages.

Catlin, however, found the sight both mesmerizing and melancholy. Although he was certainly not the first westerner to witness Native Americans swimming, he was certainly the first to pay such close attention. To him, it was personal.

Born in Wilkes Barre, Pennsylvania, in 1796, Catlin had been raised on a small farm in nearby Broome County, New York. From an early age Native American culture had fascinated him. His mother had briefly been held by a band of Iroquois, and Native Americans still roamed the nearby woods. Once, in fact, while hunting in the woods young Catlin was surprised when a shot rang out and dropped a deer before him. As Catlin later wrote, he then saw "what I never had seen before, nor ever dreamed of seeing in that place, the tall and graceful form, but half bent forward, as he pushed his red and naked shoulders and drew himself slowly over the logs and through the bushes, of a huge Indian!" Petrified, Catlin considered killing the man but when he turned his way, wrote Catlin, "I saw then (though a child), in the momentary glance of that face, what infant human nature could not fail to see, and none but human nature could express. I saw *Humanity*."

The encounter sparked a lifelong interest by Catlin in Native Americans. He studied law and briefly worked as an attorney but soon abandoned the law and turned to painting, eking out an existence as a portrait artist. Although the self-taught artist was kept busy, his work was considered crude and was a critical failure.

In 1824, however, after encountering an Indian delegation traveling to Philadelphia, Catlin had an inspiration and decided to devote his talent to documenting Native Americans as his primary subject matter. Over the next few years Catlin made plans to take an extended trip west to observe Plains tribes. But in September 1928, as Catlin tried to wrap up his affairs before beginning his journey, his younger brother Julius Catlin traveled to Rochester, New York, to deliver one of his brother's portraits. While there, he decided to sketch a waterfall along the Genesee River. On the hot day, after sitting in the sun for several hours, he found the waters too tempting and decided to cool off.

Like most other of his contemporaries, Julius Catlin's swimming skills, were, at best, rudimentary. He could float and probably paddle along a bit using the breaststroke, but was by no means an accomplished swimmer.

On this day he delicately stepped into the water. Taking care not to slip, he slowly made his way from shore, feeling, with each step, the rising tide of cool water around his body, and then a steady pull as the current increased.

Then he was gone. The current lifted him off his feet, pulled him into the Genesee, and swept him downstream. Panicked, he fought and splashed and called out, but neither Catlin himself nor anyone else had the skills needed for rescue. In only a few moments he was exhausted, slipped beneath the water, and drowned. His battered body was found days later far downstream.

George Catlin was broken. Not only was his brother dead, but he had died while making a journey on his behalf and while pursuing a vocation George Catlin himself had inspired. George Catlin then decided to make his journey westward alone, a trip that in 1832 brought him to the Mandan and Hidatsa tribes.

Catlin observed the tribes with the eye of an artist and a keen attention to detail, but he was never more precise than when he saw them swimming in the swift currents of the Knife and Missouri rivers. The Mandan and the Hidatsa took to the water every single day without incident, the women and younger children at a place above their village, and the men and older boys below. As he looked down from the surrounding bluffs and saw them cavorting in the water, laughing and shouting, he could not help but think of his brother.

"They all learn to swim well," wrote Catlin of his hosts, "and the poorest swimmer among them will dash fearlessly into the boiling and eddying current of the Missouri, and cross it with perfect ease . . . The art of swimming is known to all the American Indians, and perhaps no people on earth have taken more pains to learn it, nor any who turn it to better account.

"The mode of swimming amongst the Mandan, as well as amongst most of the other tribes, is quite different than that practiced in those parts of the civilized world which I have had the pleasure yet to visit," wrote Catlin. Unlike the Europeans, the Mandan and Hidatsa did not use the breaststroke. Instead, noted Catlin, the Native swimmer "throws his body alternately upon the left and right side, raising one arm entirely above the water and reaching as far forward as he can, to dip it, whilst his whole weight and force are spent upon the one passing under him, like a paddle propelling him along; whilst this arm is making a half circle, and is being raised out of the water behind him, the opposite arm is describing a similar arch in the air over his head, to be dipped in the water as far as he can reach before him, with the hand turned under, forming a sort of bucket, to act most effectively as it passes in its turn beneath him. By this bold and powerful mode of swimming, which may want the grace that many would wish to see, I am quite sure . . . that a man will preserve his strength and breathe much longer in this alternate rolling motion, than he can in the usual mode of swimming, in the polished world."

There, in a few brief paragraphs, was the future of an entire sport. And there it sat, in one of Catlin's notebooks, for much of the next decade, unread and unstudied, as countless men and women "in the polished world" drowned, just as Julius Catlin had. But if anyone had looked closely at the painting Catlin made the following winter entitled *Hidatsa Village, Earth Covered Lodges, on the Knife River*, they would have seen how profoundly the scene affected the painter. From the perspective of the opposite shore the scene shows more than a dozen mud dwellings atop a bluff above the river. In the foreground of the far shore, where the river runs beneath the village, four swimmers lay horizontal in the water, each with an arm stretched out or overhead, apparently swimming easily.

Yet on the near shore, almost unnoticed, in the lower right corner of the painting is an indistinct lone figure. This figure, half immersed in water, arms thrust overhead, appears to be drowning. A canoe is rushing toward the figure, water churning as it speeds to help, and several Native figures can be seen running toward the riverbank, preparing to dive into the water.

The contrast in the scene is unmistakable. The Indigenous figures can swim. The drowning figure cannot.

Over the next few years Catlin made several more journeys, eventually making contact with nearly fifty tribes, turning his sketches into paintings, opening a modest gallery to display his work, and giving lectures with little success. In the meantime the Mandan and Hidatsa were both afflicted with smallpox. The disease raced through the tribes, and only five years after Catlin's first contact barely one hundred Mandan remained alive, while nearly half the Hidatsa succumbed.

Distraught, depressed, and on his way toward bankruptcy, in 1840 Catlin gathered his paintings and other artifacts and abandoned America for England, hoping for a better reception, and self-published a two-volume collection of his writings and prints entitled *Letters and Notes on the Manners, Customs, and Conditions of the North American Indians*, a book that included Catlin's description of the Mandan and Hidatsa swimmers. For a time his gallery was quite successful, but after a few years interest began to wane. Catlin, scrambling for financial survival, then created an English version of the "Wild West" show, using family members and actors to portray Native Americans.

Then he encountered a retired member of the Canadian military, Colonel Arthur Rankin, who had befriended the Ojibwa tribe and had traveled to England with nearly a dozen members of the tribe. The Ojibwa caused a sensation in London, and Rankin and Catlin became partners as the Ojibwa became a living display in Catlin's gallery, performing actual Native dances and songs.

A short time later at the invitation of a member of the British Swimming Society, who had apparently read Catlin's book, the Ojibwa were invited to make an appearance at the swimming baths at High Holborn. The society wished to see a demonstration of Native swimming. Two Ojibwa, Wenishkaweabee (the Flying Gull) and Sahma (Tobacco), were invited to compete for a silver medal to be presented by the society.

As London's *Times* reported, "At a signal the Indians jumped into the bath, and, on a pistol being discharged, they struck out and swam to the other end, a distance of 130 feet, in less than half a minute. The Flying Gull was the victor by seven feet . . . The style of swimming is totally 'un-European.' They thrash the water violently with their arms, like sails of a windmill, and beat downward with their feet, blowing with force and grotesque antics . . . They dived from one end of the bath to the other with the rapidity of an arrow, and almost as straight as the tension of limb." Although no one in attendance realized it, they had just witnessed the first formal demonstration of a stroke that would one day be refined into the "crawl," better known today as the "freestyle." It left enough of an impression that for some decades afterward the stroke was known in England as simply "the Indian."

After a second race, again won by the Flying Gull, the two Ojibwa were challenged to swim once more by Harold Kenworthy, a member of the society and widely acknowledged as one of the best swimmers in England. For the third time in less than ten minutes, the Ojibwa swimmers dove into the water, this time joined by Kenworthy. Kenworthy, utilizing the backstroke, won easily as the Flying Gull and Tobacco, by this time exhausted, barely managed to finish. The victory satisfied the Englishman's sense of superiority, for the English would be slow to adopt "the Indian" stroke, but the days of the breaststroke as the preeminent style of swimming were numbered. All it would take was someone to recognize it.

Perhaps the first swimmer to recognize and take advantage of the style of swimming that so captivated George Catlin was John Arthur Trudgen, who, quite apart from Catlin, made his own discovery. The son of an English engineer employed in Brazil, as a boy Trudgen was taught how to swim by Indigenous Brazilians, learning a stroke that was essentially identical to that displayed by the two Ojibwa. When he returned to England he began to use the stroke, which he refined somewhat from the original, using the same double overarm stroke displayed by the Mandan and the two Ojibwa. But instead of beating "downward with their feet," as the Ojibwa had, Trudgen utilized the "frog kick" used by proponents of the breaststroke, kicking simultaneous with the downward stroke of his right arm. He then glided forward, legs together, as he stroked with his left arm. Although the result was rather jerky, as the swimmer constantly sped forward then slowed down, this slight change made the stroke palatable to the English sensibility, which was at least as concerned with grace as it was with raw speed, and Trudgen's kick resulted in less splashing than the swimming style demonstrated by the Ojibwa.

In early August 1875, representing the Alliance Swimming Club of London at Edgbaston Reservoir, in a race in which every other swimmer used the breaststroke, Trudgen captured the English 100-yard championship, traveling the distance in one minute and sixteen seconds—roughly the same pace as the Flying Gull in his first exhibition some thirty years earlier. Recalling the two Ojibwa, as a writer in the British publication the *Swimming Record* sniffed a few days later, Trudgen's "action reminds an observer of a style peculiar to the Indians."

5

The Women's Swimming Association

ONCE TRUDY LEARNED to swim, there was no keeping her out of the water. Although her parents insisted that she spend a few more sessions attached to the rope, Trudy soon learned not only the dog paddle but, with the help of Helen and Meg, the breaststroke as well. Every day of every summer the family spent in the Highlands, Trudy spent at least a few minutes in the ocean, either watching over her younger siblings or racing though the surf with Meg.

She and Meg were both intrigued by the men and boys they saw swimming farther offshore—and not just because they were men. These swimmers used a stroke the girls had heard of—the crawl— but neither girl had any idea of how, precisely, it was done, and both were too shy to ask. They tried to learn by watching, but whenever they tried the stroke themselves, churning each arm like a pinwheel, they were far more successful at splashing each other than at swimming, able to propel themselves forward only a few yards before becoming exhausted and collapsing in laughter.

Ever since the Ederles had spent their first summer in the Highlands it had become not just a second home, but something of a sanctuary, for as World War I unfolded and it became ever more likely that the United States would enter the conflict, anti-German sentiment, which in some parts of the country had even led to lynchings, began to foment and spread. Despite the long-established role German immigrants played in American culture, ex-president Theodore Roosevelt had summed up the growing climate of intolerance by referring to German immigrants that tried to retain their German heritage disparagingly, calling them "hyphenated Americans . . . not

Americans at all, but traitors to America and tools and servants of Germany against America."

The challenge for a successful, high-profile German family like the Ederles was to emphasize the American portion of their ancestry, for New York, despite its vibrant German community, was particularly reactionary—even long-established German-American families in New York were not immune to the reach of anti-German sentiment. The New York press, particularly the *New York World*, encouraged anti-German attitudes, and they were on display throughout the city in any number of ways: City College of New York cut the number of credits it awarded for the study of German language and history, city schools dropped German from the curriculum, and the Metropolitan Opera banned works by German composers. Germanic street signs were changed and foods such as sauerkraut temporarily became known as "liberty cabbage," German measles was referred to as "liberty measles," and even the most ubiquitous of American foods with a German heritage—the hamburger—temporarily became known as the "liberty sandwich." Although nearly three-quarters of a million New Yorkers were of German extraction, during the war fewer than half would publicly acknowledge their German roots. German cultural and social societies either disbanded or virtually went underground. In some parts of the city, most notably Brooklyn, anti-German sentiments ran so high that entire neighborhoods fled in fear, dispersing to elsewhere in the city. Plenty of Schmidts and Brauns suddenly became Smiths and Browns.

Henry Ederle did not hide his German heritage but neither did he flaunt it, and as the war continued, the Ederles found ways to emphasize the American portion of their German-American background. Henry Ederle had been a citizen since 1906 and openly and enthusiastically embraced his status as an American. In 1917, as required by law, he registered for the draft, willing, if called, to do battle against his former countrymen. He made a point to buy Liberty bonds and made sure the American flag and patriotic bunting were prominently displayed in the front window at Ederle Brothers Meats. And even though the social life of many German-American families centered around various German groups like the Turner societies that promoted German culture and German-only athletic competitions, wise Germans like Henry Ederle either cut their ties to such groups or kept them hidden. The Ederles did not raise their children as German-Americans, but as Americans. The Ederle girls were typical American girls to the core, thoroughly modern. To the occasional consternation of their parents, they embraced every fad and fashion. They liked listening to popular music on the gramophone, taught one another how to dance, went to the movies, and, in the winter, ice-skated in Central Park.

While the Ederles had to exercise some caution over their heritage in Manhattan, the xenophobia so common in New York was far less pronounced in the Highlands. There the Ederles didn't have to worry who they were perceived to be—they could be themselves, something that was increasingly important to Trudy.

It was hard to tell which parent she favored, for apart from a slight cleft in her chin she shared the same close-set eyes and strong chin of both parents. She was neither tall nor short for her age, although, compared to her older sisters, she was rather large-boned. Her hair was auburn and she wore it long, down to her shoulders, although in the summer the power of the sun gave her temporary blond highlights and a smattering of freckles spread across her cheeks.

In the summer of 1918, as World War I inched toward its conclusion, the war dominated newspaper headlines and dinner conversation. But Trudy was almost oblivious. Every day she spent in the Highlands revolved around the water, and all she thought of was swimming. As she became more accomplished as a swimmer, she was allowed in the water by herself, and long after Meg or Helen had left for home Trudy could be found in the water. She liked to test herself, swimming from one pier to another, or seeing just how long she could stay afloat without touching bottom. At times she seemed not to notice how much time was passing and sometimes stayed in for hours. She would even tell people, "To me, the sea is like a person— like a child that I've known a long time. It sounds crazy, I know, but when I swim in the sea I talk to it. I never feel alone when I'm out there." For the rest of her life, like the tide itself, she would return to her conversation, again and again and again, with the sea.

One reason Trudy found the sea to be such a steady companion was that as she grew older her hearing problem grew more pronounced. It didn't happen all at once, but over time Trudy slowly began to withdraw. At home, with her family, young Trudy was a typical, bubbly, feisty young girl who doted on her young siblings, George and Emma, and continued to follow her older sisters around like a puppy, but in school and away from the family she was a bit withdrawn, as if not always certain what was being said or taking place around her.

It wasn't obvious to everyone, but away from home she spoke just a little bit louder and a little less often than other girls her age, and gravitated to activities she could do by herself, like swimming, that didn't require a great deal of interaction with others. She was a good student but around strangers remained a little shy. More so than her sisters, she became a voracious reader, curling up in a chair every evening after finishing her schoolwork, devouring popular dime novels full of romance, daring, and adventure. While her doctors were alarmed by the amount of time she was spending in the water, fearing the possibility of further infections and additional damage, now that she could swim, keeping Trudy out of the water was impossible. As Trudy admitted later, "The doctors told me my hearing would get worse, but I loved the water so much I couldn't stop." Whatever damage exposure to the water might have caused to her hearing, it was more than offset by the joy she experienced in the water.

Her parents seem to have come to the same conclusion—nothing was going to keep Trudy out of the water. So when her mother saw a notice for a swimming and diving exhibition in the Highlands sponsored by something called the Women's Swimming Association (WSA), she was intrigued. But she was drawn to the group by more than the simple fact that it was about swimming. Unlike the Turner societies or other German social groups, the WSA had no ethnic identity—it was an American organization, albeit all-white, without other restrictions on membership. Perhaps, thought Gertrud Ederle, this was the kind of group Trudy might want to belong to, a place where she could meet other young women of various backgrounds just as excited about swimming as she was, and an organization that could simultaneously draw her out of her shell and help her pursue her favorite pastime.

Although the WSA was less than a year old, the organization was already revolutionary, changing the way women looked at themselves, and thereby changing the way men viewed women. It was made for the Ederle girls, who loved the water and loved all things new and American.

The roots of the organization had been born on the day of the *Slocum* tragedy. In the wake of so many deaths, all so pointless and all so avoidable, the issue of women and the morality of swimming had been thrust into the spotlight. Only a few weeks after the tragedy a letter to the editor in the *New York Times* began, " 'Self-preservation is the first law of nature,' but to teach its people the 'art of self-preservation' should be the first law of a nation and would tend to lessen the repetition of Slocum tragedies." Captain Tom Riley, Coney Island's best-known lifeguard and swimming instructor, told a reporter, "The burning of the *General Slocum* has aroused thousands of people of the necessity of learning how to swim." Riley addressed the question of women swimmers directly, telling the newspaper bluntly, "The average girl has just as much nerve as the boy in the water and will become as good a swimmer if taught properly," but he offered that "the trouble with grown up women is that sometime in their lives they have been dunked by a would-be funny idiot until they have come to regard the water with terror."

Those who were fighting for women's suffrage and women's rights viewed the tragedy as a call to arms. Suffragists and women's rights advocates immediately began to campaign for changes in women's swimming attire and recommended swimming lessons for women, but at first the movement had little traction.

The major problem was, in a sense, semantic. Over much of the next decade any call to teach women how to "swim" for its own sake inspired moral outrage. Opponents of swimming became half hysterical as they imagined the deleterious effects on public virtue if women were allowed to commingle with men in pools and on public beaches, particularly if they did so while not fully and conservatively clothed.

The reason was a young Australian woman named Annette Kellerman—or women who admired her—because to the minds and fertile imaginations of most American men, Annette Kellerman *was* women's swimming—and absolutely everything that was wrong with it.

As a child growing up in New South Wales, Kellerman suffered from some undiagnosed bone affliction, likely either polio or rickets, which left her with bowed legs, forcing her to wear heavy braces. At the suggestion of a doctor, her father insisted that Kellerman begin taking swimming lessons to strengthen her legs. In Australia, where virtually the entire population lived along the coast, taboos against swimming for both men and women were far less pronounced than elsewhere in the western world. An Englishman named Frederick Cavill and his sons pioneered the sport in Australia and were among the first swimming instructors both to teach the trudgen stroke and begin to improve upon it.

At first Kellerman found swimming impossible, later writing, "My brothers and sisters had learned to swim in four or five lessons, but eighteen were required for me. Only a cripple can understand the intense joy that I experienced when little by little I found that my legs were growing stronger, and taking on the normal shape and normal powers with which legs of other youngsters were endowed." She advanced quickly, and by age of seventeen, in 1902, Kellerman was the 100-meter champion of New South Wales. The pretty young woman, with the support of her father, parlayed her local fame into a vaudeville routine, performing a mermaid show in a glass tank, swimming with fish. She then began making more public swims, such as one down Melbourne's Yarra River, and in 1904, at age eighteen, she traveled with her father to England, where they hoped she would find a larger audience for her mermaid show.

Yet once Kellerman arrived in England no one knew who she was. While the stodgy English public was titillated by her act, they also found it morally offensive and—publicly anyway—ignored her. To generate publicity Kellerman began making long-distance swims in the Thames and other bodies of water. That was more agreeable. A newspaper, the *Daily Mirror*, became intrigued and in 1905 sponsored Kellerman in an attempt to swim the English Channel, a publicity stunt that had little chance of success. To date, the Channel had been swum successfully only once before, by the Englishman Matthew Webb in 1875. Few men, and no women, had since come close to repeating Webb's feat.

Kellerman didn't have a chance but that really didn't matter. All during the summer of 1905 stories about Kellerman's training regimen appeared in the newspaper, many of them commenting on her beauty and accompanied by illustrations, making her a public figure. She made several attempts to swim the Channel, failing each time, although during one attempt she managed to stay in the water for an impressive six hours before being forced to quit due not only to seasickness, but chafing under her arms and on her thighs as a result of the rough surface of her woolen swim dress.

The attempts made her famous but also caused her to rebel. Men who tried to swim the Channel knew full well about the dangers of chafing and avoided it altogether by swimming in the nude. Kellerman decided that simply wasn't fair.

She didn't swim nude—not yet. But she did toss out her swimming dress with its long sleeves and skirt and bought a boys' one-piece suit, similar to a leotard. To this she sewed a pair of black silk stockings to the legs that covered her bare skin and nominally adhered to prevailing standards of modesty. She called her outfit the "one piece all over black diving suit." The public didn't care what it was called but couldn't take their eyes off her when she was wearing it, for the garment revealed as much as it concealed, accentuating and even enhancing every curve on Kellerman's already curvaceous body. In an instant Kellerman became the world's first sex symbol.

The impact on her career was instantaneous. She became a sensation and soon took her act to the United States, where she attracted a huge following. Her vaudeville show was an ingenious mixture of sex and sport. Kellerman revealed herself slowly. She first threw the diablo (a form of juggling), then put on an exhibition of swimming and diving in a glass tank before "dancing" behind a backlit curtain that etched her silhouette—and more—into the mind of every man who saw her performance. For publicity reasons Kellerman also continued to make long-distance open-water swims. At Revere Beach, just north of Boston, she created a huge scandal when, in an act of defiance that guaranteed her the front page, she removed the stockings from her suit, exposing her bare thighs to onlookers. Shocked local officials charged her with public nudity. Kellerman fought the case, arguing that the modification had nothing to do with morality but everything to do with women's rights—it was safer for her to swim unrestricted by heavy stockings—and the case was dismissed. The notoriety of the case made Kellerman both more notorious and more heroic, part sex symbol and part suffragette, a combination that was both tantalizing and—to some—threatening.

Dudley Sargent, the longtime director of Harvard University's Hemenway Gymnasium, was obsessed with measuring the human body and convinced Kellerman to allow him to take her measurements. He then declared that out of ten thousand women he had measured, she was the first whose proportions matched those of Venus de Milo.

Kellerman soon began appearing in the movies and her fame only increased as she now could be seen all over the world. She created one last sensation when, in the film *Daughter of the Gods*, the movie industry's first million-dollar-plus production, Kellerman's character went skinny-dipping and she became the first big-name screen actress to appear nude.

Those who hoped to make swimming a respectable activity for women in the United States first had to overcome the licentious image created by Kellerman, one that, rightly or wrongly, found every fear confirmed by her curvaceous figure and left the impression that women's swimming—as a sport—was destined to be as much about titillation as competition.

Yet while modest men—and many women—found Kellerman threatening, other young women found her both inspirational and liberating, not for the way she exposed her body but for the way she exposed contradictions and inequality in the way women were treated. One after another, they followed her into the water.

Charlotte Epstein wanted to swim. The Jewish-born native of New York was only twenty years old when the *Slocum* burned and sank, and Epstein was mortified. A graduate of the Ethical Culture School, a nonsectarian, nontheistic religious and educational movement still in existence today, Epstein was unfettered by the restrictions and prejudices that kept most women her age in their place—at home. She firmly believed in the group's three major precepts: to teach the supremacy of moral ends above all human ends and interests; to teach that the moral law has an immediate authority not contingent on the truth of religious beliefs or of philosophical theories; and to advance the science and art of "right living," a life lived according to those standards.

To that end, Epstein was a rarity—an independent, single woman with a career. She worked as a court stenographer and was involved in women's rights and the suffragist movement, something "right living" made a moral prerogative.

For most young women of the time there were absolutely no outlets for sports of any kind, not to mention swimming. While there was still staunch resistance to teaching women to swim simply for pleasure, in the wake of the *Slocum* disaster, instruction in "lifesaving" was another thing entirely. Reluctantly, the United States Volunteer Life Saving Corps (USVLSC), a group formed after the Civil War that previously had trained male swimmers in lifesaving techniques, began to allow women to join the group.

Epstein was fully aware that being allowed to join the group was an important step in the fight for equal rights for women. An unlikely pioneer, beneath her mouse-colored hair and behind her wide-set brown eyes, the slightly built Epstein appeared quiet and demure, the model of restraint and decorum, the polar opposite of someone like Annette Kellerman. Yet in the sport of swimming and in women's athletics, Epstein would prove to have a more profound impact than the Australian bathing beauty. She immediately joined the group and soon became the Susan B. Anthony of swimming.

Epstein was one of the first of a small contingent of women who were taught to swim and then taught basic lifesaving techniques by the USVLSC. Using the breaststroke, the young women of the USVLSC learned to swim one hundred yards or more, support struggling swimmers, safely dive into the water, and free-dive to depths approaching fifty feet. The group touted its efforts in silent films and newspaper articles and held public exhibitions and races to attract new members. On occasion, women members were allowed to participate, and they proved so popular that the group began holding occasional "water shows" featuring female members. Epstein, although not the best swimmer in the group, was competitive, excelling at deep diving and relays. But this first generation of women swimmers soon became frustrated by the league. The "water shows" trivialized their skills—the women weren't allowed to swim long distances and often competed in relay races in which each woman swam only thirty yards or so.

There seemed to be little opportunity within the group to change that. The open chauvinism and prejudice that prevented women not only from competing in sports, but from breaking a sweat anywhere but in the kitchen, had become institutionalized in the United States, a factor that had its roots in the 1890s, when the Olympic movement was still in its infancy. Olympic founder Baron Pierre de Coubertin of France adamantly opposed the participation of women. Like most men of his time, particularly those involved in athletics, de Coubertin found the notion of a woman competing in athletics physically dangerous for such delicate flowers and morally offensive as well, once stating that women athletes simply did not create a "proper spectacle." De Coubertin himself personally selected the members of the first International Olympic Committee (IOC), and although not all shared his outlook in regard to women, many did, and de Coubertin found a powerful and important ally in American committeeman James Sullivan.

Sullivan was the founder of the Amateur Athletic Union (AAU), then the preeminent governing body of virtually all amateur sports in America, a position the group would hold for decades. Together, even as the membership of the IOC started to act independently, the two men managed to keep women from participating in sports in any meaningful way both in the United States and elsewhere in the world, as the IOC authorized only nominal competition for women in "proper spectacles" such as golf, yachting, tennis, archery, and figure skating.

That was it. Apart from these few pursuits and the sporadic, unorganized efforts of individual female athletes, like Boston's Eleanora Randolph Sears, who garnered headlines for long-distance walking, not only were women kept away from athletics, but they might as well have been kept locked up in a separate room away from all sporting activity. For all intents and purposes there were no women athletes in the United States, no organized sports programs for women, and, apparently, little chance of that ever changing. Most men *and* women believed that strenuous exercise was not only inappropriate for a woman of good standing, but physically dangerous.

But in 1912, much to the dismay of both de Coubertin and Sullivan, the IOC broke ranks and elected to add women's swimming as an official sport. At the 1912 games in Stockholm, Sweden, women competed in both the 100-meter freestyle swim and the 4-by-100 freestyle relay. But France and the United States stubbornly refused to accept the decision. De Coubertin was the reason France chose not to participate, and James Sullivan, who served as AAU president from 1906 to 1908 and then became executive secretary, managed to block American participation. The AAU oversaw the selection of the American Olympic team, and Sullivan simply would not allow women to join the AAU, thus effectively preventing American women from competing, not only in swimming, but in any sport for as long as he was in charge.

In 1911, while Annette Kellerman was attracting all the wrong kind of attention and the IOC was still pondering the question of adding women's swimming to the Olympics, Charlotte Epstein led an insurrection. The female members of the USVLSC broke off and formed their own group, the Women's Life-Saving League. Its aims were far loftier than those of the USVLSC. It wasn't enough that women simply had the opportunity to learn how to swim. The Women's Life-Saving League wanted to institutionalize the sport of swimming for women. It wanted lifesaving swimming instruction to be a mandatory part of school education, and it wanted to foster athletic competition among women for health benefits.

"Eppie," as Charlotte Epstein was known to her friends, became the chairman of the athletic branch of the group. She was well equipped for her position. As she sat in court every day working as a stenographer, she watched and listened as male attorneys and judges battled one another using not only their intellect, but their powers of persuasion, rhetoric, and political savvy—all skills that would come in handy in the fight for the right of women to compete in swimming. She was not intimidated by men, and she both knew how to make—and win—an argument, sometimes on the merits of her claim, but also through the shrewd manipulation of her opponent.

In 1914, after a successful visit to the United States by an organized group of Australian women swimmers, the AAU sensed that despite its efforts to suppress women's swimming as an organized sport, it was nonetheless gaining a foothold. Someone had to take charge, and, ever so reluctantly, the AAU assumed the role as the sport's governing authority, overseeing Epstein's fledgling competition wing of the Women's Life-Saving League. Although Epstein and other officials of the league grated under the AAU's domineering influence, which relegated women's swimming to second-class status within the organization and allowed the actual participants, coaches, and managers like Epstein little influence over their own sport, Epstein realized that if she openly fought the AAU, she was destined to lose. Eppie wisely chose another tack.

In Australia, a separate swimming association for women ruled their sport, and in occasional competition against American swimmers, the Australians, who used a variation of the trudgen known as the Australian crawl, were clearly far superior, beating American swimmers handily. The losses were embarrassing and offended the AAU's sense of nationalism, making the notion of an American swimming association based on the Australian model intriguing. After all, the AAU still wasn't certain it wanted to be in the business of women's athletics at all, and an American association based on the Australian model might relieve them of that responsibility.

Following the death of James Sullivan, in September 1916, Epstein sensed an opportunity. Over the next few months she worked behind the scenes and used the local press to her advantage, methodically extolling the advantages of having a women's swimming association managed by women, while deftly praising the example set by the AAU as an organizing body without peer, essentially killing the organization—and its male overseers—with kindness. She wrote the *New York Times* that while she was certain there would one day be some kind of women's association, "If we are left to our own resources now, totally unprepared to meet the situation, much harm could and probably would come to it." She was just as politic in person, at least initially. Almost waiflike in her personal appearance, underneath her complacent exterior was the heart of an athlete who did not like to lose and was determined to do what was right.

Epstein's calculated brand of passive-aggressive reasoning played on the AAU's inflated sense of superiority. In 1917 she struck out on her own again, creating the WSA, a group that slowly evolved from an idea into a working organization whose stated purpose was not to compete, but to encourage "girls and women to swim for self-protection, then to practice swimming for health, physical improvement and recreation," all ideals that made it clear that, even though Annette Kellerman was, in many ways, an authentic pioneer of the sport, America's first female swimmers had nothing to do with the swimmer herself or anything she represented. The club's slogan was similarly passive, declaring, "Good sportsmanship is greater than victory." Their goal—to be seen and appreciated as athletes rather than sex symbols—would prove to be a challenge for the sport.

Epstein deftly convinced the AAU that, for all intents and purposes, the WSA was not only subservient to the AAU but had been its idea in the first place. In this way she turned the AAU from a potential obstacle into an ally vested in the success of the group, outflanking the AAU and creating the WSA to her own liking. The best part was that the AAU was completely oblivious to what had happened.

It was a masterstroke that gave the group some instant credibility, but Epstein was savvy enough to know that unless the group quickly established itself as a legitimate athletic organization, the moral crusaders who equated all women swimmers with Annette Kellerman were certain to attack the group and bring it down. To survive, the organization needed to grow and prove that it was providing a service and not just an excuse for young women to splash around in the water half undressed.

Epstein proceeded with a zeal that was almost evangelical. To grow the group, she needed swimmers, and to get swimmers, the WSA needed to go to where the swimmers were—the beaches and resort towns around New York City. Public demonstrations such as the one it planned for that summer day in 1918 at the Highlands both gave the group publicity and served as a recruiting tool. After all, without sufficient membership, the WSA was nothing more than a grand idea.

On the day Trudy and her mother and sisters reached the pier along the estuary where the demonstration was being held, a small crowd of mostly curiosity seekers, mothers, and young children had already gathered. No one quite knew what to expect, for while the WSA was becoming a familiar name in the newspaper, few in the crowd had ever viewed a swimming competition or demonstration of any kind. Trudy like to swim, but watching swimming? Well, that was something different.

The demonstration began with diving. That was nothing new to Trudy. She and Meg often watched young men jumping from the piers and did so themselves. But as the first WSA swimmer mounted a small platform at the edge of the pier, stood on its edge with her toes curled over the side, raised her arms perfectly symmetrically over her head, then bent slightly at the knee and jumped, back arched, first up, then out and down, entering the water with hardly a splash, the crowd let out an audible gasp like they were watching the fireworks on the Fourth of July. This wasn't some show-offy young man preening for the attention of some giddy young girl. This was beautiful, athletic artistry.

One after another the young women launched themselves into the air, backward and forward and twisting through space, each dive more miraculous and more elegant than the one before. Trudy and her sisters could not help but notice, as the swimmers surfaced and returned to the pier, that they swam not the breaststroke or the dog paddle, but the overarm stroke like the men and boys used, only the women didn't thrash through the water so much as they churned through it, far more efficiently and more beautifully than Trudy had ever seen before.

Then it was time for the swimmers. During a brief demonstration of lifesaving techniques, the Ederle girls again noticed that the WSA swimmers almost always used that same overarm stroke. When the lifesaving demonstration ended and a very young girl stepped to the edge of the pier, most of the crowd thought the demonstration was coming to an end. In fact, it was just getting started. This is what Charlotte Epstein wanted everyone to see—and remember.

Most members of the WSA were teenagers and young women, but the young girl on the edge of the pier was only seven years old. Her name was Catherine Brown, and when they announced her name, some members of the crowd nodded knowingly. They had heard of her.

Catherine Brown was already something of a local celebrity. Her father, Alfred, was a commodore in the American Life Saving Society and a well-known figure himself. Several years earlier, in 1913, he had become the first person to swim from the Battery in lower Manhattan to Sandy Hook, a distance of twenty-two miles. That same year he also swam the Panama Canal before it opened to boat traffic, and those two accomplishments led him to refer to himself as the "long distance champion swimmer of the world," but even he knew that claim would ring hollow unless he accomplished the sport's Holy Grail, the swimming of the English Channel. Unfortunately any chance Brown had to accomplish that goal had been thwarted by World War I, which turned the Channel into a battle zone as the English enforced a blockade and made any attempt to swim the Channel far too dangerous. In the meantime, he turned his attention to his daughter.

When Catherine Brown was only two and a half years old, Alfred Brown had taught her how to swim the breaststroke in Long Island Sound. Something of a publicity hound, Brown made certain newspaper photographers were present whenever he took the toddler swimming, and New Yorkers soon became familiar with both Brown and his precocious daughter. When she was only four her father had her give a diving exhibition at the New York Sportsman's Show. The appearance caused a sensation. Local authorities were mortified at seeing the young girl diving into a small tank of water and dragged Commodore Brown into court, charging him with endangerment of a child. The charges were soon dismissed, but the publicity made Catherine Brown—and by extension, her father—one of the best-known swimmers in the country. Syndicated newspaper articles giving swimming instructions appeared under her byline when she was only five.

When Charlotte Epstein organized the WSA, Brown's daughter became one of the group's first members, instantly giving the fledgling organization both good press and credibility, for Epstein was savvy enough to understand that parents needed to be convinced that swimming was both safe and healthy. The sight of little Catherine Brown swimming confidently assuaged many of those concerns.

Not only was Brown a proficient diver, but since joining the WSA she had added a new stroke to her repertoire. She did more than just move gently through the water using the breaststroke, or thrash her way through the waves with the trudgen.

Brown dove from the pier, surfaced quickly, and, like Trudy so often did, began swimming for the next pier. Almost immediately the Ederle girls looked at one another and began talking excitedly back and forth. Catherine Brown plowed through the water like a steamship, using an overarm stroke many had never seen before and most did not even know existed, something known as the American crawl. She made the men and boys who'd been showing off near the next pier look like they were standing still.

Trudy and Meg weren't the only ones who were impressed. Seeing the eager look on her daughters' faces excited Gertrud Ederle as well. Although her own children could swim, Gertrud still worried and fretted when they were in the water. Yet young Catherine Brown made swimming seem as natural as running down the sidewalk and almost as safe—she seemed utterly at home in the sea.

At the end of the demonstration Charlotte Epstein gave a brief talk about the WSA and described the benefits of membership. For a nominal fee any woman or young girl of any age could join the association and take one fifty-minute lesson per week, either at its outdoor pool in the summer or an indoor pool in the winter. For a few dollars more, each member could take additional lessons, and after a swimmer became proficient she was eligible to compete in swim meets sponsored by the WSA. Eppie extolled the virtues of the group and, before calling for interested parents to enroll their children, cautioned that for the first six months membership was provisional to allow WSA officials "the opportunity to observe closely each candidate during the period of probation and ascertain whether or not she is desirable in every way as a representative of the organization."

Mrs. Ederle raced to the front and, as Charlotte Epstein later recalled, "begged her to take Gertrude in hand and develop her natural swimming powers." Mrs. Ederle then turned to young Catherine Brown, standing idly by, and blurted out, "I'll pay you a thousand dollars if you can teach my girls to swim like that," drawing a laugh from everyone and a few embarrassed looks from her own daughters. In short order, Trudy's mother had enrolled Helen, Meg, and

Trudy in the WSA. Now, for the first time in her life, Trudy would be able to swim year-round, and she might even learn to swim that overarm stroke. Eppie had a few more converts.

The ripples in the water that had formed the day the Flying Gull and Tobacco leapt into the pool at High Holborn had crossed the Atlantic and finally landed onshore.

6

The Crossing

IF SHE WASN'T DREAMING about swimming, helping Meg and Helen with their chores around the house, or watching over her younger brother and sister, Trudy Ederle could usually be found curled up with a book, losing herself in another world, this one fashioned not of water but of words.

Although she would later be drawn to more romantic works, in 1918 she was only twelve years old, and thoughts of romance were still a few years in the future. Instead, she found herself reading adventure stories, often true tales of personal courage and daring. Few of these books featured female subjects—very few such subjects existed. Most were breathless morality tales about male adventurers like Lewis and Clark overcoming great odds, or patriotic biographies of great men such as Abraham Lincoln. Trudy read these stories over and over again, nearly committing them to memory.

A favorite author of the time was Henry Llewellyn Williams, whose inspirational works included the titles *The Boys of the Bible; The Lincoln Story Book; Taking Manila: Or in the Philippines with Dewey, Giving the Life and Exploits of Admiral George Dewey, U.S.N.*; and *Buffalo Bill, the Hon. William F. Cody: Rifle and Revolver Shot, Pony Express Rider, Teamster, Buffalo Hunter Guide, and Scout, a Full Account of His Adventurous Life with the Origin of the Wild West Show.* Of course she would have preferred reading similar stories about young women, but such books featuring female subjects were all but unknown.

One Williams title, however, had particular resonance. *The Adventurous Life of Capt. Matthew Webb, Swimming Champion of the World* told the story of Matthew Webb, the first man to swim the

English Channel. Williams's thirty-page recounting of Webb's heroic battle with the English Channel, as well as other accounts of his story, which included comics, made Webb as familiar to children of Trudy's generation as the frontiersman Daniel Boone. To a young swimmer such as Trudy, Webb's story was like discovering a kindred spirit—here was someone who felt the same way she did about the sea.

Williams's account and other versions of Webb's story all told the basic story of a young man who tested himself against the elements. Webb's adventure began as a thrilling act of selfless heroism and hooked Trudy immediately. She was never going to be a great explorer like Lewis and Clark, or president of the Unites States like Abraham Lincoln, but like Matthew Webb, she was a swimmer.

On April 28, 1873, while he served as a merchant seaman on the crew of Cunard steamship *Russia*, Webb's vessel, en route between England and the United States, hit a patch of rough weather. On deck, a crewman lost his footing and fell into the frigid seas of the North Atlantic. While the ship's captain continued steaming onward at sixteen knots, oblivious to the accident, the barrel-chested Webb, who stood only five foot seven, sported a walruslike mustache, and weighed nearly two hundred pounds, kept his eye trained on the sea and raced the length of the ship before he courageously—and foolishly—dove into the waters in an effort to rescue his fellow crewman.

Webb saw the man's head suspended above the waves and swam toward his companion, but as he reached out for him and grasped his head, Webb discovered that the man had already slipped beneath the waves and perished—all that remained was the sailor's cap bobbing on the surface of the water.

Now Webb was alone—the *Russia* steaming off toward the horizon. Although the captain of the *Russia* was soon informed of the accident and launched a lifesaving boat to search for both men, Webb's chances of being saved in the frigid seas were nearly nil—he would be nearly impossible to spot between waves, and it would be only minutes before hypothermia would send him to the depths.

But Webb thought fast. Knowing his clothing was weighing him down, Webb stripped off his garments and started to swim after the *Russia*, trying to follow the boat's wake. After more than half an hour in the water, Webb, rising on a wave, spotted the rescue vessel and the men in it spotted him. He was pulled out of the water a moment later, some thirty-seven minutes after he first leapt overboard.

When the gallant sailor, half frozen, returned to the ship, the captain, crew, and passengers all hailed him as a hero. When the story of his courageous effort reached the press, Webb was again hailed as a hero, earning the Stanhope Gold Medal, Britain's highest civilian award for heroism, awarded by the Royal Humane Society.

Webb was no fool. He had not only survived for nearly an hour in the frigid waters of the open ocean, something few other men had ever done before, but despite the cold water and rough seas he had swum for more than a mile. He immediately realized that not only had he just experienced a life-altering event, but he had discovered a unique talent, one that could free him from the drudgery of the merchant service.

While Webb remained a member of the merchant service, he made the decision to stake his future on his prowess as a swimmer and sought out a challenge equal to his aspirations. The English Channel, which to date had been crossed only by boat and by balloon, was the obvious goal. Webb declared that he would be the first man to swim from England to France.

Observers reacted skeptically. Although boat and balloon crossings of all kinds were commonplace, the notion of swimming across the English Channel was almost unthinkable. No one, absolutely no one, except for a handful of swimmers themselves thought that it would be done or ever could be done. Even then, few swimmers had even dared take more than a few strokes in the water, and most of those were men in a drunken stupor who quickly found sobriety in the cold Channel waters. A foolish few had drowned, but most were pulled out of the water by their less-inebriated companions and nursed their failure with brandy. A handful of sailors claimed to have swum across the Channel, but none could provide any witnesses or documentation and weren't taken seriously. In 1862 a merchant seaman named William Hoskins claimed to cross the Channel clutching a bale of straw, but if he did, his crossing more resembled that of a cork than a true competitor.

In fact, it was not until 1872 that anyone made a serious attempt to swim the Channel, and that effort made it seem even more unlikely than ever before. The English swimmer J. B. Johnson, twenty-three years old, well built and handsome, had already swum his way to fame by winning a variety of swimming medals as a member of the Serpentine Club, London's first swimming club, then barely a decade old. Something of a publicity hound, Johnson made a very public rescue of an elderly man, diving from the London Bridge to save him, which made him the best-known swimmer in England, although observers later learned the man he saved was quite a good swimmer and really hadn't needed saving at all. When someone laid a wager of one thousand pounds versus thirty that Johnson couldn't swim the Channel, he saw his opportunity and he took it.

He made certain all of England knew about his plans, plastering London with placards touting his attempt, identifying himself as "Hero of London Bridge and Champion Swimmer of the World," and on the morning of August 25, 1875, he drew a crowd of several thousand people to the Admiralty Pier in Dover to witness his departure. Johnson pulled out all the stops, hiring a brass band to entertain the crowd, and made an entrance worthy of a monarch, wearing a fine blue coat trimmed in white braid and brandishing upward of thirty swimming medals on his chest. After several hours of self-serving pomp and circumstance, Johnson finally climbed aboard a steamship, changed into his swimming suit, and, when the steamer was two hundred yards offshore, dove off the paddle box and into the sea. The crowd hung around for a while as Johnson swam out of sight and the boat began to fade on the horizon.

Only sixty-five minutes into his swim, with the coast of France still well out of sight over the horizon, Johnson swam over to the steamer and asked for something to eat. Then, realizing the tide had turned and his attempt was futile, Johnson climbed aboard and the boat continued on its way to Calais, France. As the boat entered the harbor Johnson had sufficiently recovered from his time in the cold waters of the Channel to entertain taking another dip. He leapt back into the water and swam to shore, leaving the impression that he had indeed swum all the way from England, and he was briefly hailed as a hero before his hoax was revealed. He soon left the country to remake himself in America and left the impression that anyone who tried to swim the English Channel was either a quack or a con man, or both.

Johnson's failure seemed to answer the question of whether it was possible to swim the Channel—if Johnson could not, it was likely no one else could. Still, among other swimmers his effort made the notion of swimming the Channel the Holy Grail of swimming. Like the running of a marathon, it captured the imagination of athletes and dreamers alike—a one-way ticket to renown, a way to stand out from the crowd.

Three years later Paul Boyton, an American, became the next man to test the Channel, and his effort underscored just how difficult a task it was and how eager the pubic was to embrace a hero. Boyton became the first person to cross the Channel without either a balloon or a boat—sort of.

Boyton, an Irish-American who served in the U.S. Navy in the Civil War before first becoming a mercenary and then operating a lifesaving service in Atlantic City, was hired by the inventor C. S. Merriman to demonstrate his latest creation, a "patent waterproof life-saving apparatus," essentially a primitive dry suit. Weighing nearly thirty-five pounds, Merriman's suit was made of vulcanized rubber and, save for the face, covered the body completely. The suit contained a series of inflatable air chambers and was capable of supporting three hundred pounds, a man, and up to nine days of provisions stored in a special pouch. The wearer of the suit carried a paddle to propel himself through the water, and it was even possible to attach a small sail to an iron hook that protruded from the sole of one of the suit's rubberized feet.

Boyton made demonstrating the suit something of a cottage industry, wearing the suit, which he referred to as the "lifesaving dress," to accomplish all sorts of stunts, ranging from having himself thrown overboard from a boat during a storm to taking extended trips down rivers, sometimes paddling, sometimes sailing, and sometimes kicking with his feet and flailing his arms to propel himself along, but usually depending upon the current as much as anything else to send him downstream. In April 1875 he decided to try to cross the Channel.

His first attempt ended in failure due to a combination of bad weather and unfavorable tides that nearly swept him and his escort boat into the North Sea. Nevertheless, he had spent an extraordinary fifteen hours in the water and upon his return to shore was greeted like a hero, receiving dozens of congratulatory telegrams, including one from Queen Victoria herself. Over the next month he cashed in, making public appearances in the suit, earning about $250 for only a half hour's work. Then Boyton decided to make a second attempt. This time he traveled to France, choosing to leave from Cape Gris-Nez and swim to England, to take advantage of what he hoped were favorable tides, currents, and, just as important, wind.

Press reports noted that Boyton looked "like a giant porpoise" when he waded into the water at 3:00 A.M. and began to paddle his way through choppy seas toward England, floating on his back in a horizontal position, a human boat. He looked completely absurd in the suit, an odd marriage of a sailboat, a kayak, and a diving suit, but it was nonetheless effective. Twenty-four hours later Boyton landed at Fan Bay, just west of the South Foreland Lights. Boyton was hailed as a bona fide national hero, and he basked in the attention.

Matthew Webb, however, was aghast. He had spent the last several years in training and had even secured a wealthy patron to back his plan to swim the Channel. To Webb, Boyton's achievement was an embarrassment, a stunt that was offensive both because of its crass commercialism and because of the use of the suit. He now became more determined than ever.

Four months later, at 12:55 P.M. on August 24, 1875, after a breakfast of eggs, bacon, and claret, Webb, his body glistening under a coating of porpoise fat to hold his body heat that caused everyone downwind to give him a wide berth, entered the water at Dover, diving from the Admiralty Pier. He was accompanied by two boats, a dory and a sailboat, bearing a total of fifteen witnesses, including members of the press.

Under relatively calm conditions and in waters of about sixty degrees, near the upper limit for the Channel, for the next twenty hours Webb, his head held high, relentlessly pushed his arms out ahead and kicked with his feet, gulping air and occasionally swigging brandy, beef tea, coffee, and ale and eating stale bread. The tide and currents of the Channel first pushed him to the southwest, then almost due east, then south and east again, like so much human flotsam. Yet even as the weather deteriorated, with each stroke Webb inched ever closer to his goal.

He was near the point of collapse when he stumbled onshore at

Calais at 10:35 A.M. the next morning. Indeed, he needed assistance to stay on his feet as he waded out of the surf, an indiscretion that today, under official Channel-crossing guidelines that prohibit any physical contact with the swimmer in the water, would disqualify his accomplishment. His success was more a demonstration of stamina, good fortune, and stubborn determination than true aquatic skill. Nevertheless he had made the twenty-one-mile crossing without material assistance, swimming for what was variously reported as twenty-one hours and forty or forty-five minutes, covering more than thirty miles as he plodded along at a pace of a bit less than a mile and a half an hour.

Webb's accomplishment made Boyton insignificant. At a time when few people walked twenty miles, swimming that distance seemed superhuman. Webb's success earned him worldwide fame. Swimming the English Channel was instantly recognized as the world's supreme athletic achievement, the standard against which all else was measured and compared. Ever since that day every swimmer of any ability has had to answer the question, "Do you think you could swim the Channel?"

Unfortunately for Webb, swimming the Channel would prove to be his undoing, creating unrealistic expectations over the remainder of his life. After swimming the Channel he was forced to try to attempt swims that were even more daring and dangerous, but none had the resonance of the English Channel. In 1883, while attempting to swim across the rapids of the Niagara River beneath Niagara Falls, Webb was swept up in the current and carried downstream. When he reached a famous whirlpool he went under and didn't reappear until his body was discovered four days later several miles downstream.

For a young reader like Trudy, however, it was easy to overlook Webb's tragic death and focus on the heroic figure of the man himself, someone who against all odds had done something that everyone had previously thought to be impossible. Trudy was not alone. Soon other men and women would follow in Webb's wake and take on mankind's most challenging individual endeavor.

7

The Teacher

WHEN TRUDY EDERLE walked into a WSA pool for her first formal lesson in the fall of 1918, in the basement of a Brooklyn Heights apartment building, sharing space with the building's boiler room, she had no idea that she was walking in on the start of a revolution. Not only was the WSA virtually the first athletic organization for women, but it was one of the few organizations anywhere that young girls and teenagers like Trudy and her sisters could belong to—even the Girls Scouts had been in existence only since 1916.

With peace in Europe a few short weeks away, it was becoming clear that the world was changing, and changing rapidly. The women's suffragist movement was on the precipice of success, as most states had given women the right to vote. The Nineteenth Amendment to the Constitution, which would extend the right to vote to all women, had the support of President Woodrow Wilson, had passed the House of Representatives, and needed only Senate approval before being ratified by the states.

While that process would take two long years, what the Nineteenth Amendment did for women's voting rights, the WSA would do for women's athletics. Sports would no longer be for men only.

When Trudy, Meg, and Helen arrived at the pool, nothing was familiar. Indoor pools were rare, and none of the girls had ever seen one before, much less swum in one. Although in time the organization would eventually have its own pool in a building on West Fifty-fifth Street in Manhattan, as the group approached its first anniversary the organization rented a pool every Wednesday and Friday evening.

After changing into their swimming attire in a small dressing room, when Trudy and her sisters first pushed through the heavy doors that opened to the pool, they were hit with a blast of air as hot and heavy as that of a sauna, acrid with the smell of chlorine, which rapidly caused any untiled surface not covered in a heavy coat of paint to rust and corrode. The pool, only thirty feet long and so shallow that except at one end all but the youngest girls could stand upright with their head and chest out of the water, was surrounded by a narrow tiled walkway and a few wooden benches. It hardly seemed sufficient for more than the most basic instruction. Compared to the open ocean, it was absolutely claustrophobic.

As Trudy and her sisters stood alongside the pool waiting for their first lesson, among the dozens of swimmers and instructors from the previous session crowded in and around the pool, she couldn't help but notice that one person stood out—a man. Unlike all the young women, this man—tall, fit, and with a shock of graying hair—was not wearing swimming attire. Despite the near tropical heat in the basement, he was dressed formally, in business attire, wearing a starched white shirt with a high collar, a tie knotted in a taut Windsor knot, a vest, a jacket, and a bowler. His only concession to the oppressive conditions in the basement was, on rare occasions, to remove his jacket.

The other girls called him "Mr. Handley," and as Trudy watched, Handley was clearly in charge, keeping dozens of swimmers, swimmers to be, and instructors busy at once. One group of girls at the far, deep end of the pool practiced diving from a small platform. Another group alongside the pool lay down with their stomachs supported by chairs and practiced kicking and stroking with their arms, turning their heads and pretending to take in and release their breath. Others simply held onto the side of the pool and kicked, and more accomplished swimmers swam back and forth. As they did the man in the business suit strode between groups, leaning down to give advice. Sometimes he pantomimed the movement he expected. At other times he stood before everyone, even the other instructors, and with a swimmer at his side pointed out proper arm and hand positions, making small adjustments as he spoke. He moved back and forth between all swimmers and spent the same amount of time with each one, speaking formally in a firm yet gentle voice that still contained more than a hint of fine breeding and exposure to the continent.

To Trudy and her sisters it seemed as if the water was full of Catherine Browns, because every swimmer in the water sped back and forth with a speed they found astonishing and had not seen since that day of the exhibition at the Highlands. Absolutely no one was using the dog paddle, and even the few swimmers using the breaststroke were obviously already far more accomplished swimmers than anyone Trudy had ever seen at the Highlands.

It was all due to Louis de Breda Handley. A generation before he had revolutionized the sport of swimming for men by helping to develop an improvement on the trudgen, known as the crawl, an advance in swimming that was as dramatic and profound as learning to run after a lifetime of walking. And now he was teaching the exact same stroke to women swimmers. In fact, at the time he was probably not only the only person in the world teaching the stroke to women, but the only person who thought women could even have the ability to learn it. Despite the fact that the WSA was a women's organization, few people would have more to do with the cause of women's athletics or with the career of Trudy Ederle than the man standing at the side of the pool that fall evening.

At last the pool cleared and the Ederle girls, as well as a few dozen other swimmers, were allowed into the pool to begin the new session. Handley and the other WSA instructors had to assess the skills of the girls, as new members of the group, before they were assigned to classes.

After learning her name, Handley systematically asked each girl to get into the water and swim. Helen and Meg both went before Trudy and, compared to the other girls, seemed to do well. When he came to Trudy, he said simply, "Well, Gertrude, get in and swim as fast as you can."

Trudy lowered herself in the water. Ever since the demonstration at the pier, she and Meg and Helen had been trying to swim like Catherine Brown, and although Trudy knew she wasn't nearly as fast as the young swimmer, she was quite proud of her progress. She took a deep breath, stretched out in the water and began to swim for the opposite side of the pool, only thirty feet away.

There were cruise ships plying the North Atlantic that didn't create so much havoc on the water. Legs and arms thrashing wildly, Trudy laboriously plowed through the pool. Every so often she lifted her head, and like a whale, took a great deep breath before she went back under the surface. The end result was a great deal of splashing but little progress.

After what seemed like an eternity, Trudy reached the far end of the pool, turned around, and after another period of extended flogging of the water, finally made it back to where she started, panting and out of breath. Then she looked up expectantly to Handley, who had stood by calmly, watching, with the WSA diving instructor.

The other instructor turned to Handley and said, "Oh, she'll *never* make a swimmer. She's too wild," and suggested instead that perhaps Trudy might make a better diver than a swimmer.

Handley, however, disagreed. He wasn't interested in how much Trudy knew about swimming and how well she did. In fact, he actually preferred working with swimmers like Trudy who were so raw they hadn't developed any bad habits, and he was impressed by the way all the Ederle girls had tried to swim the crawl, even though they really didn't know how.

He would teach, she would learn, and in time Trudy Ederle would be a swimmer.

Like Henry Ederle, Louis de Breda Handley's first glimpse of America had probably been that of the Twin Lights of the Highlands. He was born in 1874 in Rome, his mother was Italian, and his name on his birth certificate was Luigi de Breda. His American-born father, Francis Montague Handley, was a sculptor, specializing in marble, capable of producing exquisite figures in the classical style. The elder Handley, whose family was already prominent, became attached to the Vatican as a palace official, serving as a Privy Chamberlain of Sword and Cape to both Popes Pius X and Leo XII—their private butler—and becoming the first American to be made a commander in the Order of Saint Gregory. Of the five pontifical orders of knighthood in the Catholic Church, to be appointed to that group is the highest honor that a layman can attain, an honor given in recognition of extraordinary service to the church.

One of three children, Louis de Breda Handley's two sisters later became nuns. Educated by the Christian Brothers in Rome, Handley received a classical education in the most formal sense, learning Latin, Greek, French, Spanish, and Italian, and earned a reputation as a persuasive and elegant writer. But for all his academic prowess, he adhered to the classical notion of "healthy mind, healthy body" and took physical training as seriously as he took his studies. He learned to swim in the Tiber River.

In 1896, at the age of twenty-two, Handley, who adopted the anglicized version of his name, left Rome to live in the United States. Upon his arrival he went into the importing business. A gentleman, he spent most of his time pursuing pastimes appropriate to his status.

He joined the prestigious Knickerbocker Athletic Club, for whom he competed in sweeps and sculls, swimming, and water polo, but he also trained and bred dogs, raced sailboats, hunted, rode, and played football. When the club disbanded after the notorious Molineaux murder case, a scandal in which one club member tried to poison the club's athletic director and accidentally killed the director's aunt instead, Handley quietly changed allegiances and joined the New York Athletic Club.

Despite his mannered appearance and upbringing, Handley was one of the finest all-around athletes of the era, recognized as the world champion in an event known as the "medley race," a event popular at the turn of the century, which combined aspects of both the decathlon and the modern triathlon. Racers competed against one another in a series of consecutive, quarter-mile races, walking, running, cycling, riding, swimming, and rowing in sequence, a feat Handley accomplished in a remarkable sixteen minutes and twenty-seven seconds.

Handley, however, made his greatest mark as an athlete in the water. Like Trudy Ederle, swimming fulfilled him like nothing else and served his life the same way the church had once served his father. His reverence for the sport of swimming bordered on the spiritual, and he once wrote, "There is no better form of physical culture. Swimming brings into action the entire system, giving every part of the body its proportionate share of work; it develops thoroughly and symmetrically, producing supple, resilient, well rounded muscles; it makes for grace of carriage and ease of movement; it activates and strengthens the functional organs, it ensures robust good health and good spirits." When teaching, either in print or in person, he often proceeded in the manner of the Catholic catechism, asking questions and then providing the answer himself, all the while cautioning that while the desire to win was natural, that was never the sole goal of sport. "If undue importance is attached to them so that victory becomes the paramount consideration and defeat leaves a feeling of disappointment and humiliation," wrote Handley, "then the zest goes out of the game and it no longer represents pastime and recreation, as it should."

This did not mean that Handley was any kind of milquetoast, for to do anything but one's best was not only unacceptable, but essentially immoral, a betrayal of one's physical gifts as delivered by God, and Handley himself played to win, an attitude he fostered in Trudy and every other swimmer under his direction. During an era in which the sport of water polo was considerably more violent than it is today, Handley was considered the greatest player of his era. He served as captain of both the swimming and water polo teams for first the Knickerbocker Athletic Club and then the New York Athletic Club and led the American water polo team to victory at the 1904 Olympics. In over a decade of competitive water polo, teams captained by Handley lost exactly twice.

He constantly strove to be better, and he studied swimming as if it were a subject taught to him by the Christian Brothers. When word of a new stroke known as the Australian crawl made its way to the United States in 1903, Handley sought not only to understand and learn the new stroke, but to improve upon it.

Like the trudgen, the new stroke had its beginnings in the style of Native people, although the specific circumstances are still debated by swimming historians. Some trace the origination to a ten-year-old boy, Alick Wickham, who had been reared in the Solomon Islands by his English father and Native mother, where he learned to swim. When he was then sent to boarding school in Australia he inadvertently imported an entirely new stroke, one that combined the arm action of the trudgen with an up-and-down leg kick used by Solomon Island Natives. A swimming coach named George Farmer saw the boy swimming in a race at Sydney and allegedly called out, "Look at that boy crawling over the water!" thus giving the stroke its name.

But at about the same time, three brothers by the name of Cavill also began using the stroke, which their father, Frederick Cavill, later claimed to have learned from a Samoan woman while traveling through the Samoan Islands. The Cavills refined the stroke some-what, so that as one arm came over and pulled down, the opposite leg kicked downward. However the stroke originated, male swim-mers using the so-called Australian crawl began winning races in Australia in times never seen before. The days of the trudgen were just about over.

Handley first learned of the stroke through written descriptions and diagrams in newspapers and magazines and tried to teach him-self in the indoor pool of the New York Athletic Club, at the time one of only a few indoor pools in New York. Yet no matter how fast he stroked with his arms and kicked with his feet, Handley, already one of the best swimmers in America, equally proficient in the back-stroke, the trudgen, and the breaststroke, could not manage the Aus-tralian crawl. In fact, after only a few strokes his legs kept sinking under the water, bringing him to almost a complete stop. Other club members who tried the stroke were no more successful and after only a few tries returned to the more familiar trudgen, dismissing the Australian crawl as some unexplained foreign novelty, leaving Handley to learn the stroke on his own.

He studied the problem as if it were an issue of science, which, in effect, it was. He concluded that the problem he was having stemmed not from the arm stroke, which was almost identical to that used in the trudgen, but from the unique kick. In the Australian crawl, the swimmer kicked at the knee, as Handley himself once described it, "lifting the feet high above the water and beating them down just once to every arm stroke." Over and over and over again Handley tried to master the kick, only to falter as if he had never been in the water before. It was embarrassing and the cause of no small amount of amusement to other club members, for Handley had rarely expe-rienced failure of any kind.

He was nearly ready to give up, concluding that either the Cavill brothers were freaks of nature or that the descriptions of the stroke were simply wrong.

Then it came to him. In Australia, competitive swimming events took place in so-called ocean pools—outdoor swimming pools filled with water from tidal tanks or even from the tide itself simply spill-ing over the sides of the pool. Competitive swimming was done in seawater. But the indoor pool at the New York Athletic Club was filled with fresh water, which Handley knew provided far less buoyancy than the salt water of the sea.

Out of the sea, in fresh water, the kick used in the Australian crawl was not sufficient to keep Handley's lower body above the water. When one leg left the water to begin the kick down, the other leg—and the rest of the swimmer's body below the waist—sank. Each subsequent kick only made the problem worse, for as the leg raised up to kick back down, it drove the swimmer farther under water. In only a few strokes all forward progress stopped.

Now that he knew what the problem was, Handley puzzled over the solution. In seawater the Australian crawl kick had already proven superior to any other kind used at the time, such as the frog kick used by the breaststroke and the scissor kick of the trudgen, so Handley knew he had to develop a kick that would prove equally superior in fresh water. One day while he was in the pool experimenting, he discussed the issue with Gus Sundstrom, the club's veteran swimming instructor. Sundstrom instructed Handley to watch him closely and then demonstrated what he referred to as the "swordfish kick," a kick he used in training demonstrations with novice swimmers to convince them of the importance of using their legs while swimming. Stretching his arms forward in front of him, Sundstrom locked his thumbs so that he was unable to either stroke or paddle with his arms. He then stretched out in the water and began kicking furiously, not from the knee, using the lower leg as in the Australian crawl, but from the hip, keeping his legs straight and using his feet as if they were flippers. In this way he was able to propel himself across the width of the pool without using his arms at all.

For Handley, it was a "Eureka!" moment. In an instant, he combined the overhand arm stroke with Sundstrom's swordfish kick. That changed everything. His lower body stayed buoyant and Handley moved through the water with a speed that he had never thought was possible. It wasn't easy, but it worked.

Over the next few months and years, Handley and another club member, Austrian-born Otto Wahle, spent hours perfecting the new stroke, over time adding several other adaptations, and timing the stroke with breathing. Handley discovered that since the swordfish kick, which he preferred to refer to as the "thrash," provided the swimmer with more forward momentum, it was possible to reach out farther with the arms than was standard in the trudgen stroke, and that the swimmer need not stroke quite as quickly to maintain speed. Although Handley and Wahle initially tried to time the thrash precisely with the arm action, they discovered that was of absolutely no benefit. For consistency, all the swimmer needed to do was make sure that he or she kept kicking at a regular pace, usually four or six times for each stroke of the arms, but it didn't matter a wit whether the downward leg kick matched the downward motion of the arm, or if the kick of the left leg took place simultaneously with the stroke of either arm. All that mattered was that both the arms and the legs remained in motion the entire time. The result was the first swimming stroke in history in which the arms and legs were in motion independent of one another. The "American crawl" was born, and Louis de Breda Handley became its evangelist.

Over the next few years, with help from Sundstrom, Wahle, and Handley, a younger member of the club, Charles Daniels, became the first swimmer to perfect this new stroke. In 1904 he won three gold medals at the Olympic Games, easily defeating swimmers using versions of both the trudgen and the Australian crawl, and in one four-day stretch in 1905, he set a remarkable fourteen world records.

Yet despite Daniels's success, the new stroke had a hard time catching on. Swimmers already trained in the breaststroke and trudgen found it difficult to break old habits and learn new ones, and many instructors, unable to break old habits themselves, considered it a gimmick that might be fine for world-class swimmers but was of little benefit to those who swam less frequently. Others simply did not know how to teach it or else refused to abandon the notion that the leg kick must somehow be directly tied to the arm stroke, unnecessarily complicating the procedure, while many Australians stubbornly stuck with their own version of the stroke.

Nevertheless, Daniels's success secured Handley's reputation as an innovative teacher, and as his own competitive athletic career began to wind down as he reached his midthirties, Handley began to spend more and more time teaching others. When American water polo enthusiasts chose to abandon the rougher American version of the game in favor of the tamer European model in 1911, Handley retired from the sport and began devoting more of his time to swimming. Over the next decade Yale, Princeton, New York University, and the

New York Athletic Club all asked for his help and expertise. Handley said yes to them all, refusing to take a salary from any of them. He still viewed athletics as a higher calling, and taking a salary to teach swimming would have violated his commitment to amateurism. At the same time, however, he began writing about swimming, penning short articles and instructionals for newspapers and magazines. In a short time be became the best—and best-known—swimming coach in the entire country.

In 1917, shortly after she created the WSA, Charlotte Epstein asked Handley if he would serve as head coach for the group. In the context of the day, it was like asking the New York Giants legendary manager John McGraw to teach women how to play baseball. But Handley was completely unfettered by prejudice or, by all accounts, sexism. He thought everybody, everywhere, should learn to swim, and quickly agreed.

He may not have realized it at the time, but the opportunity to teach under the auspices of the WSA was an ideal situation. Few members of the association knew how to swim before joining the group, and many were youngsters not even in their teens, with no bad habits to break or preconceived notions to dissuade. The WSA provided Handley with a perfect laboratory in which to perfect his training methods, and an unending stream of subjects of every athletic ability and type upon which to try them out.

Moreover, the group's organizational philosophy, epitomized by the motto Sportsmanship Before Winning, matched Handley's classical notions about the nature of sport. The main focus of the WSA was never the girls and young women with the most talent, but those who could not swim at all, and the development of character was more important than any timed trial. Swimming in competition, and even giving public demonstrations like the one Trudy Ederle attended at Highlands, was done primarily to publicize the larger group and help the WSA reach more and more young women and give them the opportunity to learn how to swim.

After their first session with Handley, the Ederle girls soon became regulars at the basement pool, showing up every Wednesday and Friday evening for their fifty-minute session. They looked forward to seeing Handley calmly walking back and forth along the edge of the pool, never in a rush, completely unhurried, as patient with the novice as he was with the more experienced, completely unbothered by the conditions in the basement pool in Brooklyn—in fact, he barely noticed them. Handley understood that there was no alternative. Except for the rare swim meet, women were simply not allowed in the pools of private clubs such as the New York Athletic Club or the YMCA, and once fall arrived, ocean pools were not a viable alternative for training. Handley was there to teach swimming, and he was determined to do so without regard to either physical conditions or the prejudices that to this point had prevented women from participating in sports.

Of the three Ederle girls, Margaret was initially the most advanced and the most promising. Helen, the oldest, had the most bad habits to break, was less athletic, and although she enjoyed swimming, was not quite as enamored of the sport as her two younger sisters. Trudy clearly loved to swim but was timid, still more of a child than a young woman and, as of yet, lacked her sisters' discipline and drive to learn. But Meg, age fourteen, was at the perfect age for a young woman to join the WSA. She was just going through her adolescent growth spurt and growing stronger and more confident in herself every day. In the WSA she found a host of girls just like herself and responded to the emerging camaraderie of the group.

Handley was convinced that the American crawl was not only the fastest swimming stroke, but, in the long run, the easiest to learn and the most efficient. Few other swimming instructors outside the WSA shared his belief, for few had mastered the stroke themselves. Most believed that the crawl was too advanced for beginners and doggedly taught students the dog paddle, the breaststroke, and then the trudgen, in succession. Handley took the opposite approach, teaching the crawl first, even to those who previously could not swim at all. He later cautioned female swimmers "not to be misled into thinking that old fashioned strokes are the best for them." He may not have known it, but at the time he was probably the only swimming coach in the world who was teaching the American crawl to women.

His method was methodical. Even though Trudy could swim, in her first few sessions he treated her as if she had never even gotten wet before. That could have put Trudy off, but Helen and Meg received the same treatment. The first thing Handley had everyone do was learn to float, to relax in the water and become accustomed to their own buoyancy.

Even Trudy found that a bit difficult at first. Even though she had already spent hours and hours in the water, at nearly every moment she was moving her arms, legs, and hands keeping herself afloat. She had to learn to float without the assistance of her arms and legs, to feel herself half in and half out of the water, to float without having her heart race a thousand miles an hour and without gasping for breath, but breathing as easily as she did when she was reading.

Handley then taught his students how to kick, using the "thrash," so they could gain a sense of just how much their forward movement depended on their legs, and not their arms. This was almost brand-new for Trudy. Although she used her legs when she swam they were something of an afterthought, and this was, perhaps, the most difficult part of the crawl for Trudy to learn. In fact, as she grew older, if there was one flaw in her style, it was her occasional failure to make the most of her leg kick, an imperfection that was offset somewhat by her feet. Trudy's feet were not long, but they were extremely wide and acted almost as paddles when she swam.

Not until Trudy learned the kick to Handley's satisfaction did he even mention the arm stroke, something he first had his students learn by standing in the water—easy to do at the basement pool—bending at the waist until submerged and practicing stroking while walking forward, so they grew accustomed to the feel of the arms pulling through the water. Like most young swimmers, at first Trudy kept her arms too straight and reached out too far, giving her stroke little strength. She had to learn the proper arm position and how to turn her body slightly as her stroke shifted from side to side so she could take full advantage of her shoulder, chest, and back muscles.

The next piece of the puzzle was breathing, which Handley referred to as "deep inspiration," a phrase that not only reminded his students to take full, rather than shallow, breaths, but reinforced his view that one swam primarily for well-being and health than for any other reason. He taught Trudy to breathe in much the same way in which he taught the arm stroke, by having her and the other students stand in the pool then bend at the waist, so their face was in the water.

Once each of the four elements was learned, swimming the crawl was just a matter of putting those four elements together. Of course it wasn't quite that easy, but that was another part of Handley's genius. By breaking the crawl down into its component parts, and having students learn each component isolated from the other, he made the stroke seem easy to learn. When he asked his students to pull all the parts together, since they were already proficient in each element beforehand, learning to use them in combination was far less overwhelming than if they had tried to learn the kick and arm stroke and breathing method simultaneously. All the while, he emphasized keeping the body relaxed and the movements slow and deliberate, concentrating on form. Speed would come with experience.

Every week, Trudy learned something new and gained ever more confidence. And that was Handley's real talent. He was a master motivator, smiling easily, gaining the girls' trust, and from the very beginning working on the girls' mental attitude and self-confidence as much as their swimming skills. Despite the prevailing belief that women were—by far—the weaker sex, Handley was his own man and rejected that assessment. Each week he saw more and more young women who only needed an opportunity and some confidence to thrive. The more time he spent with the young women the more convinced he became that they were just as capable of swimming as men were, and perhaps even more so.

Physically, he recognized that due to a higher percentage of body fat women were more buoyant than men and that this gave them a great advantage in the water—it took less energy for a woman to stay afloat than it did for a man. At a time when others were debating the medical wisdom of women doing any kind of physical labor, Handley believed, as he later wrote in his book *Swimming for Women*, "Any normal girl and woman who is proficient in swimming, healthy and in good condition, will profit by going in [the water] as often as she pleases, even daily." He saw nothing wrong with female swimmers swimming as much as a thousand yards a day if they had the opportunity, suggesting only that any swimmer "rest as soon as one feels tired."

In this way, as Handley taught swimming technique, he also began breaking down psychological obstacles that few women even recognized existed, teaching his students that there were no barriers to their potential achievements. While some of the adult swimmers found such freedom a bit intimidating and began their lessons thinking "I don't think I can" rather than "I can and I will," many of the younger girls, already being raised in a world in which, for the first time, the equality of women was actually being debated and gaining some credence, accepted Handley at his word. His own personal manner exuded confidence. If he thought the girls could do something and told them so, well, they believed they could. It was that simple, and everything he had them do reinforced that notion, for his incremental method of teaching left no place for failure. Some students learned faster than others, and some were more adept, but absolutely everyone learned.

The sessions in the pool were only a beginning. Even during his weekly lessons, half the time he didn't even have the swimmers in the water. At first Trudy and some of the other girls were more than a little puzzled over that—they wanted to swim, after all—but in a very short period of time Trudy realized that Handley's methods worked. The proof was in the pool.

Because access to the water was so limited, Handley gave his students exercises they could do the rest of the week when they had no access to the water at all. He showed them simple drills they could do at home, like sitting in a chair and sticking their legs out and practicing the thrash kick, or bending at the waist and practicing the arm stroke in front of a mirror. He didn't use the term, but all these dryland drills reinforced the muscle memory that today is recognized as important to any athletic achievement.

Trudy, Meg, and Helen spent hours practicing the drills at home, standing or sitting in front of a mirror. They would giggle at one another as they pantomimed the various drills, criticize and cajole one another, all competing with one another for the words they hoped to hear the next time they saw Mr. Handley. A simple "Very good, Miss Ederle, very good," was the greatest praise imaginable and did wonders for Trudy's self-confidence.

Handley did not just teach the students, either. He also taught the other instructors. All WSA coaches, including Handley, were volunteers, and as swimmers became more proficient, they were expected to contribute their time to teach others, and Handley's training routines and methods of instruction were adopted throughout the organization. In short order the WSA created a virtual assembly line of swimming instruction and spat out swimmers and teachers in rapid succession, all of them swimming and teaching Handley's American crawl, the only women in the world who could do so.

For Trudy, almost from the moment she first joined the WSA and fell under the influence of Louis de Breda Handley, if he told her she could do something, she simply accepted it as a fact, without any hesitation. And away from the pool, where Trudy and her two sisters were naturally competitive, they reinforced for one another each and every lesson, physical and mental, Handley was teaching. His manner of coaching swimming was just as influential as his work on the development of the American crawl.

Although none of them knew it at the time, all of Handley's students, including the three Ederle girls, were learning at the hand of a master. In only one short year the best WSA students were already well on their way to becoming the best female swimmers in the world. That was, after all, Handley's goal. The Olympics were on the horizon, and the former Olympian, a true believer in the Olympic ideal, was already preparing his charges to reveal the American crawl to the rest of the world.

While Handley took care of the swimming instruction, Charlotte Epstein handled the administration of the organization, continuing to tout the work of the WSA at every opportunity. Now that the WSA had the blessing of the AAU, Eppie moved quickly. She sensed that the death of the AAU's James Sullivan had removed the biggest impediment to the participation of American women in the Olympics. The 1916 Olympics had been canceled due to World War I, and now there was increased interest in and awareness of the 1920 Olympics scheduled for Antwerp, Belgium, as the entire world looked toward the games as evidence that the recent nightmare had ended and that it was possible for enemies to come together, put political differences aside, and battle peaceably in the athletic arena.

In the fall and winter of 1918, just as the Ederle girls joined the group, Epstein organized swim meet after swim meet and demonstration after demonstration, raising the profile not only of the WSA and WSA swimmers, but of women's swimming in general. A small cascade of stories in New York's newspapers made women's swim meets almost as common as the baseball box scores and rapidly began moving the sport into the mainstream.

By the beginning of 1919 WSA swimmers, all of whom were learning the American crawl under the tutelage of Handley, were clearly the best in the world, collecting world records at every distance like seashells on the beach. The IOC was already planning to hold women's competitions in the 100- and 300-meter freestyle swims, the 4-by-100-meter relay, and both platform and springboard diving in the 1920 Olympic Games, and in a time of increasing nationalism, the American Olympic Committee (AOC) was feeling pressure to field a women's swimming team to Antwerp.

Although the emphasis on winning went against both her background and the stated goals of the WSA, Charlotte Epstein knew that an appearance in the Olympics would raise the profile not only of women's swimming, but of women's athletics in general. She wanted to make certain that American girls would not only be included in the games, but that they could win, for she knew that if it appeared that the American women's swimming team was likely to medal at the games, the AOC would be far more likely to send a women's team to Antwerp. Besides, as they began to talk about the Olympics to the members of the WSA, and Handley regaled them with his memories of past Olympics, they could sense that young girls like Trudy were beginning to dream, chattering to one another about what it would be like to perform in front of thousands of people and meet athletes from all over the world.

As WSA swimmers continued to dominate every competition and set nearly every record at nearly every distance, in April 1919 the AAU announced that in 1920 it would sponsor Olympic tryouts and that the AOC would send a women's swimming and diving team to the Olympics. The decision, which only a few years before would have met staunch resistance, scarcely caused a ripple. Dozens of other fledgling women's swimming groups were hastily created all over the country. The first wave of American swimming talent was poised to take on the world.

The Ederle girls, particularly Margaret and Trudy, were beginning to move up in the ranks of WSA swimmers, but none was as yet in the top echelon of the group and under consideration for the Olympic team. Those swimmers who would participate in the Olympic tryouts would be the swimmers that Handley had the most success with, primarily girls who had joined the group soon after it had first formed and had done so while still quite young. Ethelda (Thelda) Bleibtrey, after contracting polio in 1917, which led to a curvature of her spine, had joined the WSA at the age of sixteen early in 1918, as part of her recovery, and within a year was the best swimmer in the group, undefeated at any distance. Young Aileen Riggin, only thirteen, had joined after surviving the Spanish flu to help with her recuperation. Already an accomplished dancer, the sprightly Riggin was not only one of the group's best swimmers but excelled at diving as well. Trudy and Margaret were improving, but were a year behind the groups' best swimmers.

All the WSA girls, including Trudy and her sisters, were among the crowd that gathered for the Olympic swimming and diving trials held at the Manhattan Beach ocean pool on July 10, 1920, the same pool that served as the home of the WSA during the late spring and summer. In addition to WSA swimmers such as Bleibtrey, Riggin, and the WSA's two other most accomplished swimmers, Charlotte Boyle and Helen Wainwright, the trials also included representatives of Philadelphia's Meadowlark Club, the Detroit Athletic Club, the Multnomah Athletic Club of Portland, Oregon, and several other groups.

It wasn't close. The WSA girls, with their mastery of the American crawl, dominated the contests: Thelda Bleibtrey beat the existing world record in the 100 meters in a trial heat, and then set the record again in the finals, knocking another half second off the mark. Aileen Riggin, now fourteen, and Helen Wainwright, another fourteen-year-old, dominated the diving competition despite the fact that both girls had been diving only a short time. Had the Olympic team been selected on the basis of the trials alone, the entire team could have been created from the roster of WSA swimmers; but for political reasons the AOC selected six girls from the WSA trained by Handley, and six swimmers not connected to the WSA.

Even so, it hardly mattered. With Charlotte Epstein serving as team manager and Handley's old colleague Otto Wahle acting as coach, the WSA swimmers were just as dominant in Antwerp as they had been at Manhattan Beach. Although conditions were horrible—the swimming competition was held in a frigid, silt-filled canal that left the girls shivering—Bleibtrey won the gold medal in both the 100- and 300-meter freestyle, winning the shorter distance in 1 minute 13⅗ seconds, more than three seconds faster than second-place finisher Irene Guest of Detroit. She then won the 300-meter freestyle in 4 minutes 34 seconds, nearly eight seconds better than American Mary Woodbridge and nearly ten seconds faster than any non-American. In the 400-meter relay the American team, paced by Bleibtrey, finished an incredible twenty-nine seconds ahead of runner-up Great Britain. Aileen Riggin, Helen Wainwright, and Helen Meany, all of the WSA, swept the springboard diving competition. As Riggin later recalled, the Americans' advantage was due almost solely to the crawl stroke developed by Handley. "We were the first girls to do it," she said, "and we won everything. That stroke took the world by storm." And in the wake of the Olympics, it also swept up Trudy Ederle.

As the first American women to win a medal at the Olympic Games, when Bleibtrey, Riggin, Wainwright, and the others returned to America they were greeted as heroes. For weeks they attended a steady stream of banquets and luncheons and parades, met politicians and other celebrities, and were even offered work as swimming coaches. To their fellow members of the WSA, like Trudy and her sisters, it was all a bit hard to believe that the girls who they swam alongside in the basement pool were famous. Trudy was particularly close to both Riggin and Wainwright, and she loved hearing their descriptions of the Olympic opening ceremonies, where thousands of white pigeons were released into the air and the swimmers wore white flannel pleated skirts and smart-looking navy blue jackets. Although Trudy had already traveled to Europe when her family visited relatives in Germany, she still hung on every word when Riggin and Wainwright described the nearly two-week trip across the Atlantic, where the swimmers, the only women among the hundreds of male athletes, were the object of constant attention from such well-known athletes as the Hawaiian swimming champ Duke Kahanamoku.

Although Trudy found it hard to imagine that she would ever

swim well enough to make the Olympic team, at the same time the message was clear: if a girl was one of the top swimmers in the WSA, she was also one of the best swimmers in the world. For Trudy Ederle, that meant that anything, absolutely anything, was possible.

8

The Channel

THE ENGLISH CHANNEL is like no other body of water in the world.

Only twenty-one miles across at its narrowest point between Cape Gris-Nez (Cape Gray Nose) and Dover, those twenty-one miles can be the most treacherous waters in the world. The reason is the tide, for were it not for the tides, swimming the English Channel would have all the allure of swimming back and forth in a backyard pool for half a day or more in the middle of November. It is the tide that makes swimming the Channel so challenging, and the tide that has made swimming the Channel not only one of the most difficult athletic feats on the face of the earth, but also one of the best known and most romantic, a challenge that, once it takes hold of a swimmer, refuses to let go.

And to understand the tides one must understand the creation of the Channel itself.

The English Channel began in a flood. For eons, since the very first formation of Pangea—the ancient supercontinent that once included virtually the entire land surface of the earth—the land mass that eventually included all of the British Isles was not an island at all. As sea levels went up and down and the mechanics of plate tectonics alternately split continents apart and drove them back together, much of the island was alternately exposed and buried and exposed again as if a great tide were rising and falling, shaping it with each wave. Yet Britain itself remained fixed to the larger continent of Europe, its eastern and southern coasts folded into France.

During one such metaphorical wave about 205 million years ago, the south and east of England were covered by a warm, shallow sea absolutely teeming with microscopic marine life—plankton—that swirled in the currents and tides, rising and falling in the water column until death. Over time these infinitesimal remains inexorably drifted to the bottom of the sea, a slow but steady rain of calcium carbonate, its depth growing by one millimeter per century until the cumulative weight and pressure fused the remains together into a single massive strata, one that over some thirty-five million years eventually created a seafloor that in places measured more than three hundred meters deep.

The result—built up over those thirty-five million years—was chalk. It can be seen today not only in the white cliffs of Dover that reveal the full dimension of this incessant rain of microscopic life, but just inches beneath the ground in much of the south of England, in northwestern France, and elsewhere in western Europe. Each place there is chalk was once the bottom of the same vast primordial sea.

Then, over time, as ocean levels dropped and this sea began to recede, a vast portion of southern Britain, France, and northern Europe was exposed, a single land mass sandwiched between the North Sea and the northern Atlantic that scientists dubbed "Doggerland." As seas levels rose and fell and rivers carved their way through the chalk and poured into the sea to the north and to the south, what is now Britain came to resemble a peninsula connected to France and the rest of the European continent by an isthmus, a massive chalk land bridge nearly two hundred meters high, covered by a thin layer of soil, that ran through Dover in England and Calais in France. Known to geologists as the Weald-Artois ridge, flora and fauna alike flowed back and forth across this land bridge without interruption. What lived in England also lived in France.

Then came the ice. Nearly two million years ago, as the land mass that included the British Isles drifted northward almost to its present position, the Northern Hemisphere entered an epoch marked by the advance and retreat of ice, periods of cooling that featured glaciation and the subsequent lowering of the sea level, separated by warmer periods in which the glaciers retreated and seas levels rose again. England was affected dramatically by these changes. During warm periods England became a savanna resembling modern-day Africa. When the temperature cooled the savanna turned to tundra, windswept and snow covered. And each time the ice came south it scoured the earth, carving wide, deep channels. In the south of England the ice began to cut into the strata of chalk that bound Britain to the continent.

Yet Britain and the European continent still remained joined together until some 450,000 years ago, by which time early humans had reached both England and northern Europe, advancing and retreating in the wake of the ice. Then, sometime between 450,000 and 200,000 years ago as glaciers more than two thousand feet thick retreated, a lake of meltwater, trapped to the north by the retreating glaciers, built up behind the land bridge between Britain and France. Each day it grew ever larger and deeper as both the Rhine and the Thames rivers, draining an enormous watershed, combined with meltwater from the glaciers themselves to create a vast lake far larger than any ever seen on the planet before.

The land bridge, some thirty kilometers wide, became, in effect, a dam. To the north the great lake grew ever larger, while south of the bridge, the land now free of ice, the weather turned more temperate and created a mixture of grasslands, forests, marshes, and lakes. Fed by the Somme and the Seine rivers, a damp but fertile delta plain emptied into the North Atlantic. Great herds of game and vast numbers of birds and other animals took advantage of the natural bounty, as did small bands of men and women.

Had the great lake, hundreds of miles wide and far, far larger than any lake that exists on earth today, continued to fill, and had the glaciers not retreated so quickly, the lake may eventually have slowly breached the ridge, spilling over it first in a trickle and then, over time, eventually wearing down a channel and creating a massive waterfall and a river running southward, slowly draining the lake until the retreating glaciers finally created an outlet to the north that then would have allowed the waters to escape into the North Sea.

But this is not what happened. For reasons that are still not entirely clear, the land bridge between France and Britain suffered a massive, catastrophic failure, perhaps caused by an earthquake or other tectonic event.

In an instant, billions and billions of gallons of water, water that had rested placidly in the lake for thousands of years, began to move.

Those billions of gallons, which had long pressed upon the land bridge from the north, burst through in an act of watery violence the world had never before seen. The equivalent of one hundred Mississippi Rivers poured through the breach as up to *one million cubic meters of water per second* roared down into the valley and then into the North Atlantic. Water and earth were sent downstream in an unimaginable torrent, a cataclysmic event that plowed and scoured and carved away at the surface of the lowlands, tearing deep into the chalk, carving away the land bridge in huge chunks, as one scientist described it, "like a buzz saw through Styrofoam." In this case the unstoppable force—water—met nothing immovable. Gigantic sections of earth and rock acted like a bulldozer, while the torrent of water washed away everything before it like so much sand before a fire hose, scouring out a passage to the Atlantic.

And then, in only a few months, it was done. The lake was emptied and the flow of water slowed and then stopped. Now the dimension of the destruction was revealed. Every tree and blade of grass, every European bison, antelope, mammoth, wooly rhinoceros, cave lion, and deer, every member of every vast herd that lived in the valley was gone, swept into the water and washed into the sea, their existence there virtually erased. The land bridge itself was radically diminished, its center carved out in an enormous swath. Where man and animals had once roamed there was now only water. Britain became an island, separated from the European continent by what we know today as the English Channel, the path of this primordial flood.

Britain and Europe remained apart for at least the next hundred thousand years, separated by the sea, as the human residents of each place lurched toward civilization oblivious to the other. Then, ever so slowly, summers began to shorten and winter's tentacles reached out once again. The glaciers slowly returned, the sea level dropped, and the sea drained away from the valley to the south. The narrow remnants of the land bridge were exposed once more, tenuously joining England to the continent, and humans and animals and other life filled the valley one more time.

Incredibly, it all happened again. The earth warmed and as the glaciers retreated a second great lake backed up behind the land bridge to the north, growing larger and deeper each day, fed by the Rhine and the Thames, filling with water the great cuts and gouges the glaciers had cut into the earth.

And once again, the land bridge did not hold. For a second time the ground shuddered and lurched and the waters broke through, instantly and catastrophically, in a flood even larger than before, a deluge contemporary scientists believe was the largest flood in history, releasing even more water than before, scouring the Channel floor even deeper, this time creating troughs and gouges in the earth as much as ten kilometers in width and some fifty meters deep, turning the waters of the North Atlantic brown with earth and sediment for months.

For all intents and purposes, Britain was now an island, as on only a few subsequent occasions has ice caused sea levels to drop far enough to expose the remnant of the land bridge and reconnect England to Europe, and then only briefly. For most of this time Britain and Europe have been separated by the confluence of the North Sea and the North Atlantic.

The result of these two floods was the English Channel, a great basin through which the ocean waters of the North Sea and the North Atlantic, driven by the tides, meet violently, creating massive and at times thoroughly unpredictable currents that wash back and forth and up and down and to and fro as if in a gigantic bathtub. The result is some of the roughest and most unpredictable waters in the world, waters that are calm one moment and storm tossed the next, often shrouded in fog and driven by winds, waters that for eons isolated Britain from the rest of the world, and left human beings on each side, wondering how to get across.

Every six hours, as the moon orbits the earth, the ocean tides change. In the English Channel, currents powered by the tides speed up, slow down, and then reverse course, and the tide rises and falls. For about an hour and half before the high tide to about four and a half hours after—known as the "flood tide"—the water rushes through the Channel in a northeasterly direction as the waters of the North Atlantic flow toward the North Sea. Then the ebb tide takes over, and the water first slows, then, forming a series of channels in slack water, reverses its course before moving again en masse in the opposite direction, flowing southwesterly as the waters of the North Sea come rushing back in a rough imitation of the primordial flood that shaped the Channel in the first place.

The effect is most pronounced in the Strait of Dover, the narrowest part of the Channel and where the Channel waters, in effect, act something like the water in a river. For as the waters from the North Sea and the North Atlantic move through the narrows between England and France, they are squeezed between both coasts, increasing in speed. At their peak during the flood and ebb tides, the waters of the Channel flow astonishingly fast—as much as four miles per hour.

The intensity of the tide does not remain static but changes as the moon completes its twenty-eight-day orbital cycle around the earth. Every two weeks, when the moon is new or full and the tidal pull strongest, what is called a "spring tide" is in effect. Over the course of one twelve-hour cycle, there is an eighteen-foot difference between high tide and low tide, resulting in an enormous volume of water rushing back and forth. During the spring tide an otherwise stationary object will float some thirteen nautical miles northeastward during the flood tide, then be pushed back to the southeast fifteen nautical miles on the ebb tide. Even during neap tides—when there is a half moon and tides are somewhat weaker—the difference between high water and low water is still nearly ten feet, and a stationary object will still be carried some seven or eight miles in each direction as the tide floods and ebbs.

To this day even experienced mariners using gas- or diesel-powered vessels have a difficult time navigating these treacherous waters. For a Channel swimmer, the problem is exponentially worse. He or she is virtually at the mercy of the tides and wholly dependent upon the accompanying pilot boat to remain on course. The swimmer must simultaneously make use of the tides and at the same time swim through and against them, somehow maintaining a course that, in the end, will take the swimmer perpendicular to and across the direction of the tidal currents. The swimmer must work with the tides, at various points racing with the rush of water back and forth to tack across the Channel in a manner not unlike a sailboat running before the wind, and then take advantage of slack water between tides to gain ground toward the opposite shore before tacking with the tide once more.

As a result the swimmer's route across the Channel is never a straight line. Depending upon the speed of the swimmer and tidal conditions, the path across—if made under sixteen or seventeen hours—much resembles the letter Z, a serpentine course with at least two near-180-degree turns, a route that can add as much as ten or twenty miles to the twenty-one-mile distance the crow flies between Dover and the French coast. But if one swims more slowly and becomes caught in another tidal change, the route becomes even more tangled. Matthew Webb for instance, who took nearly twenty-two hours to make his crossing, made no less than four reverses of direction with the tides—his course resembled two squat Z's stacked on top of each other—and he traveled much farther within the Channel itself, back and forth, than the twenty-one miles across.

That is the reason swimming the Channel is so difficult and the reason so many swimmers have come so close to succeeding only to be turned back, for when the tide turns on an exhausted swimmer, even one only a few hundred yards from completing the swim, he or she often lacks the strength and energy to overcome the changing tidal current and can be carried off, either parallel to shore, or, in some conditions, even backward, back toward where he or she first started, a reversal with a devastating psychological impact. The hardest and most difficult part of the swim is often the final few hundred yards, when the tide combines with exhaustion and the cold to keep the swimmer from shore as surely as if he or she were anchored in place.

In the years following Webb's crossing, as one swimmer after another tried and failed to swim the Channel, those who pondered crossing the Channel would often spend as much time studying the tides and the currents as they would in training. But even the tides alone do not tell the entire story. In the same way that the waters of a river, when encountering shallows, can increase in speed and change direction, so too does the depth of the Channel waters impact the current in the ebb and flow of the tides, for as the depth of the water changes, so does the speed of the currents. Due to those two primordial floods in the Strait of Dover, the depth of the Channel varies wildly, from more than 120 feet in places to less than 6 feet in others. Around the Goodwin Sands, a ten-mile-long sandbank just northeast of Dover, the water is dangerously shallow, and a combination of storms and tides can make the waters around and over the sands surprisingly swift and uncertain. The Goodwin Sands, in fact, is even exposed at low tide, a condition that can create dangerous eddies and rough water in otherwise calm seas. The area is such a hazard that more than two thousand ships are known to have met their fate there. Even today an anchored vessel that serves as a lighthouse—a lightship—is permanently stationed atop the massive sandbank, yet ships still run aground with frightening regularity.

As if all this did not combine to make the crossing difficult enough, the weather adds another uncomfortable dimension. The clash of the waters often results in fog, a year-round hazard, one that not only can make the experience of swimming the Channel psychologically difficult, making it impossible for a swimmer to detect their own progress, but dangerous as well. The fog can be so dense that the accompanying pilot boats can and have lost sight of swimmers entirely, sometimes for hours, turning an already risky proposition into a potentially deadly one. Not only is it possible for a "lost" swimmer to drown, but due to the amount of boat traffic in the Channel, without the aid of a pilot boat a swimmer risks being run down by a passing vessel oblivious to the swimmer's presence.

Then there are the storms. Fronts moving in from the North Atlantic and funneled through the Channel can create winds that can reach hurricane force and waves that regularly reach two meters and occasionally much, much more. With every increase in wave action swimmers must struggle to breathe without swallowing seawater, which can cause nausea, while the constant rising and falling with each swell can make swimmers seasick. In short, crossing the Channel requires not only conditioning, physical fitness, and a measure of luck, but an experienced boat pilot and a complete and thorough understanding of the Channel itself.

For these reasons most attempts to swim the Channel have taken place during what early swimmers referred to as the "mystic season," August and September. Then, for two brief periods of three days each, the neap tides are at their weakest and the water temperature its warmest. If the weather cooperates, a virtually impossible task becomes only a nearly impossible one. For some swimmers that slender chance of success has made swimming the Channel completely irresistible.

Soon after Matthew Webb staggered onto the shore in Calais in August 1875, other swimmers began lining up for their chance at glory, for Webb's crossing made him wealthy, a fact that did not go unnoticed. In the weeks immediately after the crossing Webb made nearly fifty thousand dollars—the Prince of Wales alone gave him an award of twenty-five thousand dollars in honor of his accomplishment. For the remainder of his life Webb earned upward of one thousand dollars per personal appearance, and for the swim that killed him in the Niagara River he was scheduled to make fifteen thousand dollars.

Swimming the English Channel suddenly became the Victorian equivalent of winning the lottery. It had the potential of taking an otherwise normal bloke and, in less than twenty-four hours, not only making him famous, but rich. And Webb's success, in only his second try, made what had once seemed impossible not only plausible, but even likely.

The first swimmer to follow Webb into the cold Channel waters was Frederick Cavill, the same Frederick Cavill who would later help develop the Australian crawl. Already a well-known swimmer and, like J. B. Johnson, a member of the Serpentine Club, Cavill prepared for his crossing by completing a twenty-mile swim in the Thames and afterward was confident that the Channel would prove to be little more difficult. But Cavill—and others—soon discovered that Webb had either been extraordinarily lucky or extraordinarily talented. It would take more than thirty years before another person would be able to duplicate Webb's accomplishment.

Cavill made his first attempt in 1876 using the breaststroke but had to be pulled from the water, exhausted, three miles short of his goal. One year later he tried again and made it excruciatingly close—220 meters—before collapsing from the effort and requiring assistance to get out of the water. Although the Serpentine Club recognized his crossing, no one else did—then, as now, swimming the Channel does not mean stopping 220 meters short. Cavill tried to claim success but tired of defending himself in the public eye and eventually immigrated to Australia, opened a pool, and became known as the father of Australian swimming.

Over the next twenty-five years at least a dozen other swimmers made a serious attempt at duplicating Webb's feat. Yet no matter how hard they trained or how prepared they appeared to be, none succeeded. In almost every instance the tides conspired to defeat them, often teasing them to within sight of their goal and then, with solid ground and glory reaching out a hand, stopping them cold, slapping them back, and even pushing the swimmers away from shore toward where they had first started. To many Channel swimmers the tides have proven to be a barrier nearly as impenetrable as the thick stone walls of Dover Castle.

Most swimmers who tried to swim the Channel in the first few decades following Webb's crossing followed his course, leaving from England and swimming toward France, but as more and more swimmers tried and failed to make a successful crossing, swimmers began to look the other direction, some leaving from France and heading toward England. The problem with the former course is that a swimmer leaving from England often takes aim on Cape Gris-Nez, the nearest point to England but a relatively small target jutting out into the Channel. But if a swimmer and the captain of the pilot boat miscalculate the tidal shifts and current as they near the French shore, it is entirely possible to sweep completely past Gris-Nez and then face certain failure. Swimming from France to England, while offering a wider landing area, also makes it necessary to time the swim with the tides so that the swimmer doesn't get hung up on the Goodwin Sands, just east of Dover, or swept along parallel to the coast.

Yet even when the weather and tidal conditions are the most favorable—even today—failure is as common as success. Swimming the English Channel remains a challenge even for the most fit and committed swimmer.

In fact in the first few decades after Webb's crossing, as swimmer after swimmer tried and failed to match his accomplishment, many began to doubt that anyone had ever swum the Channel at all, or ever could. Some even began to think that Webb was a fraud who somehow had faked his deed. To quell such rumors, surviving witnesses aboard Webb's pilot boat eventually made sworn depositions attesting to his feat.

With every passing year, as newspapers and various patrons offered cash prizes and other incentives to the first man to match Webb, the stature of the quest only increased. While some swimmers tried once, failed, and then left the Channel experience behind as a memory they cared not to revisit, to others swimming the Channel became something of an obsession.

Of all the swimmers who tried to duplicate Webb's feat, none were more committed and determined than Jabez Wolffe and Thomas William Burgess. Like Matthew Webb, Wolffe and Burgess each looked across the Strait of Dover and saw not only a personal challenge, but a way toward fame and fortune waiting on the other side.

9

The Best Girl

It was raining.

Just before 2:00 on the afternoon of Tuesday, August 1, 1922, what local newspapers still referred to as fifty-two "mermaids" assembled near the shoreline at Manhattan Beach, a resort community on the eastern edge of Coney Island, the southernmost point of the borough of Brooklyn. Dressed in competition swimwear consisting of one-piece, form-fitting, woolen "athletic tank suits," which began just above the knee and extended over the shoulders, and holding bathing caps, the young women, mostly in their teens and early twenties, huddled together in bunches beneath umbrellas, trying, for the time being, to stay dry.

Although it was midsummer, the weather along the shore was not cooperating. A storm system had stalled just off the coast. The forecast called for thunderstorms inland, but along the shore a brisk wind spinning in from the northeast delivered a steady, driving rain. The air temperature barely reached seventy degrees. The breeze raised a few whitecaps in the channel between Coney Island and the Rockaways, and the air smelled of the sea. On most such summer days, the beach normally would have been all but empty but for a few hardy vacationers determined to be outside. Some might have chosen to duck in and out of the attractions along the boardwalk at Coney Island, or else have a relaxing lunch at one of the nearby resort hotels and watch the surf.

But today a crowd of several hundred men, women, and children braved the rain and stood beneath umbrellas on the beach. Many in the crowd were friends and family of the young "mermaids," but a fair number—mostly men—had no personal connection to the young ladies at all. Many had come to Manhattan Beach just to see what all the fuss was about.

For much of the past month New Yorkers who were close readers of the *Tribune* had had their curiosity piqued by a series of stories touting what the newspaper referred to as the "international women's long distance swimming championship," a three and a half mile open-water swimming race for women, sponsored by the newspaper and Joseph P. Day, a wealthy New York real estate developer. The first such race had been held ten years before, in 1912, and was sponsored by the Women's Life-Saving League. Apart from a hiatus during World War I, the competition had been held annually ever since but generally had drawn little attention.

In the four years since Trudy Ederle and her sisters joined the WSA, much had changed. The success of the American women swimmers at the 1920 Olympic Games had provided the sport of women's swimming with a beachhead. Although women's swimming was hardly a popular spectator sport, in the wake of the Olympics even critics of female athletics had come to accept the reality that women were going to swim and compete. In 1921 the annual long-distance race even acquired a sponsor, the Brighton Beach Baths, a nearby private club that Day himself had rebuilt after the original Baths burned. That race had been won by Thelda Bleibtrey, winner of three gold medals in swimming at the 1920 Olympics. Bleibtrey, an attractive blonde, had drawn significant press attention to the event, not just for her appearance, but because the press loved repeating her inspirational story about taking up swimming and joining the WSA as therapy for curvature of the spine. Her participation in the race had drawn a surprisingly large crowd to the long-distance swim. Indeed, soon after her victory she announced that she intended to become a professional and left the ranks of amateur swimming. She worked as an instructor, purchased Annette Kellerman's indoor swimming tank, and created a vaudeville act—and even got the attention of the motion picture industry, which gave her a screen test.

Joseph P. Day duly noted the size of the crowd in 1921 and, in 1922, took over personal sponsorship of the event, awarding a trophy known as the Day Cup to the best team of swimmers to complete the course. The developer had recently completed a 114-home development on Manhattan Beach. He had extensive plans for more such developments in the surrounding area and wanted to draw attention both to his properties and the surrounding community. All summer long the Businessman's League in nearby Atlantic City, New Jersey, had been touting its Fall Frolic, a five-day celebration that would take place in September and culminate in a bathing beauty contest, the winner of which would be dubbed "Miss America." So far the ploy had resulted in plenty of publicity for Atlantic City, even before the contest. Day likely drew some inspiration from this event and concluded that the presence of four dozen young beauties in swimwear at Manhattan Beach would prove to be a sure-fire attraction.

He was right. Most of the crowd in Manhattan Beach had not assembled due to their deep love of the sport of swimming. Apart from friends and family members of the swimmers, the attraction for many was, to be blunt, still the girls themselves. Only in the last few years had it finally become acceptable for a woman to wear a bathing suit that was even remotely practical, or exposed any flesh whatsoever, and then only if she was swimming in an athletic competition. At the very least, most "respectable" women still wore tank suits that extended to the knee and kept their woolen stockings pulled up high, leaving only the face and arms exposed, and many still wore the cumbersome and even dangerous suits that consisted of long-sleeved heavy wool blouses, long flowing skirts, and stockings.

But the "mermaids" participating in swimming competitions held to a more relaxed standard. They were allowed to swim bare legged and wear tank suits that were somewhat more comfortable and revealing than those worn for simple recreation. The athletic tank suit was often made from a lighter woolen knit, fit the body closer, and stopped at midthigh.

Nowhere else, not even on the stage, were women allowed to wear such revealing outfits. Although the era of the flapper was beginning, skirts had yet to rise above the knee. Indeed, even modest tank suits were still legally banned from being worn at many public beaches, and women who entered the water wearing anything less than the standard swimming skirt and blouse still risked arrest. Each summer in and around New York, several women were arrested for doing just that. In fact in 1919 two WSA swimmers,

Thelda Bleibtrey and Charlotte Boyle, had been arrested not only for wearing the still-risqué tank suit at a public beach, but for removing their stockings.

The WSA recognized the controversy and, in an attempt to deflect criticism, made certain that the suits worn by its members were plain and dully colored, unadorned by any decoration apart from the WSA emblem on the front of each suit. Furthermore, each member of the group had to adhere to a strict moral code and strict standards of behavior and were always chaperoned at WSA events. The only place WSA swimmers were allowed to be "fast" was in the water.

The curious among the crowd that gathered along the beach or in pleasure boats just offshore were not held to the same moral standards. The binoculars and opera glasses carried by some of the many men in the crowd were not intended to be used to examine the swimming styles of the participants as much as they were to examine the stylish participants themselves.

One after another, long wooden rowboats meant for ocean travel, known as dories, were pushed into the water, each one manned by an oarsman and a pilot and carrying a swimmer. Eventually more than four dozen such boats, one for each competitor, were all headed southeast, across Rockaway Inlet, toward a destination just off Riche's Point. As the dories pulled away from shore, dozens of pleasure boats anchored offshore set sail after them.

Few spectators even knew the names of many of the swimmers, and if they did, it was only because of a series of prerace stories in the *Tribune* and other New York newspapers. Most stories tried to drum up interest in the race by touting the swimming achievements of the favorites—and reprinting their photographs.

The main attraction was seventeen-year-old Hilda James of England. The Liverpool native, widely acknowledged as Europe's greatest woman swimmer, had been a medalist at the 1920 Olympics and was the world record holder in both the 300- and 440-yard swims. It didn't hurt that in the photographs in the newspapers James appeared to be quite attractive. Even though the newspapers published only a head shot of the young swimmer, that was enough to tantalize male readers into showing up to see the rest of her in person. Like most swimmers of the era, James wore her hair in a kind of bob, the hairstyle currently favored in the motion picture industry. With a bit of imagination it was possible to look at a photograph of James and see a bit of film star Mary Pickford in her features.

The press touted the race as a showdown between James and her American Olympian counterparts, Helen Wainwright, Aileen Riggin, and a precocious young teammate, fourteen-year-old sensation Ethel McGary, who had recently set the American 300-yard record. Yet while the four swimmers were, in fact, among the most accomplished of the era, in truth the main attraction to the event was as much due to young womanhood on display as it was to competition.

It was a forgone conclusion that a team from the WSA would win the coveted Cup. Wainwright, Riggin, and McGary made up the first of two three-girl teams representing the club in Cup competition, but thirty-three of the remaining forty-seven swimmers competing as individuals wore suits bearing the "WSA" emblem on their chests.

After a good thirty minutes of hard pulling, for each dory was running against the changing tide, each boat slowed as it approached Riche's Point, where a tug waited. On board were Joseph P. Day himself, several newspaper reporters, and assorted race officials, including Epstein and Louis de Breda Handley. As the dories pulled up alongside the boat, Epstein checked off each swimmer, making certain that all fifty-two entrants were at the start. It then took another twenty or thirty minutes to assemble the boats in something approaching order, stretched in a line across nearly a quarter mile of open ocean, facing northward toward Point Breeze, parallel with the far shore.

The rain and accompanying wind and chop made keeping the dories in place something of a challenge, but they were an absolute necessity in such a race. Many of the swimmers had never before competed in a race of more than five hundred yards, and even then they had done so only in the protected confines of a pool. This race was something else entirely, an open-ocean course of three and a half miles. The swimmers would be subjected to the tides and currents and whatever other surprises the water might hold. For safety reasons, each swimmer would be trailed by a dory. Not only would the pilot of the boat shout instructions and help keep each swimmer on course, but at the first sign of trouble he could pluck the swimmer from the water.

One by one, as the scheduled 3:00 P.M. start of the race approached, each girl climbed over the side of her dory and entered the water, swimming a few strokes back and forth, then dog-paddling to stay warm, before returning to the boat and clinging to the side while awaiting the start of the race. Although it was August, the water had not quite reached its warmest temperature of the season—that would not come until September. Still, the temperature of the shallow waters of the inlet was comfortable, hovering around seventy degrees, warm enough for the swimmers to remain in the water for an hour or more on the muggy afternoon, despite the wind and the rain, without risking hypothermia.

The course was simple: It began from Riche's Point and extended a half mile due north toward Point Breeze, just over a mile east of Manhattan Beach, where spar buoy number 9, marking the local shipping lane, was anchored offshore. From there each swimmer would round the buoy and head west, swimming parallel to the shore for another three miles, past Manhattan Beach, before turning north and swimming back to shore directly in front of the Brighton Beach Baths. Two temporary towers erected in the shallows served as the finish line.

As laid out, the course was not particularly dangerous, but it could be. Only seven years before, in 1915, when the race had been sponsored by the Women's Life-Saving League, race officials had neglected to account for the influence of the tide and local currents, which impacted swimmers just as the tides in the English Channel did. Swimmers found themselves either swimming in place or being swept out to sea. Every single swimmer had to be pulled from the water, causing those who thought swimming was beyond the capability of women to smile with knowing satisfaction. But the race was then rescheduled during a more fortuitous tide and went off without incident. Organizers learned their lessons and in subsequent years made certain to consult tidal charts far ahead of time to make sure the race would run with the tide. Only at the start of the race, when swimmers would be at a right angle to the current, would the tide prove to be a problem. The poor weather made the waters of the inlet a bit choppy, but that was more a nuisance than a real danger.

As the start of the race approached a few pleasure boats strung out along the course, although most hung near the start, jockeying for position. Many planned to shadow the swimmers, sailing a parallel course that kept as many girls as possible within sight.

Finally, at 3:30 P.M., all the swimmers were in the water and the dories were more or less even. On the main boat a race official raised a starter's pistol into the air and fired a shot signaling the start of the race. In an instant, fifty-two young women let loose of the dories and started to swim toward Point Breeze.

For a few moments the water fairly churned with swimmers as each girl set off, arms whirling and legs kicking. Some spectators unfamiliar with modern swimming methods couldn't resist pointing and shaking their head in befuddlement, for although Handley's American crawl had been used by WSA swimmers from the very start of the organization, the stroke was still something of a novelty to the general public and was seldom seen outside sparsely attended swim meets.

There was some early anxiety among race officials for the girls' safety, for it was difficult to see in the gloom and it would be several minutes before the field stretched out and each dory pilot could locate his swimmer and follow behind. The start was the most dangerous point of the race, for in such close quarters, water splashing all around, a swimmer could accidentally get kicked in the head or be struck by an oar, lose consciousness, and even drown before anyone noticed. Almost immediately race officials began counting heads, making sure every swimmer was accounted for.

Undoubtedly there were still some in the crowd who, upon seeing more than fifty women swimming in the water at once in the start of the race, recalled the *Slocum* tragedy. Here, nearly twenty years after that event, the folly and needless tragedy of that day was fully exposed. Fifty-two young women were now swimming in the open ocean toward channel buoy number 9, in the wind and the rain, oblivious to the white caps, not just staying afloat but sprinting through the water at a speed most observers found absolutely astonishing.

At first all eyes of the spectators and the press on board the tug were drawn to the favorites, Hilda James, Aileen Riggin, Helen Wainwright, and Ethel McGary, all of whom had started the race in close proximity to one another on one side of the course. The race was but a few minutes old when Wainwright appeared in open water out front, swimming powerfully a few yards ahead of McGary, Riggin, and then James, as the other swimmers all fell back.

It was at this point that someone on the officials' boat looked across to the other side of the course and spotted another swimmer, all alone, out in front of everyone, even leading Helen Wainwright by some twenty yards. Her identity was, at first, a mystery. Then a member of the WSA put a name with the face and blurted out, "It's that Ederle girl!"

Most thought she was referring to Margaret Ederle, now eighteen years old. That was a mild surprise, for although Margaret was a fine swimmer who had finished seventh in the long-distance race in 1921, finishing seven minutes behind Bleibtrey, she was nowhere near as accomplished as Wainwright, Riggin, or at least a dozen other WSA swimmers. Her appearance at the front was truly astonishing.

But after another moment someone blurted out that the Ederle out front was not Margaret Ederle at all. It was her little sister, Trudy.

That was truly astounding. Although Trudy had been a member of the club since the day she accompanied her mother and sisters to the demonstration in the Highlands and had shown some promise as a swimmer, she was not considered to be among the club's best. In 1921 she had won a few junior races and, in fact, had competed in the 1921 distance race but finished well back. In September at Madison Square Garden, in a complete surprise, she had finished second in a 220-yard race won by teammate Charlotte Boyle, in which Boyle set a new world record, and had later teamed with Boyle, Riggin, and Wainwright in a relay that had set a record in the quarter mile, but such performances were the exception. More often she performed indifferently and had even quit a few races before the finish. In the weeks before the Day Cup race she hadn't even been training with the other girls and seemed disinterested in competition. When Trudy did compete it was only because Meg had filled out the forms for her and then cajoled her into appearing.

In fact, Trudy apparently hadn't been scheduled to compete in the Day Cup race at all. Earlier in the week the WSA sent out a press release that read, "Family strife threatens to add considerable interest to the Day Cup race," and cited four sets of swimming sisters scheduled to compete—the O'Maras, the Chesters, the Delaneys, and the Donahues. The two Ederle girls were not even mentioned.

Yet here was Trudy, out in front and swimming strongly. At first most observers thought that she must have been the fortunate beneficiary of a tidal surge in shallower water that pushed her ahead. They expected her to soon fall back, but as the swimmers drew together as they approached the buoy off Point Breeze ten minutes into the race, it became clear that her lead, which now approached an astounding fifty yards, was genuine. She appeared as if she were simply out for a weekday swim, without a care in the world, while some of her better-known competitors were struggling. Given the quality of the competition, it was as if a schoolboy had stepped from the stands at the ballpark, toed the rubber on the pitcher's mound, and without warming up, blew fastballs past Babe Ruth.

As the swimmers rounded the buoy and turned west, parallel to the shore, Ethel McGary, unaccustomed to such choppy conditions, got off course and had to be retrieved by her dory and set back on track. So, too, did Hilda James drift off, fighting with the water instead of swimming with it, battling to stay abreast of both Helen Wainwright and Aileen Riggin. Some of the lesser swimmers also struggled. Most were far more accustomed to swimming in more controlled conditions, in tidal baths, freshwater pools, or more-protected bays. Out in the open water, however, the swells that looked inconsequential from shore lifted the swimmers up and down relentlessly. Some were getting queasy, particularly those who had inadvertently swallowed seawater as their bodies heaved up and down.

This situation was little better on the boats that kept pace with the swimmers. Even those spectators who were accustomed to spending time on the water were not necessarily accustomed to moving at a snail's pace, which subjected the boats to the swells as well. The water wasn't very rough, but it was enough to send some bending over the rail.

Only one person really seemed to be enjoying herself, and that was Trudy. She swam along like a happy machine, never showing any distress and hardly showing any effort. She plowed steadily through the waves, never stopping to rest or look back.

It was nothing new to her, this long-distance ocean swimming, even in the wind and the rain. No one outside her family knew it at the time, but of all the swimmers in the race, none had more experience swimming in the ocean. What was a new and somewhat intimidating challenge for most of the swimmers was, for Trudy, as familiar as an evening bath. Summer after summer swimming at the Highlands made her completely comfortable in the open water. Unlike some other swimmers, the thought that she was swimming in twenty, forty, or a hundred or more feet of water did not frighten her, and she was not bothered by the lively waters of the open sea or burdened by thoughts of what possibly lurked beneath. To Trudy, crossing Amsterdam Avenue when it was choked with vehicles was scary, swimming in the ocean was not.

She forgot herself there. It was that simple. The other girls swam to get back to land, but Trudy swam, well, to get away from everything, and in doing so, out in the water she found own true self, the place where she felt most comfortable, where she did not think or worry but simply felt the water holding her up and pushing her along.

The race to shore, such as it was, was over. Wainwright and James each made several charges to try to head Trudy off, but after a minute or two of sprinting saw them gain only one or two hard-earned yards, neither was able to keep up the pace and had to drop back. Observers noted that, unlike the competition, Ederle's stroke never varied. In fact, if anything, as she approached the finish she seemed to swim even faster than at the start, as if more time spent in the water somehow allowed her to increase her momentum.

As she turned toward shore at the Brighton Beach Baths, she led Helen Wainwright by a comfortable sixty yards. Trudy then sped past the finish line between the two stationary towers in front of the Brighton Beach Baths nearly a minute ahead of her more accomplished teammate, finishing the course in one hour, one minute, and thirty-four seconds. Although that was five minutes slower than the winning time of Thelda Bleibtrey one year earlier, observers were far more impressed by Ederle's effort, which had been made under much poorer weather conditions.

The crowd on the beach clapped and cheered as she emerged from the water, an embarrassed smile on her face as if she was surprised to be first. She looked as if she had just come out after taking a quick, cooling dip. Even those who had come to gawk were impressed. Far from exhausted, Trudy bounded out of the water, scanned the crowd, spotted some girlfriends waiting, and joined them before startled race officials could even congratulate her on her victory.

Helen Wainwright struggled from the water a full forty-five seconds behind Trudy to finished second ahead of third-place finisher Hilda James, who waded to shore nearly three minutes later, followed by Aileen Riggin and Ethel McGary, but only five other swimmers managed to finish the course within ten minutes of Ederle's winning time. Yet despite the conditions, all fifty-two swimmers who started the race completed the course, the last being ten-year-old Julia Mannostein, the youngest swimmer in the field.

The Day Cup went to the WSA team of Wainwright, Riggin, and McGary, but Trudy Ederle's stunning individual victory made the team trophy seem like some booby prize given away by some sympathetic Coney Island carnival barker. But after the race Trudy was so nonplussed by her achievement that when the press went looking for her she was nowhere to be found, perhaps because her parents, in Germany visiting relatives, had left the girls in the custody of their aunt and uncle.

Hilda James, heretofore considered the greatest all-around female swimmer in the world, was left to meet with reporters and give her estimation of young Trudy Ederle, a girl neither she nor anyone else outside the WSA had ever heard of before.

"The best girl won," gasped an exasperated James. "Of that I have no doubt."

10

The Next Man

No two figures in the history of Channel swimming are more emblematic of both the great pull the English Channel can exert on the human spirit, and the personal cost, than Jabez Wolffe and Thomas William "Bill" Burgess. From the time each man first entered the Channel waters, the quest to swim the Channel proved to be an attraction as strong and relentless as the flood tide. For nearly three decades, over and over and over again, Wolffe and Burgess tested themselves against the same twenty-one-mile stretch of water.

On August 24, 1901, the anniversary of Matthew Webb's crossing, the British cyclist and swimmer Montague Holbein made the first of several of his own unsuccessful attempts to swim the Channel. He employed a Yorkshire-born resident of Paris, a blacksmith named Thomas William Burgess, to serve as one of several pacesetters. The son of a cook and a blacksmith who had been employed as a tire maker by the Earl of Shrewsbury, Burgess had been sent to France by the earl to open another branch of the tire business. Well known in Parisian swimming circles, Burgess had been a member of the British Olympic team in the 1900 Paris games, competing in the 1,000- and 4,000-meter freestyle competition and the 200-meter backstroke, and in water polo, winning a bronze medal in the final event. He stood a full six feet and weighed 210 pounds, with a barrel chest and arms that reflected his long use of the blacksmith's hammer, and a natty Vandyke beard that gave him a distinguished, if somewhat well-worn, air. Burgess, primarily using the sidestroke that Holbein favored, swam alongside Holbein for a time, providing the swimmer with some company during the monotonous ordeal and helping him maintain a steady stroke rate.

Although Holbein failed in this quest despite spending more than twelve hours in the water, he nevertheless made a significant contribution to all those who followed him into the Channel. Instead of depending solely upon the skill of a local boat captain, Holbein was the first Channel swimmer to make use of available scientific evidence concerning the tides and currents, utilizing British governmental records and reports to create complex charts and maps as he tried to use the tides and current to his advantage.

Holbein refused to give up and made another five attempts to swim the Channel, each time learning a bit more about the currents. On August 28, 1902, swimming from France to England, Holbein came within one mile of success, closer than any man since Frederick Cavill.

Bill Burgess paid attention. He emerged from the Channel waters full of ambition and determined to become the second man to swim the Channel. Taking his cue from Holbein, he took an almost scientific approach toward his task.

He recognized that to swim the Channel one had to better understand the influence of the tides. To that end Burgess not only studied charts, but spent hours at Cape Gris-Nez looking out over Channel waters and made dozens of experimental swims to gauge the strength, direction, and duration of the tidal currents. Burgess also experimented with various oils and greases to coat his body, both to protect it from chafing in the corrosive salt water and to help retain precious body heat. Taking note of how long exposure to salt water caused his eyes to become inflamed, Burgess was one of the first Channel swimmers to wear a bathing cap, which he tied under his chin, and goggles, adapting those used by early motorists. Burgess even filled his ears with wax to prevent water from entering his ear canal.

He made his first attempt to cross the Channel in 1904 and failed, but Burgess was even more determined than Holbein. The cyclist stopped after six attempts, but Burgess kept on going, banging his head against the Channel wall more than a dozen times; each time he entered the water completely convinced that he would succeed, only to fail. If anything, however, defeat made him ever more determined.

And if he needed any further motivation, that was provided by Jabez Wolffe. Like Burgess, Wolffe was also determined to be the second man to swim the Channel.

The moon-faced Jewish Scotsman from Glasgow, who lived in London and trained in Brighton, became Burgess's main competitor. Although Wolffe, like Burgess, was powerfully built and highly motivated, compared to Burgess's more intellectual approach, Wolffe, although a fine swimmer for the era, was both quite a bit less athletic and quite a bit more pugnacious. He didn't so much try to swim the Channel as wrestle it into submission, trying to make up for what he lacked in ability with grit and fortitude. Wolffe's particular forte was self-motivation, and he recognized that if a combination of the tides, the water temperature, and the weather provided the main physical barrier to swimming the Channel, one's own mind created a similar psychological barrier.

In one sense swimming the Channel is not unlike being immersed in a sensory deprivation tank. Once a swimmer overcomes the rush of adrenaline from the initial immersion in the Channel waters and settles in to a steady pace, the remainder of the swim is often mind-numbingly the same. Until the swimmer is within a few miles of the land the view never changes, there is only the swimmer and the pilot boat, the Channel waters and the sky, cold and wet, and light and dark, for many swimmers either begin or end their journey during nightfall, and sometimes both. Swimmers often lose complete track of time, thinking hours have passed when in fact only minutes have, and as exhaustion and the cold take their toll, many swimmers slip into the early stages of hypothermia with all its attendant mental effects. Swimmers can become disoriented and hallucinate both visually and aurally, seeing and hearing what does not exist, slipping ever farther into themselves.

Just as Matthew Webb's entourage tried to keep him alert by singing, Wolffe used a similar approach, one that had the added benefit of proving of interest to the press. On his pilot boat Wolffe often employed a bagpiper to play traditional Scottish songs, giving Wolffe something else to focus on as well as helping him keep up his desired pace of around twenty-six strokes per minute.

Like Frederick Cavill, Wolffe did everything but succeed. In 1908, leaving from England, Wolffe made his way to what was variously reported as between a quarter mile and two hundred meters off the French coast, tantalizingly close, near enough to hear those onshore urging him on, their French accents serving as a siren's call. But after fifteen hours in the water, Wolffe, who was blessed with extraordinary stamina, was not strong enough a swimmer to overcome the tide and could not break its binds.

But he was not deterred and tried again and again and again. Each time, if it was not the tide that turned, pulling him away from land at a rate faster than he could swim, it was something else that stopped him short of his goal—the weather, a sudden storm, or his own body breaking down. On one swim he pulled tendons in his leg while kicking, and on another he was injured when he slammed into a timber floating just beneath the surface. Three times he made it to within one mile of success only to fail, sometimes after spending more than twenty hours in the water. Much to the swimmer's consternation and embarrassment, "Wolffe Fails in Attempt to Swim Channel" became something of a running headline—and an increasingly comic one—in English newspapers. In France they joked that watching Wolffe floundering offshore of Cape Gris-Nez was becoming a favorite summer pastime.

For a time Burgess, despite his advantages, was no more successful than Wolffe. Yet his efforts, based on the French shore, were given little notice in the British press, which favored Wolffe. Many Englishmen sniffed that despite his English birth, Burgess's marriage to a Frenchwoman and residency in Paris made him more the French poodle than the British bulldog. Even today, his accomplishments are little known in the country of his birth.

Yet like Wolffe, Burgess was determined, fixated on his goal, spending most of the year saving money and drumming up support so he could spend a month or two at the end of the summer watching the tides and the weather for an opportunity to try again.

The two men were acquainted, held a grudging, public respect for the efforts of the other, and were polite to each other on their rare encounters, but they were not friends. Wolffe thought Burgess's fetish for tidal charts and weather reports a waste of time and a way for the swimmer to have a ready-made excuse each time he failed, while Burgess thought Wolffe was foolish to ignore such information and couldn't understand why Wolffe entered the water on so many occasions when the tides and weather conditions made a crossing virtually impossible.

Although both swimmers used both the sidestroke and the breast-stroke, even their training methods were at odds. Burgess rarely trained for more than a few hours at a time in Channel waters before making an attempt, believing that extended training swims were of little help and did little more than exhaust a swimmer. Wolffe, on the other hand, spent as much time as possible in the water. He thought nothing of spending eight or ten hours in the Channel only a few days before making a serious attempt.

For nearly a decade the two competitors swam to a standoff, Wolffe making more attempts and, on a few occasions, nearly making it across. Burgess made fewer attempts, and while he never made it quite as close as Wolffe, he was somewhat more consistent. Thus far, the wisdom of their approaches and training methods had been a draw.

On September 5, 1911, the end of the "mystic season," Burgess entered Channel waters for the sixteenth time, wading into the surf at 11:15 A.M. at South Foreland, Dover. In calm seas and under a slate gray sky, conditions were nearly ideal, for there was little difference between the air temperature and the temperature of the water, and Burgess didn't have to worry about the blazing sun burning his fair skin. Using the sidestroke, Burgess had indulged in very little special training beforehand, later saying he had spent only "eighteen hours swimming in preparation," with his longest swim only six miles. His earlier efforts in the Channel had taught him that it was more important to feel fresh and not be worn down, either physically or mentally, by training. He would soon need every ounce of energy he had.

With the possible exception of Wolffe, to this point Burgess had probably spent more time in the waters of the Channel than any man on the face of the earth. Good thing, because as soon as he entered the sea the Channel threw nearly everything it had in his direction, making certain he would be tested in every way possible.

First came the fog, which settled in during the first hour and hung over the water for the remainder of the day. For the rest of the journey Burgess spent much of his swim in the disorienting soup with only his pilot boat for accompaniment.

Then came the tides. A stronger than expected flood tide swept him up and pushed him directly toward the Goodwin Sands. He was forced to make a near Herculean effort, sprinting for more than an hour to avoid the hazard and find safe water farther out. As soon as he did, as if on cue, the wind rose up, not a full-blown storm, but stiff enough to cause the spray and wash from his motorized pilot boat—forced to stay close in the fog—to shower down upon Burgess's face, causing him to swallow water, making it almost impossible for him to breathe. He was nearly ready to give up before his crew, in an act of pure dedication, launched a rowboat, cut the engine on the pilot boat, tied it fast, and, with a crew of three, *rowed* alongside Burgess for the duration of his swim, towing the motorboat and the remaining eight crew members, never stopping, a physical feat nearly as impressive as that of the swimmer himself.

Still, Burgess continued to struggle. The seawater soured his stomach and the swells made him seasick. In desperation, for a time he abandoned the sidestroke and flipped over on his back. After a while he felt better, only to get nauseous once again as soon as he resumed his usual stroke. Fortunately, a second period of time on his back settled his stomach, and he was finally able to continue.

But his struggles were not over. In mid-Channel another tidal change swept him up, and for a time he was driven back toward England; but after night fell the seas calmed, and although a layer of fog hung close to the water's surface, the moon shone through, providing him with a companion through the night. Burgess swam strongly through the darkness, bothered—or perhaps made more alert—by what he later referred to as "thousands" of stings from jellyfish.

In the early morning hours Burgess drew to within five miles of the French shoreline, entering what Channel swimmers euphemistically referred to as the "swimmer's mile," the last leg of the journey, and the part of the swim that is usually most difficult, for in those last few miles success or failure depends almost entirely upon the swimmer's will and talent.

At 4:30 A.M., however, when first light began to show on the horizon, Burgess began to break. Exhausted after spending nearly fifteen hours in the water, Burgess was barely conscious and began to hallucinate. But his crew, invigorated by the sight of the French coast only three miles in the distance and the specter that their work was soon done, began singing, trying to keep Burgess alert for the final push.

Now, after thousands of arm strokes, a muscle in his chest began to spasm and cramp, causing him to slow down. When the cramp finally passed, Burgess began vomiting again, unable to keep down his provisions of so-called patent food (canned goods), chicken, chocolate, and tea, occasionally spiced by a cautious measure of twenty drops of champagne, for Burgess was at the time a teetotaler who in any other circumstance would not drink at all.

At 7:00, each time the swells lifted him up, Burgess could see Cape Gris-Nez looming before him, looking for all the world like a gray nose poised over the horizon. Burgess had planned to land at Calais, but at 8:00, his energy waning, Burgess took a chance, changing course and aiming straight for the nearer shores of Gris-Nez.

The tide had another idea. While each stroke pulled him closer to his goal, he miscalculated the current, which pushed him sideways a quarter mile past the cape. Desperate to finish, Burgess turned back toward shore and, using the cape itself to shield him from rough water, headed to shore in a small bay just to the east of Cape Gris-Nez.

Bathers on the shore spotted him swimming, and by the time his feet touched ground at 9:50 A.M., more than twenty-two hours after he started his swim, a sizable crowd had assembled on the beach. As he reached the shallows and stood, stumbling and crying uncontrollably, the crowd came to his aid, hoisting him to their shoulders while, to the disgust of the British press, they sang the French anthem, "La Marseillaise." The so-called swimmer's mile had taken Burgess seven and a half excruciating hours to complete. But thirty-six years after Matthew Webb's successful crossing, a swimmer had once again conquered the English Channel.

After he recovered from his ordeal Burgess was understandably ecstatic, terming the swim "the hardest fight I have ever had all the way through." That was an understatement. He estimated that in his twenty-two hours in the water, during which he fought his way through three tidal sets, he had traveled a circuitous course of some sixty miles, likely an exaggeration, but not dramatically so, and still indicative of the impact the tides played on a swimmer.

While Burgess reached a certain measure of fame, due to his split citizenship he was denied the full acclaim that had been delivered to Matthew Webb. Still, Burgess's celebrity was still sufficient that before long the blacksmith became the owner of a Parisian garage and then purchased a small cottage atop Cape Gris-Nez, where he was able to look down upon the scene of his triumph.

And from that peak, for much of the next decade—apart from the war years—he may well have scanned the horizon for Jabez Wolffe. For Burgess's accomplishment did not deter Wolffe. He continued his quixotic quest unabated, even as he slipped toward middle age and his chances of success became smaller with each passing year.

But the name of Jabez Wolffe was not meant to appear on the roster of those who have successfully swum the Channel, but atop another list, one that measured futility. After his success Burgess chose not to test the Channel waters again, but Wolffe, as if offended by Burgess's success, kept trying over and over and over. He tried and failed at least twenty-two times and perhaps as many as forty, both figures far more than any other swimmer. By the time of his final attempt in 1921, however, the waters of the Channel were beginning to get crowded as a new generation of athletes made plans to take to the water. Wisely, most of these aspirants would seek advice and counsel from both Bill Burgess and Jabez Wolffe.

The competition between the two men would turn vicarious, and soon begin anew.

11

Goals

THE DAY AFTER Trudy's victory in the Day Cup, columnist Marguerite Mooers Marshall of the *New York Evening Herald*, one of the leading female journalists of the day, interviewed her at the Ederle home in the Highlands, where, as usual, Trudy was spending the waning days of summer. Accompanied by a photograph, Marshall's profile would introduce Trudy Ederle to the world.

The interview had all the earmarks of being set up through Charlotte Epstein and the WSA, and Epstein was likely in attendance—she rarely left the girls unchaperoned, much less let them meet with the press alone. Besides, all of a sudden Trudy Ederle was the new face of the WSA, and it was Epstein's responsibility to ensure that both Ederle and the WSA were put in the best possible light.

She needn't have worried. When Marshall arrived at the Ederle bungalow, Trudy was dressed in a worn and slightly faded tank suit, the same one that she wore often during training, and a sweater to ward off the morning chill. She was in the middle of her daily chores, ironing clothes in the kitchen while she looked after her little brother Henry, who was not yet three. Her parents were still away in Germany, leaving all the Ederle children in the care of relatives, but the girls, as usual, kept close watch over their younger siblings.

Trudy Ederle was on the cusp of womanhood. Marshall, who penned an influential column entitled "The Women of It," was thoroughly enthralled by the young swimmer and tagged Trudy as "that almost extinct person—if we may believe the cynics—the normal, healthy, pretty, sport-loving, fun-loving, home-and-family-loving

American girl. She is everything that is the converse of the flighty flapper."

Now standing five foot six and weighing perhaps 140 pounds, Trudy was no movie star, but she was unquestionably pretty and, only one day after swimming three and a half miles, displayed absolutely no fatigue. Marshall described her as a "glowingly tanned, brown-eyed, yellow-haired youngster"—her auburn hair, recently cut into a modern bob, was bleached by a summer in the sun—"tall with square sturdy shoulders and symmetrical limbs; a beauty by right, utterly unpretentious . . . [with] frank, beautiful eyes, brown, with a glint in them, like brook water on which the sun shines."

In short, the scene was pure Americana. Her education had recently ended with her graduation from grammar school at Public School 69, and now Trudy was, as Marshall described her, "an old-fashioned domestic daughter" who "stays at home and helps mother." Trudy Ederle came off as a poster child for wholesomeness, even telling Marshall that she personally didn't believe women should wear one-piece suits, similar to the suits she herself wore in competition, at public beaches. "I like the other suits better," she said, speaking of the less-revealing swimming dresses nominally still in vogue, but then, as if telling a secret, added, "although I don't wear stockings." Then, with a giggle she admitted that she usually removed the bathing skirt when she was ready to enter the water, making her appear both traditionally modest and modern at the same time.

With a day to reflect on her achievement, Trudy was absolutely effervescent, full of nervous chatter, answering each question, and then asking and answering another one or two or three more questions herself before Marshall could get another word in. For Trudy, that was something of a habit. She was already compensating for her partial deafness in subtle ways, and one strategy was to anticipate questions before they were asked to save her from the embarrassment of asking the speaker to repeat the question. On this day, giddy with excitement, the words poured out of Trudy in a flood of giggles and unintentional, genuine charm. After all, she had never been interviewed for a newspaper before and had rarely been the center of attention, even within her own family. As the third of what would eventually be seven children, she was sometimes lost in the family drama as her parents understandably paid more personal attention to her older sisters, both of whom were dating and embarking on a social life of their own, and her younger brothers, who still needed plenty of supervision. It was not intentional or reflective of anything but the dynamics of a large and growing family, but the self-reliant Trudy was often a bit overlooked.

She had been in a similar position within the WSA, where to this point she was viewed as simply a good swimmer of some promise but was not held in anything close to the same regard as Aileen Riggin or Helen Wainwright or any of the girls who had competed in the 1920 Olympics, or even her sister Margaret. But now, finally, it was Trudy's turn to talk and she loved it.

"I don't train," she offered as she ironed and folded and ironed some more, "if you mean eating special food or anything like that. And I don't practice much. The girls in the swimming association simply can't get me to practice. For a day or two before a race—yes— but not every day. Down here at the beach I am in the water an hour or two daily, because I love it and it's such fun. But the swimming association has an indoor pool for winter work, and do I go every day? I should say not!"

That was another reason why Trudy's victory had been such a surprise. Compared to the other top swimmers in the WSA, like Wainwright, Trudy was something of a slacker who did not appear to take swimming seriously, at least in her training sessions at the pool. In fact, though, once summer started and she was on her own in the Highlands, she was swimming more than most of the other girls because she swam every day, for fun, rather than confining her efforts to a concentrated period of training. In that way she was lucky, for few of the other girls had as much unfettered access to the water as Trudy.

That was the key to her success, for Trudy's training "method" was, in fact, just as revolutionary as Louis de Breda Handley's improvements to the Australian crawl. She was in and out of the water all day long at the Highlands, reinforcing Handley's teachings and building her stamina. Purely by accident, as she went through puberty, her daily routine had allowed her skills to keep pace with her changing body. By swimming virtually every day, she had not only grown markedly stronger, but had retained and even enhanced her coordination at an age in which many adolescents become awkward and gawky.

And by rowing and canoeing, she had also been cross-training, adding to her strength and fitness level. She had energy to spare, as she also told Marshall, "I love to row a boat or paddle around in a canoe. I love basketball and all the things you do in a gymnasium. I love—LOVE—dancing. But swimming is the best of all.

"I think it's the most splendid sport in the world. It develops you all over, not just one or two sets of muscles. It improves your general health—I never was really ill," she said, perhaps alluding to her bout with measles, and then thinking better of it, for as yet her hearing trouble was known only to her family and close friends, "but I've been ever so much better since I took up swimming. It strengthens your lungs and tones up your nerves. And it's such a clean sport!"

Then Marshall, obviously smitten, asked Ederle, "What is your secret? What made you swim away so easily from those other world beaters?"

Trudy grinned broadly before answering, "I just did the best I could, and I never thought of winning. I guess I swim as easily as I breathe or walk. And I truly think it ought to be just as natural for everybody. The scientists say we were all water animals to begin with, then why shouldn't we go back, now and then, to our first home—the ocean?"

Neither she nor perhaps even Marshall realized it, but Trudy had just articulated what made her different from swimmers like Hilda James or many of the other girls who swam in competition of the WSA. Most of them had come to swimming later in life, first learning for safety reasons, then, as their skills improved, competing, and then continuing to swim only to compete. When swimming became a sport it also became something that was practiced like a chore—a pleasant one perhaps, but nevertheless a chore, something that they had to work at to become good.

But to Trudy Ederle, swimming was something else altogether. It was play transformed, a way to herself. She never thought of winning while she was swimming because, well, she really never thought of anything when she was swimming. And that was the best part.

Ironically enough, although Louis de Breda Handley deserved credit for the American performance in the 1920 games, he bore little direct responsibility for Trudy's victory in the Day Cup. Handley was not even aware that she had regularly been swimming long distances and afterward didn't even recall that she had tried the swim in 1921, telling reporters she was "a rank outsider never having competed in a race longer than 220 yards."

At the end of the interview with Marshall, Trudy was photographed in athletic poses, touching her toes and, oddly enough, boxing. Although she is wearing a sweater over her suit in the photographs, compared to swimmers like Aileen Riggen or Helen Wainwright, whose bodies still resembled those of children, Trudy was much more athletic, with powerful arms, legs, and shoulders.

For a few days anyway, Trudy's Day Cup win made her nearly as well known as Olympians such as Thelda Bleibtrey and Helen Wainwright, girls that she had always looked up to. Swimming had always been fun for her, but now Trudy seemed to sense that it was something more. Near the end of the interview, Marshall asked her "What else do you want to do?" Trudy, who just a few minutes earlier had confided to Marshall about the Day Cup that "I never dreamed I could win. It never occurred to me that I could beat the other girls," now had an answer.

"Win some more races," she blurted out with a grin. "And I want to go to the Olympic Games."

Now that Trudy Ederle had a goal, she might even start trying to win.

12

Rivals

AFTER THE GREAT WAR some looked out upon the English Channel and were reminded of the recent conflagration, others thought of shipping and commerce, and artists saw a subject for their work. Jabez Wolffe and Bill Burgess, however, saw something else.

Money. As soon as the war ended, swimmer after swimmer traveled to the English Channel, desperate to be the next, next man, after Burgess, to cross the waters. To that end, both Burgess and Jabez Wolffe suddenly found themselves not only popular among these new aspirants, but in competition once again. This time they would not compete against each other directly to see who could first cross the Channel, but compete they still would, through the men—and women—who had decided the take up the challenge.

By 1920, in fact, it was even beginning to get a bit crowded, both in Dover and on Cape Gris-Nez, as it sometimes seemed that anyone who could stay afloat for more than fifteen minutes suddenly wanted to swim the Channel, or at least announce that they did and for a brief time bask in the spotlight. To Jabez Wolffe and Bill Burgess, that was the best news possible at a time when the European economy was in tough shape. For much of the next decade Wolffe and Burgess spent almost as much time in Channel waters assisting others who wanted to swim the Channel as they had when each was trying to do so himself.

Before World War I the English Channel was little more than a name to most Americans. Most were almost completely unaware of the great naval battles that had taken place on its waters during the

Napoleonic Wars or when the British fleet repelled the Spanish Armada. If they knew anything about the Channel at all, they knew it only as a simple fact of geography, that it separated England from France. For most, the Channel was a place with little romance and absolutely no story.

The Great War changed that. Early in the war German destroyers, U-boats (submarines), and other vessels roamed the Channel waters like sharks, sinking vessels of all nationalities, including those sailing under American flags. In February 1915 the German government declared "the waters around Great Britain and Ireland, including the whole English Channel, a war zone from and after February 18," daring any vessel to test the prowess of its navy. Early in the war there was even speculation that if Germany could gain control of Calais it would use the port to launch an invasion of Britain across the Channel.

Both sides also made use of mines to deter boat traffic. The German navy laid mine fields at the mouth of many Channel harbors, while the British navy, hoping to prevent U-boats from roaming Channel waters in a pack, seeking out and destroying ships at will, maintained a mine field across the Strait of Dover from Dover to Cape Gris-Nez. For much of the war all but the most necessary military and transport boat traffic stayed in port. It was simply too dangerous to be exposed in open water, and those that did venture forth usually did so with military escorts.

Aspiring Channel swimmers were likewise confined to port, as the war made any notion of swimming the Channel an act of pure madness. And even after the war ended in November 1918, it was more than a year before the Channel was cleared of mines—even then the occasional rogue mine sank ships, or, still dangerous, washed up on the beach. Not until 1920 did swimmers again venture into the Channel waters and once more dream of reaching the other side.

Although the list of Channel aspirants before the war had almost exclusively been confined to swimmers of either English or French citizenship, after the war the nature of the combatants changed. The Americans were not only coming, they were already there and they were staying.

By then the English Channel meant much more to the American public than it had before the war. Now they understood not only its geography, but its recent political and military importance. Hundreds of Americans and dozens of American vessels had been lost in the Channel during the war, and thousands of American soldiers had either crossed the Channel on their way to fight in Europe, breathing its heavy, salt air and looking in wonder at the white cliffs of Dover, or else stood on the French coast, weary of battle, and dreamed of the end of the war and a return to peacetime. The reopening of the Channel after the war to both boat traffic and swimmers marked not only a return to normalcy, but a shift in world view. The Channel was no longer seen solely as a barrier that separated England from France, but as a passage that united England—and America—not only to the European continent, but to the future.

The war had changed everything. As soon as the passage was cleared of mines, swimming the Channel suddenly took on a significance that it had previously lacked. Before the war men like Webb, Holbein, Wolffe, and Burgess had been celebrated—and occasionally castigated—as individuals. Their desire to swim the Channel had been seen as a kind of partly eccentric, partly exotic, somewhat quixotic pursuit. But the Great War had spawned a strong sense of nationalism among all combatants, and now those that came to swim the Channel did so not only as individuals but as representatives of both their country and their culture. The next generation of swimmers to test the Channel did not try so much to cross the Channel as they tried to conquer it.

Unburdened by war, in the 1920s citizens on both the American continent and in Europe, eager to forget, found themselves spellbound by athletes and athletic achievements, giving attempts to swim the Channel new significance. The Channel Swimming Club was formed to oversee and support Channel swimmers, and the London tabloid the *Daily Sketch* made a standing offer of one thousand pounds to any swimmer who could match the efforts of Webb and Burgess. Over the next few years the *Sketch* would give Channel swimmers more and more ink, leading newspapers on both continents to do the same. In a few short years Channel swimming would evolve from an act of madness to a sport and even something of a craze.

No one was more in need of that than Wolffe and Burgess. The already modest fortunes of each had taken a hit during the war, and each man was scrambling to pay the bills. Although in the wake of his successful crossing Burgess had received a modest windfall—the Nestle Company paid him to endorse its chocolate, and even Wolffe had received an endorsement opportunity from Shredded Wheat cereal—those days had long since passed. He had given up life as a blacksmith in favor of operating a Paris garage, but the war virtually destroyed his business. When Channel swimmers waving not pound notes or francs but dollar bills began knocking on the doors of both men—Wolffe in Brighton, on the English coast, and Burgess in his cottage atop Cape Gris-Nez—they were invited inside. Each man soon discovered that, in the summer at least, training Channel swimmers could be something like a full-time occupation. It certainly beat working.

The first swimmer of note to return to the Channel waters was the first serious American contestant, Henry Sullivan of Lowell, Massachusetts. The portly son of a Lowell businessman, Sullivan, like Matthew Webb, favored the breaststroke. He had tried and failed to swim the Channel in 1913 but as soon as the mines were cleared he announced his intention to try again in 1920.

He wasn't alone. Jabez Wolffe himself still entertained his own dim dream of making it across, and there was a growing list of others determined to try the swim, among them a waiter from Boston named Charles Toth, the Canadian Omer Perrault, Georges Michel from France, and Enrique Sebastian Tirabocchi, a native of Genoa, Italy, who was now a citizen of Argentina. Over the next few years all these swimmers and more would make repeated attempts to swim the Channel.

It was no accident that so many were now determined to try. Before the war, for those few men who were determined to swim the Channel, the biggest impediment to the swim—apart from the tide and the weather—had been money. It was costly to spend the better part of two months in either England or France, training and awaiting the proper conditions. But after the war the European economy had collapsed, and most of Europe was in the throes of a deep recession. In 1923 one U.S. dollar was worth about seventeen French francs, or nearly four English pounds, making a middle-class American wealthy. Suddenly one didn't need to be a millionaire to finance a swim across the Channel.

What a swimmer did need was the funds to provide for room and board either in Dover or, if one chose to swim from France, in Calais or Boulogne or the village of Gris-Nez. Apart from that the only requirement was an accompanying pilot boat and crew, and there were plenty of boats and boat captains of varying ability available to escort swimmers across the Channel.

That was where Wolffe and Burgess came in. Although nothing beyond their experience in Channel waters really qualified either man as a swimming coach, they were still invaluable. In addition to their experience in the water each man had extensive contacts with boat captains on each side of the Channel, for each had made the crossing himself by boat many, many times. These local mariners had an intimate knowledge of the tides and weather conditions and were more than willing to assist a crossing in exchange for cash. Once a swimmer was in the water the boat captain became almost solely responsible for navigating the swimmer across the Channel.

Beginning in 1920, and for the next several summers, each man was kept busy. Burgess found more or less part-time employment from Henry Sullivan, because after Sullivan failed in 1920 he kept returning and kept trying. He was something of a throwback, for while most swimmers had given up the breaststroke in favor of the sidestroke, or a combination, Sullivan, although he occasionally used both the sidestroke and the old trudgen, much favored the breaststroke.

Finally, on August 9, 1923, in his sixth attempt, Henry Sullivan became the third man to swim the Channel. But he didn't so much swim it as bob across in one of the most grueling efforts in the history of Channel swimming. The *New York Times* reported that at times he "drifted, scarcely making progress," and "sometimes he lost distance for hours at a time," for Sullivan simply wasn't a powerful enough swimmer to swim either against or across the current. As such it took him more than a full day—twenty-six hours and fifty minutes—to cross, so long that by the time the normally clean-shaven swimmer walked ashore, he had grown a beard.

Both Wolffe and Burgess took some credit for his success—at various times Sullivan had consulted with each man—but Burgess received the greatest acclaim. He, and not Wolffe, had been on board the pilot boat for Sullivan's entire journey.

Although Sullivan collected his one thousand pounds from the *Sketch* and hustled off to London for what he hoped were some lucrative opportunities, he had precious little time to enjoy his accomplishment. Only three days later, Enrique Tirabocchi, leaving from France, crossed in only sixteen hours and twenty-three minutes, cutting more than five hours from Webb's record. His achievement was stunning, and again Burgess basked in the afterglow—once again, he had been aboard one of the pilot boats. Wolffe had been in the water, but had been accompanying another swimmer, one of four who tried to swim the Channel that day. Only Tirabocchi—and Burgess—found success.

Incredibly, one month later, on September 9, another one of those swimmers, Charles Toth of Boston, who was trained by Burgess, became the third person to successfully swim the Channel, nearly matching Tirabocchi's mark with a time of sixteen hours and fifty minutes. Unlike Sullivan and Tirabocchi, however, Toth gained little from his achievement apart from the satisfaction of having done it. The *Daily Sketch*, after paying out two one-thousand-pound offers in a matter of days, had withdrawn the prize before Toth's swim. Swimming the Channel was suddenly becoming almost commonplace.

In just a few short weeks the entire nature of crossing the Channel had changed. Three successful swims in such close proximity seemed to indicate that, somehow, swimming the Channel had been "solved" and simply wasn't as challenging as it once had been. To the great dismay of Jabez Wolffe, Bill Burgess was the common denominator for all three successful swims, and it appeared as if he somehow possessed a secret key to crossing the Channel.

That wasn't entirely true. Part of the reason the three swimmers had succeeded was the weather, which had been unusually favorable, and the fact that so many swimmers were in the water trying at the same time. The 1923 season had been the busiest in Channel history—nearly twenty separate swims had been attempted—increasing the odds that someone would succeed.

There had also been an enormous amount of luck involved. Both Tirabocchi and Toth had landed on a tiny point of land that extended into the Channel between Cape Margaret's Bay and Kingsdown—literally a spit of sand only about a yard wide at the base of a sheer cliff. Had either man missed the point, each would have been swept several miles farther down the coast and may not have finished at all.

Yet luck was not the only reason. The era of the breaststroke and sidestroke was beginning to end, for despite Sullivan's success, both Tirabocchi and Toth used a variety of strokes but primarily depended upon the trudgen, which allowed both to swim far faster than previous Channel conquerors. In so doing, each was able to avoid a tidal change, allowing both men to swim the Channel in a course that more resembled the single letter Z rather than the squat double Z that Webb and Sullivan had followed.

Still, swimming the Channel remained a significant challenge. Over the next few years the goal of many swimmers would not be so much to swim the Channel, but to swim the Channel faster or in some kind of novel way.

Five men had already conquered the Channel. As the *Boston Globe* asked after Toth's swim, "Who will be the first woman to swim the English Channel?"

13

Records

ON THE MORNING of Saturday, August 5, 1922, dawn in Manhattan revealed one of those rare perfect days that happen only a few times each summer and make New York seem the center of the season. Blue skies, a gentle breeze, and a few puffy white clouds sent New Yorkers outside in droves. For sports fans—and nearly everyone was a sports fan—there was, truly, something for everyone.

In Sea Bright, New Jersey, just south of the Highlands on the Jersey Shore, some three thousand spectators turned out to see Boston's Leslie Bancroft try to knock off women's tennis champion Molla Mallory. Several thousand more traveled a bit farther south to Spring Lake where U.S. Open golf champion Gene Sarazen was scheduled to play the English champion Long Jim Barnes in thirty-six holes of match play. Excursion trains heading up the Hudson River were packed to overflowing as the biggest crowd of the racing season, more than fifteen thousand strong, pressed through the gates at Saratoga Springs to see thoroughbred sensation Martingale race in the prestigious U.S. Hotel Stakes for two-year-old thoroughbreds. A similar number of fans poured from the Ninth Avenue elevated train station near the Polo Grounds in Manhattan to see the New York Giants, in a pitched battle for first place in the National League, play host for the Chicago Cubs. And in Brooklyn, even though the Dodgers—then better known as the Robins—were in sixth place, another eight thousand fans packed Ebbets Field for a doubleheader between Brooklyn's nine and the Reds of Cincinnati. Just outside New York parks and beaches were packed to overflowing, while those who remained in the city flocked to Central Park and to Prospect Park in Brooklyn.

In later years, the dean of American sportswriters, Grantland Rice, would refer to the decade of the 1920s as a golden age that spawned "sport's first tidal wave of popularity."

Rice was correct, for in the 1920s, America was sports mad. For the first time in the nation's history both participating in and watching sports became something of a national obsession.

Despite the restrictions of Prohibition after the war, America not only cut loose and cut ties with the repressive Victorian era and its restrictive sense of morality, but shed its insularity and became part of the world. The biplane heralded a new era in transportation, radio broadcasts and telephones began to become commonplace. News traveled faster and farther. What happened today could be known halfway across the globe in a matter of minutes. The world had become smaller almost overnight.

Returning servicemen had seen Gay Paree and weren't turning back, while those they had left behind when they joined the service—women—had entered the workplace and emerged from the war with a newfound sense of independence and self-esteem. Hemlines started to rise, and women who had run households and worked during the war weren't satisfied to resume their place before the hearth, darning socks.

Americans suddenly felt unbound and embarked on a headlong rush to have as much fun as possible. They didn't want to sit around, either. The economy was booming, and for the first time in American history a significant number of Americans had both the time and the money to indulge themselves. With the possible exception of the speakeasy, spectator sports suddenly became America's favorite pastime. Before the war, only baseball, boxing, horse racing, and bicycling had much of a fan following. But after the war, sports of all kinds grew exponentially, in terms of both spectators and participants. Even lesser sports such as yachting, wrestling, billiards, and rowing enjoyed newfound popularity. Daredevils such as Alvin "Shipwreck" Kelley became celebrities and elevated stunts like flagpole sitting to near respectability, while ersatz sports, like dance marathons and six-day bicycle races, attracted thousands of spectators. With no television and still-limited access to radio broadcasts, most sports fans had to either attend the event in person or read about it in the paper.

Even swimming was on the precipice of a boom. Within a decade, water shows and carnivals that mixed athletic competition and artistry would draw thousands of fans to outdoor pools and indoor arenas. As yet, however, women's swimming was still something of a fringe sport, drawing press attention and the occasional curious crowd, such as that at the Day Cup race; but unless an international star such as Hilda James was participating, swimming attracted few spectators.

But as the surprisingly large turnout to the Day Cup race had indicated, that was about to change. All the sport needed was a catalyst, the swimming equivalent of a Babe Ruth or Red Grange, a charismatic figure who would give the sport a personality.

To no surprise, among the hundreds of thousands of New Yorkers who set off that morning to enjoy the fine summer weather, thousands descended on Brighton Beach and the Brighton Beach Baths, most arriving by either train or subway. But what was shocking was that despite the fine weather several thousand of the visitors showed no interested whatsoever in the beach or in the Baths' several public pools, at least not at first. Instead they gathered around the twenty-five-yard competition pool, pressing forward until it appeared as if were one person to fall in, hundreds more might follow in a massive chain reaction.

They had all come to see Trudy. Five days before she hadn't even been worthy of a mention in all the press buildup to the Day Cup, but now people who had never cared a wit for swimming were willing to give up half their weekend just to see her. The WSA had been so stunned by the public interest in Trudy that she was quickly added to the roster of WSA swimmers invited to compete against Hilda James in a special 300-meter invitational race. In the last few days the race had been touted as a return test between "the victor and the vanquished," Trudy Ederle versus everyone else.

Trudy herself hadn't quite known what to think when her name was quickly added to the race, but Meg was absolutely thrilled to see her sister suddenly considered one of the WSA's top talents. The past few days had been a whirlwind in the Highlands. With Trudy's parents still overseas neither Trudy nor her family quite knew how to deal with her sudden fame.

Apart from the 1920 Olympics, never before in the history of women's swimming had any true swimming race drawn more than a few hundred spectators, not even those featuring bathing beauties such as Annette Kellerman and Hilda James. Even then, many in the crowd were generally friends and the families of the swimmers themselves. Even the Day Cup race, which had been the subject of weeks of prerace publicity in the *Tribune*, had drawn a crowd of only three or four hundred dedicated souls.

Yet on this day several thousand spectators turned out to see, of all things, a swimming race between women. At the time it was perhaps the largest crowd ever to attend a swim meet in the United States.

Hilda James was looking for retribution. Her loss to the unknown Ederle had been a shock. She hadn't expected to lose and was hoping to regain her reputation before she embarked on a short tour of the Midwest. Helen Wainwright, Aileen Riggin, and several other accomplished WSA swimmers were scheduled to accompany her and swim in meets against the best swimmers in the Midwest before James was scheduled to return to the East Coast and set sail for Europe in early September. Trudy Ederle had not even been invited.

Like James, Aileen Riggin and Ethel McGary were also hoping to prove that the loss to Ederle had been an anomaly. Ever since the 1920 Olympic gold medal winner Thelda Bleibtrey had turned professional, working as a coach, Riggin and McGary, along with Helen Wainwright, had been in an intense yet friendly battle to become the WSA's next golden girl. Wainwright wasn't scheduled to compete in the invitational, but Riggin and McGary, who had finished fourth and fifth in the Day Cup race behind Ederle, Wainwright, and James, were looking to stay on top. Although Trudy had been their superior over the course of three and a half miles, the girls were confident that over the shorter distance she would provide them with little competition.

But as the swimmers warmed up before the race, a rumor swept through the crowd that Trudy was under the weather. A few days after the Day Cup race she got a touch of the flu and was still home in the Highlands. As the spectators learned that she would not compete, there was disappointment, but only a few left. After all it was a fine day, there would still be a race, and afterward there was still time to take a stroll on the beach or nearby boardwalk.

Although Trudy Ederle was not in attendance, the instant the swimmers hit the water her presence was felt. James had been so shaken by her loss that in only four short days she had changed her stroke completely, abandoning the trudgen for her version of the American crawl, which she used in competition for the first time in this race. Although she hadn't found the new stroke easy, and at several points seemed to lose her rhythm as both Riggin and McGary nearly overtook her, the results were irrefutable. She didn't just win the race, she set a new world record at 300 meters, as race officials with stopwatches concluded she had bettered Bleibtrey's mark of 4 minutes 34 seconds by one-fifth of a second. Riggin and McGary had pushed her hard, however, and finished only three yards behind James, about a foot apart. Armed with the new stroke, for a moment, anyway, Hilda James was once again the best swimmer in the world. Trudy Ederle was just another contender.

Over the next month, as they embarked on the midwestern tour, James and Wainwright gathered all the headlines. Like James, Wainwright seemed motivated by her loss to Trudy and responded with some record-setting performances and staked her own claim as the world's best female swimmer. She broke James's world record in the 300-meter freestyle race, beating James by several yards and clipping four seconds from James's preexisting record, winning in 4 minutes 29²/₅ seconds. In the process she set an American record for 300 yards and eclipsed the world mark over 500 yards, beating James by ten yards and finishing in 7 minutes 9²/₅ seconds, ten seconds faster than the previous mark. Although James dominated in 100-yard races in the freestyle, backstroke, and breaststroke, when the swimmers returned to New York, Wainwright competed in the national AAU mile championships at the ocean pool in Manhattan Beach. Over a two-day period, on August 18 and 19, Wainwright smashed five more records including the world record in the mile, winning in 26 minutes 44³/₅ seconds, more than four minutes better than the previous mark, and also setting a new standard over 100 yards, 120 yards, 150 yards, and the half mile. Her performance pushed her to the forefront of the world of women's swimming. For the time being everyone forgot about Trudy Ederle.

That was probably just as well. Despite her Day Cup win, Trudy hardly seemed prepared to compete at their level in shorter distances. But the tour gave her a chance to catch up, and while James and Wainwright pursued records Trudy did more than tread water.

For all his commitment to swimming, Louis de Breda Handley did have his import business to run. He remained in New York, taking care of his trade and coaching WSA swimmers in the outdoor pool. While Wainwright, Riggin, and the other WSA stars were on tour, Handley was able to focus on Trudy. Before, she had just been another girl in the water, someone Handley worked with in a group with other girls. Now, all during the month of August she received individual attention as Handley worked with her to determine a pace she could maintain at distances ranging from 100 to 500 yards.

As Trudy trained she seemed almost oblivious to the extra attention and completely nonchalant about her recent success. Although she had enjoyed winning, she was a true believer and took the lessons of the WSA and its adage "good sportsmanship is greater than victory" to heart—Trudy was the ultimate good sport.

Handley, however, couldn't help but notice that Trudy was an entirely different swimmer than she had been only a few months earlier when she had been training indoors, an environment she had never been particularly fond of. But after spending the better part of two months swimming for hours every day in the Highlands, Trudy was simply in much better shape than the other swimmers.

Even though she was younger than either Wainwright or Riggin, Trudy had an entirely different body than either, more stoutly built, with broader shoulders. And now Handley noticed that she simply swam *differently* than most of the other girls. Even in longer races, most swimmers started out fast, in a near full sprint, then, as their bodies tired, they slowed over the course of the race, like a toy boat with a propeller powered by a twisted rubber band. Trudy, Handley noted, demonstrated a different approach. Although she lacked the pure sprinter's speed of swimmers such as Wainwright and Riggin, once she got going, Trudy didn't slow down. She was able to maintain a much faster pace for much, much longer, making her something of sprinting tortoise to everyone else's panting hare. She swam as if she needn't ever stop and maintained the same pace almost indefinitely, as if she simply turned a dial to the desired speed and then took off.

Handley's challenge was to harness her newfound strength and refine her stroke to take advantage of her stamina and make her competitive over shorter distances. As Meg had long known, Trudy needed a little pushing. For much of the past year Meg realized that her sister was the better swimmer, but something seemed to hold her back. Trudy was not lazy, but at times she simply seemed unaware of anything outside herself, perhaps as a result of her hearing problem and her tendency to turn inward. Trudy herself also found it a little hard to believe that after a lifetime of chasing after Meg in the water, she could now beat her sister with ease. Meg had to assure her again and again that it was okay.

Unlike most athletes, Trudy was not primarily motivated by her own ego or quest for personal glory—her win during the Day Cup had been something of an accident, but she'd been thrilled afterward to discover how excited her win had made Meg and other members of her family. She craved only the approval of others, and now that both Meg and Mr. Handley were telling her she could do more and asking her to do more, she was determined not to let them down.

It was almost funny. All Handley had to do was ask Trudy to concentrate a little more, increase her pace a little bit, push herself a little harder, and she did, instantly. In fact, he was almost a little embarrassed by her success, realizing that he had probably been underestimating her all along. A few words of praise—"Very good, Miss Ederle. Fine job."—went a long, long way.

Handley was astonished at how quickly she seemed to improve, but not completely surprised. The years he had spent as a teacher of swimming had taught him that at times during adolescence, as their bodies quickly change, athletes can make sudden and extreme changes. Many lose their coordination almost overnight. With Trudy, however, the opposite was happening. Over the course of one summer her body seemed to mature, becoming stronger and more muscular. Combined with her new focus and desire to win the approval of her family and coaches, she had completely changed. It was as if she was coming out of her cocoon and using her wings for the first time.

On August 27 at Seaside Park in Bridgeport, Connecticut, the world of swimming began to find out exactly what that meant. Despite the fact that she had never before competed in a national championship, Trudy was entered in the national 220-yard freestyle swim, an event that was supposed to include both Hilda James and Helen

Wainwright. This time, however, it was Helen Wainwright who was forced to withdraw before the event. Long exposure to the water had left her with a painful ear infection, and there was some concern that she might have to undergo an operation. Her absence made James the heavy favorite at the start of the race. No one, apart from Handley perhaps, and Meg, had any idea just how good Trudy Ederle had become.

It was no contest. After the first few strokes Trudy settled into a rapid pace that James, even at the start, could neither match nor maintain. Ederle moved through the water almost mechanically, each stroke identical to the last, her speed never wavering, as James slowly and inexorably dropped back. Trudy finished the race in 2 minutes 49$^1/_5$ seconds, three seconds faster than the old mark set by Thelda Bleibtrey. James, who only one month before had held the title as the best female swimmer in the world, wasn't even close. Although she finished in second place, she splashed her way to the finish line more than thirteen seconds behind Trudy. It was humiliating.

The win put Ederle—and women's swimming—back in the headlines. The three-way competition between James, Wainwright, and Ederle was starting to attract some attention. In the world of women's swimming it was as if the baseball Yankees, Giants, and Dodgers were all fighting for the pennant together for the first time.

The WSA was wise enough to recognize what was taking place. Never before had there been so much interest in the group, or its swimmers. Before the summer swimming season ended and James returned to England, the group decided to take full advantage of the public's growing fascination with its sport and its three best-known swimmers by holding a special Labor Day competition at Brighton Beach to include 50-yard and 100-yard freestyle races, fancy diving, and, most significantly, a special 500-meter invitation race that would include Ederle, Wainwright, and James.

Although the weather forecast that day called for partly cloudy conditions with gentle, variable winds and a temperature of near eighty degrees, weather forecasting was an inexact science. By midmorning New York and Long Island were experiencing a slow-moving, almost tropical downpour, marked by distant thunder and occasional flashes of lightning. At Brighton Beach worried WSA officials pondered canceling the swim meet.

Then the crowd started to arrive, first in a trickle and then, like the rain, in a torrent. Despite the poor weather more than two thousand spectators—mothers and daughters and fathers and sons—braved the elements, carrying umbrellas and wearing raincoats and slickers. Once again they pushed their way to poolside, surrounding the seventy-five-foot pool in a crowd that in places was more than fifty people deep, all standing patiently as the rain pounded down and a surprisingly cool wind whipped the waters of the pool, at times nearly raising white caps on its surface.

Charlotte Epstein and other WSA officials looked to the sky and virtually pleaded with the rains to stop, for they knew that if the race were not held, an important opportunity would likely slip away, for in only a few short weeks it would be impossible to hold a swim meet outdoors. Fortunately, just as it appeared that they might have to cancel the meet, the rains ended. Although it remained overcast, the thunder and lightning slowly dissipated. The race would go on.

Since Helen Wainwright was also scheduled to compete in the "fancy diving" event, the 500-meter swim was the first scheduled race. As the swimmers warmed up, four capable officials, led by Louis Handley, staked out positions staggered alongside the pool. They were meticulous in their planning. The race was destined to be a record setter, for there was, as yet, no official women's record for the 500-meter freestyle. Along the way, given the strength of the field, everyone expected at least a few other records to fall, and officials were determined to time the swimmers at various intervals in both yards and meters. While it was easy enough simply to count laps in the twenty-five-yard pool to time the swimmers over every fifty- or one-hundred-yard interval, doing so in meters as well took some calculations. At various points one or more of the timers would have to change position alongside the pool as various distances were eclipsed.

Of course the whole business of swimming records was something of a mess. Claims of American and world records were just that—claims—until they were verified and accepted by the AAU and the International Record Committee, which set standards concerning the methodology used to measure time and distances. But as yet there was no agreement on a standardized set of competition distances, meaning that in virtually any race that included some of the nations' best swimmers it was possible to claim some kind of new record, depending on factors such as the distance of the race, whether the race was held indoors or outdoors, the length of the pool, and other variables.

From race to race, however, conditions varied widely and rendered many of these marks almost meaningless. The competitive environments for races held in closed pools, ocean pools, and open water all varied wildly, and a world record set in one environment was not remotely the same as one set in another—a 100-yard race held in the open ocean was not the same as one held in a twenty-yard indoor pool or a fifty-yard ocean pool. In reality, the only standard that really meant anything was a swimmer's record in head-to-head competition versus other swimmers, on the same day, under the same conditions, in the same race.

On this day Trudy Ederle, Hilda James, and Helen Wainwright were the only swimmers invited to compete in the 500-meter invitational. At the end of the race the better swimmer would be obvious to everyone. As each girl took her place before her lane at the end of the pool, the crowd cheered and clapped in anticipation.

For most of the spectators, this was their first real look at the swimmers they had been reading about for more than a month. And although Wainwright and James were more experienced and somewhat better known, Marguerite Mooers Marshall's profile of Ederle had done a fine job of exposing her to the public, and it responded to her bubbly personality. Trudy was still the crowd favorite.

It also didn't hurt that when spectators saw Trudy alongside Wainwright and James, they found her much better looking than James and more voluptuous than Helen Wainwright. In person James was not quite the beauty her publicity pictures made her appear to be, while Trudy appeared as the quintessential American teenager.

At the start of the race the three swimmers stood side by side, each dressed similarly in a competition suit, Wainwright and Ederle's both sporting the red, white, and blue logo of the WSA. Hands out front, each was poised at the edge of the pool listening for the report of the starter's pistol that signaled the beginning of the race.

At the gun, Wainwright and James took to the air a heartbeat before Trudy, but by the time each woman had reached the surface and started to stroke, Trudy already had a slight lead. Observers later noted that she began the race as if it were a fifty-yard sprint, showing early speed that she had never before demonstrated. At the first turn she held a slight lead over both Wainwright and James, and at the end of fifty yards still swam as if she were in a sprint, while James and Wainwright began to slow. Pushing ahead of the others, Trudy also had little trouble staying in her lane. She swam straight as a string, while both Wainwright and James occasionally wavered and continually had to correct their course.

Over the next fifty yards, Trudy slowly pulled ahead as Wainwright, who had been third at the fifty-yard mark, went into a sprint and passed Hilda James, putting her within reach of Trudy. But if Ederle felt the pressure, she didn't show it. In fact, she swam as if she were in the pool by herself, apparently unconcerned about the whereabouts of the other swimmers, never varying her stroke or taking a glance their way. She may as well have been at the Highlands, swimming along and humming to herself in the surf.

At the two-hundred-yard mark she led Wainwright by more than a yard, with James another five feet back. Ederle was in command, but the race was still relatively close. Over the next fifty yards, however, both Wainwright and James began to flag as Ederle kept up the same inexorable pace she assumed at the start of the race. With each stroke she increased her lead by a precious inch or two.

As she approached the turn to mark three hundred yards, the lead over Wainwright approached five yards, and race officials took their first timed measurement. They were astonished.

The existing record over three hundred yards was 4 minutes $8^3/_5$ seconds. Yet Trudy had covered the distance in ten and one-fifth fewer seconds—3 minutes $58^2/_5$ seconds. She had not just broken the record, she had nearly broken the stopwatch as the incredulous timekeeper looked at his watch again and again before recording the time. In fact, officials were so shocked that they failed to get a time for Ederle at the three-hundred-meter mark—she was swimming so swiftly that she outraced the timer to the mark, a factor that undoubtedly prevented her from breaking Helen Wainwright's recent record at the distance.

From then on it was as if Trudy Ederle swam with the current while Wainwright and James fought against a riptide. On each lap Trudy added another yard or two to her lead as Wainwright and James dropped farther and farther behind.

And each time she passed a milestone, the same scene was repeated as the timekeeper checked his watch again and again as if unable to believe the numbers. At four hundred yards she was timed at 5 minutes 22^2/$_5$ seconds, an incredible forty seconds faster than the existing mark, and she passed the four-hundred-meter line at 5 minutes 53 seconds, forty-three seconds faster than the record, and the 440-yard mark in 5 minutes 54^3/$_5$ seconds, twenty-three seconds better than Hilda James's world best.

While the crowd roared, sensing from both her growing lead and the behavior of race officials that something extraordinary was happening, Trudy swam merrily along, oblivious to nearly everything, utterly relaxed, wholly and completely in her element.

And she *was* oblivious. She had not even bothered to keep track of her number of laps, and when she made the next turn, she rolled over on her side for a moment, spotted a race official, and without stopping asked how many more laps she still needed to swim. One observer later noted that she spoke as if "she were addressing a bystander at a club practice session." The startled official blurted out "two" and Ederle, without comment, put her face back in the water and resumed her pace.

Leading Helen Wainwright by fifteen yards with only one lap remaining, Ederle finished in a flourish, sprinting on top of what already had looked like a sprint. She added another five yards to her lead, swimming her strongest lap yet, and touched the end of the pool just a few beats after Wainwright made the final turn. Trudy was timed at 7 minutes 22^1/$_5$ seconds for the 500-meter race, her sixth record of the day. She covered the final hundred meters in eighty-eight seconds, almost the same pace at which she had covered each of the first four hundred meters, a remarkable demonstration of her stamina and strength. Even more significant, however, was the fact that she beat Helen Wainwright by twenty yards, and bettered Hilda James by twice that distance. It was the most extraordinary performance by a woman swimmer to date, a tour de force performance that in historical terms was akin to the day in 1935 that track star sprinter Jesse Owens set world records in the long jump, 100 yards, 220 yards, and 220-yard low hurdles. There was no doubt whatsoever that Trudy Ederle was the best female swimmer in the world.

And she was still a teenager.

14

Girl in the Water

THERE MAY AS WELL have been a sign on each shore of the English Channel stating the obvious: For Men Only.

Despite the fact that Matthew Webb had swum the Channel in 1875, it had remained virtually off-limits to women swimmers of any ability. No woman even made a serious attempt to swim the Channel until 1900, when Walburga von Icacescu, an Austrian, spent ten and a half hours in the water, alternating between the breaststroke and the sidestroke, reportedly covering twenty miles before giving up. Five years later Annette Kellerman made the first of her two attempts to swim the Channel using the trudgen stroke. She failed each time but garnered massive amounts of publicity for her other ventures.

"I had the endurance," said Kellerman afterward, "but not the brute strength." For much of the next two decades that statement encompassed the prevailing attitude toward any woman who even hazarded to dream of swimming the Channel. It was considered completely out of reach, beyond a woman's physical capability, about as likely as a woman fighting for and winning the heavyweight boxing title. Just as women were once considered far too frail to run a marathon, even as more and more women learned to swim, they were considered too weak to challenge the strong tides and currents of the Channel—Kellerman's admission seemed to underscore that fact. After her failures, as Wolffe and Burgess and several dozen men tested the cold Channel waters again and again and again, the English Channel remained an all-male domain. For the next decade no other woman made a serious attempt to swim the Channel.

Then the war, the suffragist movement, the success of women's swimming at the 1920 Olympics, and economic conditions on both sides of the Atlantic all combined to make the Channel more accessible to women. Female swimmers suddenly took to the waters of the Channel as if it were an extension of the WSA swimming pool. The moral, physical, and even psychological barriers that had prevented women from competing in sports like swimming, while not entirely erased, were no longer as rigid—and neither were the swimming suits, as more and more women swimmers opted for less-confining garments more like those used by swimmers in the WSA. Women finally had the license to swim as athletes, for their health, and, increasingly, in competition. Now—finally—they could swim simply because they chose to.

The first woman to enter the Channel after the war was Mrs. Arthur Hamilton, the daughter of the English baron Sir Charles Fairlie-Cuninghame, a confirmed member of the upper crust. Although Hamilton's effort is little known today, her attempt was hugely important in the history of women's long-distance swimming. Hamilton, whose family was known for its eccentricity and independence, had been the first woman to swim the Solent, the four-mile stretch of water between the Isle of Wight and the English mainland. During the war she became notable for her work with soldiers, helping to develop the so-called trench sock to help prevent trench foot.

In the spring of 1920, as soon as the Channel was cleared of mines, she announced that she intended to duplicate Webb's feat and become the first woman to swim the Channel. She took her task seriously, spending months training in the Channel waters, posing for British newsreel photographers both in the water and out, modeling bathing suits—including a revealing unitard.

Hamilton failed—due to convention, the press never even bothered to refer to her by her own given name, but as either Mrs. Hamilton or even more anonymously as "the Baron's daughter"—but although she barely made it halfway across the Channel she nevertheless stayed in the water for twelve hours, considered an unofficial record for women swimmers at the time. Although her effort was greeted with some skepticism—a Margate businessman who provided a motorboat to accompany her claimed she spent much of her swim inside the boat, a charge Hamilton vigorously denied—few argued that she did not have the right to try, even as they may have considered the attempt foolhardy. As it was, Hamilton's swim opened Channel waters to women, and when she tried again the following summer, leaving from Cape Gris-Nez, over twenty hours she managed to make it to within three miles of Deal using the trudgen stroke, an effort no one questioned. With each stroke of her arms she supplied increasing evidence that swimming the Channel was within a woman's capacity.

The next female Channel swimmer of note was Amelia "Mille" Gade of Denmark. As a young woman Gade grew up in Vejle, a fjord on Denmark's east coast. Gade, although she stood only five feet four, was built more like a football lineman, squat with large bones and, for a woman, heavily muscled. Although her parents hoped she would become a musician like her father, she was more athletically inclined. She learned to swim and as a young woman worked as a swimming instructor and lifeguard, reportedly rescuing no fewer than three swimmers from drowning in the waters near Vejle. On one occasion she even retrieved a young girl who had gone under for the last time in twenty feet of water. Gade managed not only to bring her to the surface, but to haul her seventy-five feet to shore, where she was resuscitated and survived. Her act of heroism earned a decoration from King Christian X.

It was not, however, enough to make Gade remain in Denmark. Like the rest of Europe, Denmark's economy was in a shambles after the war. In the fall of 1919, at age twenty-two, she immigrated to the United States, passing through Ellis Island and joining her older sister Helga. Gade, who spoke some English, was soon hired as a swimming instructor at the Harlem branch of the YWCA.

Teaching swimming, however, was little challenge to Gade, who missed the attention that had been hers in Denmark, as she once explained, "It was funny, very funny to come to this big country where nobody knew me. At home, all the people know who I am—a big swimmer in a country with many." All over America, it seemed, young people were swept up in all manner of fads and stunts, from marathon dancing to flagpole sitting and other nonsensical pursuits. In the summer of 1921, Gade, who was determined, as she put it, "to do something fine in my line," stared at the waters of the Harlem River and was suddenly seized by the notion to swim around the island of Manhattan.

She stopped a passerby and asked how far it was. He shrugged and told her it was probably thirty or forty miles. "Right then" she later said, "I decided to swim." It wasn't a particularly original idea—Robert Dowling had been the first to accomplish the feat in 1915, and a woman, Ida Elionsky, had done the same in 1916, completing the swim in eleven hours and thirty-five minutes, two hours faster than Dowling. The swim was challenging but was as much a matter of planning as athletic skill. To succeed a swimmer had to make the best use of the tides and currents that swept around Manhattan, riding the outgoing tide south and hoping to catch the incoming tide back north.

This did not deter Gade. She boldly approached the naval vessel USS *Illinois*, docked at the foot of West Ninety-sixth Street in the Hudson River for use by the New York state naval militia, and asked for maps and tidal charts to assist her in planning her swim.

She received all that and even more, meeting Lieutenant Clemington Corson, a thirty-seven-year-old career navy man. Corson not only helped her out with maps, but the two quickly became an item. He taught her how to read the charts, assisted her in her training, and a few months later accompanied her on her swim, trailing her in a rowboat. Gade, primarily using the breaststroke, succeeded, finishing her swim in fifteen hours and fifty-seven minutes, while covering a distance of some forty miles. But in a world increasingly impressed by fads, she received far more attention for her swim than either Elionsky or Dowling had received for theirs, even though Gade was by far the slowest of the three.

Gade was undeterred. Thrilled with the spotlight, in September she set her sights on another swim heavily impacted by the tides and current. She announced that she would swim down the Hudson River from Albany to New York, a distance of some 150 miles. Once more she rode the tide, and she reached Manhattan 153 hours after leaving Albany, spending 63 hours in the water—the first person to accomplish the swim in more than twenty-five years.

The six-day journey kept her in the headlines for a week, and this second swim made Gade famous. Each day she spent in the water she drew more attention, and as she approached New York more and more spectators turned out to watch her pass, and whenever Gade was aware of the crowd she wisely stayed close to shore.

The press loved her. It didn't hurt that Gade, despite her size, photographed well, her blond hair and high cheekbones accentuating a bright and open smile. The story of the immigrant who fell in love with the doughboy was ready-made for the postwar press, and only a few weeks after the swim she and Corson married, using the occasion to announce that Gade—who retained her maiden name in swimming events—next intended to swim the English Channel.

It would be two years, however, before Gade Corson made good on her promised intention. She quickly became pregnant and gave birth to a son, then was hired as swimming instructor on her husband's naval vessel, essentially providing sponsorship for her swimming career, and began training with Louis Leibgold, well-known race walker and physical director of the *Illinois*. In the summer of 1923 she finally made it to England, training with Henry Sullivan and several other men who planned to try to swim the Channel.

She made her first attempt to swim the Channel on August 9, 1923, just a day after Henry Sullivan's successful crossing. But with the French coast in sight, the water turned rough, the tide turned, and Gade Corson was pushed back some seven miles before abandoning her attempt after spending fourteen and a half hours in the water and covering twenty-one miles. Although few made note of it at the time, until the moment she left the water Gade Corson had actually outperformed Sullivan, swimming much faster than the American man.

Like a sand castle facing a rising tide, the barriers that barred women from competing in sports were beginning to fall. As Thelda Bleibtrey had told the *Ladies' Home Journal* earlier that summer, "The tremendous advance of women in athletics during the past twenty years, and especially in the past five years, has been a thrilling drama to me." Just a few weeks earlier Sybil Bauer, an eighteen-year-old student at Northwestern University, had shocked the world by unofficially breaking the *men's* world record for the 440-yard backstroke. Although the new record was never officially recognized due to the fact she swam in an unsanctioned meet and used the new "alternate arm" backstroke rather than then standard double arm method in which both arms were used in tandem, it nevertheless represented a stunning achievement.

That was part of the reason that Gade Corson's presence in Channel waters had caused so little comment or controversy. Due to the efforts of the WSA, at least as far as the sport of swimming was concerned, women swimmers were no longer a novelty. As one anonymous writer in the *Literary Digest* cautioned at the time, "Masculine holders of championships in athletics, look to your laurels. Sundry members of the so called weaker sex, having obtained the vote and many other things upon which they had set their dear fluttering little hearts, are now out for far bigger game. Frankly, they are making what may be called Herculean efforts to overcome the vaunted superiority of their brothers."

Everywhere one looked, all of a sudden it seemed as if there was a girl in the water, swimming faster than ever before.

Why should the English Channel be any different?

15

Trials

TRUDY WAS SO GOOD it was almost getting monotonous.

After her record-setting performance on Labor Day, Trudy Ederle was still a long, long way from swimming the English Channel, although she may have started entertaining the notion as she shared space on the sports page the next day with Charles Toth, who had just become the third man to swim the Channel that summer, and the fifth of all time. But for the next year and a half, all she did was swim and win, at any distance, under any conditions, against any competition, setting world records with nearly every breath and kick. Fifty yards in an indoor pool against the world record holder? Check. One hundred and twenty yards in an outdoor pool in Bermuda against Britain's best swimmers? Check. A half mile in an ocean pool? Check. With the wind in her face? Check. When she was sick? Check. In Boston? Check. When it was hot? In Indianapolis? Honolulu? Bermuda? Over four hundred meters, the quarter mile, the half mile, in a relay, in a sixty-foot pool, over 50 yards, 100, 120, 150, 200, 400, a half mile, in a handicap, giving every other swimmer a head start? Check, check, check, check, check, check, check, check. "Ederle Sets World Record" became as common a headline in the sports pages as "Ruth Hits Home Run."

Few athletes of any kind and of any gender have ever dominated a sport the way Trudy Ederle did from the fall of 1922 through the summer of 1924—she held virtually every imaginable women's world record in swimming at distances that ranged from fifty yards to one mile, losing only twice—each time to teammate Helen Wainwright, and even then she defeated Wainwright in a later rematch. The few records she did not hold were only because she had failed to swim those distances under the particular set of conditions required—such as swimming one hundred yards in a seventy-five-foot pool, as opposed to a sixty- or one-hundred-foot pool—or, as in her Labor Day swim, when race officials had failed to time her.

In male sporting terms she was Tiger Woods, Babe Ruth, Wayne Gretzky, LeBron James, and Michael Phelps all rolled into one, her only possible female equivalents such legends as Babe Didrikson, Martina Navratilova, and Serena Williams. But when one considers that Trudy was as successful swimming sprints as she was long distances, her performance is more impressive than that of any of these other athletes. It was as if the world record holder in the 100-meter sprint was simultaneously the world champion in the quarter mile, mile, and 10,000-meter steeplechase, and winner of the Boston Marathon, and that most of those marks had been set in the same race.

Under the tutelage of Louis Handley, using and perfecting the American crawl, for nearly two years Trudy Ederle hardly knew how to lose. The only thing that stopped her was the ice—she wasn't quite as good swimming indoors in the winter, which sometimes gave her opponents a slim chance at victory; but outdoors in the open ocean she played the sleek porpoise to their meandering turtle.

When Trudy's parents returned to New York from their extended visit to Germany just a few weeks after her Labor Day victory, they discovered that their daughter was a star.

They were not completely surprised by her accomplishments, for they had been kept informed of her remarkable performances by letters and cables and were aware of the fame she had gained. Still, it was not until they returned to New York that they realized just what that meant and how much their lives—and hers—had changed. In only a few short months she had gone from a complete unknown to a young woman many New Yorkers now felt that they knew—and cared about.

She didn't just belong to her family anymore, but also to the WSA, to the women and young girls who looked up to her as an example of what a woman could achieve, and to all New Yorkers, who loved to tout the accomplishments of their own. In her own neighborhood Trudy was a star, and the Ederles' retail butcher shop became an impromptu salon for neighbors to discuss her accomplishments and find out when she was competing next. Elsewhere in New York, when Trudy walked down the street, strangers started to point and whisper.

In an era in which the very notion of being a celebrity was still newly minted, Trudy was one of the first. America had never really had a female athletic hero before. Other WSA swimmers, like Thelda Bleibtrey, had their careers end just as they began to reach success, and tennis champ Helen Wills, who would soon become the women's national champion, was still a schoolgirl. French tennis star Suzanne Lenglen, although wildly popular in France, was little known in the United States. Women had yet to compete in track and field, and other sports that later came to be identified with female athletes, such as figure skating, as yet had little popular appeal or public profile.

There was only Trudy. Never again would her life be hers alone. At a time when most other girls her age were still in school, Trudy, for all intents and purposes, was now a full-time swimmer. Although she still detested indoor work, by now the WSA had secured a pool in Manhattan, on Fifty-fifth Street, and she no longer had to make the long jaunt to Brooklyn just to practice.

Significantly, Ederle had the full support of her family. Her father, in particular, burst with pride at his daughter's accomplishments and accompanied her to nearly every meet. Since she had already stopped going to school and the Ederles were well off, there was no pressure on Trudy to work or otherwise support the family apart from her household chores. Nothing stood in the way of her swimming career. She turned her life over to the WSA, to Charlotte Epstein and Lou Handley.

But *everyone* wanted her. The British Amateur Swimming Association extended an invitation to the WSA to send a team to Bermuda in October 1922 to participate in a water carnival in the new natatorium at the Hotel St. George, but the invitation was just a veiled excuse to get a look at Trudy Ederle, the girl who had beaten Hilda James so badly. The WSA accepted, and to no surprise Trudy collected another set of records, a performance that earned an invitation from a British promoter who wanted Trudy and Helen Wainwright to tour Europe the following summer and swim in nearly two dozen events all over Europe.

That was the first sign of what would soon become a larger conflict between the WSA and the AAU, both of which were beginning to battle for control over the young swimming star. She was a valuable property in terms of both publicity and real dollars. While the WSA accepted the invitation almost immediately, the AAU withheld approval.

All the while Trudy kept her head down in the water and focused on swimming. With each new victory she seemed to thrive, becoming ever more dedicated as each win built upon the next, and the approval she received from everyone—Meg, Handley, her parents, and other swimmers in the WSA—increased. The Olympics were only two years distant and provided Trudy with a goal beyond the pursuit of records. Now she could swim for the approval of an entire nation.

In 1923 she picked up right where she had left off in 1922. In a year in which Trudy, like a boxer taking on all comers, seemed to set a record every few weeks, one performance stood out from all the others.

Near the end of the summer season, on September 3, she participated in yet another water carnival at the Olympic Baths, a sixty-foot pool in Long Beach on Long Island. For once she actually had some competition: Johnny Weissmuller.

Weissmuller, like Trudy, was of German heritage, born in what is now Romania in what was then Austria-Hungary, in 1904. In 1905 he immigrated to the United States with his parents, living first in western Pennsylvania before the family finally settled in Chicago, where his father ran a bar and worked in a brewery and his mother worked as a cook. Weissmuller learned to swim in Lake Michigan, eventually joining the YMCA swim team and becoming a junior champion. At age seventeen he began to work with famed swim coach William Bachrach at the Illinois Athletic Club and in 1921 began to compete in AAU-sanctioned races.

He was, in many ways, the male swimming equivalent of Trudy Ederle, with one exception: Weissmuller, from the time he first started swimming competitively as a young boy, never, ever lost a freestyle race, not even once. He explained his success nonchalantly, saying, "I could make good time because I was so long and skinny, shooting through the water like a stick," but his physical skills were matched by unparalleled determination and a competitive instinct that refused to admit—or allow—defeat. He burst upon the national scene in the summer of 1922 when he set the men's record in the

100-meter freestyle, and for the next two years he grappled Trudy Ederle for his share of the headlines.

Weissmuller, charismatic and already movie-star handsome, would prove to be of benefit to Trudy's career. He made swimming even more popular and brought even more attention to the sport in the mainstream press, thereby helping to make Trudy Ederle a household name as well. By the summer of 1923 half of America was already gaga over Weissmuller. He'd been ill, and for a time doctors feared heart trouble. They were wrong, but that just made Weissmuller more heroic and more popular.

He was also a cogent observer of Trudy Ederle, once noting, "She has such powerful arms and shoulders that she gets practically ninety-nine percent of her propelling progress out of them—she swims more with her arms and less with her feet than any other swimmer I know . . . [her] feet are nothing but trailers . . . I believe she could swim just as fast with her feet tied together."

Swim meets that featured both Weissmuller and Ederle drew crowds unlike any the sport had ever seen. Young girls and women swooned before Weissmuller and looked up to Trudy as a kind of role model. Not until Mark Spitz emerged in the early 1970s did the sport of swimming enjoy such a figure as dominant and charismatic as either Weissmuller or Ederle.

At Long Beach the crowds were enormous. Weissmuller and Ederle were the reason. Weissmuller didn't disappoint—he defeated Ranger Mills, the metropolitan New York one-hundred-yard champion, by more than two seconds in their one-hundred-yard race. But it was Trudy who won the battle of the headlines.

Hers was a five-hundred-yard handicap event against two other WSA swimmers, Virginia Whitenack and Ethel McGary. Both were accomplished—Whitenack, one of the WSA's up and coming stars, was the metropolitan champion over 880 yards, while McGary held a variety of titles from 100 to 500 yards and earlier in the week had won the national AAU long-distance championship, a three-mile race in which Trudy, now focusing on shorter events in advance of the Olympics, had not competed.

Nevertheless, when racing against Trudy, each girl was provided with a head start in a handicap race. Whitenack received a fourteen-second lead and McGary a nine-second jump. By the time

Trudy entered the water, Whitenack had already made the first turn and McGary was in the process of doing so.

It wasn't enough.

Trudy responded with the best single-day performance of her career to date, at least equal to her Labor Day effort in 1922. She set world short-pool records at every imaginable distance officials had thought to time—200 yards, 220 yards, 300 yards, 300 meters, 400 yards, 440 yards, and 500 yards, lowering the record over 500 yards by nearly three seconds, finishing the course in 5 minutes 52 seconds. Moreover, despite giving the other girls a head start, she managed to beat Whitenack by seven yards and McGary by fifteen feet.

It was an absolutely stunning, jaw-dropping performance, made even more so by the apparent ease with which she had swum. The *New York Times* reporter covering the event described her as swimming "a slow, easy crawl. She seemed to be putting such little effort into it that the crowd was amazed when the times were announced." A month later she traveled to Hawaii to face members of the famed Huimakani Club, a Hawaiian team that some swim observers believed was better than the WSA, and whose top swimmer, Mariechen Wehselau, some believed was even better than Trudy.

Not so. Over a three-day period Trudy broke her own world records in the 100, 200, and 400 meters. She was the most dominant athlete in her sport in the world—no one else, not even Johnny Weissmuller, was even close.

Although many men failed to recognize her abilities, those who did did not bother to hedge their words. At the end of the year Grantland Rice, who had earlier accompanied Trudy and the other WSA swimmers to Bermuda, wrote a syndicated column in which he tried to select "the single greatest competitive achievement of 1923." Rice offered a laundry list of some fifteen accomplishments, ranging from Helen Wills's victory in the American women's tennis championship to golfer Bobby Jones's victory at the U.S. Open, Bill Tilden's fourth consecutive U.S. title in men's singles, and Babe Ruth's two home runs in one World Series game.

But in Rice's estimation no one quite matched Trudy Ederle. "Breaking one record is often a great year's work," he wrote. "Smashing seven in one year is a monumental affair."

16

Agony

THERE WAS NO PLACE like Paris.

As the 1924 Olympics approached, the French government and the IOC were determined to show the world that Europe was on the move and had rebounded from years of wanton carnage. Later romanticized by expatriate American writers such as Ernest Hemingway, F. Scott Fitzgerald, and Gertrude Stein, in the 1920s Paris was the most exotic city in the world, in Hemingway's terms "a moveable feast," a place where culture flourished, where the jazz was hot, wine flowed, and talk of art and literature filled the air. The Olympics promised to be yet one more beacon for the City of Light, and after the dismal conditions that plagued the 1920 Olympics in Antwerp, where swimmers and divers competed in a murky canal full of fetid water of dubious origin, the French pulled out all the stops to make the 1924 Olympics a celebration not only of France and French culture, but of the world itself.

After her stellar performance in 1923, all that remained for Trudy to accomplish in her sport was to earn a place on the Olympic team and then win the expected gold medals. She spent the winter training in Miami with Helen Wainwright, Aileen Riggin, and other WSA stars and then embarked on an abbreviated indoor schedule that took her to such exotic locales as Omaha, Nebraska, Brookline, Massachusetts, Buffalo, and Chicago, where she continued her streak of spectacular swimming. In April her Olympic prospects achieved another boost when Lou Handley was named the coach of the women's swimming team; Johnny Weissmuller's coach, William Bachrach, was named coach of the men's squad, thus ensuring that the two top

American prospects for winning medals would be accompanied by their own personal coaches. As summer approached, Trudy cut back on the number of meets in which she competed in order to focus on the upcoming Olympic trials.

Trudy's place on the team was not a given—despite her multiple world records there was no mechanism to name her to the team unless she qualified at the trials. She still had to earn her place, one of 135 young women from all around the country vying for one of the coveted eighteen spots on the swimming and diving team, plus six alternates, more than three times the number of entrants who competed for a place on the 1920 squad. What she had done in the past didn't matter—now she had to perform.

In early June Trudy and most of the other girls gathered at the site of the trials, the Briarcliff Lodge, a hotel and resort in Briarcliff Manor, New York, in Westchester County, just north of New York City. The resort, which offered to host the trials in exchange for the publicity, featured an outdoor pool. On June 7 and 8 the women would swim a series of trials to determine the makeup of the team for the full compliment of Olympic events open to them: the 400-meter relay, 400-meter freestyle, 200-meter breaststroke, 100-meter freestyle, 100-meter backstroke, and both platform and springboard diving. The *Times* accurately referred to the group, which included swimmers from as far off as Hawaii, as "the greatest aggregation of girl swimmers ever."

When Trudy awoke on the morning of June 7, it was raining. Those conditions brought a smile to her eyes, and at breakfast, while other competitors looked glumly out the rain-smeared windows at the downpour, Trudy bubbled with confidence and nervous energy. She loved the rain, absolutely loved it, for over the past few years, beginning with the Day Cup, rain had always been a portent of good fortune, and many of her greatest victories had come during a deluge. Had she been a thoroughbred racehorse she would have been known as a "mudder," one whose performance improved in adverse weather. Both the weather and the outdoor pool in Briarcliff played to her strength.

There was pressure on Trudy to win, and not just because she was expected to. While a top two or three finish was generally thought to be good enough to make the team, one never knew for sure. Funds were tight, and while the trials were being held, the AOC was meeting in New York to discuss Olympic financing. Expenses for the American team were expected to cost about $350,000, but the committee had less than $250,000 in hand and was already $53,000 in debt to its president, Robert Thompson, who reportedly had paid housing expenses in Paris in advance out of his own pocket. Already the committee was cutting back on the number of athletes it was sending to the games—slashing the fencing team from eighteen to fourteen men, the boxing squad from twenty-five to sixteen, and choosing to create a water polo team from among the men's swim team rather than send a separate squad—and there were rumors of more cuts to come. Since women's swimming was a relatively new event, and some members of the AOC still viewed female athletes with disdain, there was a real chance the team might be cut to the bone. Even a second-place finish at the trial might not secure passage to Paris.

That wasn't the only concern. Some competitors showed up for the trials with a checkbook, from their own family or club, or in the name of a well-heeled patron. Large donations to the AOC often came attached to very strong string—they were dependent on whether certain entrants made the team, and Olympics officials were far from immune to such pressure. In the past, lesser athletes had been selected for the Olympic team almost entirely due to the amount of money their selection promised to deliver. It often explained the selection of alternates, many of whom held a purse string. This allowed the AOC to take the money and still retain some integrity.

For Trudy, the bar was even a little bit higher. She was not only expected to win her trials, but to drum up publicity and raise funds. During the trials, Olympics officials decided to hold a special 150-meter race between Trudy and Helen Wainwright, despite the fact there wasn't even Olympic competition at that distance. It would be the first time that event had ever been held in the United States, where apart from the Olympic trials, most races were measured by yards rather than the international standard of meters.

As if her task wasn't hard enough already, the special race made it a bit more difficult, but Trudy didn't really mind. Over the past two years she had slowly grown into her role as the face of the WSA, and as she grew and matured she was beginning to come out of her shell a bit, although she disliked being left alone around strangers without her sister, her coaches, or her friends to act as a buffer. But the young girl who had dashed out of the surf after winning the Day Cup was now a young woman who realized her responsibilities to others and was ever more cautious about the kind of impression she left. She had grown accustomed to being in the public eye and watched what she said and did, but around the other WSA girls Trudy never put on any airs and behaved as if she were just another novice. Still, Trudy would have to swim to win a place on the Olympic team. There would be no coasting, and for the first time in her life she would be competing under real pressure.

Fortunately, she had an advocate in Coach Handley, and he did what he could to make things easier for her. He had the latitude to select the members of the 400-meter relay team himself, in team trials to be held in Paris, and he saw no need for Trudy to overtax herself at the trials at Briarcliff. After all, if the unexpected happened—an injury, illness, cramps, and the like—and Trudy lost, she risked not qualifying at all. That would be a disaster, for there was already talk that she should win three gold medals at the Olympics—not *could* win, but *should* win. Although the 400-meter individual race was scheduled for the first day of the trials, both the 100-meter race and special 150-meter race were scheduled for day two, a tough schedule. But Handley had an idea.

He had Trudy skip the 100-meter trials entirely. There was still time for her to earn her spot in the 100-meter swim at more team trials in Paris, and if she held back now, that would open up room on the team for several alternates. He could always name Trudy to the 100-meter squad after the team arrived in France, keeping everyone relatively happy.

As expected, on the first day of the trials, in the rain, Trudy won the 400-meter race handily, with Helen Wainwright finishing a distant second. Like Trudy, Handley also held Wainwright out of the 100-meter race on day two as well. Now both girls could focus on the 150-meter race.

The rivalry between the two girls, while outwardly pleasant, was intense. If not for Trudy, Helen Wainwright would have been considered the greatest swimmer in world. And Wainwright, from Corona in Queens, was all that stood between Trudy and perfection—Ederle's only defeat in the last year and half had been against Wainwright, in a 50-yard sprint, and she was the only swimmer in the world to regularly challenge her. Neither girl treated the 150-meter contest like an exhibition.

Well, not quite. Trudy swam as if she hadn't a care in world and was never challenged in the race. She beat Wainwright by five yards, establishing a new world record in 1 minute 58³/₅ seconds.

At the end of the trials Trudy, along with other notable WSA members such as Wainwright and Riggin, was one of twenty-four American women named to the women's team. Apart from two female fencers, they were the only American female athletes going to Paris. While only one-third of the squad was made up of girls from the WSA, with only a few exceptions they represented the best swimmers of the lot. Most of the other picks for the team were made for political reasons, a payback for donations, to appease other swim clubs, and to placate AAU officials.

Neither Trudy nor anyone else had much time to celebrate. The boat to France was scheduled to leave in a week. They'd be gone for over a month, and Trudy had lots of packing to do. As with every other member of the team, the notion of spending weeks in Paris was absolutely intoxicating to her. But before she left, the AOC milked her popularity one more time. Only two days before the team left for Paris, on June 14, the AOC held a special water carnival for both male and female Olympians at the Olympic pool in Long Beach.

The weather was terrible again, with cold winds and rain more reminiscent of March than June, conditions that once again put a smile on Trudy's face and a song on her lips. Trudy raced in a 100-yard event against only one other swimmer, her own teammate, Martha Norelius, winning in a time of 1 minute 7²/₅ seconds. But the highlight of the day was a rare 160-yard mixed relay featuring members of both the men's and women's team—usually, men and women didn't even compete at the same meet, much less in the same event, but the AOC was eager to cash in on its two biggest stars, Trudy and Johnny Weissmuller. Both swimmers were put on the same team, Trudy swimming the third, forty-yard leg while Weissmuller swam anchor, a relay dream team. But despite the presence of both Ederle and Weissmuller on the same squad, they lost to the team anchored by Hawaiian champion swimmer and surfing legend Duke Kahanamoku. For Trudy Ederle the race was perhaps the first sign that the Olympics would not go quite as planned.

The next day the entire U.S. Olympic team of more than three hundred athletes assembled on the USS *America*, a steam-powered cruise ship leased by the AOC at the cost of $160,000 to transport the American team to France for the games. Six hundred and ninety-nine feet from stem to stern, the vessel, which had a capacity of more than 1,600 passengers, had been the largest ship in the world when it was first launched in 1905.

Yet the ship always sailed under something of a black cloud. Built for the German Hamburg line, the ship was initially called the *Amerika* and for nearly a decade traveled back and forth across the North Atlantic without incident—some of Trudy's German relatives immigrated to the United States on the same vessel. But on April 14, 1912, while sailing in the North Atlantic, the ship's captain noted the presence of two large icebergs. He transmitted a message to the U.S. Hydrological Office in Washington noting the position of the icebergs and remained vigilant—he knew a run-in with an iceberg could be catastrophic.

Tragically the message was never forwarded to the bridge of the *Titanic*, which struck the icebergs a short time later and sank. Then, a few months later while sailing through the English Channel, the *Amerika* inadvertently struck an English submarine, sinking the vessel and killing fifteen of sixteen crew members. During the war the United States confiscated the boat while it was docked in Boston, renamed it the *America*, and used it as a troop transport. It sank in an accident while at dock, was then repaired and updated, and was put back into service after the war as a cruise ship for the United States Lines, only to burn in 1926 and end its useful life back in military service as a floating barracks and troop transport.

In 1924, despite the fact that it was still one of the best-known passenger ships in the world, the *America* would not prove lucky for Trudy Ederle. Even on their own boat, Trudy and her fellow Olympians were treated something like second-class citizens, for in addition to the more than three hundred athletes on board, they were joined by several hundred officials, trainers, chaperones, journalists, photographers, coaches, and various other VIPs, including film

Trudy, age thirteen, in the Highlands.
(*Boston Public Library*)

Louis de Breda Handley, swimming coach of the Women's Swimming Association.

The United States Women's Olympic Swim Team, 1924. Trudy Ederle is in the center.

Trudy in 1925, just before making her first attempt to swim the English Channel. (*Boston Public Library*)

Trudy Ederle, training to swim the Channel. (*Library of Congress*)

Trudy Ederle signing her contract with the *Tribune-News* syndicate, flanked by Dudley Field Malone (left) and her father (standing, right).

Trudy (left), her father, and her sister Meg (right), aboard the *Berengaria* just before leaving for France, 1926.
(*Boston Public Library*)

Trudy meeting the press before leaving for Europe for her successful attempt. (*Library of Congress*)

Aileen Riggin (left) and Helen Wainwright (right) see Trudy off aboard the *Berengaria* as she returns to Europe to make her second attempt to swim the Channel. (*Library of Congress*)

Thomas William "Bill" Burgess, the second man to swim the Channel, 1909.

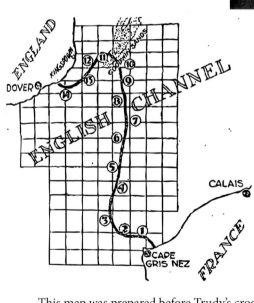

This map was prepared before Trudy's crossing and shows what Bill Burgess hoped would be her hourly progress on her route across the English Channel. Incredibly, and despite poor weather, Trudy Ederle managed to stay close to this course until the final hours, when tidal currents forced her to the northeast before she finally struck out for the beach at Kingsdown.

Trudy's famous goggles, now a part of the collection of the Smithsonian Institution.

Trainer Bill Burgess coats Trudy with grease before her successful crossing of the Channel. (*New-York Historical Society*)

Trudy, moments after being reunited with her mother aboard the tug *Macom* after returning to New York, August 27, 1926. (*Boston Public Library*)

Crowds surround Trudy during the ticker-tape parade following her return to the United States after conquering the English Channel.

Trudy is lost in the crowd and ticker tape as New York celebrates her achievement. (*Library of Congress*)

Trudy's house on Amsterdam Avenue, decorated to welcome her home a few days after her return from her triumphant swim. Police still guard the door to the street.

stars Mary Pickford and Douglas Fairbanks, and General Douglas MacArthur, whose courageous performance in World War I made him the most decorated American soldier of the war. The VIPs received the spacious staterooms and prime accommodations on the ship, while the athletes were given the equivalent of second- and third-class quarters.

For the first time ever, the American press and public were taking the Olympics seriously, viewing the games as a measure of American athletic prowess and a source of national pride. That hadn't been the case in 1920—the Antwerp Olympic Games had taken place while both the United States and Europe were still reeling and recovering from the war and the pandemic of the Spanish influenza. But by 1924 the whole world appeared to be looking forward—the now-familiar Olympic motto, *Citius, Altius, Fortius* (Faster, Higher, Stronger), was being used for the first time and was emblematic of the unabashed optimism and confidence each nation was trying to project.

On June 16 New York pulled out all the stops and gave the Olympians a memorable send-off. Trudy was seen off by dozens of friends and family members. Tugs and fireboats escorted the *America* out of New York Harbor beneath a fusillade of bellowing horns and cascades of water. Both sides of the ship were emblazoned with the words "American Olympic Team," in oversize script as if the size of the letters alone would be enough to intimidate athletes from the rest of the world. Absolutely everyone expected the *America* and her cargo to return bearing perhaps a hundred medals or more, many of them gold. American observers handicapping the games pronounced American athletes as the favorites in nearly every event.

No athlete was expected to be more dominant than Trudy Ederle. After two years of near total supremacy, the Olympics presented her with the perfect opportunity to provide an exclamation point to her remarkable career. Her participation in the 1924 Olympics would likely mark the end of that career as well, for it was unlikely that she would retain her amateur status much longer. Although a few Olympians, for example, Riggin and Wainwright, had been on the 1920 team, they had been schoolgirls at the time. Competitive swimming was a young woman's sport—virtually the entire team was under the age of twenty. It wasn't realistic to think that Trudy would still be competing in another four years. Thelda Bleibtrey accepted a coaching job after the 1920 games, which made her a "professional" under the standards then in place, and Trudy was likely to do the same. For Trudy, the games would in all probability be both the peak and the end of her career. No other athlete in the world entered the Olympics with higher expectations.

Trudy felt the pressure. She was at her peak and knew that in order to win she needed to maintain both her concentration and her fitness level. But from the instant the ship left New York Harbor, there was trouble. For the next nine days Trudy and the other athletes struggled to maintain their fitness and mental focus.

Olympic officials tried their best to enforce discipline and keep the athletes on a schedule, occupying their time with training and trying to keep them busy, but they had little experience running a floating gymnasium and athletic facility. While virtually the entire deck was used for training exercises, some participants found it easier to adapt than others.

The runners had it best. The deck of the ship was expansive enough to accommodate both sprinters and long-distance runners, and they could continue their training under conditions that were almost as good as those on dry land. Both the boxing and wrestling teams were able to train under conditions not dissimilar to those in a gymnasium—the boxers were provided with heavy bags, speed bags, and a ring for sparring, while the wrestlers were provided with mats for training. The fencing team had little difficulty finding room to continue their exercises, and even the pole vaulters and high jumpers were able to stay in shape, using the deck and leaping onto cushions.

Competitors in other field sports, however, had a more difficult time. Discus and shot put competitors aimed their training tosses at canvas sheets above stacks of mattresses but had to chase down errant throws before they rolled off the deck and into the sea. For safety reasons, however, javelin throwers weren't allowed to throw the spear on deck. Nevertheless, they managed to find a way. Bill Neufeld, who finished in fifth place in the javelin throw at the games, later recalled that team members attached "a 300-foot string [to the javelin] and we would throw until we reached the end of the string," tossing the javelin off the deck into the water at the back of the ship, the opposite direction that the ship was traveling. Since the ship was steaming toward Europe at fifteen knots, the athletes joked that each throw was a world record. After retrieving the javelins the athletes checked the tip, looking for blood, as their imaginations ran wild and they imagined themselves to be harpooners hunting whales and sharks.

But Trudy and the swimming and diving team were not so fortunate. Despite being surrounded by water, the *America*, unlike some more modern passenger ships of the era, was not equipped with a pool, and it was both far too dangerous and too costly to stop the ship in the middle of the ocean to allow swimmers and divers to swim in the ocean. Instead of a pool, the divers were provided with a low springboard and an enormous pile of cushions. During training each diver wore a safety belt and was supported by ropes held by teammates to prevent them from springing headlong onto the deck. The divers would leap from the board and hope their companions managed to hang on and help break their fall. If nothing else their arms and shoulders got a workout trying to keep each other from breaking their necks.

Back on land, training under Mr. Handley, Trudy was, by now, accustomed to the routine. Although she still didn't particularly care to swim indoors, she had grown to accept it. Handley still had Trudy and all his swimmers continue doing drills out of the water, but there was increased focus on their performance in the water, as Handley would have the girls alternate longer, slower swims, in which they focused almost entirely on their form, with timed trials. As they swam, Handley would walk alongside the pool calling out their times and encouraging them to either slow down or speed up, trying to teach each swimmer to monitor herself and reach the appropriate pace, for once they were in a race, they wouldn't be able to depend on him to set their pace.

All that was impossible on the boat. Trudy and the other swimmers could get wet, but that was about all. The "pool" was made of a sheet of canvas that sat in a wood timber frame, measuring about ten feet square and about four feet deep, filled with salt water.

Each time Trudy went to work out, she had to undergo the same awkward process. Each day the pool was filled with seawater and each day each girl trained under the watchful eye of Lou Handley according to a schedule that gave each swimmer on the team, male and female, the same amount of time in the water regardless of his or her chance at winning a medal. With twenty-four members of the women's team and more than thirty male swimmers all needing to stay in condition, each competitor was able to work out in the water for less than a half hour a day, hardly adequate for conditioning purposes. It mattered not that Trudy, who was competing in three events, probably should have received extra time in the water—Handley was scrupulously fair and treated every girl the same.

Each day, Trudy and another swimmer—usually Helen Wainwright—would don their suits and report to the pool at the appointed time. As one pair of swimmers left the water, another pair would get in. In a scene reminiscent of the day Trudy first learned to swim at the Highlands, after climbing into the pool each swimmer would don an elastic belt that was attached to the side of the pool by ropes that held her in place, creating a kind of primitive "endless pool." As the girls swam in place Handley would try to approximate race conditions, describing the scene, timing each stroke and marking off distances—"You have fifty meters to go. Let's pep up your stroke."

It was barely adequate and, in fact, might even have even been detrimental. The swimmers were immersed in salt water, which gave them greater buoyancy than the fresh water they would swim in at the games and most, like Trudy, had spent the past few months swimming almost exclusively in fresh water. The belt was not only uncomfortable but caused chafing and forced the girls to alter their stroke. Moreover, Trudy was accustomed to swimming for hours each day. Now, by the time she had warmed up and become accustomed to the belt, practice was over. For the first time in her life, swimming was a chore.

It had been years, since before her family moved to the Highlands, that Trudy had spent such little time in the water. At a time when she should have been peaking, she was, literally, just treading water. As each day slipped by her hard fought confidence in her own ability—and her level of physical fitness—began to slip. Although she was friendly with the other members of the team, she missed Meg. Her sister kept Trudy from turning inside herself and kept her spirits high. Now, without Meg's pep talks, Trudy's self-assurance began to waver.

Trudy and the other swimmers tried to stay in shape by walking the deck, but there was a limit to just how much walking a young athlete could do before going batty, and it was hard to stay focused during the long journey. As the trip went on, many Olympians found they were more and more easily distracted. There were, after all, more than three hundred male athletes and, including the two fencers, only twenty-six females, primarily teenagers, plus a handful of female chaperones, like Charlotte Epstein. The result was a lot of unchecked testosterone. The female athletes found themselves the object of a great deal of attention—some of which they encouraged, and some they did not. A few of the women ran the chaperones ragged as they snuck off to distant corners of the ship, basking in the attention, while others tended to hole up in their cabins to keep unwanted interest to a minimum.

Trudy preferred to stay in the background, something all her teammates noted. According to one, Doris O'Mara Murphy, on the trip Ederle "was a very quiet person She didn't hear very well and didn't like to be interviewed . . . She always sat aside." Her effusive conversation with Marguerite Mooers Marshall after the Day Cup was a thing of the past. Her hearing had continued to deteriorate and was now obvious to everyone. Although she was familiar with her teammates from the WSA, and they with her, Olympians from elsewhere in the country found her pleasant but somewhat reticent and instantly noticed she was hard of hearing. Trudy often spoke much more loudly than others and tended to ignore conversations unless she could see the speaker talking, reading lips to compensate for what she could not hear.

To keep everyone from going stir-crazy, all the athletes were provided with ample amounts of food, and, like modern cruise ship vacationers, few could resist three full meals a day. The food helped to break up the monotony, but Trudy fretted over her weight as each day her clothes seemed to fit just a little tighter. Chaperones and coaches also organized activities more common to a summer outing, just to keep everyone occupied, like potato races and other games. Douglas MacArthur gave several formal addresses and inspirational talks and led impromptu discussion groups on politics and world affairs. At night the athletes participated in sing-alongs and even held one formal dance, which for many of the women gave them the most exercise of the entire journey, for there was no lack of willing dance partners. There was even a talent show one night at which Johnny Weissmuller gave an inadvertent peek at his future. At the end of the show, which primarily featured singers of varying abilities, Weissmuller, clearly bored with being on ship, jumped up on a table, grabbed a chandelier, and swung back and forth, scratching his side as if he were a monkey and letting out a yell, as one teammate recalled, "like he later did in *Tarzan*."

As the journey went on the athletes managed to break away and have their own kind of fun. Even Trudy got involved, and one incident in particular may have played a part in her performance in the Olympics.

Despite his diminutive size, American long-distance runner Joie Ray was one of the best runners of his era. Standing only five feet four inches and weighing less than 120 pounds, Ray, a taxi driver, was a member of the U.S. Olympic team in 1920, 1924, and 1928 and at times was the world record holder in both the mile and two-mile runs. On the journey to France, even though Ray was so heavily muscled he earned the nickname "Chesty," his teammates razzed him unmercifully over his size. When someone mentioned that they thought Trudy Ederle, who was both taller and heavier than Ray, could outwrestle him, the contest was on.

Although it ran counter to her personality, Trudy, who despite her shyness still enjoyed making friends, was goaded into accepting the challenge. Besides, she was bored stiff. Word of the impending matchup spread among the Olympians on board the ship like a juicy piece of gossip. A time was arranged for the match and without alerting chaperones, trainers, coaches, or any other officials, Ederle and Ray, dressed in their training attire, squared off in the ring.

It was anything but a fair matchup. Ray may have been small but he was also a competitive boxer, an activity that had already led to several suspensions by the AAU for participating in "unsanctioned" events. But the bored Olympians found the matchup more than titillating. Trudy and Ray reportedly wrestled several times before Olympic officials found out what was going on.

It was all in good fun, but when the chaperones and AOC officials found out about the match, they were mortified. If word escaped that males and females were wrestling *each other* on board the ship, the virtuous image of the Olympic team would be shattered. Not only were Trudy and Ray read the riot act, but everyone involved was told that not only would there be no more wrestling, but they were not even to speak of it. While the match was never reported in the press and there was no specific indication that either Ederle or Ray was injured in the tussle, later circumstances suggest that Trudy Ederle may well have been injured in the fracas.

On the final evening of the journey Douglas MacArthur addressed the entire team and gave a rousing speech. "I want you to tell you something before you leave," he said. "It's true you're all Olympians, but first and foremost you are Americans." Then, perhaps recalling the ill-advised wrestling match, he added, "Everything you say and do will reflect on your country."

The ninth and final day of the long journey brought the USS *America* into the English Channel on its way to the port at Cherbourg, France, the first time Trudy Ederle had traveled through Channel waters since her trip to Germany with her parents nearly a decade before. This time, however, she may well have looked at the Channel waters with a critical eye, for the recent performances of Sullivan, Toth, and Tirabocchi, not to mention the efforts of Mille Gade Corson, now identified the Channel as the swimmer's ultimate challenge.

The team disembarked in France on the morning of June 25 in Trudy's favorite weather, rain. The American male Olympians bounded off the ship and looked around, befuddled at their reception. General MacArthur had led them to believe they'd be greeted by scores of beautiful Frenchwomen who would deliver kisses on the cheek, a fantasy that some of the athletes had spent some time looking forward to. Instead, they were met by a group of middle-aged men in beards carrying umbrellas—customs and other French governmental officials.

Few Olympians had ever been to Europe before, and even those who had, like Trudy, were still wide-eyed as they traveled through France by train to Gare Saint Lazare, a train station in Paris made famous by both the Claude Monet painting of the same name and Henri Cartier-Bresson's famous photograph "Behind the Gare Saint Lazare." There they were greeted by quite a large crowd that included a number of Americans who now lived in Paris, but once again, no Frenchwomen raced to embrace the American men. From there the squad then boarded buses and traveled to the team headquarters at Chateau de Rocquencourt, an eighteenth-century mansion outside Paris owned by Joachim, the fifth prince of Murat.

Trudy was wide-eyed when the team arrived at the chateau. Poised on a hill overlooking the Seine, nine miles from the site of the games in Colombes, in the northwestern Parisian suburbs, the chateau was outwardly beautiful, and that was undoubtedly the reason it had been selected to house the American squad, because in almost every other way it was wholly inappropriate. But the men on the team didn't even get to stay in a permanent building. They were housed in Spartan, temporary huts made of pressboard erected on the grounds of the chateau. Each "room" of the cottages wasn't even entirely separate from others, as sleeping quarters were divided by half walls similar to those of a modern-day office cubicle. They were not only cold and damp, but the lack of privacy made it almost impossible for some of the men to sleep—one man snoring kept another dozen awake. The Olympics officials, on the other hand, stayed in the opulent accommodations of the chateau itself.

Trudy and the other female athletes didn't have it much better. The women's swimming team was segregated from male athletes in two carriage houses a quarter mile away from the main house and the temporary cottages. The accommodations themselves were generally adequate, although one of the buildings lacked a bathroom. Like many of the other girls Trudy found that the high feather beds and sumptuous quilts and comforters took some getting used to, and she had a terrible time sleeping. The carriage houses bordered the main road, and the sound of automobile traffic was almost nonstop, a cacophony of beeping horns, revving engines, and squealing brakes.

Even though some events, like rugby, had been taking place for weeks, it was still ten days before the official opening ceremony and more than three weeks before the start of the swimming competition. Although at first the athletes were accepting of their surroundings, each day brought more complaints, particularly from the two swim teams and their coaches.

Lou Handley was particularly vociferous in his criticisms, if still unfailingly polite while filing them. The AOC officials had been told the swimming events would be held in a new pool in Colombes, but upon their arrival they learned that the pool was not yet finished and the swimming competition would have to be held at Les Tourelles, on the far eastern side of Paris. Handley understood that the AOC wasn't to blame for that, yet while the AOC rented spacious limousines for their own use, the swimmers were only provided with a bus. Road conditions were so poor that instead of traveling a direct route to Colombes, the buses had to detour through central Paris, making what should have been a nine-mile journey a trip of fifteen miles bouncing over cobblestones that took more than an hour. Then it was at least another hour by bus to the pool for training. Then, once they arrived, the entire team of nearly sixty athletes, male and female, had precisely one hour to practice, from 11:00 A.M. to noon. For Trudy, it was hardly an improvement on the conditions aboard the *America*. She was a swimmer, but so far she had spent precious little time in the water. On the other hand she was becoming a world-class bus passenger.

Apart from a locker room, there were no other Olympic facilities at the pool. After their brief period of training, in order to eat lunch Trudy and her teammates had to board the bus again and return to Paris, and then bus back to Les Tourelles—the AOC was petrified of leaving them alone in Paris, where they might meet a Frenchman— before returning by another bus to Rocquencourt at night. On any given day the girls spent up to six hours being driven back and forth, bouncing up and down on rough roads—hardly an idyllic situation, leaving Trudy to feel as if she were a piece of cargo being schlepped back and forth with no one to accept delivery.

She and her teammates became so desperate to train that on a few occasions they woke before sunrise then traveled to the pool at dawn to squeeze in an extra half hour or so of practice before teams from other countries arrived later in the morning. But this created as many problems as it solved. The dining staff at Rocquencourt followed their contract to the letter and refused to provide the swimmers with an early breakfast. Whenever they returned from training and missed a meal, the staff refused to feed them. To an athlete like Trudy, training without proper nutrition, particularly after the long journey to France, was yet another impediment. And even when the women did make it for dinner, the food, as Handley delicately termed it, was "ill chosen . . . totally unfit for training athletes." True enough, because when the athletes learned they were being served horsemeat, some took to spiriting away bread and celery and skipping some meals all together.

The situation was a mess, something that even the AOC eventually recognized. After only a few days even the officials themselves grew tired of the journey and many moved out of Rocquencourt and into a hotel in Colombes. They also moved many athletes, such as the men's swimming team, to other quarters, but the women's swimming team remained in a kind of exile in Rocquencourt, isolated from the rest of the Olympic Games, all but left to fend for themselves, with absolutely nothing to do after they returned to their quarters each evening. The only adjustment made in their accommodations came a few days later when the AOC ditched the ponderous buses and hired cars to transport the women. While that cut the time they spent on the Parisian roads almost in half, the AOC hired only five cars, one of which it regularly commandeered for its own use. On most days that left seven passengers piling into each of the remaining cars, hardly leaving room for the driver, as the girls sat on one another's laps and squeezed into seats made for half that number. The trip was quicker but even more uncomfortable than before.

The end result left Trudy—and the women's team—in a shambles. After gaining weight on the trip over, now Trudy was hungry all the time, but instead of getting much-needed protein, she was filling up on bread and other items. All the back and forth by bus and car to the pool left her feeling exhausted, and the more tired she felt, the less confidence she had in her own ability. She could feel herself getting out of shape, and after being crammed in the seat of a car for several hours a day, her muscles were stiff and sore. When she got out of the car before training, there was virtually no time to warm up and work out the kinks.

Trudy, partially because of her size and partially because she had to try to stay in shape for three events, was more adversely affected than any other swimmer. The lack of practice, a possible injury, cramped muscles, and difficulty adapting back to fresh water all combined to prove disastrous. Instead of the Olympic motto Faster, Higher, Stronger, Trudy's motto might as well have been "Slower, Weaker, Less Confident."

Her only respite was the Olympic Games themselves. As im-

mortalized in the 1981 film *Chariots of Fire*, the memorable opening ceremony, held on July 3 under a crystalline blue sky after two
days of heavy rain, left an impression on everyone. In a sense, the
1924 Olympics were the first modern Olympic Games, and today's
opening ceremonies are in many ways based on the 1924 model. The
United States team was the seventeenth nation in the parade of athletes that was the centerpiece of the ceremony, and the American
team took over Colombes Stadium as if it were a conquering army—
the American contingent of more than three hundred athletes was
more than that of the first sixteen nations put together. The athletes'
only complaint was with their dress—both men and women were
garbed in navy blue jackets and wore straw hats, which Trudy and
the other members of the women's team found entirely lacking in
style.

Fortunately the pool at Les Tourelles was a gem. The six-lane,
fifty-meter Olympic pool surrounded by stands capable of seating
more than five thousand spectators was more than adequate for
competition. Set on a hillside overlooking Paris, the view was spectacular. For most of the girls it was the finest pool they had ever had
the pleasure to use. Unfortunately they saw the pool far more often
than they were actually allowed to swim in it.

For nearly two weeks Trudy and many of her teammates slowly
fell further out of shape. Lou Handley knew what was happening but
was powerless to do much about it. The swimmers from Hawaii had
brought along a trainer who specialized in massage, and a few days
before the competition began he went to work on Trudy's legs, trying
to knead them into shape. But he told her the knots in her thighs
and calves felt "like walnuts" beneath his hands—it was too late to do
much, and his description made her feel even worse. How could she
swim with walnuts for muscles?

As expected, at the team trials Trudy nevertheless earned a spot
in both the 100-meter freestyle and the 400-meter relay team—
even in diminished condition she was still one of the best swimmers in the world, and the opportunity to swim before so many
people initially gave her and the other swimmers a much-needed
shot of adrenaline.

Trudy's Olympic Games finally began on July 13. Racing in one of
three 400-meter heats, she won her race easily in a time of 6 minutes

$12^1/_5$ seconds, but that was nearly twenty seconds slower than her best time over the same distance. The following day she won her semifinal heat without being pressed, but she was even slower, finishing in 6 minutes $23^4/_5$ seconds, still nearly thirty seconds off her best. Nevertheless her two times were still the best times in the trials, and she became one of three Americans, along with Helen Wainwright and Martha Norelius, to qualify for the finals.

But the travel back and forth—and perhaps that lingering injury stemming from her wrestling match with Joie Ray—was beginning to take its toll. By all rights, the 400-meter freestyle was her race—over the past two years she'd never been seriously challenged over the distance, and her performance in the two preliminary heats seemed to indicate that her physical ailments were behind her. News reports confidently predicted an American sweep asking only, "Which American girl will win?" then answering that question by predicting a victory by Trudy with Wainwright likely to finish second ahead of Martha Norelius.

Trudy's strategy in the race was the same as it had always been—if one could criticize her method of competition, it was that it never varied. In most races of any distance she simply ground her opponents down, setting a pace no other swimmer could maintain and then relentlessly pushing on as they dropped back. Thus far no one had ever really been able to keep up. But on this day the plan went awry.

Trudy led early but Martha Norelius, in a surprise, hung with her through the midpoint of the race and then began to pull ahead as Trudy, for the first time in her life, seemed to lack stamina and instead of growing stronger, began to fade. In the final lap, as she fought to keep Norelius within reach, Helen Wainwright, who had trailed both swimmers for the entire race, finished with a flourish. Martha Norelius beat Trudy by almost the length of her body, and Wainwright edged out Ederle for second place by nearly a meter, in a winning time of 6 minutes $2^1/_5$ seconds, faster than Trudy's time in the preliminary, but still far off her best.

Trudy finished third, good enough for the bronze medal, but she was crushed. As soon as she was alone she broke down in tears. The ceremony at the stadium at Colombes, where the girls received their medals and watched the American flag being raised as a band played

"The Star-Spangled Banner," helped soften the blow, but the aura of invincibility that she had built over the previous two years was gone, as well as her self-confidence.

Trudy received a measure of revenge the next day, giving the American team a five-yard lead in her opening leg of the 400-meter relay, as the American women swept to victory in 4 minutes 58⁴/₅ seconds, earning Trudy a gold medal, but it was an empty victory, for the American team was so far advanced in comparison to swimmers from the rest of the world that any other swimmer on the American squad could have swum in Trudy's place, and the United States still would have won the gold medal. She was little more than a place-holder, and she knew it. The medal may have been gold on the outside, but to Trudy it seemed like plated tin.

She had one last chance, in the 100-meter freestyle race. Perhaps, she hoped, swimming a shorter distance her tight muscles might not prove to be as much of an impediment as they had been over four hundred meters.

Once again, Trudy easily made it through the preliminary heats and into the finals, as all three American swimmers, Trudy and teammates Mariechen Wehselau of Hawaii and Ethel Lackie, broke the world record in the preliminaries as each girl pushed the other to her best performance. Trudy drew the favored lane three for the finals, and a second gold medal appeared in her grasp—this time an individual award. If she could come away with a second gold medal she could still look at her Olympic experience as a success.

The stands at Les Tourelles were full for the finale, and with all Paris for a backdrop the scene was set for Trudy to end the Olympics on a high note, basking on the victory stand before an adoring crowd of thousands, looking out over Paris, the best female swimmer in the world. At the start she stood poised on the edge of the pool, hands overhead, hoping for a good start.

But there was something wrong with the scene. The race official who held the starting gun stood directly behind Trudy. Although she could easily hear the report of a gun, she could not do so quite as well as if the starter had been offset slightly to either side, and in any race, particularly one over such a short distance that matched three swimmers of nearly the same ability, each millisecond matters.

At the sound of the gun the six swimmers leapt into the water. Five made the initial splash simultaneously. One—Trudy—was a heartbeat late. She was the last swimmer into the water and spent the entire race trying to catch up. Usually, it was the other way around.

She tried to push herself, to send the messages to her muscles that would make her go faster, despite the knots and soreness, but her muscles resisted, and with each stroke she began to tighten up and even panic. For years she had always been able to draw upon reserves of strength and stamina that she seemed to have in abundance, but now, suddenly, all that was gone. Water that had always felt fast and light to her limbs now seemed slow and thick. She was unable to swim automatically, on muscle memory, but had to think, trying to push herself to perform.

Stroke by stroke she fought on, passing the other swimmers to move into third place behind Ethel Lackie and Mariechen Wehselau, then, as she made her turn for the final leg, she could sense that Wehselau was tiring and, inch by inch, Trudy finally began to gain some ground, closing in a rush.

Yet just as she drew abreast of the swimmer, with the end of the pool only a few short yards away, Ethel Lackie surged past both swimmers, and the hand of all three Americans touched the end of the pool in rapid succession. Trudy lifted her head and looked imploringly to the official standing above her, but she could see the verdict in his eyes and in the smiles of the other swimmers. She had finished third. That was worth another bronze medal, but Trudy did not feel as if she had won anything. In a matter of only a few seconds Trudy had seen a possible gold medal slip from her neck and disappear beneath the water. For any other athlete, winning three medals would have been a tremendous accomplishment, but for Trudy it was devastating. For the first time since she had won the Day Cup, Trudy had entered the water and, instead of finding peace, had encountered only disappointment.

She later termed the Olympics "the greatest disappointment of my life," an experience she found so profoundly painful that for the rest of her life she found watching or reading about the Olympics to be a gut-wrenching experience. She identified with the favorites, cheered for them, and prayed for them to meet expectations. "How do they say it?" she later described the experience, "The agony of defeat?

When a champion is defeated in the Olympics? I went through that agony every year since. I cry when I watch it. I should have had three golds. I definitely should have."

Her Olympics were over and so too, perhaps, was her swimming career. The one goal she had kept in her sights had eluded her. Now, as adulthood approached, what was there left for her to do?

17

Comeback

THE ONLY WRESTLING Trudy did on the return trip aboard the *America* was with the voice in her own head that kept asking what had gone wrong.

After her defeat Trudy Ederle initially had precious little time to dwell on her failure. Olympic officials were so worried about leaving young women unoccupied in Paris that after the end of the competition Charlotte Epstein and Louis Handley took the entire team to England, crossing the Channel by boat to swim an exhibition, and then crossing back again to make another appearance in Brussels before returning to Paris for the closing ceremonies and then boarding the *America* for home.

For most of her teammates, the return trip was a nonstop party. Without the pressure of competition they acted like tourists on a cruise, and no one had to worry about staying in shape. But Trudy kept to herself, replaying her races over and over in her head, wondering what had gone wrong and what she possibly could have done about it, but she had no answer. Fortunately, although the Olympics had ended with disappointment for her, America hardly noticed. Despite some pre-Olympic fears by some observers that young American athletes were more concerned with "hot" music, bobbed hairdos, and rising hemlines rather than with the raucous cheers that accompanied falling records, the United States had dominated Olympic competition in very nearly every event, leading all countries with a total of 93 medals, one-quarter of the 361 medals awarded at the games, including 45 golds. In team scoring, the United States was just as dominant, winning the overall championship in eight of the twenty sports—track and field, tennis, rowing, wrestling, shooting, boxing, rugby, and, of course, swimming.

In fact, in the water the United States had been most dominant of all, winning fully 80 percent of all medals, and the women's team failed to win gold in only one event—the 200-meter breaststroke. As the *Literary Digest* noted, quoting the *Pittsburgh Sun*, the victory "indicated that American youth, despite much head shaking and lamentation, is able to hold its own with the youth and stamina of the rest of the world . . . It indicates that an age that is commonly said to be going soft is not entirely flabby." As a result, Trudy faced little direct criticism for her personal failure. America had won, so her personal failure was virtually overlooked, but in some ways that was even worse. She had left for Paris as one of the teams' best-known stars but returned as just another competitor.

But in his official report to the AOC, Louis Handley made it clear that as far as he was concerned Trudy's performance was not her fault, but that of the AOC, the result of its poor planning in regard to transportation and accommodations for the women's team. He went out of the way to single out her experience and excuse her performance, the only individual swimmer he so cited. "I cannot say to what extent the track and field men suffered," he wrote, "but I know the swimmers were affected materially. Miss Gertrude Ederle, our reliance for women's freestyle events, went off form completely."

The Olympics had also been something of a checkered experience for both Louis Handley and the WSA. Although the WSA girls had performed relatively well, they hadn't been dominant, a fact that was simultaneously both disappointing and gratifying. While Handley and Epstein had certainly hoped that the WSA girls would win more medals, the fact other American swimmers did so well underscored the impact of the group on women's athletics. All over the country other swimming clubs had used the WSA as a model, and Handley's teaching methods were now standard. Everyone else was rapidly catching up with the WSA. The American crawl had not only utterly transformed the sport, but in doing so it was transforming the way society looked at women. They were beginning to be allowed to be athletes.

Still, for Trudy Ederle life after the Olympics was like diving into a pool and finding out it was filled with only a foot or two of water. For the past two years she had trained and trained hard, but now, with the Olympics over, everyone seemed to be taking a break. Even the WSA had cut back on holding meets and other events. Trudy didn't quite know what to do next. Ever since she had joined the WSA, swimming had been her life, but now it appeared as if sometime soon her life might have to go on without competitive swimming being a part of it. Now that it was gone she suddenly realized just how much she had enjoyed the limelight.

In mid-August she traveled to Boston and retained her national title over the half mile, but the field was weak as other big WSA stars, like Helen Wainwright and other Olympians, were still taking time off. For the rest of the fall and into the early winter, Ederle raced only intermittently, and every day it became just a little bit easier for her to decide to put off her training for another day. Already out of shape upon her return, throughout the fall, without the warm and familiar waters of the Highlands calling her out every day, her condition only deteriorated.

Her swimming career appeared to be slowly winding down. Her WSA teammate Martha Norelius, whose father swam for Sweden at the 1906 Olympics, seemed poised to become the next Gertrude Ederle. Despite all her success, Trudy was not in danger of becoming yesterday's news—in a sense, she already was.

Purely by accident, Helen Wainwright saved her.

In the wake of the Olympics Wainwright was looking for another challenge. At age nineteen and already the veteran of two Olympics, she wanted to cap off her amateur career before turning professional and becoming a coach. Likewise, with another Olympic Games nearly four long years in the future, the WSA needed to do something in the interim that would continue to bring publicity, attract donors, and reinforce the notion that the WSA was still the foremost women's athletic club in the nation. Now that the 1924 Olympics were over, and without Trudy Ederle breaking another record every time she jumped in the water, press coverage of the WSA was beginning to drop off.

The only significant swimming accomplishment in the world open to women not yet dominated by the WSA was the English Channel. For more than a year Wainwright, whom the press started to refer to as Helen "Swimright," had let WSA officials know that she thought she could change that and become the first woman to swim the Channel. Over time she earned the support of both Louis Handley and Charlotte Epstein. Handley, in particular, thought it a worthy idea. He had long pondered the challenge posed by the Channel and was eager to test his ideas. After all, no swimmer of either sex had attempted to swim the Channel using the American crawl—the Channel would prove to be the ultimate test of the stroke Handley believed was far superior to any other over any distance. Wainwright, and not Trudy Ederle, had been the WSA's most consistent swimmer over the last six months, equally skilled in both sprints and longer distances, and in the wake of the Olympics she was in top shape. Handley had recently called her "the fastest girl swimmer in the world," an indication that Trudy Ederle, who had once held that title, now did not, not even in the eyes of her own coach. It was a measure of just how far Trudy's star had fallen, for Wainwright, despite all her talent, didn't have nearly as much experience as Trudy in open water.

In the fall and winter of 1924 and 1925, Epstein began researching precisely what an excursion to swim the Channel would entail, and in January she formally presented the idea before the WSA's board of governors. Clearly and logically she laid out why she thought it was important for the group to support Wainwright and precisely what such an effort would entail—and cost. Using Wainwright's AAU record time of 26 minutes $44^4/_5$ seconds for the one-mile swim as a benchmark, Epstein and Handley told the board they believed that Wainwright could cover the twenty-one miles between England and France in about fourteen hours. By way of comparison the current record holder, Enrique Tirabocchi, who had crossed the Channel in sixteen hours and thirty-three minutes, couldn't swim a mile in less than thirty-five minutes. Epstein and Handley believed that Wainwright might not only succeed, but set a record in the process, shattering the men's mark. If she succeeded, the goals and aims of the WSA would become a worldwide quest, helping the cause of women's equality in every corner of the globe.

The board found their arguments convincing and authorized Epstein to spend upward of five thousand dollars to make all arrangements for the trial. She planned to accompany Wainwright to England in June, where the swimmer would spend at least a month training and acclimating to conditions. If all went well she would swim the Channel sometime in August.

Although Trudy had heard that the WSA decided to send Wainwright to Europe and she was hurt and disappointed at being overlooked, part of being a member of the WSA was being a good sport, and Trudy did not complain. In fact, she didn't even learn of the final decision to send Wainwright abroad until Meg, who still looked out for her younger sister and continued to push her forward, told her. She believed that Trudy was just as deserving as Wainwright to take a shot at swimming the Channel and told her younger sister just that. Trudy thought her sister was crazy, but Meg was much more animated—and persuasive—asking her, "Why can't you at least try? How do you know if you don't at least try?" Trudy had to agree, telling her sister, "Well, you have a point there, you know." Now that the seed was planted, the rest was up to Trudy.

Trudy knew that in her current condition there was no way the WSA could possibly consider sending her to the Channel. But now—for the first time since her victory at the Day Cup—she was being told she wasn't the best, and that bothered her. If she was the best swimmer, well, the Channel would take care of itself. Almost immediately she responded to the challenge and for the first time in more than six months began to show the form that once had made her almost unbeatable.

All the girls who had passed Trudy now found Trudy catching up to them again. In late January she clipped one-fifth of a second from her American record over two hundred yards in a sixty-foot pool, then finished second by fifteen yards to teammate Ethel McGary in the 500-yard nationals in a seventy-five-foot pool, a sign that although she was getting stronger she still had room to improve. In St. Augustine, Florida, in early February she began to show signs that her career was not over.

She finished second in her defense of her title in the 50-yard sprint, but only after the first final trial ended in a dead heat between Trudy and two other swimmers; in a repeat she lost by less than a foot. Twelve days later she knocked one full second off the 150-yard record, tied the world mark over 220 yards, and then, just a few days later, on February 26, broke it by a full two seconds and then broke the 200-yard record the following day. All of a sudden, and entirely unexpectedly, Trudy Ederle was the best swimmer in the world again.

Meanwhile, it was Helen Wainwright who was slipping—literally. Shortly after defending her national 220-yard title, she lost her footing while getting out of a trolley and tore a muscle in her thigh.

Trudy was training at the City Athletic Club in New York when Meg heard about Wainwright's unfortunate accident. Meg instantly thought of Trudy and rushed to the club. Trudy was still in the pool when her sister, dressed in street clothes, came rushing in and called out to get Trudy's attention, then waved her over to the end of the pool so they could talk.

Hardly able to contain herself, in a rush Meg blurted out that Wainwright had slipped and fallen while getting off a streetcar and had hurt her leg and could barely walk not to mention swim and now, isn't it terrible, just horrible, but she wouldn't be able to train, and if she could train she couldn't stay in shape and if she couldn't stay in shape, well, then, certainly, she couldn't possibly to go to England and try to swim the Channel, could she? So . . .

"Why don't you go, Trudy?"

The question hung over the pool for a moment as Trudy tried to process exactly what her sister was getting at. She shook her head. "Margaret," she said, addressing her sister by her formal name to make sure she understood that she was serious, "Are you *crazy*? I only swim 220 yards," referring to her most recent competitions and conveniently forgetting everything else. "That's the farthest I've ever raced so far. I could *never* swim across a big body of water like that."

Meg had heard that kind of talk before. That was her sister, always underestimating herself. Had she forgotten about all those hours at the Highlands? How about the Day Cup? She'd beaten Helen Wainwright by miles.

In her best "I'm your big sister and you're going to listen to me so pay attention" kind of voice, Meg knelt down along the edge of the pool and looked her little sister right in the eye, putting her face directly in front of Trudy's so there'd be no question whether or not she could hear her—when she wanted to, Trudy could pretend not to hear with the best of them. "Listen, Trudy," said Meg slowly, enunciating every word. "You are the better swimmer right *now*," she said with emphasis. "If Helen Wainwright can swim five miles, you can swim six."

Meg stared down at her sister with a look that said "you know I'm right," and Trudy stared back at her sister and knew she had already lost the argument. Meg was right. Meg was always right, and when Meg was right, well, Trudy knew better than to argue. She shook her head, raised her eyebrows, rolled her eyes, and, letting out a big sigh, said, "Oh, is *that* all I have to worry about?" Meg refused to look away and then Trudy, smiling faintly and still looking a bit uncertain, said, "Whatever you think . . . okay, okay." Then she turned and started to swim again. She had a lot of work to do.

The press had the same idea as Margaret and soon asked Trudy the same question. "I'm going," she told them, "I'm going." In a matter of days the WSA reached the same conclusion. Although it still hoped that Wainwright might recover and make the trip, Charlotte Epstein approached the board of governors at its monthly meeting in April and asked for authorization to take Trudy to England as well. Adding Trudy to the trip made a great deal of sense, and the added cost was relatively insignificant. The two girls not only could train together, but when it came time to attempt the swim, they could pace each other, and their natural competitiveness was bound to kick in and help each push the other, increasing the chance of success for both. To have two WSA swimmers become the first two women to cross the Channel, and to have both do it on the same day, would be a huge story all over the world.

The board readily agreed. Epstein booked passage for the pair, as well as for herself and her assistant, Elsie Viets, and began making arrangements for accommodations overseas. They planned to train in England then swim the Channel from Cape Gris-Nez to Dover.

To that end she needed to hire an experienced trainer who could make the necessary arrangements and oversee the girls' training while overseas. Jabez Wolffe was the best-known Channel swimmer in England, and Epstein had already made contact with him and was in the midst of negotiating a contract. Bill Burgess, the other obvious choice, was based in France, and Epstein felt that it was better to train in England. Besides, most Channel experts, despite the fact that Burgess's swimmers had been more successful, still wondered precisely how much that had to do with Burgess.

After he ushered three swimmers across in 1923, none of his charges were successful in 1924.

Until it was time to leave, both Trudy and Helen Wainwright were placed in the steady hands of Louis Handley. The swimming coach was particularly cautious with Wainwright, getting her back into shape slowly so that by the time it came for her to go to England, her leg would be completely healed.

But just a day or two after the board approved Trudy's Channel excursion, Wainwright slipped again, this time on wet pavement, tearing the same muscle in her leg. Doctors told her it wouldn't heal unless she gave her leg some rest. Swimming a lap in a sixty-foot pool was temporarily out of the question, not to mention trying to swim the Channel.

The young swimmer was crestfallen and withdrew from the trip. "Under the circumstances," she said, "I felt it would hardly be fair for me to allow the club to go to the heavy expense of sending me abroad . . . It goes without saying that I am terribly disappointed. For several years the Channel has been my greatest ambition and I hate to lose the opportunity to try it this season." While she hoped to try again at some future time, at age nineteen her competitive swimming career was just about over.

Now Trudy would have to swim alone. But that did not mean she would have the Channel to herself. Already, as spring began turning into summer, other female swimmers planned to beat Trudy across.

Mille Gade Corson, who had tested the Channel in 1923 and promised to return, was, for the time being, left on dry land, caring for her two young children. But while the eyes of the world had been focused on the Olympics in the summer of 1924, another woman, Lillian Harrison of Argentina, had been testing the Channel waters.

Harrison appeared to have all the necessary skills to complete a swim across the Channel. Born to an English father and Argentinean mother, she first garnered attention in 1923, at age twenty, when she swam across the mouth of the River Plate, a distance of thirty miles across the estuary formed by the confluence of the Uruguay and Parana rivers forming the border between Uruguay and Argentina downstream from Buenos Aires. Not only was she the first woman to swim the river at this point, she was the first person of either sex to do so. Even Enrique Tirabocchi, who had bested the Channel, failed when he tried to cross the Plate. Moreover Harrison had remained in the water for twenty-four hours and nineteen minutes, a remarkable demonstration of stamina even if the waters were many degrees warmer than those of the Channel and the currents and weather conditions far less treacherous.

Training under Bill Burgess, Harrison based her Channel crossing in France and intended to swim to England. Unfortunately, her first attempt to swim the Channel in 1924 ended in ignominy. As she gingerly tried to enter the waters along a rock-strewn beach at Cape Gris-Nez in France, she lost her balance, tumbled into the surf, and was tossed by the waves back onto the shore. She cut her leg badly on a rock and was forced to crawl back out of the water, setting a record for shortest Channel swim attempt of all time. But in a later try she had managed to stay in the water for nearly ten hours before turning back.

Despite these failures, in May 1925 Harrison again traveled to France, far in advance of Trudy, to train for another attempt. She was well aware that becoming the first woman to swim the Channel guaranteed a certain measure of fame and fortune.

Yet when Harrison arrived in France, she discovered a Frenchwoman, Jeanne Sion, already in the water. A matronly looking woman of forty-seven, Sion was nevertheless an accomplished swimmer and already familiar with Channel waters. Like Harrison, she, too, had engaged Bill Burgess as her trainer.

Trudy began training for her Channel swim in earnest in April, soon after the WSA gave approval. Rather than put in hours swimming laps in a pool, to acclimate herself to colder Channel waters as soon as it was warm enough she did the bulk of her training in open water—swimming, rowing, or making use of what was known as a "bubble boat," a contraption made of canvas and a metal frame that supported a swimmer in the water by means of four large air-filled metal "bubbles" about twice the size of a basketball. The bubble boat allowed Trudy both to work on her form without unduly fighting against the waves and surf, as well as train without the need of an accompanying boat—if she got cramps or was otherwise physically indisposed, being on the bubble boat allowed her to stay afloat.

Louis Handley was in charge of her training schedule, but Trudy needed little encouragement to train in the open water. He cautioned her to make sure she ate well and to keep her weight up. Handley knew that, particularly in open water, women benefited from extra buoyancy due to their higher fat content and that a layer of body fat was also of benefit in shielding the swimmer from the effects of cold water. Although tastes were changing and the lean figure of the flapper was now the goal of every young woman, no flapper was ever going to swim the Channel, and he wanted to make sure Trudy realized that.

But Handley's greatest contribution to Trudy's effort was the American crawl. Unlike most of the other women and men who aspired to swim the Channel, Trudy was fully committed to the American crawl—the others, at best, used the crawl only rarely and not nearly as efficiently as Trudy. Prevailing wisdom, perpetuated by the men who had succeeded in swimming the Channel, still held that the breaststroke and sidestroke were the best strokes to use in the crossing.

For the next two months Trudy hardly competed for the WSA, choosing instead to focus her efforts on training for the Channel. Already, however, some observers, looking at her background and her training methods, were predicting not only that she would succeed, but that she could set a record. As one anonymous reporter noted, "She is even faster than Miss Wainwright . . . and she possesses all other essential qualifications, including exceptional strength and stamina, imperviousness to cold water, determination and gameness. In addition she is an experienced outdoor swimmer, quite at home in rough seas." Another accurately noted that she was "the first speed champion of the modern school to undertake the quest . . . She is a faster swimmer than any man who ever set out to conquer the Channel," but admitted that task remained difficult, for "many question that any woman is possessed of the necessary qualifications to accomplish the great feat," whatever those qualifications—apart from her sex—were.

Just a few days before she was scheduled to leave, on June 14, she made one final appearance for the WSA at the Olympic Baths in Long Beach. Despite the fact that she had been focusing on the Channel, she nevertheless set a world record in the 150-yard invitational race in the sixty-foot pool. But she was just warming up. As if taking note of those who questioned whether women were even capable of swimming the Channel, less than twenty-four hours after setting the world record over 150 yards, Trudy took on another challenge.

If there was an American equivalent of the Channel, it was the swim from the Battery, Manhattan's southernmost point, to Sandy Hook, in New Jersey, the barrier beach just north of the Highlands, a distance of sixteen miles. Like the Channel, swimmers had to negotiate the tides and currents of New York Harbor, adding five or six miles to the swim. In 1914 the *New York Herald-Tribune* had sponsored the first such swim, and it had been won by George Meehan of Boston, a proponent of the sidestroke, in seven hours and eighteen minutes. An Australian woman, Nell Kenney, claimed to have completed the swim later that summer in nearly ten hours, but no one had witnessed her swim and it was discredited. No other woman, not even Mille Gade Corson, was known even to have tested herself over that distance.

Little wonder. Despite a strong tailwind, of the thirty-one men who had competed in the *Herald-Tribune* race in 1914, only four had been able to finish—the rest had been beaten by the tides and the currents and the cold water. The swim was anything but easy—swimmers first had to negotiate the waters of Upper New York Bay, where the Hudson River meets the sea and the East River commingles with the waters of Long Island Sound, then ride the swift current through the Narrows between Staten Island and Brooklyn before finally heading south through Lower New York Bay off Coney Island and then across Raritan Bay between Staten Island and Sandy Hook. The entire route was a confusing mix of currents and tides that pushed a swimmer back and forth like a rubber duck in a tub, and was made even more difficult by the amount of shipping traffic that ran nonstop along the same course, constantly sending out wakes in all directions. Just as they did in the English Channel, swimmers had to account for every change and variation of tide and current or risk being swept far away from their chosen destination, turning an already difficult and dangerous journey into an impossible and potentially deadly one.

After going to bed early in the evening on June 14, Trudy awoke around 2:00 A.M., ate a light meal of cantaloupe, cereal, toast, and coffee, and then, together with her father and sister Meg, met Charlotte Epstein, WSA president Margaret Johnson, several journalists, and a small boat crew at the pier in Battery Park. Apart from the lap of the water along the shore and the distant sound of boat traffic far offshore, it was nearly silent. Lights twinkling on the horizon marked the far shores of Staten Island and Brooklyn, and a cool, soft breeze rustled the leaves of the trees in nearby Battery Park.

At precisely 4:42 A.M., in the darkness, Trudy carefully entered the harbor, put her face in the water, and began to swim, followed first by a rowboat and then, a few minutes later, by the *Helys*, a small power-boat. Only one day before leaving to swim the Channel, and less than twenty-four hours after setting a world record over 150 yards, Trudy Ederle was attempting to swim to Sandy Hook.

To maximize the impact of the swim, the WSA had kept her attempt a secret from the general public. Far better, they believed, for the public to learn of her accomplishment after the fact. If she succeeded, her attempt to swim the Channel was certain to generate terrific publicity, yet if she failed she'd provide evidence for those who believed the Channel was too much for a woman, as well as risk destroying her own self-confidence. The swim was a gamble, but one Trudy and the WSA felt was worth it.

Although Trudy and her crew had taken care to make inquiries in regard to the tides and currents, after only a few short minutes in the water she felt the rush of water wash over her face. While her pace never varied, it felt as if she were swimming upstream in a rushing river.

She was. Her crew, which included the fire commissioner of Hoboken, New Jersey, had assured everyone that it was familiar with the tides and currents between the Battery and Sandy Hook. While that may well have been the case, familiarity didn't mean expertise. Her crew was clearly misinformed. Rather than catching the harbor in ebb tide, flowing out to sea, a strong flood tide was racing in, running directly in her face as the sea tried to push its way up the Hudson River, making Trudy's task infinitely more difficult.

For an hour and a half Trudy gamely slogged along, each stroke of her arm and pull of her hand gaining her only a few feet against the current as she slowly cut across Buttermilk Channel between the Battery and Governor's Island, and then finally clear of the island itself. She was already exhausted but had covered less than two miles and occasionally turned over on her side to relieve her muscles of cramping. In midharbor the water temperature barely reached sixty degrees. At the break of dawn, Sandy Hook was hardly any closer than it had been when she had started.

There was concern aboard the *Helys*, where Epstein and the others looked at the girl, clearly struggling, with grim faces and spoke to one another in hushed tones. They openly wondered if Trudy should abandon the attempt. There seemed little chance that Trudy, who appeared lethargic and beaten, could succeed, and they didn't want her confidence to suffer.

Then, as if the struggle jolted her awake, Trudy began picking up her pace, finally fighting the tide rather than allowing herself to be pushed around. As she did, first slowly and then in a rush, the tide turned and the sun lifted in the sky and hit the water. As the conditions changed, so did Trudy's mood. Her rate of speed in the water doubled, and then tripled as the Hudson River chased the tide out to sea in a rush and Trudy rode the current back out.

Trudy and the two accompanying vessels stayed close to the Brooklyn shore through the Narrows and then caught a current that sent her out into the deeper water of the shipping channel. Sandy Hook was still out of sight, hidden by morning fog still lingering farther out at sea, but the crew on the *Helys* directed her way with an onboard compass.

At 10:30 the fog began to lift, first revealing the Highlands, Trudy's second home, and then, finally, the low beach and dunes of Sandy Hook, a fine white line along the horizon.

Victory was in sight, barely one mile away. But over the last few hours the tide had slowed and then turned slack. Now it began to run again and was pushing back against Trudy just as her energy began to fade. The motorboat slowed to keep pace, barely crawling through the water. From her seat on the boat, Meg could see that Trudy was losing ground, and the success that a few moments before had seemed so certain now seemed far off. And no one was doing anything about it.

Meg had enough. She jumped from her seat, cupped her hands around her mouth and called to her sister. "Hey!" she shouted, startling everyone. Meg's voice cut through Trudy's fatigue and the swimmer's head snapped around. "Get going, lazy bones," Meg called out. "You're loafing!" Indignant at the insult, Trudy fixed her sister in her sights.

"Loafing, am I?" she called back. "For that I'll make it if it kills me!" Then Trudy turned back to the water, put her head down, reached out with her arms and with each stroke pulled the shore closer again, turning inside herself, swimming as if she was doing intervals in the WSA pool, her stroke strong and true. Meg watched with a satisfied smile as Trudy began to put some distance between herself and the *Helys*. The boat pilot leaned on the throttle, and as the Highlands peaked over the horizon, Meg exhorted her sister to swim even faster.

As the buildings of Fort Hancock, on the northernmost point of the Hook, began to appear, Trudy picked up her pace even more. The fort commander had been informed in advance of their plans, and a small crowd of Trudy's friends and her family were waiting onshore as she sprinted the final hundred yards before finally reaching the shallows. When her arms hit bottom she popped to her feet and began wading to shore, rubbing her eyes, which were red and raw with irritation from the salt water. She had swum for much of the last few hours with her eyes closed, all sounds muffled due to her hearing loss, her arms and legs numb from the cold, yet this had not deterred her or even caused her to slow down.

It was 11:53 A.M. She had been in the water for seven hours, eleven minutes, and thirty seconds, finishing nearly seven minutes faster than the existing record. She had not only succeeded, but she had shattered a record previously held by a man, and done so only one day after she had set a world record in a 150-yard race. As soon as their boat hit the beach, several newspapermen dashed off in search of a telephone to call the story in to the evening papers.

After spending a few moments to collect herself, Trudy pronounced herself fit—and hungry. She had neither eaten nor taken any drink during her time in the water. A reporter asked her whether she was tired and she replied, "Not much. I could have kept on going if I had to."

When another made mention of a "second wind," Trudy shook her head disparagingly. "I've heard other swimmers talk about it," she said, "but I don't think I have a second wind. I usually feel a little tired during the first mile but after that I am all right." With that she was escorted to the fort's dining room for a meal, and then boarded the boat for the journey back, where she amazed everyone as she alternately sat and stood on deck, chatting away as if she had just returned from swimming practice.

The next day her achievement made headlines in sports pages all over the country. In his nationally syndicated column "It Seems to Me," Heywood Broun of the *New York World* did not miss the significance of her achievement, writing, "When Gertrude Ederle stepped onto the beach at Sandy Hook the shake of her shoulders sent flying many things besides drips of water. As she crawled and kicked down the bay the churning of her feet beat against tradition and bruised it. In the face of the fact that she beat the best time ever made by any man over the same course the various theories about male superiority may have to be amended."

Anyone who had not known that she was about to tackle the English Channel did so now. Based on her time in the Sandy Hook swim, she was expected not only to succeed and become the first woman to swim the Channel, but to beat the existing men's record and prove, forever and for all time, not only that women could be athletes, but that they were the equal of men, if not better. As Broun noted, Trudy's swim pointed out that "the reason men excelled so markedly in sports for so long a time did not lie in any lack of potential equality among women, but was explicable rather on the ground that women didn't get the chance to try . . . Little girls were brought up to believe that the games of boys were not for them . . . But now the challenge has come, and before we know it the old legends against which we have leaned so heavily will crumble."

For the first time ever since men and women looked across the Channel and dreamed of one day swimming across it, there was finally a swimmer to whom swimming the English Channel was not just a personal challenge, but a charge and a responsibility.

18

Wolffe

THE DAY AFTER Trudy Ederle swam from the Battery to Sandy Hook, she met her chaperone, Elsie Viets, at Pier 54 at the foot of West Twelfth Street to sail for England aboard the *Berengaria*, the pride of the Cunard Line. Although Charlotte Epstein had originally intended to accompany Trudy and Helen Wainwright, when Wainwright dropped out it was decided that only Viets would make the trip with Trudy.

Even among the nearly five thousand passengers, thousand-man crew, and thousands of visitors aboard the ship to see people off, Trudy Ederle stood out. In the wake of her record-setting swim the day before, newsreel and still photographers sought her out and made certain they shot some footage of her boarding the vessel and posing on deck. By the time she reached England, moviegoers all over the United States would be made aware of her quest. When it came time to swim the Channel, the entire nation would follow Trudy's wake.

At the same time a syndicated article by Louis Handley appeared in newspapers from coast to coast. Entitled "Will 'Trudy' Be the First to Swim the Channel?" Handley, logically and dispassionately, laid out the reasons why he expected her to succeed. After citing Trudy's already substantial accomplishments from the Day Cup to the Sandy Hook swim, Handley concluded, "From every point of view then, Miss Ederle appears ready for the great venture."

Unlike for her trip to the Olympics the previous summer, conditions on board the *Berengaria* would play no role in her success or failure. She was pleased to discover that accommodations on the *Berengaria* were much more opulent than those on board the *Amer-*

ica. Like the *America*, the *Berengaria* had also been confiscated from Germany during the war and turned over to the British as reparations for the sinking of the *Lusitania.* The flagship of the Cunard Line, the enormous vessel, which measured over nine hundred feet in length, was the most luxurious liner of its day, featuring almost every creature comfort imaginable, including numerous restaurants, lounges, saloons, gymnasiums, a sauna, and a cinema.

To Trudy, however, the most significant feature of the ship was its swimming pool. Although not the first cruise ship to feature a pool, none was as lavish as that of the *Berengaria.* The indoor pool measured twelve meters by twenty-four meters, cut through two decks, and looked like it would have been more at home in a Roman villa of antiquity. In fact, it was decorated in the Pompeian style, complete with marble benches and columns, fountains, a tiled promenade, and other features that seemed entirely unlikely on a cruise ship. As Trudy limbered up in the pool, the irony must not have been lost on her—had the *America* been equipped with such a pool, perhaps Trudy would have been more successful in the 1924 Olympics. Then again, had she won three gold medals, she may well have felt no need to take on the English Channel.

The weeklong trip was uneventful, and as soon as Trudy and Miss Viets disembarked at Southampton, they traveled to Brighton and met Jabez Wolffe for the first time. They planned to train there for the next month before moving across the Channel to Boulogne, France. At the time, most Channel swimmers had concluded that the route from France to England was somewhat easier than beginning in England.

From their first meeting, the swimmer and the trainer eyed each other warily. Trudy and Viets were accustomed to the quiet, professional, polite, almost scientific approach of Louis Handley, who built a swimmer's skill and confidence slowly and incrementally. Jabez Wolffe was an entirely different creature.

He saw little need to indulge in social pleasantries and eyed Trudy like she was a racehorse, looking her up and down as if he were trying to determine if she met his standard by her shape alone. The burly old swimmer was built like a barrel, his round face in a permanent flush. He was a tough man to begin with, gruff, blunt, and short spoken, and his nearly two dozen trials in Channel waters had done little to soften his approach. Because he had failed so often, he thought failure was the norm and tried to scare swimmers with tales of the horrors they were certain to endure—the power of positive thinking was not an approach he recognized. He resented anyone who did not share his dour outlook.

From their first conversation, Wolffe underscored the notion that swimming the Channel was nearly impossible, a point that he felt he had to impress on Ederle again and again and again. He dismissed her swims in America—"The Channel is different, Miss Ederle," became a phrase Trudy would soon hear in her sleep. To hear Wolffe tell it, there was no water anywhere in the world colder than the waters of the Channel, no tide more mysterious, no current swifter, no weather less forgiving. Nothing she had previously done, insisted Wolffe, prepared her in any way for what was about to come.

Trudy, however, thought differently. Before she left the United States, Louis Handley had designed her training schedule for her, slowly increasing the time she spent in the water so she could acclimate to Channel conditions, focused on getting her in shape to maintain a steady rate of twenty-eight strokes to the minute, a rate designed to get her across the Channel in less than fourteen hours, a strategy that that would bridge only two tidal cycles so her route across would resemble the much-preferred single letter Z rather than the squat—and slower—double Z.

Wolffe rolled his eyes at that. There was no way she'd swim the Channel that quickly, he thought. In fact, he was unimpressed with almost everything Trudy did and said. He took issue with her style of swimming, her training schedule, and Handley's assumptions about the Channel. Wolffe didn't believe in the American crawl, at least for use in the rough waters of the open sea, and refused to believe that any swimmer, much less a young woman, could possibly maintain the stroke for the many hours it would take to cross the Channel. And even if a swimmer did use the crawl in the Channel, Wolffe argued, Trudy's rapid stroke rate was impossible to maintain. Handley, thought Wolffe, was a fool, a mere pool swimmer, and his belief that Trudy could swim the Channel in fourteen hours was pure fantasy.

That was only half of it. Wolffe was accustomed to young women who deferred to him because of both his gender and his status as a Channel expert. Neither Trudy nor Elsie Viets paid him the deference he felt he deserved. Trudy now wore her hair in a bob, a practical style for a swimmer but still considered risqué in some circles, and her speech was peppered with the latest slang—to Trudy, Wolffe was "all wet." Even worse, she didn't *listen* to Wolffe but had her own opinions about swimming. Although Trudy was generally shy, when it came to swimming she knew her stuff and wasn't afraid to express her opinion. Over the past few months Meg and Handley had convinced her she could succeed, and she had never felt more self-assured. Wolffe had expected to meet a malleable hunk of clay. Instead he met a young woman brimming with confidence, certain and secure.

In short, Wolffe behaved as if he was offended by the fact that Trudy was a more talented swimmer than he had ever been, or that a woman might be able to do something that he himself never could. When Trudy began to train in the waters off Brighton, Wolffe tried to change everything. He was soon disabused of that notion by Viets, who from the start served as an advocate for Trudy and as a foil between the trainer and the swimmer. She told the trainer that while they welcomed Wolffe's suggestions, his main responsibility was logistical. He was expected to lend his expertise to the actual details of the crossing—securing a support boat and an experienced captain and navigators who could direct Trudy across, taking into consideration the weather, the currents, and the tides and, based on his own knowledge of local conditions, recommending the best time to make an attempt. As far as Trudy's training went, Wolffe was to supervise her sessions and attend to her physical safety, but he was largely expected to leave the details of her training schedule alone and not make any recommendations whatsoever in regard to her swimming stroke.

Wolffe was infuriated. He was not accustomed to such treatment and reacted by berating Trudy at every opportunity. During her training swims, when Wolffe followed alongside her in his rowboat he constantly urged her to slow down and screamed at her that she'd never make it across the Channel if she failed to follow his instructions. "This isn't a 400-meter race, Miss Ederle," Wolffe called out sarcastically over and over again. Despite Viets's admonitions to leave her stroke alone, Wolffe continued to try to dissuade Trudy from Handley's notion of swimming at the rate of twenty-eight strokes per minute to a much slower rate of eighteen or twenty, a pace Trudy knew would cause her to spend at least eighteen hours in the water and therefore contend with a third tidal change. This would make the chances of her success slim. She didn't just reject his suggestions, but laughed at them, making him even angrier.

Wolffe didn't think she was working hard enough, either. Handley had recommended that Trudy swim for two hours each day and spend another two hours doing road work, walking and hiking, enough to build her stamina without wearing her out.

Wolffe thought that was crazy. He believed a person trained for swimming the Channel by swimming in the Channel, over and over again, sometimes for extended periods of time. He wanted Trudy to spend many more hours in the water and much preferred a schedule in which over a three-day period she spent ever more time in the water, then took the fourth day off, and then repeated the pattern. Then, after every workout, he wanted to give Trudy a deep and vigorous massage of her muscles, particularly those of her arms and legs. He believed that over time such massages, which took at least an hour under his rough hands, "hardened" the muscles and made them immune to fatigue.

Trudy was appalled—she wanted none of it. At her age she didn't want anyone to touch her that she didn't want to touch her, particularly a middle-aged man she didn't particularly like and already did not trust. Elsie Viets stepped in and told Wolffe that if he thought massages were so necessary, they would have to be administered by a woman.

Wolffe even found fault with the way Trudy spent her time when she wasn't training. Trudy had brought along a ukulele and when she wasn't in the water or doing road work she was teaching herself to play and could be found curled up in a corner crouched over the instrument plucking out a tune. Wolffe would look at her, and with sarcasm dripping from his voice, ask, "Playing the ukulele again, are we, Miss Ederle?" as if every second she spent with a ukulele in her hand was adding miles to her journey across the Channel. Trudy would just ignore him and play a little louder.

They might as well have dug trenches, like opposing forces in the Great War, Trudy and Viets on one side and Wolffe on the other, and a considerable breach of trust in the middle. Nevertheless, it was too late for either side to change—Wolffe had already been paid, needed the money, and was still the most experienced trainer in England. Burgess, at Cape Gris-Nez, was already engaged by other swimmers.

After nearly a month in Brighton, in the last week of July, Trudy, Viets, and Wolffe relocated across the Channel, to Boulogne, on the coast just south of Cape Gris-Nez. Now she could train in the same waters she would encounter at the start of her swim, and whenever Wolffe determined that conditions were amenable to the swim, Trudy wouldn't have to race across the Channel from England. Although she would have preferred to stay in the village of Cape Gris-Nez, where her swim would begin, there were no accommodations available—other swimmers and journalists had locked up all the space at the only two hotels in town. Wolffe had targeted two periods when he believed that tidal conditions might prove favorable for Trudy to make her attempt—August 4 to 7, and August 17 to 19. While Trudy waited for Wolffe to give the go-ahead, other Channel swimmers weren't waiting around.

Lillian Harrison had already tried and failed to swim the Channel a few weeks before but was preparing to make another attempt. A Japanese swimmer, Masanori Nakamuri, was in training, as were the World War I hero Colonel Cyril Freyburg, the Frenchwoman Jeanne Sion, and a garrulous giant of a swimmer from Egypt, Ishaq Helmi.

The son of a famous Egyptian general, Helmi, the spelling of which caused newspapermen on both sides of the Channel fits, was as close to being a professional Channel swimmer as was then humanly possible. Considered a member of Egyptian royalty with the rank of *bek*, Helmi received a stipend of some twenty-five thousand dollars a year and was in training to swim the Channel at the behest of King Fouad I, who for nationalistic reasons wanted an Egyptian to make a crossing. Helmi spent the bulk of his annual fortune on his desire to swim the Channel—in the summer of 1925 he had rented one of Cape Gris-Nez's two hotels for his use alone, effectively trying to block other swimmers from having access to the town.

Although all the swimmers in training for crossing the Channel were, in some way, in competition with one another, they were more in competition with the Channel itself. Over time the swimmers became close to one another. Despite his lease of the hotel, Helmi's broad, open face, bright smile, and gentle manner made him instantly likeable. He served as something of a social secretary and big brother among the swimmers, leading excursions to the beach and impromptu gatherings at his hotel. Nearly every time a swimmer entered the water, Helmi volunteered his services as a pacesetter. Standing six feet four inches and weighing upward of 250 pounds, although Helmi didn't swim very fast he was blessed with considerable stamina and strength, making him invaluable.

As July turned into August the swimmers began jockeying for position to make their crossing. The summer had been unusually hot, and the waters of the Channel were warmer than usual, sometimes as warm as sixty-four or sixty-five degrees, but that didn't necessarily make the trip any easier—warm water did not necessarily mean calm seas. Each time a swimmer entered the Channel the other swimmers paid close attention, eager to learn from their experience and hoping their encounter with the Channel was not so horrible as to destroy their confidence and cause them to second-guess their own efforts.

Taking advantage of a favorable tide, Jeanne Sion left from France on the morning of August 4 and swam strongly, if not terribly fast, for the better part of the day. As dusk approached, she was only one and one-quarter miles from the English coast when the tide turned and forced her from the water after some thirteen and a half hours. As she made her return to France her boat passed Colonel Freyburg, who had entered the water twelve hours after Sion. He swam through the dark and the next morning was within a quarter mile of the white cliffs of Dover, near enough to hear the crowds onshore cheering him on. One member of his party, noting that the tide was beginning to change, told a reporter, "If he can get over the next 200 yards in fifteen minutes, he'll make it."

But those two hundred yards might as well have been two hundred miles. The tide turned, and Freyburg was simply not a strong enough swimmer to go against it, yet he refused to quit. For the next two hours, despite his best effort, he was slowly but surely swept back toward France, losing more than a mile before he finally lost his bearings and, delirious, began swimming back toward France. When he was pulled from the sea he had spent nearly seventeen hours in the water.

Trudy was not put off by these failures, and the other swimmers, amazed at her speed, boosted her self-confidence when they told her they believed she would succeed. While Trudy waited for the go-ahead from Wolffe, she continued training.

In some areas Trudy did take Wolffe's advice. She took part in several "dress rehearsals" of the swim that mimicked the conditions she'd soon face for real. During these practices Trudy wore the one-piece unitard she expected to use during the swim and donned her bathing cap and goggles, which were attached to her face with latex in an attempt to create a waterproof seal. Wolffe and Trudy experimented with various types of grease and oils to cover her body, not only so she could get accustomed to the feel, but to the smell, as she tried various combinations of olive oil, petroleum jelly, lanolin, and porpoise fat to reduce chafing and help her to retain her body heat. Wolffe, who still expected that she would spend as much as twenty hours in the water, also wanted to make sure Trudy grew accustomed to swimming in the dark. He recommended that she begin her swim before sunrise so her time in the darkness would take place while she was still fresh. Wolffe not only trailed her in a rowboat, as he would during her real attempt, but even had an accompanying tug-boat shadow her so she would grow accustomed to the sound of its engines and its effect on the surf.

In any Channel crossing, due to the strain and the cold Channel waters, swimmers must take nourishment. Although Trudy had neither eaten nor drunk during the Sandy Hook swim, the journey across the Channel would be at least twice as long and in cold water, Channel swimmers can burn more than twenty thousand calories. According to the then unwritten but widely accepted rules of Channel crossing, if a swimmer was touched, even accidentally, by another human being while in the water, or sought support on a floating object, such as a boat, the swim was invalid. As a result, finding a way to eat and drink in the water posed quite a challenge, as did getting accustomed to eating and drinking while battling seasickness and the accidental ingestion of seawater. Wolffe practiced passing food and drink to Trudy from the rowboat, sometimes by hand, and sometimes by means of a long pole to cut down on the chance of an accidental touch. He made himself responsible for selecting her food and drink, convincing Trudy and Viets that he knew what would be palatable in mid-Channel.

Trudy's dress rehearsals were near perfect. During one swim she spent three hours in the water, and even though she battled an adverse tide for the first sixty minutes, she still swam nine miles from shore and her pace of twenty-six strokes per minute never varied. Observers, including the tug captain Joseph Corthes, who had captained many crossings, were stunned not only at her pace but with the ease with which she moved through the water. He called her "marvelous," and offered that he believed she would beat Tirabocchi's mark "by several hours."

Trudy did find one of Wolffe's suggestions utterly baffling, at least at first. For each of Wolffe's many attempts, he tried to swim to the accompaniment of a bagpiper on his support boat playing familiar tunes, helping him battle boredom and maintain the proper pace. He wanted Trudy to do the same. "If I have anything to say about the musical program," he said, "we will have several bagpipers so that they can work in relays, a fresh man to take up the tune as fast as the piper is exhausted," adding that he had the bagpiper play different tunes during meals and when he needed extra motivation requested his favorite tune, "I Love a Lassie."

Trudy, however, shuddered at the thought of swimming to bagpipers for the better part of a day and countered by asking if it might be possible to listen to a radio on deck of the tug instead. But Wolffe vetoed the idea, explaining that it would be impossible to ensure that the radio would broadcast music in the precise rhythm required. Once again, Wolffe and Trudy were at a standoff.

The solution to the quandary was provided by the French swimmer Jeanne Sion. Sion told Trudy that "music is as essential to a channel swimmer as food," and suggested that she swim to music she enjoyed, as Sion had, and hire a band, recommending that she get one that included a cornet, a clarinet, a trombone, and a concertina. Trudy, a true fan of popular music, liked that idea, saying she wanted to make sure they band played "real American jazz—hard boiled music. Nothing in a minor chord for me."

While that solved one issue, it still did not mean that Trudy and Jabez Wolffe were rowing together in the same boat. Wolffe had previously told some observers, like Alec Rutherford, an English sportswriter who was widely considered to be an expert on Channel swimming, that "if conditions are favorable . . . I firmly believe that Miss Ederle will succeed, and if she does I think she will lower the record," and he made tentative plans for Trudy to make an attempt on August 7. On that day, however, Trudy had a touch of the flu, and the swim had to be put off until August 17, the next date the tides would be favorable. Wolffe was clearly miffed—he acted as if he thought she'd faked her illness and now changed his tune, telling a reporter, "I do not expect her to succeed . . . She refuses to train and plays the ukulele all day . . . [and] she is too fast a swimmer for such a great distance. If she swims fast she will collapse, and she cannot swim slowly because her feet have a trick of hanging down when she is swimming slowly."

It almost appeared as if Wolffe didn't *want* her to succeed. Ederle's presence in France had captured the interest of the press on both sides of the Channel—never before had so much press attention been foisted on the Channel swimmers and their coaches. Wolffe not only enjoyed the attention, but as a result he now regularly fielded inquiries from other Channel swimmers—including some women—who were interested in hiring him in the event Ederle either failed completely or failed to better Tirabocchi's mark. However, if Trudy succeeded, few of these swimmers were likely to continue their quest, providing Wolffe with a financial incentive for her to fail. And if she did fail, Wolffe would likely be hired in the summer of 1926 by even more swimmers eager to swim the Channel.

There was also the matter of wagers. Insurance bookmakers in London started out giving odds of 1 to 10 against Ederle making it across, but in recent days, due in part to Wolffe's original pronouncement that "Miss Ederle will succeed," the odds changed precipitously. Now the odds were only 1 in 4 against Trudy. While there is no direct evidence that Wolffe had placed a bet or was trying to manipulate the odds, his contradictory statements are suspicious.

Then again, it just may have been Trudy's sex that turned the old Scotsman against her. It galled Wolffe, who had tried and failed so many times in the Channel waters, to see Trudy, a woman, and a far better swimmer than he could ever dream of being, cut through the water at a speed he found both astonishing and—this is what really got to him—almost effortless, surrounded on land by reporters and supporters who treated her with a measure of respect and deference that was no longer his. Wolffe continued to complain to reporters that she hadn't followed his training methods and then added bitterly, "I have told her that this marathon swim is different from anything she has tried. But what man can argue successfully with a woman?"

While Trudy recuperated, Lillian Harrison made another attempt to swim the Channel, but when she was approximately halfway across she passed out from the cold water. Fortunately for her, at the time she was being paced by Ishaq Helmi, who managed to grab hold of her and keep her afloat until she could be pulled back on the boat.

That was enough for Harrison. When she recovered she said, "I've had my fling at this old channel; I'm going to turn it over to Gertrude Ederle now to see what she can do." Harrison never tried to swim the Channel again.

Ederle's illness kept her out of the water until August 12, when she resumed training, but she appeared no worse for wear. Wolffe, however, was at the end of his rope and now complained to reporters about interference from Trudy's chaperone, Elsie Viets. Just one day before Trudy was scheduled to enter the water, on August 16, he became so incensed that he stalked off and tried to board the ferry from Boulogne back to England, only to be hauled off the ship by some friends who urged him to reconsider. He chose to remain, but he still wasn't happy.

In fact, Wolffe seemed determined to undermine Trudy's confidence even further, for later that day Wolffe chose to sound an alarm. Two fishermen from Boulogne came back into port with two sharks they'd caught in the Channel, which they hung from huge hooks on the dock so the entire town could see the fearsome creatures on display.

Although biologists have determined that the Channel is, in fact, the occasional home of several shark species, including the thrasher shark, blue shark, basking shark, and, on rare occasions, even the great white, attacks are virtually unknown. Most shark sightings in the Channel were, in reality, of porpoises, and at the time some Channel residents used the terms interchangeably.

Trudy had little reaction to the news—this was the first she had heard of sharks from Wolffe, and other swimmers had told her there was nothing to be concerned about; of the many hazards that swimmers face in the Channel, shark attacks are among the most remote. But still, even entertaining the thought before attempting to swim the Channel, which required everything a person had, was a distraction, and the fact that Wolffe was bringing it up hardly made her feel better about him. If success was the goal, giving Trudy any reason to doubt both herself and the wisdom of her effort served no useful purpose whatsoever.

That is why it is strange that Jabez Wolffe chose not only to tell Trudy about the sharks, describing them in all their toothsome glory, but even added that he himself had been forced to cut short a Channel swim due to a shark attack, which was news even to those who had known Wolffe a long time. Less than twenty-four hours before she would test herself in the Channel waters for the first time, Trudy had to worry about not only the sharks in the water, but also, perhaps, the shark who was serving as her own trainer.

19

Touched

IF TRUDY WAS TROUBLED by visions of sharks and blood in the water the night before beginning her swim, she didn't let on. At 6:00 on the evening of August 16, after a dinner of her favorite meal, beefsteak—no horsemeat on this trip—Trudy retired early.

Ten hours later, Elsie Viets shook her awake. Trudy opened her eyes and her first words were "How I wish tomorrow was today." She knew that this day might well prove to be the most difficult and challenging of her young life.

Trudy dressed quickly, already thinking of the swim. As she stood up from a light breakfast of apple fritters and weak tea, she told Viets, "I'm ready for it. Bring on your old Channel." The women made their way to the dock in Boulogne, where the tug *La Morinie* sat waiting to bring her to Cape Gris-Nez and then follow her on her journey. Just as she began to board the vessel Viets noticed that Trudy had put her skirt on inside out and asked if she wanted to return to her room and change, but Trudy laughed it off saying, "I feel it will bring me good luck." Carrying a large American flag, she crossed the gangplank and immediately asked that it be raised.

Nearly a hundred people were milling about the dock in the dark waiting to board the boat, including cameramen, press correspondents—among them the American Minott Saunders, the Englishman Alec Rutherford, and Sydney Williams of the English-language *Paris Tribune*—assorted crew, well-wishers, and friends. The scene more resembled the controlled chaos of a departing cruise ship than the departure of a Channel swimmer. Just after 5:00 A.M., the tug pulled away from the dock for the short trip up the coast to Cape Gris-Nez.

Never before in the history of Channel swimming had a swimmer received so much attention and support. Not only was the band on board the tug, but the WSA had sent over a gramophone, just in case. The tug was equipped with advanced wireless and radio equipment to send bulletins back to shore, and no less than four motorboats had been hired by journalists to ferry written dispatches back to land from mid-Channel to provide almost a minute-by-minute account of Trudy's swim. If all that somehow failed to keep the world informed, Jabez Wolffe had even insisted that the boat be equipped with carrier pigeons.

As the tug chugged toward Cape Gris-Nez in the early morning light, Trudy sipped a hot drink as reporters, wearing heavy sweaters, tussled on deck for choice space to set up their typewriters, as did the band. The weather, to a novice, seemed near perfect—a hazy sun rose over the highlands along the French shore and revealed the Channel in repose, cast in a rosy, peaceful glow, as if waiting, with no swell in her waters and the lightest breeze blowing from the southeast. To most observers it looked to be a fine summer day. The water was even warmer than usual, an almost balmy sixty-four. Somewhere through the mist was England, just over twenty miles off, and, for Trudy, perhaps, lasting fame.

But to those who knew the Channel, and knew the sea, there were signs of trouble. A crimson streak shone on the horizon, reminding some of the old sailor's adage "Red sky at morning, sailors take warning."

As was customary, Trudy was joined by many of the other swimmers who either planned to swim the Channel themselves or were considering doing so. They had been engaged to help Trudy maintain her pace, and in so doing received valuable training time in mid-Channel, the kind of experience that was certain to help them with their own efforts. Helmi, Lillian Harrison, Jeanne Sion, the English swimmer Vera Tanner, and two male swimmers representing the British and French military, respectively, a Captain Annison and a Lieutenant Destrees, were all on board.

As the tug approached Gris-Nez, Jeanne Sion, who served as something of a surrogate parent for Trudy, accompanied her below decks to the boiler room, where she first donned her one-piece unitard bearing an American flag on the breast, and then, with the help of Sion, Elsie Viets, Vera Tanner, and Wolffe, her goggles were fixed to her face with latex and her body was covered in a quarter inch of lanolin, topped with another quarter inch of Vaseline, and then another quarter inch of Wolffe's own special formulation—primarily lard—and other compounds, leading Trudy, whose hands were covered and couldn't touch anything, to pronounce with a grimace, "I hate this sticky stuff." If she performed as she expected, she would never have to wear it again.

The tug reached Gris-Nez just before 7:00 A.M. and anchored about a quarter mile from the outmost tip of old Gray Nose. Trudy, Wolffe, Lillian Harrison, and several crewmen gathered on deck, and Trudy read a telegram just received on ship from her parents: "Swim to Victory. Lots of Love, Mother and Dad." A rowboat was lowered to the water, and Trudy and her crew climbed in. As she did, she saluted the American flag flying over the tug, and as the boat's occupants cheered her on, a powerboat owned by United Press towed the rowboat to where Bill Burgess waited for her onshore. Wolffe didn't want a repeat of the bad luck that had befallen Lillian Harrison when she had slipped and cut her leg, and Burgess, in a show of camaraderie, had agreed to help with the start, knowing that Wolffe, despite their differences, would do the same for him in a similar situation.

Just off the rocky promontory, Trudy, her pink bathing cap tight over her head, slipped over the edge of the rowboat and into the water, followed close behind by Jabez Wolffe. She swam a few strokes toward Burgess, waded toward shore, and then touched a rock jutting out of the water to establish the start of her swim. According to their plans, Burgess was supposed to lead her out to open water, with Wolffe trailing her from behind to make sure she didn't get swept upon the rocks.

Trudy couldn't wait. Despite her recent illness and Wolffe's complaints, she felt terrific, excited but in top shape. A moment later, at 7:12 A.M. Trudy turned back toward England, stretched out in the water, lifted first her right arm and then her left arm, first overhead then outward, and began to swim, leaving Burgess behind. Only a generation before, the thought of a woman swimming the English Channel would have seemed ludicrous. Now, it seemed not only possible, but for the first time in history, even likely.

She had four hours and twenty minutes before the tide would

turn, and she didn't waste a moment. She struck out at a pace of twenty-eight strokes per minute, reaching and then passing the tug after only twelve minutes as the boat pulled anchor and began to chug along some ten or fifteen yards off her lee side, close enough for those on board to watch, but not so close as to interfere with her swim.

On cue, as she swam alongside the tug, the band began to play "March of the Allies," Trudy looked up, laughed, and said, "Give me 'Yes, We Have No Bananas,'" then struck off. Wolffe, in the rowboat only a few yards away, his head covered with a towel to protect his scalp and forehead from sunburn, was heard to bellow, "This is not a 1,000-yard race Miss Ederle!" already trying to slow her down. She paid him little attention but mocked him by swimming the breast-stroke for a time, as he preferred, before she resumed her rapid pace. At various intervals other swimmers occasionally slipped into the water alongside her and swam for a time to help her maintain her pace before each of them left the water, exhausted, as none could maintain her speed for long. Every hour or so a motorboat drew alongside the tug, gathered up the written dispatches from the journalists on board, then raced on to deliver word of her progress to the world. Back in the Highlands, her parents, sisters Meg, Helen, and Emma, and even her little brothers, Henry and George, were all up and awake, anxious to receive "bulletins" by telephone from the WSA, which forwarded to the Ederles any information it received by cable.

When the tide turned nearly five hours into her swim, she was already in mid-Channel, having covered eight miles in the first three hours, and even as the tide began to slow and turn, she continued to make steady progress. The only difficulty she was having was with Jabez Wolffe.

He fought her at nearly every instance. When she first complained of being hungry and asked for food, he balked at giving her anything and told her it was too early to eat or drink. When he finally did, passing her a bottle of beef broth by way of a long pole, she popped off the cork top with her teeth, and, floating on her back, lost her grip and the bottle slipped away. "Five shillings worth of nourishment gone to Neptune," grunted Wolffe before he provided another. Later, when he gave her a bottle of hot coffee and she held the bottle in her hands for a moment, enjoying the warmth, he mocked her, first asking if the coffee was too hot, then grinned and said, "Is it nice and warm in there?" referring to the Channel waters.

"Yes," snapped Trudy, unable to contain her dislike of the trainer. "It's a real treat." Then, when she asked that a swimmer be sent in the water to help her keep her pace, Wolffe derisively referred to such companions as her "playmates." When Vera Tanner joined Trudy in the water and the two women chatted as they swam to pass the time, Wolffe barked out, "Cut off that talking, girls," and whenever Trudy asked for an update on her progress, instead of telling her how well she was doing, he continually admonished her for going too fast, asking, "Would you like to go back to France, Miss Ederle?"

If Trudy needed any more motivation, Wolffe was providing it. She was determined to finish if for no other reason than to spite him and prove to him that she could. She wanted nothing more than to walk on England's shore and leave Wolffe behind.

At about 1:00 P.M., after nearly six hours in the water, the warning from the red sky began to turn into reality. The wind suddenly turned and blew harder from the southwest, covering the sun in clouds and kicking up the sea. It was as if the English Channel itself had decided, now that Trudy was almost halfway to England, it was time to remind her that there was a reason only five swimmers had ever preceded her across, and that this swim, was, indeed, different from all others.

Almost immediately, those on board the ship began to feel the effects of the swells that now rolled in incessantly and that lifted the slow-going tug up and down like a cork. The passengers had started the trip with a liberal supply of food and two barrels of beer, much of which had already been consumed and was now about to be returned to the sea. The music was the first casualty as the musicians fell out first, playing in fits and starts before each man finally dropped out and abandoned his instrument to grip the rail and bow over the side, soon followed by some journalists and other observers.

In the water, Trudy also began to turn a bit green. The rougher seas caused her to slow down a bit, and she occasionally rolled over on her back to stretch and rub her arms. The Channel is full of jellyfish and Trudy had been stung, but although her arms were sore, the stings were more an annoyance than anything else. But she was not immune to the sea swells and soon began to complain of a sour stomach—she could still taste the beef broth she had consumed earlier. She was beginning to cramp, too, which was a bit strange for this stage of the swim—she sometimes cramped up during her first minutes in the open water, before her body adjusted to the temperature and effort. Yet all in all, she was okay. Dover was only eleven miles off.

Over the next hour conditions deteriorated, and it became difficult to tell if it was raining or if the air was simply full of wind-whipped mist. Trudy slowed to a pace of about a mile and a half an hour, but she did not stop, and at 2:30 P.M., with the musicians now huddled below deck with their heads between their knees, some bored journalists took up their instruments and began to play, not as well, but with great enthusiasm. That momentarily cheered Trudy, who over the course of the last hour had become a little lethargic.

Yet at around 3:00 P.M., as conditions turned even rougher, Helmi joined her in the water. Trudy was fond of the big swimmer and felt at ease in the rough seas with him at her side. After all, he had recently been credited with saving both Lillian Harrison and Jeanne Sion, grabbing the former swimmer as she lost consciousness during one of her attempts, and pulling Sion into a boat when she was too weak to climb in herself, and others couldn't gain a grip on her due to her coating of grease and lanolin.

Trudy didn't quite understand it, but she didn't feel right. She wasn't exactly seasick, but she felt woozy and light-headed. Every time she told herself to pick up the pace, there seemed to be a slight delay before her body responded, and even when it did, it was as if the message faded. Despite her best efforts she kept slowing down.

She had never quite felt that way before, not during the Sandy Hook swim, not at the Highlands, and not during any of her training swims. Of course, she'd never been in the Channel quite as long as this before, but still . . . she just didn't feel right.

Those aboard the tug could tell that Trudy was beginning to labor. She would swim strongly for a hundred yards or so, then slow and occasionally roll over in the water as the rough seas washed over her head. Then she'd turn back over and start up again, a pattern that was completely out of character.

She was at a critical time in the swim, like a mountaineer about to make the final push to scale a peak and then head downhill. Those aboard the tug could see the English coast just coming into view and knew that in a short time the tide would turn again in Trudy's favor and rush her toward her goal.

Yet while Trudy had certainly been struggling as conditions deteriorated, from the tugboat she didn't appear to be in great trouble. Those who had spent any time in Gris-Nez had seen her swim in similar conditions many times. Then, as they watched from twenty-five feet away, observers on the tug saw a series of great swells roll in and swamp both swimmers.

Helmi, bigger than Trudy and much fresher, managed to duck under and stay atop the water. But the seas hit as Trudy was taking a breath and she breathed in and then swallowed some seawater. Helmi noticed her spitting and sputtering. "Steady, Gertie," he told her, "Steady. Take it easy." Then as Trudy rolled over on her back, seawater and a trickle of vomit streamed from her mouth.

She acted as if she hadn't even heard Helmi, and looked up, her eyes glazed and her skin pale. She wasn't swimming anymore, but simply floating.

For the next moment or two those on the tug watched with curiosity as Trudy bobbed in the water, her face turned to the sky, and Helmi dog-paddled around her. Wolffe rowed closer, fixing the swimmer in his gaze, a bitter look on his face.

Trudy knew what was happening—sort of—but she was a bit nauseous, dizzy and disoriented, and suddenly as tired as she had ever been in her life. She just wanted to float for a moment, to rest. She was so tired all of a sudden, so very very tired.

Jabez Wolffe watched from the rowboat only a few yards away, his stare never wavering as his boat lifted and fell with the two swimmers in the water.

Wolffe then turned his head to Helmi and spoke, barking out an order in a tone of voice the big Egyptian knew better than to ignore. "Take her out," spat Wolffe. "That's enough."

The swimmer reached out and put his great arm around Trudy's chest. She felt the pressure, and the warmth, and then her mind began processing precisely what was happening, and it was as if she were waking from a deep sleep and slowly becoming aware of her surroundings.

It was 3:58 P.M., and the instant Helmi touched her, the swim was over, a realization that was only slowly making its way into her consciousness. She had been in the water just short of nine hours. Dover was six and one-half miles away, near enough for those on the tug to see the coastline jutting up out of the sea.

20

Poison

TRUDY DID NOT RESIST, could not resist. By the time she realized that Ishaq Helmi had touched her, it was too late—the swim was over. With a few sweeps of his arm Helmi drew the bewildered swimmer to the rowboat. Wolffe swung a towel out over the water, and Helmi wrapped it under Trudy's arms so Wolffe could gain some leverage on Trudy's greased body, then Helmi pushed and Wolffe pulled and Trudy, passive, was pulled into the boat like an exhausted fish after a long battle. She sat, and Jeanne Sion put her arm around her shoulder and pulled her close.

From the tug, where observers watched closely and a newsreel cameraman captured Trudy's few moments in the rowboat, it was at first unclear precisely what had just happened. Why had she stopped? Trudy was clearly conscious, eyes wide open, and sat upright in the boat, but she didn't look at anyone, barely moved, and seemed almost emotionless, oblivious to everything—either too exhausted, too disappointed, or too stunned to react. She didn't move at all until Wolffe tugged at the towel around her waist. At that Trudy's head snapped back, as if startled, and with a look of utter disgust on her face, she called out that it was too tight and he was hurting her.

For a moment the journalists and observers on board the escort tug were as stunned as Trudy. For days they'd been preparing to write a tale of success, and for the last eight hours they'd been filling in the blanks of that story. Now they had to reverse course and beat one another to the scoop as to why she had been stopped. As the rowboat approached the tug, the scribes on board grappled for position along the rail and called out questions.

Elsie Viets pushed her way past, and when the rowboat drew alongside the tug, she helped Trudy climb on board, and then, as reporters gathered around with their notebooks at the ready, Trudy stalked off to the opposite side of the ship, livid, before Viets spirited her away below decks. Trudy's only recorded comment at the time was somewhat ambiguous. She didn't mention being pulled from the water but according to Alec Rutherford, probably the most dispassionate and trustworthy of the observers on board the tug, said only, "It was the roughest going I have ever known. I was going well till the storm came up."

Her sudden unavailability didn't stop the presses as the scribes created a scene far more dramatic than what actually took place, and half-baked bulletins were sent crackling to shore over the wireless as others prepared finished copy to be ferried back on the next motorboat. One account insisted that Trudy had passed out in the water, only to be saved by Helmi's heroic action. Another writer suggested that she was hauled aboard the tug "limp and crying" and insisted that she blamed her failure on the ingestion of "too much salt water." Most overstated the bad weather. No one mentioned the fact that she had covered an incredible twenty-three miles in eight hours, a performance no other human being in the history of Channel swimming had come close to.

Since Trudy wasn't talking, Jabez Wolffe did. He told reporters that "she was two hours going in the worst possible channel conditions," before adding the expected bromides about her effort and perseverance, a dramatic turnaround from his statements only a few days before that questioned her fortitude and her physical condition. Ishaq Helmi made only a brief comment, stating that he reached out for Trudy at the direct instruction of Wolffe.

But to Elsie Viets, who knew Trudy better than anyone else, her behavior after boarding the tug was so odd as to arouse suspicion. After her Sandy Hook swim for example, Trudy had been energetic—she usually was after a swim, even a long one in cold water. This time, however, Trudy was sluggish and closedmouthed. She seemed to have a hard time focusing, as if only dimly aware of her surroundings. She asked Viets for a piece of chocolate and then curled up under a blanket below decks and, despite the choppy seas and swells, fell into a deep sleep, her breathing long and laborious. When the boat finally made it back to Boulogne at 6:30 P.M. Viets had some difficulty rousing her from her slumber, and the chaperone spirited her off to her quarters without additional comment, further frustrating the press, who were impatient to get Trudy's account of the swim. As soon as Trudy reached her room she collapsed on her bed and once again fell asleep.

Trudy didn't emerge until late the following morning, at 9:00, nearly seventeen hours after she first fell asleep. She hardly resembled the girl who had been pulled from the water less than twenty-four hours before.

She felt fine and wasn't even sore from the swim. She went for a brisk walk through town and then ate an enormous breakfast, for her stomach had settled down completely. Apart from a few jellyfish stings and some chafing under her arms, she felt fine.

Although Viets still kept the press away from her, one reporter did manage to corner Trudy for a moment and get her to comment. She seemed as curious about what had happened as they were, asking rhetorically, "It was funny how I sank, wasn't it?" even though no one on the tug had seen her sink, and Trudy said she remembered crying a little after being stopped—again, something no one remembered her doing—but added, "I don't know why. I wasn't sad. I wanted to go on."

Viets was able to keep her sequestered for one more day, but the press was relentless, and Trudy made another brief statement. Now with two full days to reflect on her effort, Trudy seemed even more mystified than ever, telling a reporter, "You guys are crazy, saying I collapsed," she said. "You must have been affected by seasickness. I thought I was going good." With that she and Viets left for Dunkirk, where Jeanne Sion had invited her to get away from everything for a day or two at her home.

When they returned to Boulogne, everything had changed. Viets fired Wolffe, and despite the fact that just a few days before Trudy's attempt Viets had indicated that whether Trudy was successful or not, she would make only one attempt to swim the Channel, those plans had now changed. Viets had been in contact with the WSA. It had authorized her not only to fire Wolffe, but to hire Bill Burgess to oversee Trudy's training in anticipation of a second attempt if conditions allowed. But Viets still prevented Trudy from speaking to the press.

Over the past two days, with time to reflect on what had happened, Viets and Trudy had reached a disturbing conclusion. They thought she had been poisoned, that Wolffe—or someone—had poisoned the beef tea she had consumed either before or during her swim. All Trudy knew was that she had felt fine before drinking the tea, and then became increasingly queasy and lethargic until she had nearly passed out in the water. She barely remembered her final moments in the Channel, and her memories of the swim were hazy.

Viets concurred. Things seemed to be adding up. Wolffe had already made it clear that he didn't think Trudy would succeed and had plenty of reasons to want her to fail. He alone had been in charge of the logistics of her swim—including providing her nourishment that day—and when he had given Trudy her first bottle of beef tea and she had dropped it, he had become angry all out of proportion. Early in her swim Trudy had commented that the beef tea had unsettled her stomach, saying she could still taste it, and as her swim had continued, Trudy had slowly become increasingly unresponsive. Her collapse after boarding the tug and her near-eighteen-hour nap afterward were both completely out of character. Her symptoms—lethargy, nausea, and confusion—can also be symptomatic of drugs such as opiates and barbiturates, and within twenty-four hours she was fine, enough time for such drugs to pass through her system. Whatever her problem was that day, the WSA decided that Trudy deserved another chance away from the odious influence of Wolffe. But it was sensitive to public perception and said nothing about its suspicions. Trudy was not to speak of it.

As Trudy recuperated, she soon learned that Bill Burgess was not Jabez Wolffe, either in form or content. When they voiced their suspicions about the poison to Burgess, he didn't dismiss them out of hand but allowed that it was possible, immediately gaining the trust of both Viets and Trudy.

The more time she spent in his company, the more Trudy liked Burgess. The Channel almost seemed to haunt Wolffe, but in contrast, Burgess seemed to celebrate the body of water, not as an adversary but as a demanding and worthy partner in a quest for greatness. Sometimes he'd gaze out across the water and claim he could see "the twinkle in a young girl's eye on the streets of Dover," and he liked to joke that since he had swum the Channel, "I've been trying to get back to England ever since," a reference to his French wife and home in Paris, something that still caused the British press to sometimes eye him with suspicion. The personality of the two men could not have been more different. There was an impish light in Burgess's eyes, and he expressed a joie de vivre that was entirely lacking in Wolffe, who exuded suspicion and arrogance. Burgess laughed and smiled easily, was far more supportive of his swimmers than Wolffe, and shied away from the spotlight. And where Wolffe looked at the Channel and saw only struggle and failure, Burgess saw triumph and success—he even had a small house on Cape Gris-Nez that overlooked the Channel, as if to watch over his achievement.

Not that he didn't have his own notions about swimming the Channel—he did—but he was flexible and did not assert his views like a dictator. Instead, he managed to involve his swimmers in the process, guiding them along in the months and weeks before a swim in the same tough yet gentle manner he did when they were in the water, teaching them about the Channel rather than ordering them about. In short, Wolffe acted as if he were the general and the swimmer simply a lowly private; Burgess and his swimmers were partners in the same quest. Even better, he wasn't bothered in the least or threatened by women, women swimmers, or the American crawl. As the second person ever to swim the Channel, his place in history was secure. The success of Trudy—or that of any other swimmer he trained—only enhanced his stature, and under any circumstances he was particularly delighted to snag a client away from Wolffe, particularly one as famous and well funded as Trudy.

After a few days Trudy resumed training with Burgess and waited for another break in the weather, but the wind she had encountered during her first attempt marked a shift in the weather pattern. Time after time over the next few weeks Trudy and Burgess tentatively scheduled an attempt only to be thwarted by the weather. In the meantime other swimmers who made the mistake of entering the rough seas were just as roughly tossed out—an Englishwoman, Mercedes Gleitze, lasted only five hours in the water, while Masanori Nakamuri of Japan lasted barely three. In the first week of September both Jeanne Sion and Lillian Harrison announced they'd make no further attempts in 1925, leaving Trudy and Ishaq Helmi as the only swimmers still scanning Channel waters for a break in the weather.

It was not to be. Despite the fact that Trudy got along much, much better with Burgess, calling him "a grand old man and a channel genius," and pronouncing herself in the best shape of her life, the weather refused to cooperate. A cold front moved through the Channel in the first week of September and, as one paper reported, left conditions "positively Arctic," as the temperature of the water dropped to below sixty degrees and the wind continued to blow. On September 10, Ederle reluctantly made the decision to abandon her attempt to swim the Channel that year. On September 12, she and Elsie Viets boarded the cruise ship *Mauretania* in Cherbourg to return to New York.

Yet Trudy had, in some ways, still managed to come out on top. The passenger list published in the New York newspapers pending the arrival of the *Mauretania* made special mention of Trudy's presence on the ship, an honor generally reserved for politicians, motion picture stars, and members of high society, perhaps the first sign that Trudy was becoming better known as a celebrity, a person known principally for her fame, than for her actual achievements as an athlete. Coverage of her attempt to cross the Channel had become something of a regular feature in New York newspapers. Even in failure she had become better known than ever before.

Purely by accident she was the beneficiary of evolving technology that was impacting American journalism. After World War I, advances in wireless communication made it possible to send news around the world. Guglielmo Marconi had perfected wireless telegraphy more than two decades earlier, and since then it had become easier and easier to transmit information almost instantaneously. News was not just what happened anymore, but what had *just* happened, a far more dynamic source of information.

That had been made clear only a few months before. On January 30, 1925, a man named Floyd Collins became trapped in a Kentucky cavern. Over the next two weeks newspapers and radio, which was rapidly becoming a staple in American homes, reported on efforts to free Collins from the cave. Day by day, as rescuers tried to dig a tunnel to reach the man, the public's appetite for the story grew exponentially, and it was possible to transmit bulletins to the entire nation around the clock. By the time Collins was finally located, on Febru--

ary 17, he was dead, but for more than two weeks his story dominated every news report.

The tragedy taught newspaper editors and radio reporters a valuable lesson—such "serialized" news stories that took place over days were wildly popular with the general public. The coverage of Trudy Ederle's attempt to swim the Channel in 1925, reported in newspaper stories around the country and in countless updates on the radio, tapped into the same phenomenon—the already sports mad public had a bottomless appetite for the news, and swimming the Channel was inherently far more dramatic than a pennant race or boxing match. As one reporter noted in verse, "But here is the point I would like to stress / She furnished some news for the press—/ And we, at some distance away / Have something to read every day." Once the public got hooked on a story, it couldn't get enough.

Yet at the same time, Trudy's failure gave new ammunition to those who still believed not only that swimming the Channel was beyond the capacity of women, but that athletics was both inappropriate and even a waste of time for women. Before her failure, no less a figure than Will Rogers had favorably compared Trudy's attempt to swim the Channel to that of heavyweight boxer Jack Dempsey's quest for a boxing title, observing, "Nobody is paying her anything, nobody is guaranteeing her anything . . . that is what I call a Sport; a Sport worthy of the admiration of the entire world." Whereas "the most he [Dempsey] can fight anybody is fifteen rounds, three minutes to a round, with a minute's rest between . . . Can you imagine Gertrude Ederle being able to stop every three minutes sit down in a chair and have somebody massage her legs?" But upon Trudy's return, those who were against women's athletics again felt empowered; her failure gave them some new ammunition. One syndicated story that appeared nationwide was entitled "Science Warns the New Strong-Arm Beauty." The article cautioned that because of exercise, "the new Strong-Arm Beauty—the girl athlete of 1925" (clearly a reference to Trudy) "endangers her chances of motherhood," her natural physical symmetry, and her girlish approach to life. Even worse, such women could also result in an "emasculated race of men." Furthermore, the article argued that there was a "real likelihood of such women taking on masculine traits to the point where the feminine in their natures may be forced into abeyance." Upon Trudy's return to the United States, such criticism only increased.

Everything was fine until the *Mauretania* arrived in New York on September 18. On the dock waiting for Trudy were not only her family, but Charlotte Epstein and other members of the WSA. On the journey from England, as one paper noted, Trudy had been "held on the ship incommunicado," by Elsie Viets, who told reporters on board that Trudy would make no statement "until after certain matters have been cleared up." Passengers on the ship reported that Trudy told them that she blamed her trouble on the fact that her bathing cap and goggles had been too tight, clearly an excuse to deflect further questions

Afraid that Trudy might speak without thinking and escalate a controversy that, as yet, was still very much a secret, as soon as the ship reached the pier, WSA president Margaret Johnson, Charlotte Epstein, and Louis Handley boarded the vessel. They were fully aware of what had taken place overseas and, perhaps fearing that the WSA would be adversely affected if word of the possible poisoning got out, wanted to protect both Trudy and the organization from any unwanted scrutiny from the press. As Epstein later said, "I did not want any half-baked statements," and she spoke to Trudy and cautioned her to watch her tongue. From the perspective of the WSA, trading insults with Jabez Wolffe was pointless—what was done was done.

Yet over the next few days Charlotte Epstein and the WSA proved that while they were adept at teaching women to swim and at running large swimming events, they were as yet still amateurs when dealing with a controversy in the press. When Trudy disembarked from the ship, after first embracing her mother, she was greeted on the pier by hundreds of well-wishers and reporters who expected, even demanded, that she speak. At first, Viets stood in the way and would not allow Trudy to respond, but as the press began to grow restless and push closer, shoving cameras and notebooks in Trudy's face, Charlotte Epstein caved in and allowed Trudy to take a few questions.

When one reporter asked if she felt she could have gone on, Trudy answered that she felt she could but couldn't say for sure whether that would have meant success. When another asked, "What caused you to stop?" Trudy was far more blunt.

"Because Helmi touched me," she snapped, and when the reporter followed up by asking, "What made him do that?" Trudy bounced the ball back across the Channel, spitting out a two-word answer: "Ask Wolffe." Those two words soon sparked a cross-Atlantic argument that readers found nearly as engaging as Trudy's attempt to swim the Channel itself.

Trudy then went on to provide even more ammunition for the story, saying, "There was no truth to the story that I collapsed, Helmy [*sic*] was swimming with me and I was going strong when Wolffe suddenly called 'Grab her.' Of course as soon as I was touched I was disqualified. I don't know if I could have gone across but I could have gone further."

Handley and Epstein then stepped in and continued to answer questions as Trudy, who was beginning to tear up, was hustled away. Handley, speaking in the same calm manner in which he always did, said that he was appalled by much of what he had heard about Wolffe, in particular his demeanor toward Trudy, and asked rhetorically, "Just imagine him coming into her training quarters one day and exclaiming 'What do you know, Gertie, I saw a shark today?' Imagine the effect that would have on a young girl."

Epstein was even more direct, yet refused to be specific. "There have been many things," she said, "which should be investigated."

"The suspicion is indicated," added Handley, "that Miss Ederle was taken out of the water prematurely." The WSA then announced it planned to mount an investigation over the circumstances that led to her being touched and taken from the water and then issue a full report on the matter.

While Trudy was reunited with her family in the Highlands, word traveled fast across the Atlantic, and Wolffe fired back in full fury. For the next few days newspapers on both sides of the Atlantic printed charge and countercharge in banner headlines.

Wolffe lied, and had no problem doing so. He denied ever telling Helmi to touch her, "But as there was a risk of her being drowned, Helmi went to her aid."

He refuted everything Trudy said, saying, "Her statements are quite untrue," and explained that "I take it her story was meant to cover her non-compliance with my repeated efforts to get her to train." Then he repeated his previous statement that she had spent much of her time playing the ukulele, leading Trudy to fire back immediately from the Highlands, telling a reporter "That is all a lie. Of course I played my uke, but I played it only in the evenings after my training had been concluded. I did everything Wolffe told me to do."

Meanwhile, the WSA proceeded with its investigation, contacting Alec Rutherford, Burgess, Ishaq Helmi, and other observers, including some other reporters. By and large they tended to back Ederle's account, as did Elsie Viets, as they all stated that despite the rough seas and the obvious trouble the conditions were causing, Trudy never appeared to be unconscious, although she had rolled over on her back and expelled some seawater. They all found Wolffe's behavior toward her deplorable, although Burgess, trying to be diplomatic and stay out of any public controversy, added that he did believe Trudy was "in trouble" when rescued by Helmi. Significantly, he didn't bother to define precisely what he meant by "in trouble." He could have been referring to the fact that she was in the company of Wolffe.

The only real dissenting voice—apart from Jabez Wolffe—was that of Ishaq Helmi—sort of. Reached by reporters in Paris, he contradicted Wolffe, saying that the trainer had, in fact, ordered him to pull Trudy from the water, but he also said, "Miss Ederle was completely finished and unconscious when I gathered her in. She never objected to my touching her . . . I believe she was too far gone to know what was going on," but even then he admitted that after only a few moments she had recovered completely. No one ever brought up the fact that Trudy's growing deafness may well have played a role in the incident. After eight hours in the water, amid engine noise and the wind, she may not have been able to hear very well and might not have been as responsive as normal, particularly if she were under the influence of some kind of drug.

Helmi was in a tough spot. In mid-September he'd failed in his own attempt to swim the Channel and desperately wanted to try again in 1926. But his status in England was precarious. Just a few weeks earlier he'd been questioned by Scotland Yard in regard to his possible involvement in the escape of an Egyptian prince who had been incarcerated in London. He still wanted to swim the Channel and was hardly in a position to alienate Wolffe and or anger British authorities. Although they could not prevent him from beginning a swim in France, they could certainly prevent him from landing. In that light his statement seems couched in an attempt to play both sides, agreeing with elements of both Wolffe's and Trudy's account, as if trying not to completely alienate anyone, particularly the British.

The WSA released a statement on September 21 that backed Trudy to the hilt. It was doing so, stated the report, "in justice to Miss Ederle who has been placed in a false light before the American public by statements of her English trainer [Wolffe]." The statement went on to attack Wolffe at every opportunity, charging not only that he did have her pulled from the water prematurely, but that the tug he enlisted did not have a compass on board, which forced Trudy to swim a circuitous route much farther than necessary, that he tried to get her to abandon the crawl stroke in favor of the sidestroke, that he unnecessarily frightened her about sharks, undercut her confidence, due to his own reticence wouldn't allow her to train far offshore for long periods of time, and "gave her absolutely no encouragement and found fault with everything she did." As evidence, the WSA claimed to have written statements from Helmi and a number of newspaper reporters who had been on board the tug, who informed the WSA that before they had even left Boulogne, Wolffe had given them a statement to be released "after she failed in her attempt." But the report made no mention of any poisoning.

Later that evening the WSA hosted a welcome back gala for Trudy at the famous Hippodrome, a five-thousand-seat theater on Sixth Avenue. Beneath a banner that ran the length of the stage and read "Good Sportsmanship Is Greater Than Victory"—a statement that in the light of her experience in the Channel Trudy must have found bittersweet—the theater's eight-thousand-gallon glass water tank was raised to stage level on hydraulic pistons. Annette Kellerman, Aileen Riggin, and several other WSA stars all gave a swimming and diving exhibition in Trudy's honor. Afterward a number of VIPs for the WSA and the AAU took the stage. Trudy was asked to come up out of her seat in the front row and speak to the crowd, but she refused. She was tired of the scrutiny and was already wary about speaking in public, for as she grew older not only was her hearing deteriorating, particularly when she was in training, but she was increasingly aware that she sometimes spoke too loudly, and in large crowds she some-times misheard what was said. She didn't want to take the stage and then risk being asked a question she could not hear. A representative of the WSA then walked over to where she sat and surprised her with the gift of a diamond bracelet in honor of her achievement. Trudy clearly had the WSA's full support. Speaking from the stage, even the president of the AAU, Murray Hulbert, said that while Trudy had been warned of sharks in the water, no one warned her of "a Wolffe."

That should have been the end of the controversy—and almost was—but Trudy wasn't quite finished. In a radio interview on WOR a day later she threatened that if the WSA didn't make public the "many suspicions and even facts" that she had against Wolffe, "I will do it myself." There were already whispers that there was more to the story in the press, as Joe Williams, sports columnist for the *New York World Telegram* wrote, "Gertrude Ederle hints that a dastardly plot conceived in the fiendish noodle of an English trainer robbed her of victory in the English Channel." For his part, Jabez Wolffe had had it. Of Trudy's continuing insistence that he had told Helmi to pull her from the water, Wolffe said, "I shall treat the report with the contempt it deserves, and say nothing."

Trudy never followed through on her threat to go public with her concerns, and with good reason. Although most of the American public had sided with her during the spat with Wolffe, that wasn't true of everyone in the press. An editorial in the *New York Herald-Tribune* opined, "To us the controversy seems to be undignified and against not only the best interest of sports but pleasant relations be-tween two friendly peoples . . . Defeat is often a bitter pill but the true sportsman takes it without grimace." Reaction in England, predictably, was even harsher. Cecil Hadley, sports editor of British newspaper the *People*, called Trudy "a petulant miss" and, citing the tendency of American athletes to blame defeat on outside influences, asked, "When will Americans learn to lose?"

Even worse, however, was the reaction of some women to Tru-dy's plight. While many were sympathetic to her cause, they were troubled by her attitude. The journalist Dorothy Greene authored an influential monthly column in the *Washington Post* called "The Sportswoman," one of the first regular features on women's sports to appear in an American newspaper. In a scathing column that appeared at the end of September, she hit Trudy hard, writing, "Diana's dress has at last been soiled. The post-failure channel swim war which is being waged between Gertrude Ederle and Jabez Wolffe, with its mingled whining and mud slinging, is becoming just a bit wearisome . . . To those who entertained a belief that woman's sports would be immune to the petty quarrels and bad sportsmanship which has been known to mark men's contests, the whole altercation comes as a blow . . . She is not only a disappointment to those who had supported her but she is the first to mar the good reputation of women's sports." Although Greene accepted that Wolffe may well have been lacking as a coach, in the end she concluded that "the whole matter is not worth a fiftieth of the publicity which it has received, and we are tempted to agree that 'woman's place, though it may not be in the home, is certainly not in the English Channel.' "

21

Cape Gris-Nez

"WE SWIMMERS HAVE to keep in strict training," read the magazine advertisement. "When I first got started a veteran swimmer advised me that I could smoke *Lucky Strikes* without affecting my wind or throat. I tried them and found he was right. They're great! They have never affected my throat and they taste fine."

The testimonial was signed by Helen Wainwright, "Olympic Champion," and appeared next to a photograph of the smiling swimmer.

Apart from entertainers and a few other athletes such as tennis champ Helen Wills, the WSA swimming stars were the best-known women in America. Young, attractive, modern, and vivacious, they were trendsetters and role models for a generation of young women.

In the fall of 1925, under the direction of public relations pioneer Edward Bernays, Sigmund Freud's nephew, the American Tobacco Company decided to target women in an advertising campaign and looked to America's female swimming stars to pitch its product. An endorsement from a notable swimmer was better than one from an entertainer—due to the efforts of the WSA, the swimmers, unlike motion picture stars, were still considered wholesome. Who better to convince women to smoke than a paragon of health and virtue, a swimmer?

Although she didn't smoke, Helen Wainwright was made an offer she couldn't refuse. The American Tobacco Company contacted her and offered her a five-figure contract to endorse Lucky Strike cigarettes and appear on billboards and in magazine and newspaper advertisements.

Thus did Wainwright, completely by accident and for the second year in a row, provide a solution to the quandary facing Trudy Ederle.

Trudy felt wronged by her experience in 1925 and wanted to try to swim the Channel again in 1926. Besides, after spending the past two years preparing first for the Olympics and then the English Channel, training to compete in races against schoolgirls didn't seem very exciting anymore, and Trudy had gained some fifteen pounds while overseas. Even if she wanted to, she was no longer in the proper shape to swim competitively at shorter distances. While she had been overseas another group of WSA swimming stars had taken over and were setting records nearly every time they entered the pool. Trudy had little left to prove competing for the WSA. From her perspective it made much more sense to use what she had learned about the Channel in 1925 and take aim on swimming the Channel in 1926.

Wainwright had come to a similar conclusion. Through no fault of her own, Trudy had received a chance that had first been offered to Wainwright. Now Helen Wainwright also wanted to take crack at the Channel.

That put the WSA in an awkward spot. In the end, Trudy's effort had cost the organization nine thousand dollars, an enormous sum of money, and more than the group had originally budgeted for the journey. While some in the organization felt that Trudy deserved another chance, the disagreement with Wolffe had soured some other members on financing another Channel quest at all, while still others thought it was only right that the organization send Wainwright, who was nearly as accomplished as Trudy.

Both women made their desire clear to the WSA, but while Trudy and Wainwright waited for the WSA to make a decision, the American Tobacco Company came to the rescue. English Channel or not, Helen Wainwright could not afford to refuse. She accepted its offer, thus becoming a professional and relieving the WSA of any responsibility for financing any attempt she might make to swim the Channel. If Wainwright ever did decide to swim the Channel, she would now have to do so on her own. And if she did, the contract with the American Tobacco Company provided her with the means.

Wainwright's decision to turn pro also pointed the way for Trudy. Thelda Bleibtrey had been the first WSA star to parlay her career into a professional engagement when she took a job as a swimming coach and agreed to take a screen test. But Trudy was already much more famous than Bleibtrey had ever been, and women's swimming was now much more established as a bona fide sport. As the Wainwright endorsement proved, there were now opportunities available to Trudy that just a few years before had been unthinkable.

Ederle was soon approached by the Deauville Casino and Hotel in Miami, Florida. The Miami area was booming, and beach resorts and casinos were all the rage. The new hotel, an enormous three-story structure on the beach that featured two large spires and an interior courtyard and pool, wanted to hire Trudy, Aileen Riggin, and several other WSA stars to give lessons, entertain guests with swimming and diving exhibitions, and generally be seen in swimwear around the pool. The money was good and the Florida sunshine tempting. Besides, it was becoming ever more apparent that the WSA was less than enthusiastic over sending Trudy back to the English Channel, and the casino led Trudy to believe that it just might decide to finance her trip in exchange for the publicity.

That was the clincher. Now there was absolutely no reason to remain an amateur. In November, Riggin, Trudy, and two other swimmers, Eleanor Coleman and Alma Wycoff, all signed contracts to spend the winter in Deauville, a decision that cost both Trudy and Riggin their amateur status. Wainwright took a similar position in Tampa.

On January 1, 1926, Trudy Ederle's contract went into effect, and she became a professional. The WSA, although disappointed to lose Riggin, Ederle, and Wainwright in such close proximity, was also a bit relieved not to have to choose who to support in another venture across the Channel. Both swimmers were made honorary members of the organization for life.

Trudy was now a professional, living on her own for the first time, although she had her old friend Aileen Riggin for support. Over the next few months she enjoyed her stay at Deauville, which gave her plenty of time to swim and required little else. Whenever possible she abandoned the hotel pool for the ocean and even found time to compete in the annual Miami River swim, a seven-mile race that she won in two hours and three minutes, boosting her self-confidence and proving she was still a swimmer of considerable talent. Like Wainwright, she also was approached by advertisers and agreed to lend her name and image to tout the new Reo Roadster, so named from the initials of Ransom E. Olds, president of Oldsmobile. In the ad Trudy stood on the running board in—what else?—a bathing suit, and the copy stated that when Trudy returned to America and went home to the Highlands after trying to swim the Channel, "she didn't walk to the scene of her first plunge . . . She rode in a Reo Roadster, proving that her judgment, so keen in matters of the tides, waves and winds, is just as much alert when she is selecting her motor cars." She didn't earn nearly as much as Wainwright did for her tobacco ad, but for Trudy, who loved cars, it was easy money.

In March she told reporters that she was training for another attempt at the Channel. As yet, however, she didn't quite know just how she was going to do that. Too many casinos and resorts had opened at nearly the same time. Crowds were smaller than anticipated that winter, and the swimmers hadn't proven to be quite as big a draw as the casino hoped, so it was now reneging on its promise to finance Trudy's swim. She'd have to find another way, and even if she could, without the support of the WSA, getting to Europe and making the many arrangements needed for the swim would be an enormous undertaking. Yet there was no time to wait, for it was becoming clear that if she were to attempt the Channel again, it would have to be in the summer of 1926. Although Helen Wainwright had decided to forgo the Channel, at least for the time being, inspired by Trudy's attempt of the previous year there were already upward of a dozen other female swimmers from America and elsewhere who had announced their intention to take a crack at the Channel, increasing the chances that one might be successful and making it imperative that Trudy get in the water as soon as possible.

This time Trudy would get to make the decisions—there would be no chance of ingesting any poison—if she ever got there. She wanted both her father and Meg to accompany her, and even though Meg had recently become Mrs. Margaret Deuschle, she had already agreed to go along. Furthermore Trudy wanted to train not in Dover, but in France, at Cape Gris-Nez, under the tutelage of Burgess. Since accommodations in Gris-Nez were limited and Burgess's services were in demand, if she were to swim the Channel in 1926 she needed to find a way to do so—and fast.

A swimmer from Baltimore provided some inspiration. Lillian

Day, a professional lifeguard who also gave swimming and diving exhibitions and made occasional appearances in a vaudeville swim show under her maiden name, Lillian Cannon, had recently gained some local fame by swimming across Chesapeake Bay. The local newspaper, the *Baltimore Post*, had taken note of the way Trudy's story had dominated the newspapers the previous summer, and the Scripps-Howard syndicate, of which the *Post* was a part, signed Cannon to a contract. In exchange for exclusive rights to her story the syndicate agreed to provide financial support for her attempt to swim the Channel. It mattered little that the chances of Cannon succeeding were slim. She used a combination of the sidestroke and the breaststroke, and despite her swim across Chesapeake Bay, she was hardly in Trudy's class as a swimmer. But the mere fact that she was going to try guaranteed several months of breathless copy. The *Post* and other papers in the chain hoped that Lillian Cannon would prove to be their Floyd Collins.

The Scripps-Howard syndicate wasn't the only news operation that wanted to create its own Collins-like story, albeit one with a happier ending. In only a few short years since its founding in 1919 by Joseph Medill Patterson, the New York tabloid the *Daily News* had become one of the biggest newspapers in the country, selling nearly one million copies per day. Patterson, whose grandfather had served as both the editor of the *Chicago Tribune* and mayor of the city of Chicago, had previously operated the *Tribune*, and his family still retained a stake in the paper. An innovative publisher, Patterson brought the tabloid format to America from England, where subway commuters found the garish headlines and oversized pictures—many of attractive women—perfect for browsing on their way to work.

Patterson, who had been an avowed socialist as a young man, was possessed of a pronounced populist streak. He saw the value of a serialized story that appealed to the workingman. He could not have helped but notice the press attention Trudy's Channel effort had attracted in 1925. Her story was perfect for his paper—she was Floyd Collins in a swimsuit.

At about the same time, dismayed by the casino's broken promise, Trudy and her father engaged the services of an attorney, Dudley Field Malone. She and her father had signed the original professional contract with the Deauville Casino without fully examining the terms. Trudy had since learned that the contract also bound her to an agent who had no plans to do anything for her except take the bulk of her income. Enter Malone, who had been born in the same Upper West Side neighborhood as Trudy and was married to the suffragette Dorothy Stevens. He may well have been put in touch with the Ederles either through Henry Ederle's political connections on the West Side or through Charlotte Epstein, who herself was well known in suffragette circles.

Malone was one of a kind, a hard-drinking yet pleasant and glib raconteur, the kind of man who appeared to lead several lives, each one more remarkable than the last. Malone's first wife was the daughter of Senator James O'Gorman, and Malone became a protégé of Woodrow Wilson, parlaying his connections first into a role in Wilson's administration and then as collector of the Port of New York. In 1921, when he and his first wife decided to part, Malone traveled to Paris and managed to secure a divorce, something almost unheard of for two Catholics, and an act that brought him more business than he could imagine. For the remainder of the decade Malone was the world's "greatest international divorce lawyer." But while he was freeing couples from the bonds of matrimony he still found time to take on a host of liberal causes. He defended suffragettes—which is how he met his second wife—fought Tammany Hall and Prohibition, and in 1925 assisted Clarence Darrow in the famous Scopes "monkey" trial over the teaching of evolution. Later in his life he placed the name of Franklin Delano Roosevelt before the delegates at the 1932 Democratic convention, and after World War II, due to his resemblance to Winston Churchill, he became an actor, playing Churchill in several films, and served as counsel for Twentieth Century Fox.

Yet even in the context of Malone's full life, his involvement with the affairs of Trudy Ederle would eventually come to represent a rare failure, although at first he seemed to work magic. In 1925 a theater manager named C. C. Pyle took over the affairs of University of Illinois football star Red Grange and made a killing in endorsements and other financial opportunities. Malone took note and fancied himself as another Pyle, viewing Trudy as the female equivalent of Grange.

Malone traveled all the way to Miami to meet with Trudy and used his legal magic to extricate her from her disadvantageous contract.

Malone then started trying to peddle Trudy's story. In the spring of 1926, probably inspired by Cannon's arrangement with Scripps-Howard, several New York papers were grappling for the attention of Henry Ederle, all of them trying to secure the exclusive rights to the story of Trudy's attempt to swim the Channel in 1926, if she made such an attempt. Malone stepped in and made sure of that. He handled all the negotiations, getting Trudy a contract variously reported as either $5,000 or $7,500 from Joseph Medill Patterson and the *Tribune-News* syndicate, plus a bonus if she succeeded. Malone not only sealed the deal, but became Trudy's agent himself and advanced her five thousand dollars to help underwrite the cost of swimming the Channel, money he expected to earn back from his percentage of her earnings. Problem solved. Trudy was fond of Malone, at least at first, and understandably thrilled. She called him "Uncle Dudley."

Soon after Trudy returned to New York in April she and her father began to make arrangements for her to make another attempt to swim the Channel. They contacted Bill Burgess and hired him to serve as Trudy's trainer in 1926 for a sum reported to be ten thousands francs, a significant amount of money in postwar France but the equivalent of only 250 American dollars. They also made reservations to take the *Berengaria* to Cherbourg and planned to set sail on June 2. In the meantime Trudy continued to more than earn her keep, appearing in a popular water show at the Hippodrome, where she shared the billing with Aileen Riggin and Helen Wainwright.

The only loose end that needed to be tied up was for the *Tribune-News* syndicate to select a journalist to accompany Trudy on her journey to ghostwrite Trudy's dispatches. Joseph Medill Patterson wisely chose a woman: vivacious, twenty-nine-year-old Julia Harpman. A native of Memphis, Tennessee, Harpman had been a reporter with the *Commercial Appeal* in Knoxville before Patterson recruited her in 1919 to write for the *Daily News*. She was put on the crime beat, where her hard-boiled accounts often appeared under the nom de plume "The Investigator." The most notable crime she covered was the infamous murder of Joseph Elwell, a bridge champion and spy whose body was discovered in a room locked from the inside and whose murderer was never identified. The case inspired S. S. Van Dyne's mystery novel *The Benson Murder Case*, the first in a series featuring the character Philo Vance. But Elwell's murder was notable to Harpman for another reason. While sitting on Elwell's front stoop, working the story, she met fellow journalist Westbrook Pegler.

Pegler, who at the time was writing for the *Chicago Tribune* and just beginning to gain a national reputation, later aptly dubbed the 1920s the "Era of Wonderful Nonsense." Although he appreciated athletes such as Trudy, he looked disdainfully at stunts like flagpole sitting and dance marathons and couldn't understand their attraction. His acerbic, somewhat jaundiced, world-weary view would one day make him one of the most famous American journalists of his era. A muckraking columnist who won the Pulitzer Prize in 1941 for an exposé of racketeering in Hollywood labor unions—the first columnist ever to win the award—Pegler finished third in reader nominations as *Time*'s 1941 Man of the Year, behind President Roosevelt and Joseph Stalin. After World War II Pegler grew increasingly vindictive, and, particularly after Julia's death from heart disease in 1955, he became consumed by his own vitriol and personal prejudices. In his later years Pegler, who had been an early critic of Hitler and Mussolini, became an anti-Semite who eventually ended his career writing for *American Opinion*, an organ of the uberconservative John Birch Society. Yet when he met Harpman (who, ironically enough, was Jewish) during the Elwell investigation he had not yet become the jaded and embittered journalist of his later years—it was love at first sight and the two married in 1922. Pegler was a *Tribune* sports columnist at the time and was soon named the paper's East Coast sports editor.

Harpman may not have quite been Pegler's equal as a journalist, but in an era in which few women earned bylines in the daily press, Harpman was one of the best, a dogged reporter who knew how to tell a story and turn a phrase—her review of the Louise Brooks film *American Venus* included the memorable line, "has small plot—also few clothes." By 1926, Hartman, not unlike the Rosalind Russell character in the classic newsroom comedy *His Girl Friday* whom she vaguely resembled, was ready to put her writing career on hold for her husband. When Patterson asked her to accompany Trudy and ghostwrite her accounts of the swim, she agreed only because of the understanding that it would be her final journalism assignment—and that Pegler could accompany her on the trip. Although he wasn't assigned to cover Ederle's Channel attempt per se, Pegler was still a journalist, and he knew a good story when he encountered one. His periodic dispatches from Cape Gris-Nez would prove to be revealing.

For Trudy, everything was now in place. While her second assault of the English Channel would cost more than her compensation from the syndicate, if need be Henry Ederle could afford to make up the difference. Besides, in the previous year Trudy's eyes—and, more acutely, her father's—had been opened to the potential financial windfall that being the first woman to cross the English Channel could deliver. If Helen Wainwright, a mere Olympian, could earn five figures endorsing cigarettes, what would the first woman to swim the English Channel be worth?

The Ederles were not alone in making that kind of calculation. Joseph Corthes, described as the "magnate who cornered the sea-going tugs of Boulogne" and the "czar of Channel swimming" told a reporter, "I look for the busiest season in history." He was right, for a record number of swimmers of both sexes were making plans to spend the summer in the Channel, and in the case of the women, they were not doing so for their health. On the opposite shore they expected to find the proverbial pot of gold. In addition to Trudy and Lillian Cannon, Jeanne Sion and Lillian Harrison were likely to take on the Channel once more and were expected to be joined by Clarabelle Barrett of the United States, who had originally competed as a member of the WSA, Eva Morrison of Nova Scotia and Boston, Mille Gade Corson, Suzanne Wurtz of France, Mercedes Gleitze of England, and a host of lesser-known swimmers of little credibility.

Things were just as busy in the men's camp. Helmi was planning to return, and he was likely to be joined by several American men—Norman Ross of Detroit and Dick Howell of Northwestern University—Omer Perrault of Canada, Georges Michel and Georges Polley of France, and Colonel Freyburg. As summer wore on others were certain to enter the surf. Corthes, who had witnessed Trudy's attempt in 1925, gave her best chance of the bunch and said, "Followers of the sport expect to see Miss Ederle cross successfully this summer . . . She knows something about the coldness of the water and the treachery of the tides."

If Trudy was looking for a portent for her second attempt to swim the English Channel, as she made her way to the pier with her father and sister to board the *Berengaria* en route to Cherbourg, the sun shone bright and warm and the waters of the Hudson River were a dazzling blue. Before the boat even left the dock Trudy already felt better and far more confident than she had one year before.

This time, she would be in control, staying where she wanted, training with Burgess, and with her father and sister Meg, whom Trudy referred to as her "rock" and "inspiration," for support and company. As Trudy posed for pictures on the deck of the ship, receiving a kiss goodbye from friends like Aileen Riggin and from her mother, she absolutely glowed, resplendent in her serge suit, clutching a bouquet of flowers, a smart cloche hat perched on her head, and a rare extravagance, a fox stole wrapped around her neck.

The ship left the dock at 11:00 A.M. and steamed out of New York Harbor under near-perfect conditions. Even the trip aboard the *Berengaria* was an improvement on Trudy's journey a year before. Her name led the passenger manifest published in the New York papers, ahead of such luminaries as Mrs. Zane Grey, wife of the author and adventurer, Prince and Princess Basil Mirski of Russia, and Vicometress deJonghe of Belgium. As soon as the *Berengaria* left the dock the crew of the British-based liner distributed champagne, something not widely available in the United States during Prohibition, lending a festive air to the journey. Although Trudy did not drink she was treated as a celebrity as she and her father and sister received the best of everything from the boat's crew.

There were no demands on Trudy's time during the six-day journey to France. She did her best to stay in shape, walking the deck, knocking golf balls into the North Atlantic, swimming in the ship's pool, even giving swimming demonstrations and posing for pictures boxing with the ship's athletic director. She spent much of her time with Meg and with Harpman, getting to know her ghostwriter.

Harpman liked her young subject. She found Trudy full of personality, even if she was a bit shy at the outset and it took a bit of effort to become accustomed to talking with her. Like others who spent much time in Trudy's company, from the volume of her voice Harpman couldn't help but notice that Trudy's hearing was deteriorating, but in every other way she was a typical young woman of the era. Although Trudy was no flapper, she used the latest slang, was fashion conscious to a fault, and together with her sister Meg practiced all the latest dances. She could be a bit moody, and her moods often depended on her superstitions, which were many. Trudy disliked the number thirteen and much preferred the color red. Most of her bathing caps and hats and dresses were, in fact, red, and her father promised her a red roadster if she successfully crossed the Channel, a prize she chattered about constantly. She believed it was good fortune to see the new moon over the right shoulder and that after one spilled salt it had to be thrown over the left shoulder or else it was certain to cause a quarrel.

Good luck was indicated by broken glassware and rain, as Trudy accurately told Harpman, "Whenever I entered a swimming competition on a rainy day, I won." But as Harpman got to know Trudy even better, another characteristic stood out.

Trudy, wrote Harpman later, "seems to withdraw herself from the world and drift into some personal sphere," particularly when she was in the water, swimming. Harpman assumed that it was because of her deafness, but as Harpman spent more time in Trudy's company she found it astounding that Trudy could swim for hours without ever stopping, not saying a word, apparently oblivious to everything else.

Harpman was an acute observer. Trudy did, in fact, "withdraw from the world" in the water, but it was not so much an escape from the world as a journey to another place. In the water, Trudy truly felt completely at peace. As she herself later said, when swimming she always felt that she could go "on and on . . . when we're in the water, we're not in this world." In a sense, she had developed a real relationship with the water, once saying about swimming in the open ocean, "To me, the sea is like a person—like a child that I've known a long time. It sounds crazy, I know, but when I swim in the sea I talk to it. I never feel alone when I'm out there."

Together, Trudy and Harpman produced the first few of what would eventually be several dozen dispatches recounting her quest to swim the Channel. They hardly qualified as literature—the WSA had taught Trudy well and she generally measured her words. Trudy was not drawn to hyperbole and rarely spoke in terms that were anything but modest—even if she had, Harpman knew her job was to present Trudy to the her readers as a subject worthy of their interest and sympathy. As Trudy "wrote" in one early dispatch, "I am determined to swim the Channel. I want to do so more than anything in the world. I hope I will swim across this time and I feel that I am going to do it." Still, Harpman occasionally managed to write some more lively copy. In one ghostwritten dispatch Trudy wrote, "Every day is Christmas afloat," and went on to describe in copious detail her diet aboard the vessel, which consisted of eating as many as five meals a day. She weighed 149 pounds upon her departure and intended to gain at least an additional ten pounds to protect her from the cold water, writing, "Some trainers probably would have hysterics seeing the amount of food I consume . . . Most girls fear gaining an ounce worse than they do a mouse; but I'm not worrying about my figure."

The ship reached Cherbourg on June 8, and the Channel welcomed Trudy as if reminding her she wasn't in the Highlands anymore. The sea was choppy and rough and the sky hung low, the color of a mollusk. It wasn't chilly—it was cold, and Trudy and her entourage immediately boarded a train to Paris, where they stayed for a day before taking another train to Cape Gris-Nez.

Unlike her previous attempt, this time Trudy would spend all her time in France, at Gris-Nez. Her father had booked several rooms in the rustic, almost primitive Hotel du Phare—the Hotel of the Lighthouse—under the shadow of Cape Gris-Nez.

The headland—Cape Gray Nose—topped by a lighthouse built in 1837, dominated the landscape, and the name belied the Channel itself, for on dank gray days the headland, indeed, vaguely resembled a gray nose sitting just above the waterline sniffing the salt air. Although today the area is primarily a tourist destination due to its raw natural beauty, when Trudy first visited Cape Gris-Nez it was known more for its desolation and poverty. The cape and the small village tucked in its shadow to the east barely drew enough visitors to keep the two hotels in business, and peasants who lived in the few dozen homes scattered along the main road up from the beach eked out a meager existence, primarily from farming. Residents regularly scavenged the cape itself for goods that washed ashore from shipwrecks, and abandoned gun batteries dating from the Great War dotted the headlands. A generation before it was not unknown for the local peasants to be seen gathering seaweed, which they used as fertilizer during times of plenty and sometimes consumed during tougher times. Although nearby towns and villages along the shore supported a vibrant commercial fishery, only a few fishermen were based in and around Cape Gris-Nez itself. The waters were rough, and the rock-strewn shores of the cape lacked a safe harbor suitable for large vessels.

Still, the area's rough beauty held a certain exotic charm. Julia Harpman was absolutely captivated, waxing rhapsodic over the "cluster of stone houses, all neatly whitewashed," some with thatched roofs, and the "gardens which are dark with undergrowth and dotted with beds of beautiful flowers."

Accommodations at the hotel, which was situated almost a mile from the beach on the road that ran to the sea from the village, were Spartan at best. The three-story stone and stucco building didn't have electricity, but Trudy was pleased to note in her initial dispatch from Cape Gris-Nez that Monsieur Blondeau, the proprietor, "had acquired modern ideas since last year. The Hotel now has a wash basin and plumbing in each room and a community bath tub," all improvements designed to accommodate the growing number of Channel aspirants coming to Gris-Nez each summer. Unfortunately, these items, as yet, were for show only—none of the plumbing was connected to a water source.

Under Burgess's direction, Trudy began training on June 11 with a brief swim to reacquaint herself with Channel waters. But all was not well between Trudy and her trainer.

Even before leaving New York, Trudy had heard that Burgess was training another swimmer, Lillian Cannon. Cannon had told her as much when Trudy, as a courtesy, saw her off when she had left New York for France in mid-May. That nugget of information left Trudy "greatly surprised," and over the next few weeks press reports had confirmed that it was true.

Immediately upon arriving in Cape Gris-Nez, Trudy and her father confronted Burgess. He was not only under contract for ten thousand francs, but months before he had been sent a retainer to train Trudy and Trudy alone.

Burgess reacted sheepishly. When he had signed the contract to train Trudy he had not foreseen that the summer of 1926 would be the busiest Channel season yet, and with all the questions surrounding Wolffe after Trudy's swim, other swimmers were steering clear of the Scotsman, making Burgess everyone's first choice. When Lillian

Cannon, flush with cash from her newspaper deal, had contacted him, he had been unable to resist either her charms or her checkbook. Reluctantly, he admitted to the Ederles that he had also agreed to train Cannon, and tried to convince them there was little harm in that.

But the Ederles had a contract, and now they held Burgess to his agreement and told him he would have to drop Cannon. It made sense, for as Trudy explained, "Suppose one man handles two women . . . one is a slow swimmer and the other a sprinter. Obviously it would be impossible for this trainer to accompany both in the water." In this instance, Trudy was the sprinter, as Cannon, like virtually every other woman apart from Ederle who was planning on swimming the Channel, still depended upon the breaststroke and occasionally the sidestroke. In addition, were he to train both women, which of the two would receive priority when it came to actually swimming the Channel? There was simply no practical way for Burgess to train them both. Besides, after the trouble with Wolffe the year before, Trudy wanted no trouble from her new trainer. She needed someone she could trust without the slightest hesitation, and if Burgess was training two swimmers, how could she ever know for sure if he was acting in her best interests? When Burgess complained about the loss of income after he dropped Cannon, the Ederles reportedly increased his salary to make up the difference.

Westbrook Pegler watched the proceedings with detached amusement, as the disagreement reminded him of the shenanigans that sometimes went on between boxers and their trainers. He noted that the real issue at stake was not so much Burgess's ability as a trainer as much as it was his knowledge of the Channel. According to Pegler, after the disagreement, "Trudy didn't trust Bill as far as she could see him through a stone wall on a dark night . . . She went along with him . . . only because she thought he had the best route." Pop Ederle shared her distrust and was far blunter about it. Each evening, many of the hotel's residents and the locals took their leave in the hotel's primitive bar, which featured an ancient beer pump that operated on the honor system. According to Pegler, Pop Ederle was a regular, as were both Joe Corthes and Burgess, and "Ederle is a pretty outspoken gentlemen who becomes more outspoken as the evening wears along." Whenever Corthes and Burgess spoke French with each other,

Ederle would burst from his chair, shouting, "We all speak English at this table. Burgess speaks English. Corthes speaks English. Then talk United States. We ain't a bunch of dummies."

Trudy's insistence on holding Burgess to his contract was the cause of a great deal of foot stomping in the Cannon camp. Lillian Cannon was now without a trainer. They'd had Cape Gris-Nez to themselves for nearly a month, but now that Trudy was in town she was getting all the attention—from the press and everyone else—leaving Cannon feeling like she'd been stood up at the altar.

Despite her newspaper deal, in reality Cannon had very little chance of swimming the Channel. Compared to Trudy, she simply wasn't that strong a swimmer. Pegler, who knew a thing or two about athletes, took one look at Cannon and immediately dismissed her chances of ever successfully swimming the Channel. He called her a "warm water swimmer" and described her as "short, like Trudie [sic] Ederle, but, unlike Trudie, she seems thin and insufficiently upholstered to stand the cold of the Channel water. Lillian's hands are feminine and experts who follow the Channel swims year after year hold that no person with delicate hands can ever swim across because after only a few hours in the water thin hands fold up into fists and can't be opened to make the strokes." Pegler was correct. A woman of Cannon's build and stature utilizing the breaststroke had virtually no chance of swimming the Channel—it simply took too long and the swimmer became too cold. Even Burgess seemed to sense that, as he had tried to convince Cannon to experiment with overarm strokes. Neither Cannon nor her ghostwriter, the Scripps-Howard newsman Minott Saunders, would admit it, but her effort was doomed before it even started. As a swimmer, Cannon was a fiction while Trudy, on the other hand, was the genuine article, a world-class athlete.

While some have argued that during the summer of 1926 there was a great competition between Ederle, Cannon, and several other female swimmers who were all trying to become the first woman to swim the Channel, that was far more the artificial hyperbole of a few newspaper reporters than fact. Among all the men and women trying to swim the Channel in the summer of 1926, Trudy Ederle's only real competition was history itself. The other female contenders at the Channel that year were not nearly as accomplished or talented, and as later events would demonstrate, their approach was far different and their chances of success far less likely. Only Trudy looked at the Channel and swam it like she was in a race, with the expectation she would finish. Everyone else just hoped to survive.

The dispute over Burgess created something of a chill between Cannon and Trudy, at least in Cannon's mind. A few days later, in a snit, she moved out of the Hotel du Phare, taking up residency in the small and even more primitive Hotel du Sirene directly on the beach.

Now that Trudy had Burgess to herself, she began training in earnest. Of all the swimmers on either side of the Strait of Dover planning a swim, Trudy was the clear favorite to succeed. Bookmakers were more than happy to take wagers on any of the swimmers, giving long odds for everyone but Trudy. A year before, she'd opened at 10 to 1 and the smart money pushed the odds down to 2 to 1 by the time she finally entered the water. This year betting on Trudy opened at 3.5 to 1, and after a flurry of bets against her pushed the odds up to 6 to 1, press reports indicated that bookmakers eventually expected Trudy to go off at even money. The smart money got their bets down early.

One man who did was Henry Ederle. No one seemed more aware of the financial impact a successful crossing would create—sometimes it was all he talked about. Before leaving New York he'd heard an erroneous report that the odds against Trudy were 50 to 1 and was prepared to bet $25,000, ensuring a payout of $1.25 million if Trudy succeeded. Although Henry was disappointed to learn that the odds were far less lucrative, he still bet the full amount on Trudy to succeed. Even though Henry Ederle was wealthy, the Ederles had always lived somewhat frugally, their only real extravagance the cottage in the Highlands. But Pop Ederle anticipated that that was about to change. He'd always been a big supporter of Trudy's swimming career, but as her fame and her earning potential increased, Pop Ederle focused more and more upon the money. Although he had been driving the same car for years, now that he had promised Trudy that red roadster if she swam the Channel, he was also thinking that "maybe we get a new sedan for Momma and me."

Trudy's actual training schedule hardly varied from that of the previous year, consisting of increasingly longer swims in Channel waters, with Burgess either swimming alongside, trying desperately to keep up, or, more often, following Trudy in a rowboat. Meg often joined Trudy in the water, helping the time pass as the girls chattered away like they were back in the Highlands.

Burgess, unlike Wolffe, knew his role and knew better than to try to get Trudy to abandon the crawl. In fact, before Trudy had left New York, Louis Handley, while seeing her off at the pier, told Trudy, "Do me one big favor. Don't change your stroke. Never once do the backstroke, or the sidestroke." Then, looking her directly in the eyes and measuring every word he added, "Maintain your straight American crawl. It is faster and better, no matter how long the swim." Trudy promised Handley she would, and made certain Burgess realized that point was absolutely nonnegotiable.

Burgess had targeted several time periods when the tides would be favorable to make an attempt, focusing on a few small windows of neap tides surrounding July 26, August 10, and August 21, but although the weather was delightful when Trudy first reached Cape Gris-Nez, conditions soon turned terrible. The sun stayed behind the clouds, and it was cold and damp—some days the temperature never even reached fifty degrees. Old-timers who knew the Channel well believed the weather would remain off all summer and doubted that anyone would make it across. Even Trudy, who rarely complained about the weather, groused, "It seems like November."

While waiting for a break in conditions she tried to keep occupied. Once again she spent her spare time golfing on the beach on what she termed the "national course," one she laid out at low tide on the odd afternoon when it wasn't raining, and Trudy even introduced her father to the game. When the weather allowed they sometimes held cookouts, but otherwise there was little to do on Cape Gris-Nez apart from playing one of two Victrolas at the hotel—Trudy had left one behind in 1925 and brought another with her in 1926. Since Victrolas didn't get seasick, this time she planned to leave the band onshore and swim to the accompaniment of a gramophone instead.

As June dragged on everyone was getting a bit bored, particularly the journalists at the hotel bar, who had little to do but look at the Channel every day. Sydney Williams of the *Paris Herald* tried to break the monotony. He resorted to writing profiles about a fictitious swimmer of his own invention, an Eskimo he dubbed Itchy Guk, who found the Channel waters too warm and was waiting for them to cool. Then Helmi arrived in mid-June for his annual run at the Channel and was welcomed warmly, even by Trudy—she didn't blame him for the trouble the previous summer. The big Egyptian livened things up at the hotel, for he drank the same way he swam—slowly and for a long time—and he liked to talk and joke. His nickname for Trudy was "the Kid," and he told her a friend of his had named a thoroughbred "the Kid" after her, but joked that it was the slowest horse in the stable.

Apart from his effect on Trudy's mood, Helmi gave Meg a break by providing Trudy with another training partner. Once the two ventured so far out into the Channel that, as a cruise ship approached, Helmi had to warn her not to get too close. He was afraid she'd be spotted, mistaken for some poor soul who had fallen overboard from another vessel, rescued, and then taken back to New York.

Trudy continued to train and prepare herself for the ordeal ahead. To that end she sent her sister to Paris with instructions to buy some silk. Trudy and Meg had been experimenting.

When she had tried to swim the Channel the previous year she noticed that the longer she stayed in the water the more her swimsuit had bothered her. The one-piece singlet had caused significant chafing around her arms and had lost its shape over the course of her swim. By the time she was in mid-Channel, the neckline of the suit was gaping open like the mouth of the basking shark, creating considerable drag on Trudy as she tried to pull herself through the water.

Although many male swimmers, and even some female aspirants, swam either nude or topless, Trudy was far too modest to try that approach. This year she had brought with her a suit made of silk, which helped with the chafing, but the scoop neck still slowed her down.

She and Meg took matters into their own hands and came up with their own design. The original suit featured a small skirt, which they removed, and, using the skirt and additional material Meg bought in Paris, they fashioned a two-piece suit, rich blue in color, consisting of a brassiere that opened and closed in the front, and a bottom, akin to a pair of tight-fitting briefs. The clasps on the brassiere would allow Trudy to make adjustments in the water in the event the material stretched and began to bother her.

The result worked beautifully—Trudy could stay in the water day after day for hours. The tight-fitting top caused comparatively little drag, and she didn't have to worry about chafing. Although they did not realize it at the time, the two sisters had created the world's first bikini some two decades before Louis Reard and Jacques Heim received credit for it. Unfortunately, neither Trudy nor her sister realized they had created not only something brand-new but something with such commercial potential. They never thought to trademark or patent the design and lost the opportunity to earn untold millions of dollars.

As June turned into July the weather remained unforgiving. With the baseball season in full swing and an upcoming bout between Jack Dempsey and Gene Tunney for the heavyweight championship of the world, Westbrook Pegler returned to the United States, leaving Harpman behind until Trudy either swam or failed to swim the Channel. Apart from a holiday party on July 4, Trudy was beginning to get a little stir-crazy as day after day passed with the same rough combination of rain, wind, and clouds. The residents of the Hotel du Phare, virtually all of whom were either waiting to swim the Channel, working with someone waiting to swim the Channel, or journalists covering the Channel swimmers, began to experience the Cape Gris-Nez equivalent of cabin fever. Virtually every conversation, no matter how innocuous, ended up being a conversation about either conditions in the Channel or the weather. Trudy wanted to leave Cape Gris-Nez to spend a few days in Paris herself, perhaps even to participate in a swim down the Seine, but was afraid that if she did she might either miss a brief period of fine weather or that in her absence Burgess just might return to Lillian Cannon. In the meantime, as she told Harpman, "I am fed up on the Channel swim talk. It seems as though everybody I meet insists on talking about no other subject. Especially am I weary of those who delight in telling how terrible the Channel is to swim.

"I think," she added, "about half the difficulty of swimming the Channel is caused by having to listen to so much discouraging talk before you get started. Then, when you're in the middle of the Channel, you are apt to think all of this that you have heard and you lose your nerve."

One of those people full of discouraging talk was Jabez Wolffe. He showed up in late June, looking for a swimmer to train. Despite the huge number of competitors in Cape Gris-Nez, word had traveled fast since the previous summer, and no one, not even Lillian Cannon, who was still without a trainer, wanted to sign on with Wolffe. He even took up residence in the Hotel du Phare and made regular appearances in the bar. Trudy and Wolffe had brokered a public and, from Trudy's side of things, ghostwritten peace accord, but the two still had little use for each other. Trudy remained wary of her former trainer, and Wolffe wanted nothing more than to coach another swimmer across the water and thereby beat Ederle to her goal. He thought he had been hired by Clarabelle Barrett, who was financing her quest on a shoestring through a series of one-hundred-dollar subscriptions from family friends, but Barrett had yet to show. While he waited he simply added to the poisonous atmosphere in the hotel.

It didn't help the mood that the first swimmers of the season all failed in excruciating fashion. Frank Perks of England, who had been training in Dover, made the first attempt of the season on July 14. A day or two before the weather had changed abruptly, and now the Channel was experiencing a heat wave. Perks left at nearly midnight, but fourteen and half hours later he was spit back out—the weather had turned stormy and he'd been caught by the tides. Mercedes Gleitze was the next to try—she lasted five hours before being pulled from the water, violently ill; then Helmi and then Perks tried again and failed, as did Colonel Freyburg and several other men. Their stories were monotonously similar. All experienced strong starts before encountering weather conditions that continued to deteriorate until the Channel finally rejected each swimmer outright, each going down like the local tough guy against the carnival kangaroo. In the Hotel du Phare, the word *impossible* began to be heard. Even if the warm temperatures held, the weather was so unsettled that good conditions rarely lasted for more than a few hours before the wind picked up, then rain and even lightning danced on the horizon. Hardly anyone in Cape Gris-Nez thought the Channel would be crossed in 1926 by anyone, much less a woman.

Trudy was getting increasingly impatient, and in a dispatch dated July 31 she wrote, "All you hear is talk of the weather, the wind and the tide. It has reached a stage now where I bring a book to the table and when I am not eating I sit with my fingers in my ears, impolitely burying myself. People here are channel crazy and it seems their pesky task and desire is to frighten swimmers."

Back in the United States, readers of the newspapers were beginning to wonder just when—or if—Trudy would finally enter the Channel waters. After all, she had been in France for nearly two months, and interest in dispatches that focused on what she was eating was beginning to wane.

With so many female swimmers vying to become the first to cross the Channel, there was a great deal of gamesmanship going on— Mille Gade Corson, like Barrett, was training in Dover yet was planning to begin her swim from Cape Gris-Nez. Away from everyone else, no one knew when she might appear. Each swimmer hoped to get the jump on the others, getting in the water first as soon as conditions were favorable, and no one was planning to announce in advance precisely when that would be.

The next big splash was made by the enormous Clarabelle Barrett. She'd been training on the cheap in Dover while Jabez Wolffe had been waiting in vain in France. On August 2, with little fanfare, she left without him, entering the waters of Shakespeare Beach and slowly lumbering through the water. Although Barrett had learned the American crawl as a member of the WSA and had taught swimming, she was not nearly as fast as Trudy and was in comparatively poor condition. If Barrett succeeded in crossing the Channel it would be because her great size and bulk—she was six feet tall and weighed more than two hundred pounds, with enormous thighs— allowed her to remain in the cold for hours, not because of her athletic prowess.

For more than twenty hours she plodded through the fogbound waters of the Channel as if she were in some dream, because for most of her journey she could see virtually nothing and depended on her escort boat to keep her on course. Finally, even though she was within two miles of Cape Gris-Nez, she left the water after twenty-one hours and forty-five minutes. She simply didn't swim quickly enough to cut through another tide change. For the final few hours she had been doing little more than swimming in place, caught in the world's largest endless pool.

Barrett failed, but she had made it to within two miles, near enough to break the logjam of swimmers onshore and for Ederle and Burgess to both worry and gain confidence. If nothing else, Barrett's swim indicated that the water had finally warmed to a point that a swimmer could stand it for an extended period of time. Her near success also made them anxious—no one thought she'd come so close—but if Barrett could come within two miles of success, Trudy, Burgess, and Trudy's father were all confident that Trudy would make it all the way across.

On August 5 the moon reached its last quarter, signaling the peak of a neap tide, when the tidal fluctuation was at its lowest point and the period of slack water at its greatest. Earlier Burgess had occasionally intimated that he might have Trudy make her swim when the moon was full or new, during a spring tide, because she was such a strong swimmer that the increased current would work to her advantage, but few observers believed him. Still, the gambit may have worked. As August 5 approached, no other swimmer seemed to be preparing to take on the Channel, choosing instead to wait another two weeks when the water would be a bit warmer.

There was just one problem. Ever since arriving at Cape Gris-Nez, Trudy had been struggling with her goggles. No matter what she did or how tightly she strapped them to her face, they still leaked, and Trudy found the Channel waters burned her eyes "like acid."

In 1925 her goggles, which featured two lenses, had given her all sorts of trouble and been more of an impediment than a help. So before she left New York in 1926 she went to an optical company on Fifth Avenue and gave them her own design for a set of goggles consisting of a single piece of glass that went over both eyes, giving her a single view of the water. Thinking in practical terms, Trudy thought that if she could avoid having the goggles around her nose she might prevent them from leaking.

The optical company fashioned the goggles to her standard using a single piece of amber-colored glass set in metal and leather with a strap holding them tight to her head, but it told her bluntly, "We cannot guarantee they'll be waterproof."

During her time at Cape Gris-Nez that disclaimer had been proven correct. The seal simply would not keep water out. Trudy and Meg experimented with all kinds of methods to try to seal the goggles, adding extra chamois to help them seal around her face, and paint along the edge of the metal frame, but every time they got the mask to seal to her face, it leaked around the lens. The goggles weren't much of an issue during training—she could stand the leaks and salt water for a few hours, but the longer she stayed in Cape Gris-Nez the more she worried about using her goggles during the swim itself, later saying, "I had a real mental block about swimming with leaky goggles." The last thing she needed while swimming the Channel was to repeatedly stop and empty water from her eyepiece.

On August 4 Burgess gave her the word. If the weather held he wanted her to make the swim on Friday, August 6. Training was over. Trudy had two days to prepare herself for the ordeal ahead.

That night in the hotel, as she sat with Meg and ate dinner under the flickering candlelight in the hotel's dining room, she again started to obsess over the condition of her goggles. Then her eyes focused on a candle at the dinner table. She watched a drop of hot wax slowly drip down the side of the candle, then stop as it cooled.

"Gee, Meg," she said, "maybe we should melt a candle on the inside of the goggles," and the two sisters discussed how that might work. The next morning Burgess sought Trudy out and made it official. "If the weather holds like this," he told her, "you're going tomorrow." There was no time to wait. Trudy and Meg scoured the hotel for some more candles, then went back to their room where they melted the candles down to wax and carefully applied it around the edges of the amber glass.

Trudy then went down to the water, put the goggles on and dove into the water, swimming up the coast then back. With each stroke of her arms she began to feel more confident, certain, and relaxed.

When she came out of the water she was overjoyed. "Meg," she called out to her sister, "Meg, I think we have them waterproof!" To the superstitious young woman, the goggles were a sign.

Trudy was ready, but in London the editorial writer of the *London Daily News* was still unimpressed with female athletes. He was in the midst of writing an editorial that would appear the next day. "Even the most uncompromising champion of the rights of women," he wrote, "must admit that in contests of physical skill, speed and endurance they must forever remain the weaker sex."

22

What For?

TRUDY SPENT THE DAY before the most important day of her life quietly, saving her strength, and staying in her room with Meg and Julia and away from the crowd at the hotel who discussed her chances of crossing the Channel as if she were a racehorse. Late in the afternoon, as a dim sun tried to burn through the low clouds and haze, she took a walk along the beach with Meg and her father. As the three made small talk and joked about the red roadster Trudy hoped would be waiting for her on the other side, Trudy turned to look at the sea, searching for England on the horizon.

She was ready. Back in her room at the hotel her bathing suit and goggles were already laid out for her. When they finished the walk, her father and Meg prepared to leave. They would spend the night in Boulogne and help prepare the escort tug, the *Alsace*, and then rise early and sail back to Cape Gris-Nez before sunrise. Burgess wanted Trudy to start her swim just before 7:00 A.M. She would wake at dawn.

As her father and sister prepared to board their car for Boulogne, Meg carrying the gramophone and Trudy's precious collection of records, Trudy had a few final words for her father. While Meg would return to shore the following morning, Trudy would not see Henry Ederle again until the next day, aboard the *Alsace*. "Remember," she said to her father after a quick embrace, "Don't let anyone take me out of the water."

Before she retired she poked her head into the hotel bar where Bill Burgess and some journalists and locals were all gathered, toasting the effort to come, and she bid everyone a quick goodnight. A few hours before, Burgess had received the latest weather report form the Meteorological Office in Bracknell, in the south of England. It was brief and to the point.

"For the 24 Hours commencing 1500 GMT Thurs. 5th August 1926," read the report, "light indefinite winds, fine, visibility mainly good, warmer." If the forecast held, the weather would be nearly perfect, the air temperature a few degrees warmer than the waters of the Channel, which varied from sixty-three or sixty-four degrees along the coast to sixty-one farther out, where the water was deeper. A bit of haze would keep the glare down, and the light, variable breeze would keep the seas calm.

No rain was in the forecast, a report that delighted Burgess but one that Trudy found a little wanting. As she had told Julia Harpman, she had never lost a race when it rained.

Before Trudy retired for the night, her ghostwriter sat with her a while. Trudy chattered away as Harpman let her talk and burn off the nervous energy as Trudy did her best to bolster her own self-confidence.

She was a true believer, in herself, in the concept of sportsmanship she'd learned from the WSA, and in the patriotism she had felt during the Olympics and after. She knew this swim was not just important to her, but to everyone—her father and mother, her country, her friends in the WSA, and women everywhere. It was as if she were just a vessel being pushed along in the current, carrying all those dreams to the opposite shore.

But when she thought about all that, it began to make the swim seem a little overwhelming, even impossible. Personally, she tried to keep any self-doubt at bay simply by thinking about that promised red roadster, one she hoped to find at the bottom of a rainbow across the Channel. That was it. In her mind she was not swimming for anything but the car, which made the whole swim seem smaller, as if she were in competition for a medal or a trophy instead of everything else. The more she thought about that, and the detailed logistics of the swim, the calmer and more confident it made her feel. Everything was in place—her new suit, her goggles, her father and sister on the boat, her trainer, everything. All she had to do was swim, and if there was one thing Trudy knew she could do, it was that.

" 'England or drown' is my motto," she brashly told Harpman before turning in for the night at 11:00 P.M. "I could never face the people at home again unless I had got across."

Cape Gris-Nez (France) Aug 5. (Associated Press)—Miss Gertrude Ederle of New York will start shortly before 7 o'clock tomorrow morning on her attempt to swim the English Channel. She will take to the water at Gris-Nez Beach.

It was a short night for Meg and Trudy's father in Boulogne. They boarded the *Alsace* well before dawn, and by the time the sky at Gris-Nez began to brighten at 4:30 A.M. "summer time" in France, the French equivalent of daylight saving time, Joe Corthes had already put the anchor of the *Alsace* down several hundred yards offshore. Meg was ferried ashore and the rowboat, which would carry her, Burgess, and several others back to the boat, was pulled up on the beach past the high-tide mark.

Meg was met by a car, which took her to the hotel, where she met Burgess and woke Trudy. The swimmer blinked her eyes open and asked her sister simply, "Do we go?" Meg nodded yes. Trudy bounced downstairs in her pajamas to the dining room for breakfast—coffee, a bowl of cornflakes, a half a chicken, and over Burgess's protestations, a peach for dessert—and then sat by the kitchen stove with Meg and tried to ward off the morning chill.

Soon after sunrise, at 5:37, the white cliffs of Dover slowly appeared through the morning haze. There was already a crowd of several dozen journalists and curious onlookers gathered on the beach, and every few moments another two or three or four arrived, making small talk, glancing at the sky, and looking out to sea. Another rowboat was lowered from the *Alsace* and began to make its way to the beach, and a little dog jumped from the tug and swam behind, drawing laughs from the crowd as the Channel seemed no match for the energetic pup, which beat the boat to the beach. The day was clear to start, but hazy, and as the sun glowed red on the horizon there was some cause for concern. The old sailor's adage was in the air again—"Red sky at morning, sailors take warning." The sky itself was not red, but the sun was. Burgess hoped it would soon lose its color, and that the weather report would hold.

He had arranged for Trudy to make her final preparations to swim the Channel at the Hotel du Sirene, on the beach, but before she left the Hotel du Phare, Meg applied the first coating of olive oil to Trudy's body as Burgess hovered outside her door and admonished her to hurry up. Then Trudy donned her innovative, two-piece suit—the WSA logo and an American flag patch sewn onto the front of her brassiere—her red bathing cap, and a robe. It was 6:45 A.M. As soon as she was dressed they all hopped back into taxis and private cars and made their way to the beach, where Trudy, Meg, and Burgess went into the garage of the hotel and applied still more grease to her body, this time a darker, tarry substance that left Trudy looking and smelling like she had just left Burgess's garage back in Paris. Before Trudy began her short walk to the beach from the hotel, Meg helped her pull her goggles on over her head and pulled the strap tight.

Then Trudy strode purposefully to the beach, where the crowd now numbered nearly a hundred people, like she was out for a morning constitutional. She walked briskly, taking deep breaths, and carefully adjusted the goggles to her face, taking care not to smear grease over the glass surface. As the crowd gathered around, Burgess stood barefoot in the sand, his sleeves and pant legs rolled up, a plaid driver's cap perched on his head. He opened a can of lanolin and applied yet another layer of grease on Trudy's body, rubbing the thick substance up and down Trudy's legs, around her neck and under her arms, everywhere and anywhere he thought might be susceptible to chafing. The newsmen called greetings to Trudy, and she responded with good-natured humor. "I'll make it this time," she predicted. Then, looking at her hands, she held her arms wide and with a huge smile on her face she held her fingers, heavy with grease, apart and quipped, "I feel just like a grease ball!" At the prodding of a cameraman, Lillian Cannon, wearing a full-length coat to ward off the morning chill, stepped from the crowd and gingerly shook Trudy's hand and wished her good luck. As a newsreel cameraman captured the scene, the little dog that had swum ashore from the boat stuck its nose in the can of grease and slurped down great gobs of lanolin, drawing laughs from those on the shore.

For some, that was all they found amusing. Most of the forty journalists or so on the beach, roughly equal in number from the United States, England, and France, had assumed they'd be able to board the *Alsace* and accompany Trudy on her journey—that had been the

custom when others tried to swim the Channel, and no one had indicated that wouldn't be the case this time. But the *Tribune-News*
syndicate was protective of its story. It had paid for the boat, and only
Julia Harpman and a few others—the photographer Arthur Sorenson, John Hayward, a journalist from the British newspaper the *Daily
Sketch*, who would serve as the official observer, Meg, Helmi, Henry
Ederle, and a few crew members—were authorized to board the ship.
The rest were left, quite literally, high and dry. Unless another boat
could hastily be hired, they would all have some explaining to do to
their editors and would witness only the start of the swim.

By the time Burgess finished coating Trudy with grease it was already just after 7:00 A.M., and the trainer was anxious to get going.
He had plotted her course to take advantage of his knowledge of the
tides, and every minute mattered.

No other swimmer had ever tried the course Burgess intended to
have Trudy follow, but he was absolutely convinced that after nearly
three decades of observation of the Channel, and untold hours spent
in its waters, he had finally figured out the best way across. A year
before, as was customary, Trudy had clambered into the waters from
the rocks at the base of Cape Gris-Nez itself, the nearest point to Dover, a starting point that seemed to make common sense. If a swimmer left at the right time, after only a few strokes he or she was able
to take advantage of the current.

Burgess, however, had recently reached a different conclusion.
The previous summer he had watched not only Trudy's swim, but
the swims of both Lillian Harrison and Jeanne Sion, and he had since
taken to the water himself dozens of times and checked his theory
personally, feeling the pull of the current on his own body.

Unlike Ederle, in 1925 Lillian Harrison had started her swim from
the small sand beach near the Hotel du Sirene. As a result she had
begun her journey in the calmer waters, protected by Cape Gris-Nez
itself, giving her an opportunity to set her pace before being buffeted
by open water. She had not entered the current until she cleared the
cape, and as a result, she had not been pushed quite so far to the west,
so that when the tide changed and turned back she had not quite
so much distance to cover. Later, when Jeanne Sion had left from
the cape itself, like Ederle, Burgess simultaneously started swimming
from the beach just so he could gauge how much that small change

would impact the route toward England. As he suspected, he found the route much easier and more efficient. He had, in fact, lingered in the water and eventually been picked up by Sion's escort vessel when she finally made her way to his position. Later that day when Burgess returned to shore, he told Alec Rutherford that after more than twenty-five years of splashing around in the Channel he believed he had "solved the riddle of the tides." Trudy would test his theory.

His plan was for her to swim to England following the familiar Z-shaped route. Ideally, four hours and twenty minutes before high tide in Dover, Trudy would enter the water at the beach and strike out due north for twenty minutes. Once she cleared Cape Gris-Nez she would encounter the westward-flowing rising tide, then change her heading to the northwest for two hours—more or less running with the tide while swimming farther out into the Channel, a course that would carry her some three or four miles west of Gris-Nez.

Then it was time to change course again, steering north-northwest, quarter north for the next seven hours. Even though this seemed somewhat counterintuitive, by keeping that bearing she would gain ground toward England even as she was swept along. As the tide would turn and begin sweeping the Channel waters through the Strait of Dover and into the North Sea, Trudy would cut cross the current and swim closer to England even as she was being swept to the northeast.

If all went well, at the end of seven hours the swimmer would be about three miles east of the South Goodwin lightship and in position to make for the coast on the last leg of the Z, first through slack water and then the next rising tide, landing on the coast somewhere between Dover and Folkestone. If she swam particularly well she might be even closer to the lightship, leaving even less distance to cover to make a successful landing and less of a chance of being overcome by fatigue, which could result in being caught too far offshore and then swept past Dover and even farther down the coast.

According to Burgess's calculations, if Trudy swam to her ability she could make the English coast in about fourteen hours, a record time, but one Burgess thought was achievable, based on her strength as a swimmer. He distributed a map to the press that showed her route and his projection of her progress each hour. Of course, the wind and the weather could wreak havoc with any plan, but this was where Burgess's years of experience might prove critical—if something went wrong, he could make adjustments on the fly. His only real concern was if the weather changed and slowed her down, for if she was too far south of the Goodwin Sands when the tide began running, she would be pushed to the west, nearly parallel to the English coast. Not even Trudy, thought Burgess, was a strong enough swimmer to cut perpendicularly across such a strong tide.

It was time to go. Trudy was already fifteen, almost twenty minutes late getting into the water, and as Burgess well knew, a few minutes could be the difference between making the shore and coming excruciatingly close, between success and failure, and potentially, life and death. There was no margin.

Quickly, with little fanfare, he urged Trudy toward the sea, then gave her a quick peck on the cheek before she reached the water, taking care not to touch her once she began to wade in the surf, for if he did, even in waters only ankle deep, that would, according to tradition, be enough to void her effort. Trudy then walked confidently to the water's edge near the two rowboats waiting to ferry those lucky enough to have passage on board the *Alsace*.

As Burgess and several others waded through the shallow water and cautiously climbed into the boats, each of which bore both an American and a French flag, Trudy turned to Meg, trailing behind and carrying her purse, and gave a little wave. Then she turned her back on France and waded into the surf.

England was ahead of her, she knew that, but the day had already turned so hazy that only the barest outline of the cliffs on the opposite coast could be seen, appearing more as an apparition than a tangible landscape, the same tantalizing view that had called so many before her to cross the waters. Breathing deeply, gathering herself, Trudy plowed through the water, walking, feeling the sand beneath her feet, and then, as the water rose past her waist to her chest, she began to feel lighter. When a small wave tossed water up to her chin, she lifted her head to the sky, whispered, "Please, God, help me," then bent her head, reached out with her arms, and dove in beneath the waters.

On board the *Alsace* and on the shore, the first wireless reports crackled out through the atmosphere, telling the world she had started to swim.

Cape Gris-Nez., Aug 6. (By the Associated Press)—Gertrude Ederle, the American Swimmer, started at 7:09 o'clock this morning in an attempt to swim the English Channel. The weather conditions when she took her plunge were fine.

"Please, God, help me." As her head left the air, Trudy tried to think of nothing else—nothing important, nothing that mattered, and nothing that didn't touch her at that instant. Nothing but the water and the air, the sea and the sky, her hands and arms reaching out, her legs kicking, her face turning toward the sky breathing in, then turning, under the water, breathing out.

The start, she knew, was the hardest part. As she plunged into the water and began to swim, her body, swept over by the cold, was still in pieces—her arms felt stiff, each stroke still uncertain, wavering, irregular, and as she kicked her legs she went at first too fast, then too slow, then back and forth, holding them too stiffly, then too relaxed, as she tried to find the place where her arms and hands and legs and feet were all one piece, in harmony. She tried to find that special place atop the water and in her mind where she did not feel the cold or the spray or the difference between the air and the water, lightness and dark, day or night. A place where there was no time at all.

In . . . out . . . in . . . out . . . this was the worst. In shorter swims—one hundred yards, two hundred yards, three hundred, she hardly ever thought of breathing, and never thought of anything but going fast, breathing fast, reaching out, and kicking and breathing. Then all she did was pull with her arms and feel the water slip away as she churned along for a minute or two or three, taking deep breaths and exhaling, one after the other, until she moved through the water like running downhill, so fast that it felt like it was over before she started, before she even felt tired, before she even had time to think.

This was different, far different from the long swims she took during training, or back in the Highlands with Meg, where she didn't think about swimming at all but laughed and giggled and talked about a million things as she swam. It was hard not to swim as fast as she could, by herself for now, and even as it pained her to admit it, she knew that today, in order to go fast she somehow had to go slow. It was funny, but the farther she had to swim the slower she had to swim, and the slower she swam the harder it was for her to find that place, the place Julia Harpman called her "personal sphere." The writer had tried to talk to her about it, tried to ask her what she felt and what she thought of when she was in the water for hours, but Trudy had no words for what she thought or felt because when she reached that place there *were* no words for what she thought or what she felt, just the feeling of being lifted up and held from below, a soft hand carrying her away, deeper and farther . . .

She was not there yet, and as she stroked and kicked and breathed, she had not reached that place. She could still hear the gulls, and the splash and the slap of water had not faded the way the sound of the wind faded when it blew hard all night through an open window, or the way the sound of the rain on the rooftops slipped into a single soft surface, or the way the sound of the cars going past her home on Amsterdam Avenue ran together and made a kind of music.

It was hard for her to hear things. She knew this, but she did not know what it was like to hear everything. She did not know that everything she heard was softer and rounder and muffled, that words ran together sometimes, and that music soared and lifted and sank, like the water, like the sea, a single sound like a river running past, or a stream, all rapids and falls and quiet corners. She knew it was hard, but sometimes she thought that by being partially deaf it was actually easier for her to hear, because even though she heard less she listened more. She heard enough to know when voices were talking over hers, not waiting for her ears to hear, and she knew there were sounds that stayed with her that others missed, low rumbles and hums and whispers and laughs, secrets she heard and kept to herself.

Then it happened. For a few moments she had not thought of her arms or her legs or the water or air. For a moment she had been there, away in her place. She simply listened to the sea and spoke to it not with words but thoughts, and felt the water ride over the sea bottom and sensed the way the wind pushed the waves flat and pressed her flesh as she slipped between the sea and the air. It was like sliding into bed and finding that place, that comfortable spot between the sheet and the coverlet, her head on the pillow, and slipping into sleep.

That's how it was, swimming like this—not thinking to sleep but starting to. For a second, a moment, she had been there but now she was not, her breath was now too deep, then too shallow, and her arms were out of sync—she reached too far, pulled too hard, and her internal metronome started to wobble as she sped up and slowed down, then sped up again. And there was a sound, a low rumble like gauze unwrapping around her head that pulled her back and took her away.

It was the tug. Of course, it was the *Alsace* and Meg and Pop and Julia and Helmi and Burgess, the dark shape waiting offshore, growing larger now, her partner for—how long? Fourteen hours? Sixteen? More? She tried not to think, not of time, not of the past or of the future but here and now and what was there, just ahead, that hand ahead of hers, just out of reach, holding her, leading her, pulling her along.

Phhhuh! Salt in her mouth and her lungs spasmed and shuddered, all salt and spit and she sputtered for a second, lifted her head a little more and spit out the water and spit out the salt, then breathed again, deeply. She cleared her nose and drifted for a second before starting again and tried trying to crawl back to that place, her head now felt as if it were full of sand.

What was that taste? Could she tell? Was her stomach awake, cramping, pulling her back? No, no, not yet. But then, sh-ah! Yuk.

A sharp, deep pain in her side and a sweet and sour taste in her mouth, as if her breakfast wanted to leave her. She clenched her teeth, tried to breathe deeply. Not again, she thought, not again. She did not want the sickness to grow and spread from her belly to her brain and back again. Not like last year, not again. Please, God, help me.

And then she remembered. Meg was on the boat, and Pop and Julia. Not Wolffe, not him, not his sour beef tea or his sour puss. There had been something in the tea last year, something that made her sick. She knew it she knew it she knew it. But not today, no not today. Meg had prepared her food. Like the man had said, she had been prepared for a shark but not for a Wolffe. She almost laughed. It was silly, now really, silly that someone had cared so much to slip something in her drink, silly that someone had done that, had tried to stop her. Silly.

But there was still the sweet and sour taste in her mouth and the pain in her side and the thoughts racing through her head. What was it? The peach! Of course it was the peach, the one Burgess told her not to eat but she had grabbed anyway, the sweetness that exploded inside her mouth, delicious, then dripped down her chin and onto her hands. And now she swallowed a bit of water and the peach grabbed her in the side and now it just wouldn't let go.

But no one would know. She would tell no one this time, ever, no matter how bad her stomach felt, how bad it hurt or how long, she would never let on. This time she wasn't going to stop, not once, not ever. No one would touch her and take her away, not this time, not once she found her place.

On the tug, they didn't know—they couldn't tell she was sick. She slowed her pace, breathed deeply, stretched from one side to another, and twisted as she approached the boat, slowing her pace from twenty-eight strokes a minute to twenty-six then twenty-four and, as she drew closer to the boat, to twenty-two slow strokes a minute, the metronome winding down.

Burgess would like that, he was always, always asking her to slow down, and she never, ever did for long, but now she would, just until, just until . . .

There! As she breathed out, the pain in her side began to slip away. There. She stretched and breathed, stretched and breathed, relaxed, and with each breath she pushed the pain away, out from her side and into the water, where she kicked it away, not looking back but pressing on . . .

Ahead of her, the tug lifted slightly in the swells, its single smoke-stack spewing black smoke and the big engine almost on idle as Corthes held his position. A moment before, the rowboat bearing Burgess, Lillian Cannon, and Julia Harpman had pulled alongside, and they had all climbed on board. Now they all stood on the deck waving at Trudy and calling out to her as she swam slowly, and according to plan, drew along the port side of the *Alsace* at midships, keeping the boat off to her side, ten or fifteen, twenty feet away, close but not too close.

Burgess and Trudy had made a decision. On this trip there would be no rowboat in the water next to her, and no chance that some-one would reach out and grab her and pull her in the boat, or that the boat would crest a wave and then tumble toward her, or that she would veer off course and touch the boat accidentally, or that any-one could touch her if she didn't want them to. A year before, when Wolffe was in the boat, Trudy felt as if she had spent half her time worrying that it would come too close, causing her to sprint away, then slow down so Wolffe could catch back up after falling behind.

This time there was only the tug. She would swim alongside it, in the lee of the ship according to the current, close enough so she could see and sense the vessel beside her, but not so close that they would touch, or she would struggle in its wake or in the wash of its propellers. When she needed nourishment or drink, Burgess or Meg or Pop would attach it to a line, lean over the rail, reach out, and lower it over the side, where Trudy would play fish to the bait. This time there would be no chance, no chance at all, that anyone would touch her. It was a bit more dangerous for Trudy—if she collapsed or became unconscious, unless someone was swimming next to her there was little chance that she'd be saved, but that had never happened, not once, since she had learned to swim. This time she was in control. It was her swim, all hers.

What was that? On the side near the bow, beneath the rail where she could see Meg and her father and Helmi and Burgess? It looked like a scratch on the side of the boat, then like chalk, like words.

It was! She read the words and laughed. That Meg, she was her champion, why if it wasn't for Meg, well, she'd have never done anything, never starting racing, never tried to swim the Channel—she knew that. She owed Meg everything. And the night before, or maybe early this morning, it looked as if Meg had taken some chalk, walked along the pier where the boat was tied up, on the bow of the port side, and drawn a big arrow pointing forward and the words "This Way, Ole Girl!" And now Trudy read it and laughed. This way, ole girl, this way . . .

As Trudy drew alongside the vessel, Captain Corthes touched the throttle and the boat jumped to life, propeller churning in the water, and waves started to slap at the bow. As the tug slowly churned to the northwest, Cape Gris-Nez loomed off the port, nose on the water, and then slowly started to grow smaller, as if watching. They could all tell Trudy was swimming strongly, and after a few minutes they all stopped watching and prepared themselves for the rest of the day, Harpman with her typewriter and table, her notebooks, and Meg with the gramophone, the records in a case, the speaker horn aimed over the water. Arthur Sorenson, the photographer, dashed to and fro along the rail, snapping pictures. Pop Ederle, a scarf around his neck, walked the deck, and Burgess was everywhere, back and forth, now on the rail, now in the steering house talking with Corthes, now back on deck talking with Pop Ederle. And every few minutes the old swimmer tilted his head back, scanned the horizon, and sniffed the air. The forecast said one thing—"light indefinite winds, visibility mainly good, warmer"—but that was in an office in Bracknall. This was the English Channel, which did not pay attention to words, and Burgess scanned the horizon and kept sniffing the air.

He did not smile.

As she swam along the tug, she could feel the sea now, and sense that she was not along the shore, fighting the surf in the shallows, but in the sea itself. The swells were deeper and longer and—now she could feel it! It was hard to explain but she knew the water and knew what it did and what it was going to do before anyone else ever did, her whole life, she said once much later, "too much water, swim, swim, swim." Hours in the water at the Highlands, the tide running in and out, gave her this sense. From somewhere deep inside she could feel the moon pull at the water, reaching all the way from space to draw the water from the North Sea to the North Atlantic, as the waters behind the cape gave way to the tidal current, every atom starting to race past.

She loved it. Ooh, how she loved it, this feeling in the water, swimming with the tide, speed like she was sprinting even though she wasn't, even though she was back to twenty-six to twenty-eight strokes a minute. The water felt soft, light, and her hands pulled through it easily.

She loved it loved it LOVED it. Now that they were going, finally going, she could slip away into "her sphere," and stop thinking. This was fun, now. All she needed to do was keep the big shadow of the tug in the same place, not too close and not too far away, and swim.

After a few moments she and the tug were one, the speed of each identical to the other. Trudy swam at a pace of twenty-eight strokes to the minute, and the *Alsace*, its engines running just ahead of the current, matched Trudy's pace, two and a half to three knots an hour.

Burgess thought she was going too fast—he always did—but he

said little. This time most of the communication with Trudy during her swim would be done by way of a chalkboard lowered off the aside—the combination of her poor hearing, her distance off the ship, and the sounds of the boat's engine and the water slapping against the tug made talking back and forth, while not impossible, difficult. There was no sense having Trudy yell back and forth all day. That would only make her tired.

As the tedium of the day settled in, there was silence on board. Channel swimming is a spectator sport only for the most dedicated, for apart from the relative excitement of the start and the finish, the success of a swim is often marked by monotony and the lack of drama. No news is good news.

That sentiment was not shared by everyone. All the drama, such as it was, was back onshore at the beach at Gris-Nez. As soon as Trudy entered the water and the rowboats bearing Burgess and the others left the shore, the remaining press contingent got busy. Just because they weren't being allowed aboard the *Alsace* didn't mean they were abandoning their coverage of the swim. The *Alsace*, after all, wasn't the only boat in the English Channel.

In Boulogne, another tug, *La Morinie*, had been engaged by Lillian Cannon for her Channel swim sometime in the future. There had been speculation that Cannon might swim today as well, but she had chosen to wait. Minott Saunders, the reporter assigned by the syndicate to cover Cannon and who served as her protector, hastily contacted the boat captain, and within only a few moments of Trudy's departure, *La Morinie* was steaming to Cape Gris-Nez to pick up its cargo of reporters and cameramen.

Cape Gris-Nez., Aug 6.—(By the United Press)—8:09 A.M.— About one and a half miles off shore; sea calm, sky hazy, and storm clouds off England.

Burgess didn't like it. The weather report, now nearly eighteen hours old, was not holding true. He was not surprised—this was the Channel, after all, and if his years of experience had taught him anything it was that the weather forecast was as much fiction as science—but he wished it were otherwise. Ahead toward England, the sky, which should have been growing brighter, was turning dark, and ever so slowly, seas were starting to rise as the wind, variable at the start, began to shift and blow more steadily. Almost impercepti-bly at first, a fresh breeze of only a few knots began to press from the southwest. As it did, the sea, nearly quiet at the start, and smooth except for the usual swells, began to awake as wind and current met head on. For the next few hours, Burgess's attention was divided as he kept one eye on the swimmer and the other on the sky.

Then he heard the music. Meg had sorted through the heavy platters of recordings, cranked up the gramophone, and turned it up loud. She knew her sister, watched her, and knew when Trudy needed a lift. She could just tell. Not that Trudy was slowing down—she wasn't—but every so often she had to be reminded, had to be prodded, had to be pushed. She was sluggish and Meg could tell, and now it was time to wake her up. "Rosie O'Grady." "Yes, We Have No Bananas." "Always." "No More Worrying." "Sweet Georgia Brown." "The Sidewalks of New York." "Let Me Call You Sweetheart"—"hot" American jazz, mostly, the pop songs Trudy liked best, and some New York favorites.

"No More Worrying." Sam Lanin and His Orchestra, that was the song, a new one only a few months old and already one of Trudy's favorites. Meg placed the record on the turntable and set the heavy needle on the recording, which bounced and scratched then settled in the groove.

With the first sound of the drum and blare of the trumpet, Trudy's head snapped toward the boat. She was awake now, and she could hear the music. No more worrying!

Even from the boat, they could see Trudy's smile, and she couldn't resist sprinting for a second, coming closer to the boat, where she could see Meg and see Burgess.

"There'll not be any worrying," she shouted over the music, al-most singing, "if we get to Dover tonight!" Then she rolled over and swam away, not faster but more lively, her arm movement quicker, her leg kick more brisk. Burgess yelled for her to slow down, but Trudy could not hear him.

Cape Gris-Nez France 9:09 A.M. (United Press)—The French vessel *Nicole Schafling* exchanged salutes with the tug *Alsace*, accompanying Gertrude Ederle.

News traveled quickly. After two months of waiting, word that Trudy was now in the water had traveled the globe and was being reported everywhere. On both coasts, in England and France, ferryboats and transports pulled away from the piers, and binoculars scanned the horizon as the curious tried to spot the tug and the young woman in the sea, swimming. When they did, they changed course, swung past, tooted their horn, and watched for a moment, crew and passengers waving as their wake crashed against the side of the tug and washed over Trudy. Then the vessels pulled away, leaving Trudy and the tug alone again in the ocean.

Just after 9:00 A.M. a smudge of smoke on the horizon started steaming closer, and at 9:40 it drew alongside Trudy, pacing her, opposite the *Alsace.*

It was *La Morinie*, and the deck was almost black with people as desperate photographers snapped pictures and the newsreel cameramen cranked their cameras and trained them on Trudy, while the reporters handed out brief dispatches to the wireless operator who sent their bulletins crackling through the air.

As the boat pulled alongside her, Trudy was distracted, and looked first over one shoulder and then the other as she tried to keep both boats in sight and those aboard both vessels could see the annoyance on her face. Although the captain of *La Morinie* tried to stay away from Trudy and remain slightly behind the *Alsace*, keeping her twenty or thirty yards away, he was being paid to bring his passengers close, and now that the sea was starting to run and the swells were starting to grow, it was difficult to maintain a safe distance. Every so often the boat nearly drew abreast of the swimmer, and in the slow waters the wake of the two boats sometimes combined and lifted her up and then dropped her down suddenly. Even worse, the sound of a second engine in the water was distracting and made the music hard to hear. For Trudy, it was as if she were the jam in a sandwich being squeezed out, and it made swimming seem more like walking down a crowded sidewalk in New York, dodging pedestrians. She found herself distracted, making sure she stayed in the middle and didn't drift into either vessel.

Every so often a motorboat roared in, pulled close to the *Alsace*, and Arthur Sorenson passed a package over the side. Then the boat sped off again, ferrying the cargo to shore—photographs of her journey to be transmitted to American newspapers for the next edition. But one boat delivered a passenger, a young man and Channel aspirant, a swimmer from Boston named Louis Timson.

Oh no, thought Trudy, not Louis, not *him*. He was a grand swimmer and a nice fellow, but he had a crush on her. She was so embarrassed about that. He was too old for her, and almost bald! Why, she didn't even have a sweetheart. Not yet. Swim, swim, swim. Maybe that was why she liked the song so much. It would be nice, one day, to call somebody sweetheart, but when she thought of it for too long it also made her sad. A doctor who examined her ears had told her once, "It's a shame, Miss Ederle, a shame. When your sweetheart says to you 'I love you,' you won't hear him. It's a shame."

She swam on. Meg changed the record. "Let Me Call You Sweetheart."

Of course.

Cape Gris-Nez., Aug 6.—(By the United Press)—10:35 A.M.—
Gertrude's position was five and one-half miles off the French coast. Agitation of the sea seemed to annoy the swimmer. There was a southwest wind.

Burgess was not looking at the horizon and wondering anymore. The weather had turned. Now the wind was from the southwest and rising. At 10:45 A.M. the high tide reached its apex in Dover, and the neap tide was beginning to run, helping Trudy speed into mid-Channel, but the sea swells were growing and pushed by the winds; so, too, were the waves.

Following signals from the tug, when the boat slowed a bit, Trudy cut in front, crossing the boat's path, then Corthes slowly increased his speed as Trudy moved to the starboard side of the vessel, more in the lee of the running sea, but hardly protected. *La Morinie* followed suit, dropping behind and cutting across the wake of the *Alsace*, then pulling closer again, jockeying for position as photographers on board pleaded with the boat's captain to bring them closer, and the crew aboard the *Alsace* tried to shoo them away. Julia Harpman was not pleased that the second boat had arrived, robbing her of a scoop, but there was little she could do. Besides, no one on *La Morinie* really knew what was happening aboard the *Alsace*, or how Trudy was doing. All they saw was the young woman swimming. Whether she succeeded or failed, Trudy's story would be told by Julia, and no one else.

Trudy tried to monitor all this, tried to stay out of harm's way, tried not to think. Please, God, she whispered, help me. Let me, she breathed, call you, she breathed, sweetheart.

That wasn't all there was for her to worry about. In mid-Channel one never knew what one would encounter in the water. Trudy didn't worry about sharks, not really, but there were jellyfish—large floating masses of pink, almost red jellyfish and their stinging arms—and trash, the detritus of the continent, whatever had fallen into the Channel and still remained afloat. Boat captains familiar with the Channel even spoke of the odd mine from the Great War still bobbing around, still armed and able to blow any boat out of the water.

But it was comical sometimes, what she saw float past, debris from shipwrecks and cargo washed off decks or washed down rivers and then into the sea—carrots and cabbage from an overturned farmer's cart, tree limbs blown down during storms, dolls' heads and seaweed and suitcases, broken buoys, fishing nets, floats, hats, and even shoes, all the flotsam sometimes drawn together in one big, heaving, enormous mass between channels in the current. Joe Corthes, in the steering house, peered ahead and tried to avoid most of these debris fields, but he couldn't see everything, and that was not the only worry. Somewhere just under the surface, waterlogged, perhaps there was a tree, its sharp limbs ready to scratch and stab, or maybe a timber pulled loose from some poor dock a week or a month or five years ago, now covered in barnacles and rusty bolts and nails, floating back and forth, sagging just below the water, barely seen, ready to snag and cut and gash a bare hand, a leg, or an arm thrashing though the water, just out of sight.

Cape Gris-Nez., Aug 6.—(By the United Press)—11:15 A.M.— Gertrude was swimming six and one half miles off the French coast at two miles an hour. The current was pushing her northward.

The sea was getting rougher, that much was obvious. Even though Trudy was running with the tide now, the sea continued to rise, and her pace dropped to only twenty-two strokes per minute as she fought the swells that washed her back and forth between the two boats and blew the smoke from their engines over her head.

Trudy was cold but not overly so. As long as she kept swimming, the engine of her own body kept her warm, and although the conditions had deteriorated, she remained in reasonably good humor, occasionally bantering back and forth with those on board the boat, sometimes singing aloud, at one point yelling out, "Tell me when it's noon so I can eat—twelve to two, out for lunch."

Thus far, she neither eaten nor had anything to drink, another recommendation from Burgess. He called it his "starvation" plan. Over the years he had seen swimmer after swimmer stop and eat and then become ill. It had even happened to him a few times. Although he knew Trudy would have to eat a bit of food and take some warm drinks, Burgess wanted to keep her diet as bland and Spartan as possible.

As noon approached, Trudy's stomach began to tell her it was time to eat—she had been in the water nearly five hours, and even Burgess knew she had to eat sometime. She could have lunch, but over the rest of the day he would allow her only snacks—chocolate, sugar, pineapple, and broth—food for energy and for warmth.

Trudy took a break. The tug slowed almost to a stop and Trudy drifted alongside as Burgess attached a curved glass baby bottle full of lukewarm chicken broth to the line, then leaned over the rail as far as he could and dangled it over the water. As a swell lifted her up Trudy snatched it from the air then rolled over, floating face up, and sucked on the bottle while trying not to swallow any seawater. The warmth felt good inside but the bland broth had little flavor. She wrinkled her nose and asked for something more substantial. Burgess gave her a chicken leg which she ate rapidly, doing the dog paddle with one hand to stay afloat, holding the chicken leg with the other.

Neither agreed with her. As she trod water she began to stiffen from the cold and feel the sea in her stomach again. "That was not so good," she shouted in reference to her lunch, before turning over and resuming her swim. As she did, Meg emerged from the pilothouse.

She had put on her WSA swimsuit. She climbed carefully over the rail of the boat and then dove in behind her sister and swam after her until she drew alongside, joining her sister in the water as the tug and the young woman resumed their course. With Meg at her side and—even if it fully did not agree with her—some food in her belly, Trudy swam with renewed vigor.

Aboard the *Alsace*, however, Burgess was worried. The wind was still rising, and it looked like it was about to rain.

He'd seen this before, too many times—a fast start under good conditions and then the Channel, as if offended by a swimmer moving easily in her waters, slapped back. Corthes was getting reports from other ships farther up the Channel and from the coast. Steamers on each shore were choosing to stay in port. The weather wasn't going to get any better.

A thought began to form in Burgess's mind, one he tried to push away but one that kept returning with each wave and was soon all he thought about.

He did not think Trudy would make it.

He thought now of the packet he had stashed in the pilothouse, the papers he had drawn up. Burgess had been afraid that the weather would turn and that he might have to stop the swim and take Trudy out of the water, but all he had heard for the last two months, from Trudy and Meg and Henry Ederle, was that once Trudy started to swim, she would not stop, and no one, absolutely no one, was to touch her and take her from the water, no matter what, unless she called for help herself.

Burgess did not think that was wise. He knew from his own experience that in the midst of a Channel swim, the swimmer is often the least capable person in assessing their own condition, that a combination of the cold and fatigue made the mind move like molasses and could strip a swimmer of common sense. Even Burgess had been pulled from the water over his own protestations, and later, particularly after he had successfully crossed the Channel, he was glad for it. Better to live and try again than die trying. The Channel was not going anywhere. There would always be the opportunity to take it on again.

That was why he had spoken with an attorney and had the paper drawn up. If he was not allowed to make the final decision about whether it was safe for Trudy to be in the water, he wanted proof. He had seen what had happened to Wolffe, and if something happened he wanted the world to know it was not his fault. The attorney had written a release for Henry Ederle to sign, a paper that absolved Burgess of responsibility. Yet Burgess did not plan on using the release yet. He hoped to nudge Henry Ederle to conclude on his own that it was time to stop.

Gingerly, sounding him out, Burgess approached Henry Ederle, who was still wrapped in his scarf, standing at the rail, his eyes trained on his daughter. Burgess wanted him to talk, to have a conversation, to plant the seed that it might be best to call the swim off and get Trudy out of the water before she became exhausted. There were still several more days of reasonably favorable tides, and if Trudy stopped now, she might even be able to make another try in two or three days—today had been a good test, a trial run, good for training—but the longer they stayed in the Channel, Burgess could tell that there was no way she could finish, not the way the weather was. Gesturing to the sea, Burgess spoke. He started talking about the weather, how the sea was rising, how there was now rain on the horizon, how the wind was starting to blow, how he himself had been forced from the water in conditions far better, and how he had pulled other swimmers from such waters who were half dead with exhaustion.

Then, almost wistfully, he added, "It would be a pity," he said, "to give up now." He hoped that Henry Ederle would weigh in, perhaps agree, or at least begin the discussion that would lead to stopping and turning back.

Henry Ederle remembered what his daughter told him. He said nothing.

Cape Gris-Nez., Aug 6.—(By the United Press)—12:50 P.M.— Gertrude was ten and one half miles from the French coast and still benefiting from the tide. She had been in the water five hours and forty one minutes during which she swam thirteen miles, the extra mileage being necessitated by channel currents which prevent swimming in a straight line.

After nearly an hour in the water with her sister, just before 1:00 P.M., Meg climbed back aboard the tug as Trudy stopped to eat again.

When Trudy began swimming again, Helmi joined her in the water, but after little more than an hour he began to feel seasick and returned to the tug.

From the tug, Cape Gris-Nez was fading out of sight even as the dim outline of the cliffs of Dover began to appear on the far horizon. Trudy was halfway across, or nearly so.

Then it began to rain, first a slow, intermittent drizzle, then steadier. All the while the seas were turning ever rougher. When Trudy swam alongside the boat the swells lifted her up five and six feet, then dropped her down just as dramatically. It was almost impossible to speak to her from the boat anymore—most communication was taking place on the blackboard. To buoy Trudy's spirits, they passed along wireless messages her mother was sending every hour or so from the Highlands. The whole family was gathered there, and each bulletin reached them within minutes as friends and neighbors raced from the office of the local paper with each new dispatch.

But the bulletins did not tell the whole story and made little mention of the deteriorating weather. It was dangerous, thought Burgess, for Trudy to be in the water in such conditions. But even as Joe Corthes began to express his concern over the weather to Burgess, Henry Ederle remained adamant and ignored each suggestion, each less subtle than the last, that perhaps it was time to give up—Trudy would not stop, did not *want* to stop. Helmi went back in the water and swam to *La Morinie*, asking them to back off—in the increasingly rough conditions, they were afraid the tugs might collide, either with each other, or Trudy. Helmi, who still felt the effect of the sea, also asked Lillian Cannon if she would join Trudy in the water.

Her rival agreed, and a few moments later those aboard the *Alsace* were startled to see Cannon swimming alongside Ederle. But she could not remain there for long. She had a difficult time keeping up with Ederle, and like Helmi, she quickly became ill and left the water for the relative safety of the ship.

Dover, England, Aug 6.—(By the United Press)—3:10 P.M.— Gertrude was six and one half miles off the English coast and going good. Lillian Cannon of Baltimore joined her in the water.

Now Louis Timson entered the water. Not only was he eager to get in the water with Trudy, but he was eager to make amends. When he had first boarded the boat earlier in the day, he had inadvertently sat on a stack of Trudy's records, breaking several of them in half and earning the ire of Meg.

Timson kept his lunch down, but that was about all. He couldn't even keep pace with her and after only a few moments had to leave the water. Then Meg went back in for a time, but she had already swum for an hour and couldn't stay for long. Besides, as she swam alongside Trudy for a few moments, any question she had about her sister's condition was answered.

Trudy was doing fine. Her mouth was a bit sore from the salt water, but otherwise she felt good. Her suit wasn't chafing her and her goggles were working perfectly—not a drop had leaked inside. While the sea looked rough to everyone, Trudy was hardly bothered at all. In fact, the rougher it was, the better she liked it. And besides, it was raining, and even the broken record was a good omen to Trudy.

She's going to make it, thought Meg. She is going to make it.

Dover, England, Aug 6—(By the Associated Press)—4:45 P.M.—Gertrude Ederle, plucky American girl swimmer, was about seven miles off this port on her attempt to conquer the English Channel. She was about two miles northwest of the East Goodwin light ship. The wind, which has been kicking up a bad sea here, had moderated slightly but a heavy rain was falling and the condition of the sea was far from favorable.

Burgess and Joe Corthes did not share the Ederles' confidence, confidence that each of them now thought bordered on crazy. By now the sea was so rough that the crowd on the boat deck had given up on the Victrola and was trying to entertain the swimmer by singing out loud—"The Star-Spangled Banner" was one of the few songs that everyone knew well enough to sing, and they did so, over and over. Yet as each swimmer left the water Burgess was more and more convinced that it was time to stop—Helmi, Cannon, and Timson were all accomplished swimmers who had experienced similar conditions before, and none of them had been able to stand it for much more than an hour. How could Trudy possibly finish? It was impossible.

The tide was starting to turn again, even as the wind kept the waves crashing in from the southwest. As it did, the waters of the Channel behaved as those in a bathtub occupied by an angry child slapping their hands on the water. They lifted and fell without logic for a time before beginning to turn and run against the wind, raising the waves even higher and making it even less likely that Trudy would reach England's south coast, still several miles off, held at bay by what would soon be a strong crosscurrent running down the coast toward the North Atlantic.

Captain Corthes not only shared that concern, but he was becoming worried about his boat, concerned about their course and their rapid approach to the Goodwin Sands. There was a reason, after all, that not one but two lightships were anchored along its borders, each painted a bright red, one on the southern edge and the other to the east, each sending beacons of light across the waters day and night. There was a reason, after all, they called the sands "the ship swallower," for more than two thousands vessels of all sizes were known to have met their demise there. Corthes did not want the *Alsace*, as the local saying went, to be the next boat "to set up shop on the Sands." Had he been out on his own, he would have returned to port by now. To stay out now, nearly adrift, as he tried to keep pace with Trudy and the current pushed him ever closer to the sands, was more than dangerous.

He had made this journey many times before, accompanied dozens of other swimmers who had tried to make the crossing only to fail, and Corthes, to his credit, had never lost a swimmer. None that had ever been put in his care had drowned. That was his record, his reputation, and he did not want Trudy Ederle, the most famous swimmer of them all, to be the first. Once before, when he accompanied Jeanne Sion, she had become lost in the fog only two miles off Dover's shore. It had taken Corthes an hour to find her, and by then the panicked woman was done, half mad with fear. Corthes wanted Burgess to take Trudy from the water and steam back to Boulogne.

Burgess agreed, but he was doubly disappointed—the weather was not only dangerous, but it had pushed Trudy and the *Alsace* off his preferred course. According to his plan, Trudy should not have neared the end of the middle leg of the Z quite so quickly—the plan had been to catch the tide running back to make the final jog of the

Z and land somewhere near Dover. And even then she should have been at the southern edge of the dangerous shoals, which were several miles wide and more than ten miles in length, roughly paralleling the coast.

But Trudy and the waters were both too fast—the wind had driven the seas and driven Trudy more quickly than he planned. They were already on the verge of the Goodwin Sands, and the seas were still running strong, sending them into danger. She should not have been this far along.

Even if the wind suddenly stopped and the sea calmed, there was hardly any way for her to swim to the shore now. She could not swim across the sands—that was suicide, for there was no way for the *Alsace* to pick its way across the ever-shifting shoals.

Although Ederle appeared to be swimming strongly, Burgess ignored that. He focused on the weather and the seas, and as much as he admired her determination, he knew that no one can swim in seas running five and six feet high, and in a wind of nearly twenty knots, hard enough to blow the spray from atop the waves.

There was no choice. He had no choice. She would have to stop.

Trudy couldn't even understand it, really, but the harder the wind blew and the more it rained, the more she liked it. The rain had always been lucky, and now that it was falling she felt an enormous lift inside, a swelling of confidence. She didn't even feel like she was swimming, but riding waves up then sliding down.

She sang, silently, to herself, keeping time with her strokes and with the waves, chorus after chorus of "Let Me Call You Sweetheart." When she tired and slowed she simply changed the tune, as easily as lifting the arm of a phonograph and replacing the record. "Yes, We Have No Bananas" increased the pace. "Yes Sir, She's My Baby" slowed it down. She was not simply swimming across the Channel; she was dancing across, the sea her partner.

She did not realize that Burgess and Corthes had grown more concerned, and that at times Corthes was losing sight of her between the swells. Sometimes now the waves were even crashing across the bow of the boat, drenching onlookers and driving them, dripping with seawater, from the rail to the pilothouse, where they sat with their heads between their knees, shivering. Although the photographers and movie cameramen had been taking pictures all day from both the *Alsace* and *La Morinie*, none of them were taking pictures anymore, not in these conditions. It was impossible to hold the cameras steady, and for many of them, it was impossible to lift their head off their lap.

Corthes reached a decision—he knew his boat and knew these waters and he was not going to risk his vessel in the sands. He called Burgess and Henry Ederle to the steering house and told them he was having a difficult time keeping up with the swimmer and steering his boat in her wake. The current was too strong, the wind too stiff, the waves too tall, and the light beginning to fail.

He showed them his charts, using his finger to indicate their course. They could not continue into the sands, he explained, and if Trudy tried to cut across the sands, toward shore, he could not follow her. They must either stop and return to Boulogne or make a slow steep turn, steering back around the southern edge of the sands. But if they chose that course, Trudy must swim at crosscurrent for a time, making an already difficult task virtually impossible. It would be better, explained Corthes, with Burgess nodding in agreement, to turn back now. That would be the safe, sensible thing to do. It was a pity, but Trudy should stop.

Henry Ederle agreed—not to return to Boulogne, but to take on the impossible, to make the turn and send Trudy across the current.

When he returned to the rail, they lowered the chalkboard over the side to tell Trudy they were turning. She hardly noticed.

No more worrying.

Deal, England. Aug 6.—**(By the United Press)**—**5:39 P.M.**— Gertrude was tiring and the tide was sweeping her down the coast. She ate sugar to add to her strength in an effort to stick it out until flood tide, expected at 9:00 P.M.

Incredibly, given the conditions, she was making headway, swimming across the current in the heavy seas as Corthes skirted the southern edge of the sands. They passed by the lightship anchored along its southern edge, its signature double white light and siren casting over the seas, and the waters were fierce. Later, the Meteorological Office would estimate that wind along the south coast of England that day was, according to the Beaufort scale, which measures wind speed based on sea observation, at force four. While rough, force four conditions, consisting of winds approaching twenty miles per hour and waves only three feet in height, are not particularly dangerous.

In the Channel, however, conditions were a great deal worse. Film footage taken from *La Morinie* well before the worst of the weather shows waves approaching six feet, indicating at least Beaufort force five, meaning winds of nearly twenty-five miles per hour. That was dangerous. Yet somehow Trudy was swimming in this, and somehow, with her American crawl, she was actually moving closer to England.

Burgess couldn't believe it. He refused to believe it. He had never seen such swimming before. She had been in the water more than eleven hours, nearly half a day, and although the English coast was only five or six miles distant, in these conditions he thought it might be five or six hours more before she could even think of making land. She would not make it—of that he was certain. It was impossible.

Burgess went to Henry Ederle, who was still gripping the rail, watching over his daughter, a posture he had held for nearly the entire journey. This time Burgess did not ask. Burgess knew what it was like to cross the Channel, and, more important, he knew what it was like to fail, for he tried and failed so many times himself. He knew that it did not matter how many times one failed as long as one finally reached success—there could always be another time. Half frantic, he told Henry Ederle that his daughter must be taken from the water.

But Henry Ederle still had not forgotten his promise, or his promise of the red roadster or his wager of twenty-five thousand dollars. He remembered what Trudy told him about what happened the previous year—she was swimming and she had been touched, taken out of the water against her will, even poisoned—and she did not want that to happen again.

Ederle told Burgess no. He was not taking his daughter out of the water; no one was taking his daughter out of the water, unless she asked. Burgess insisted again, and again Ederle refused. They argued for a moment while everyone on deck watched, then the trainer stormed off, sliding across the heaving deck, into the pilothouse and then back again a moment later, waving a packet in his hands.

It was the release. He had seen what had happened to Wolffe the year before, how his reputation had been ruined after Trudy had been touched and taken from her water. Burgess would not, could not risk that.

He thrust the paper toward Henry Ederle, explained what it was, and asked him to read it and then sign.

Ederle read the paper, snorted, and then scratched his name along the bottom, the ink already beginning to smear in the rain. Burgess took the paper away.

But he did not stay away for long. A year before, despite everything, he had agreed with Wolffe and thought Trudy was done, and he thought so again, right now. And even though he had the piece of paper, he still did not want to lose the swimmer. He and Henry Ederle continued to argue, and as they did the argument grew louder, with those on the deck and elsewhere on the boat weighing in and choosing sides. Burgess tried pleading with Meg and with Julia, but Meg sided with her father and Julia was just a reporter, neutral, but rooting for her story. Almost everyone else, though, already wet and sick and cold and tired, thought Trudy was done and finished and that someone should touch her and pull her from the water.

Then someone broke away, someone ran over to the rail. Someone—no one ever said precisely who, perhaps Corthes or a member of his crew, worried about saving the boat—someone had enough. In the confusion one voice broke away and spoke out above all others, one voice from someone leaning over the rail, one voice that yelled out, over the sound of the wind and the rain and the engines and the argument, as Julia Harpman wrote later that day, "Someone, losing his head, shouted from the *Alsace*."

Come on out, girl! Come on out!

She was fine. She was swimming, singing, and dancing. Fine and happy. *Fine.*

Despite the wind and the rain, she was in that place, not thinking, swimming but not trying to swim, everything in rhythm. Please, God, help me. Let me call . . . you sweetheart. . . . Yes, we have no . . . bananas.

There were bubbles before her face. All this time and her goggles had not leaked, not a drop, and the amber glass had turned the world gold. Sometimes as she swam she was lost in it, a world and sea and sky of amber and gold. She was numb, but not cold. She was fine.

She turned to breathe, and as her ear left the water she heard muffled new words from afar. The music in her mind faded.

"Come out, girl, come out of the water!"

She was back in an instant, rushing into her body, scratching the record off, adrenaline surging through her limbs. What!? Come out? Of what? She remembers. Oh yes, she remembers. She is in the water, swimming. In the English Channel. Swimming for her roadster, swimming for Mum, for Meg, and for Pop. She is fine, she tells herself, checking each part, arms and legs and lungs. She is fine, she is fine.

She turned on her back, to look at the boat and saw all the commotion on the deck—bodies scrambling over one another, pulling at one another, everyone leaning over the rail, and she heard the loud voices of the arguments and the anger and she saw hands reach out for her and beckon her and plead with her to leave the sea.

Then she rolled over, looked across over the golden sea and fixed her gaze through her goggles. She laughed to herself and floated for a moment, turning her head to look back at the boat.

Then Trudy smiled. It is too funny, really, all that commotion. Come out? Now, when she is having so much fun and is so happy? Come out? She said the first thing that popped into her head.

"What for?" she called out, her voice clear and strong and pure, a bell cutting through fog. "What for?"

Everyone stopped. They saw her smile and heard her voice and no one had an answer to her question. In the midst of such confusion, Trudy was all calm. The figures on the deck looked at one another. Pop and Meg smiled. Burgess looked incredulous, his face flushed. The boat lifted and fell. The young woman in the water was in better condition than anyone on the boat.

Trudy Ederle turned back on her belly, raised an arm, and reached out. She laughed, took a deep breath, and looked ahead toward England.

She put her face back in the water, lifted an arm, kicked, and drew away. "What for?" she asked of the ocean. "What for?"

Soon, she was singing to herself again.

"Yes, we have no bananas, we have no bananas today."

Even in the dim light, through the mist and waves, she could see the far shore.

23

Kingsdown

THAT WAS HER STORY, Julia Harpman knew it. Trudy's wind-driven words hung in the air, two words no other reporter had heard, two words that said everything that needed to be said about Trudy, about this swim, and about whether women should compete in athletics.

"What for?" She wrote the words down in her notebook.

Why stop? What *for*? No one was going to tell Trudy to stop swimming—no one was going to tell any woman to stop swimming anymore. This time, Trudy was no puppet controlled by Jabez Wolffe or anyone else, not even her father. It was her decision, and her vote—earned by days and months and years in the water—and now, for maybe the first time ever, her vote was the only one that counted.

In an instant the unconquerable Channel was subdued, and the weather, while still atrocious, didn't matter anymore. With each stroke of her arms and kick of her legs Trudy was taming the Channel. There wasn't any question about it, not any more. Trudy wasn't coming out of the water, and if she didn't come out of the water, she was not going to fail.

With each stroke, that realization took hold among those on board the ship. No other swimmer who had ever taken on the Channel could have done it in these conditions, but no other swimmer had Trudy's strength and talent, or her mastery of the American crawl. Anyone else would have failed—anyone, woman or man.

For the next hour, gaining mere inches with each stroke, Trudy did a slow pivot around the South Goodwin lightship as the landmark moved from the stern to the starboard side of the *Alsace* and Corthes fought to keep his tug alongside the young woman. He couldn't protect her from the waves anymore, and even when he tried to do so, it had not helped that much in seas as rough as these. And now, as they crawled along, the waves seemed to be coming from everywhere at once. Corthes just tried to keep the tug nearby.

What for? In a matter of minutes Burgess went from exasperation and anger to anxiety, and, finally, as Trudy began pushing past the lightship, anchored only a hundred yards or away, to excitement and exhilaration. By God, she could make it! She *would* make it.

Trudy could barely hear, but he began shouting to her from the rail, screaming the words in the face of the wind as if he couldn't quite believe it himself, "You've got it now, Gertie, you've got it now!"

Pop Ederle joined in. "Don't forget," he bellowed into the teeth of the gale, "You don't get that roadster unless you get over!"

And then, that voice again, sure and strong.

"Pop! I will have that roadster."

Deal, England, Aug. 6.—(**By the Associated Press**)—Caretakers aboard the light ship off Goodwin Sands about six miles from the English coast reported this evening that Gertrude Ederle was swimming strongly as she passed the ship in her channel swim.

They state the tide was in favor of success for the young American swimmer.

Dover, England, Aug 6—(**By the United Press**)—Ederle five and a half miles from Dover and swimming strong at 7:10 P.M.

Still, there were hours and miles yet to go, and anyone who had ever swum the Channel or studied the Channel knew that the final two miles, the final mile, the last five hundred yards could be the worst, that dozens of swimmers before had made it *that* close and then been tossed back out, returning to shore exhausted, eyes downcast, failures.

Trudy just kept singing, not thinking, not worrying. She sang the words and talked to God and the sea as she swam, and imagined herself not in the Channel but sitting in the seat of that red roadster. She could see the sun gleaming off the hood of the car, and feel the way the gears shifted easily in her hands as the car skimmed down Broadway, Meg alongside her as she waved to everyone as she drove by, going fast.

Then she stopped. Trudy was back in the sea. Even though her arms and legs and face were numb and the cold was beginning to settle in as the last thin layers of grease that helped her retain some heat began to melt and wear and drift away, she could feel it again, the drift and pull of the moon.

The tide was changing—she could tell, and she tried to understand, because she knew that this was not the right time. It was still light and the tide should not be changing so soon, but it was. Instead of pushing her down the coast so she could swim with it, toward Dover, like a sailboat tacking before the breeze, the tide was turning back.

In a moment, Corthes and Burgess could tell too, as the tug began to be pushed back up the Channel. It was rare, but not unknown, a measure of the rough weather. The wind had blown so long and so strong that it held the waters at bay and kept the flood tide short. Now the ebb tide was beginning to run again, some two hours early.

It was that final tidal change, the one that had stopped so many swimmers so close to the end, closing off the shore like a door slamming shut, sweeping them away from the coast at the last second and keeping their names off the list of Channel champions, sending them to the much longer ledger of those who had failed. That list read like the names of the dead after a great battle—Freyburg, Sion, Helmi, Barrett, Harrison, Kellerman, name after name after name, and none of that list more often than Wolffe and Burgess, each of whom tried and failed more than any other swimmers in history.

Until that moment, Burgess and Corthes had been taking aim at Saint Margaret's Bay, a small indentation in the coastline four miles to the east of Dover. Not only the nearest reasonable landing, it also offered some protection—if Trudy missed the mark and ran past the landing spot, there was still a fair chance she'd make land by Dover, or, in the worst-case scenario, by Folkestone, another peninsula jutting into the sea six miles to the west.

The premature tide, however, made that impossible. Trudy now needed to strike out for land almost immediately, across the current, before she was pushed past Deal and into the water of the North Sea.

If she did not, her chances of making it to land—anywhere—were slim.

What she faced now was the absolute worst, the swimming equivalent of finishing the last few miles of a marathon in a full-blown sprint, lungs ready to burst and leg muscles on fire, and for anyone not named Trudy Ederle, just as unfeasible. But for the young woman who was in the sea, one more completely unattainable act, another hour or two of suffering, hardly seemed like too much to ask. Burgess leaned over the rail and tried to explain, but after sensing the change in the tide, Trudy was not surprised when he told her they were changing course.

All those hours and hours she had spent in the water for more than a decade, hours that kept her away from boys and dances, that caused her hearing to deteriorate even further, that took her from school, now she needed every minute and every second, all the strength and confidence she had built from a life spent half in the water. She needed it all.

It was not *that* unfamiliar. At nearly every distance she ever swam, when others tired, Trudy did not, and when others slowed down, Trudy did not. During the Day Cup swim, only four short years before, at the end, when Helen Wainwright and Hilda James and the others were weak, Trudy had been strong; when she swam to Sandy Hook, and Meg had yelled at her toward the end, she had sprinted and finished strong and broken the old record. And how many times had she been swimming in the Highlands with Meg and her friends, farther out than almost anyone, and when the time had come to return, Trudy had put her head down and aimed toward shore, like a motorboat, and passed everyone and beaten them to the beach, where she collapsed on the sand, out of breath and happy?

She had done this before, but now, just as the coast was coming into view and she drew closer, there was still one last obstacle. It was nearly dark—the lighthouse atop Saint Margaret's Bay flashed out across the water, and lights onshore began to twinkle on the twilight.

All day long, wireless dispatches from both the *Alsace* and *La Morinie* had kept the world apprised of Trudy's progress, and now, with success at hand, the sailors aboard the South Goodwin lightship also sent word to shore that Ederle was nearing her goal. From Dover to Deal, residents of the south coast of England streamed to the shore to witness history, collecting in pockets atop the cliffs and on the narrow beaches. They scanned the seas for a sign of the tug, gathered driftwood in huge piles, and lit bonfires to ward off the chill. To the Ederles the red and blue and green flares out over the sea made it look like it was the Fourth of July at Highlands. Everyone hoped to spot the swimmer in the water and light the way to shore.

With each new report of her position the crowds picked up and moved farther up or down the coast, trying to anticipate her landing, hopscotching from Dover toward Deal, an entourage of cars and taxis full of families wearing slickers and carrying umbrellas. Local fishermen who had stayed in port all day due to the foul weather now launched their boats and likewise searched for the swimmer in the water. Even those who didn't come to the shore but stayed at home gathered around the radio or went to nearby pubs and raised a glass to her victory even before it was achieved. In Cape Gris-Nez, there was excitement as well. There, too, people received reports of her progress, and now, in the distance, it was sometimes possible, through a break in the clouds, to see the blazes onshore and impossible to think that it was anything else but Trudy making her final approach.

Sunset came, officially, at 9:34 according to the French Summer Time the press used throughout her journey to track her progress, but in the gloom and heavy cloud cover, twilight was premature, and it was nearly dark almost an hour earlier. Swimming in the dark was nothing new to Trudy—she had done so before—but never when she was so tired and cold.

Then, for the first time since she stepped into the water at Cape Gris-Nez, Trudy got a break. After hours of wind and rain and more wind, the storm in the Channel was exhausted and spent. The sea finally started to calm, lifting and falling more slowly. And the rain, too, slowed and stopped, and now the Channel itself hurried Trudy to its shores. For the first time in hours, Trudy, who had plugged along in the heavy seas using four beats—four leg kicks to each stroke—was able to increase her pace to six beats.

There was elation aboard the *Alsace*. Everyone on the tug was staying on the rail, urging her on. Pop Ederle kept reminding her of her roadster, now telling her, "If you get over I'll let you take that roadster to bed with you!" Meg stayed busy, and when Trudy complained of her sore mouth, she lowered pieces of pineapple to soothe her and give her strength, while Burgess leaned over the rail exhorting "Gertie," as he called her, to the finish. Arthur Sorenson, the photographer, ran back and forth, always keeping Trudy in sight, sometimes manning the blackboard and delivering more encouraging words from Trudy's mother, received over the wireless.

Deal, England, Aug 6.—(By the United Press)—9:30 P.M.— Tonight Gertrude Ederle's tug, the *Alsace*, was only a few hundred yards offshore, blowing the whistle, and blue and red flares were burning on the beach.

Deal, England, Aug 6.—(By the Associated Press)—Gertrude Ederle was within a mile of Kingsdown near Deal on a flood tide at 9:30 tonight on her swim across the English Channel. Kingsdown is about five miles north of Dover.

Now, even she could hear them. As light danced across the calming waters, Trudy viewed it all through her amber-colored goggles, and she began to hear, faintly at first, the honking horns of automobiles, and the blasts of the big tugs. From nearby Kingsdown Beach a mighty searchlight from the lifeboat station suddenly cast its beam over the waters and swept it back and forth as if looking for a man overboard. Then the beam of light landed on the *Alsace*, and then upon Trudy, not a man, but a woman not in danger of drowning but about to change everything, and now the crowds on the headlands could see her doggedly putting one arm over the other in the water and gaining another precious foot or two with each stroke. It was soon joined by a similar light from *La Morinie*, putting Trudy firmly in the spotlight.

Some four hundred yards offshore, Trudy slowed and swam closer to the *Alsace*, now a shadow that loomed over the water beneath the bright lights of the pilothouse. Onboard, Burgess prepared the rowboat for landing. He, Pop Ederle, and a crewman planned to row ahead of Trudy to shore, not just to see her finish, but to ensure that she would do so safely. Hundreds of people had guessed correctly and had gathered on Kingsdown Beach to greet her, and they needed to make sure that no overzealous spectator rushed out and touched

Trudy before she actually walked out of the water and took a step without a splash—if she was touched, even as she waded in water below her knees, her journey would be for naught, its veracity called into question, and neither Burgess nor Ederle wanted that to happen.

But now Trudy was not swimming toward shore but toward the *Alsace* and looking up imploringly to the rail. Burgess rushed over. "What's the matter, Gertie?" he called out over the cacophony, sudden concern etched on his face. "What's the matter, girl?

"Gee, Mr. Burgess," she answered, suddenly concerned. "I can't see. It's so dark." Burgess looked at her for a moment, concerned, and then started to laugh. She had forgotten. After fourteen hours in the water Trudy had forgotten she was wearing goggles and as the sky darkened the young swimmer who already found it hard to hear was now worrying that perhaps she was going blind as well.

Burgess called out to her to remove her goggles and for the first time in more than fourteen hours Trudy raised them from her face. Her world, which over the course of fourteen hours had gone from gray to gold and brown and now to nearly black, burst with color as flares and flames and searchlights on the beach all sought her out as if she were the center-ring attraction at some watery circus. The waters danced with color, and a jolt of energy shot through Trudy's body as she stared in wonder at the shore. For a moment she completely forgot where she was and what she was doing but was mesmerized by the scene, which somehow reminded her of some fairy story from her childhood, all magic and light and music.

"How are we doing?" bellowed Burgess.

Trudy thought for a moment, as if surprised by the question and then burst out in a laugh herself. "How are we doing?" she asked of the world, pondering the question. "How are we doing?"

Burgess spoke again and pulled her from her reverie. "Well, for God's sake, Gertie," he said to her, "swim!" He then underscored the fact, pointed the way, with a command—"Swim four hundred yards."

Now she remembered. It all rushed back, every moment of those fourteen hours in the water, all the wind and all the rain. And she was so close now, to her red roadster and some rest. So close. This way, ole girl.

"I'm not going to go this far and let four hundred yards beat me," she yelled back, "if I have a breath in my body." Then she rolled over in the water and started swimming, sprinting.

Four hundred yards? She was the fastest in the world at four hundred yards. She could swim four hundred yards in her sleep. She had swum four hundred yards a million times. Sixteen times back and forth in the old WSA pool, or a few trips around the pier in the Highlands. Four hundred yards was nothing, nothing. She had never, never ever, tried to swim four hundred yards before and failed. Funny, how a swim of more than fourteen hours, more than twenty miles, could end in a swim of four hundred yards.

Trudy was making her final push. The beach was lit almost to daylight by the bonfires and flares and was crowded with so many people it almost resembled Coney Island on a hot summer's day. While the *Alsace* dropped anchor and Trudy swam off, Burgess lowered the rowboat into the water and struck out for shore.

Trudy swam with renewed vigor. This was not the same swimmer who had been touched and allowed herself to be taken from the water a year before, but a confident young woman who with each stroke was reaching for her goal. Now she swam, not with the long, slow strokes that had marked the previous fourteen hours, or with the wild, panicked thrashing she had used when she first learned to swim, but with the quick, sure stroke she had been taught by Louis Handley. It was as if he were somehow standing there beside her, standing along the edge of the pool, pushing her along—"Use your legs, Miss Ederle. Do not forget to use your legs." And she did, upping her pace from six beats to eight, the same rate she used in any race of four hundred yards, kicking stronger now than at any time since she first stepped into the waters at Cape Gris-Nez, churning through the water, creating her own wake. Meg noticed first. In all the time she had watched her sister swim, in meet after meet after meet, never before had she seen her use her legs so well. It was beautiful, the way she carved through the black water.

Burgess and Pop Ederle raced to shore ahead of her as the oarsman rowed with all his might to beat her to land, and as the boat made the beach a crowd of men and boys reached out and grabbed the prow and pulled it up on the sand. Burgess and Henry Ederle scrambled out and looked back toward the *Alsace*. There was Trudy, spotlighted in the water, still offshore but getting closer with each stroke.

Her head stayed out of the water now, taking in the scene, and Burgess, half frantic with excitement, admonished the crowd to stay back. Trudy was almost giddy, but now she was thinking, too, and she remembered that she must not let anyone touch her.

The waves were breaking at the surf line far offshore, and when Trudy reached them, suddenly she was gone, underwater. For a heartbeat the crowd gasped, but then the waves broke and spread out on the beach and there was Trudy, on all fours for a second, sand and pebbles beneath her knees and clutching it with her hands. And then, for the first time since leaving France, she stood, sea legs wobbly, and took a short uncertain step as a wave crashed against her backside, nearly knocking her off her feet.

Henry Ederle, carrying her robe, started racing toward his daughter, but the young woman was taking no chances. She held up her hand and called out, "Stay back, Pop! Stay back!"

Her father stopped and watched as Trudy kept striding out of the water, her heavy legs feeling lighter and more sure with each step, the water shallower, step after step after step, until it swirled around her ankles. Then she took a final stride, and the surf reached out and this time it did not erase her footstep, and it did not splash around her ankles. She was out of the water, on English soil, across the Channel at last.

The crowd roared, clapping and whistling, and now it raced toward her, calling out her name. Pop Ederle reached out for his daughter, gathered her in her robe and gave her a bear hug. "Hey, Pop," said Trudy, "Do I get that red roadster?"

"Do you get the roadster?" he bellowed back in affirmation, a teary smile forming on his face.

Trudy was done. It was 9:40 P.M. and she was the first woman to swim the English Channel. Fourteen hours and thirty-one minutes after she stepped into the water in France, she stepped out of the water in England, more than two hours faster than anyone had ever done so before.

She was the first woman, and sixth person, to swim the English Channel.

By two full hours, she was faster than any man, faster than anyone, ever.

First.

BULLETIN
Deal, England, Aug 6.—(By the Associated Press)—Gertrude Ederle landed here tonight, successfully swimming the English Channel from Cape Gris-Nez, France.

24

Shore

IT WAS DAZZLING. As flares continued to rain down upon the beach and the light from the bonfires and spotlights danced upon the water, Trudy stood for a moment, transfixed in the glow. Then she took a few tentative wobbly steps, almost as if after spending so much time in the water she no longer remembered how to walk in this new world. In a sense she had just stepped out of the darkened sea into the spotlight.

As soon as her father put her robe over her shoulders, his hands were followed by a dozen others, and then two dozen, then three, and every hand reached for her and tried to touch her, asking her questions and shining lights in her face. She was being pulled, too fast, from the sea.

It was too much, Trudy thought, too much, and suddenly the place she had spent the last fourteen hours and thirty-one minutes swimming for her life seemed preferable to this new world of strangers. In an instant she realized that the woman who stepped into the English Channel fourteen hours before was not the same person who now stood on a beach in England. Yet she had not changed. It was strange, she felt the same as she always felt, a little more tired perhaps, but she didn't recognize anything. To be alone for so long with her thoughts and then to be thrust into this crowd was too much. The stunned young woman shrank back, withdrew, and pushed away, turning her back on the crowd as if to return to the sea, to the now familiar company of the *Alsace*.

She wasn't the only one eager to get into the sea. As soon as she saw her sister onshore, Margaret jumped in and swam after her, and

aboard *La Morinie*, which had lost its wireless capability in the final hour of Trudy's swim, reporter Sydney Williams, desperate for
a scoop, leapt overboard and swam toward shore as well, eager to
find a telephone and give the world the first lengthy report of her
success. Like so many reporters aboard that vessel, he'd be forced to
make up many of the details of his story, such as Trudy's first words
upon landing, which Williams inventively concluded were "I am a
proud woman." The myth-making surrounding her achievement was
already in full swing.

Trudy was bewildered. She was tired, as well, and now that she
had stopped swimming she began to feel the cold—the instructions
her brain gave to her arms and legs and lips came through in fits and
starts. After asking her father about the roadster, and then telling
him, "Mama will be so proud," she was speechless—happy, too—but
overwhelmed. She stood teetering on the shore, and Burgess and
her father steered her back away from the water. Her father held her
close, and then Meg emerged from the water and ran up to her sister,
covering her with hugs and kisses, drawing her back into the world
with her smiles and soft talk and familiar touch.

Now she saw the hands that reached for hers, and Trudy stuck
out her hand and shook them all, automatically, as one man said,
"Congrats, girl," and a boy asked, "Are you swimming back?" and a
woman said, "Give the poor girl some room to breathe, will you?"
All the voices turned into a single babbling sound, a crowd in the
lobby at intermission, and Trudy, still blinking the salt water from
her eyes, her tongue swollen and sore, mumbled a few thank-you's
and suddenly self-conscious in her suit held the robe close. Mind-
ful of her responsibilities to the *Tribune-News* syndicate, and to Julia
Harpman, after only a few minutes onshore Trudy was ushered to the
rowboat and rowed back to the *Alsace*.

With each pull of the oars and slap of the bow against the water,
Trudy began to come back. She had done it, she knew. It seemed
unreal, but she had walked into the water in France and walked out
of the water in England. Everyone was smiling at her. Her father was
beaming, happier than anyone maybe, and so were Burgess and Meg.

By the time she reached the *Alsace*, she had emerged from her stupor and could feel things again and think in words again. When the
boat pulled alongside the tug, Trudy was even able to climb aboard

unassisted. Julia Harpman waited to capture her first words, and asked Trudy how she felt.

Trudy nodded. "I'm all right," she said slowly, speech made difficult by her swollen tongue, "but I can not realize what it's all about." It was so overwhelming all of a sudden, it was as if she had never given a thought to what would come next, to what she would do after swimming the Channel. Now that time was here, the future, in its own way, suddenly seemed as daunting and dangerous as the Channel itself, another enormous gulf filled with mysterious tides and currents already pulling her in all directions at once.

"I guess everything's all right," she said, as if uncertain, "as long as I made it." Then, as if convincing herself that she really, truly had swum across the Channel she added, "I'm the first woman across, am I not?"

When Julia and Meg and everyone else laughed and assured her that yes, she was the first, their confirmation seemed to brighten Trudy's mood, but she shivered in the cold and then smiled for the first time, saying, "I can freeze now."

It was not an altogether idle thought. As the body temperature of a Channel swimmer cools during a swim, he or she is at some risk of cardiac arrest due to the stimulation of the vagus nerve, a phenomenon that continues even after a swimmer has left the water. As soon as the swimmer stops moving and the wet body is exposed to the air, body temperature can drop drastically, making the first few minutes out of the water the most dangerous.

Although no one aboard the *Alsace* knew any of this, common sense led Meg and Julia to whisk Trudy away to the relative warmth of the pilothouse, where she removed her suit and lay wrapped in blankets and Bill Burgess's coat, eating more pineapple to soothe her tongue. Harpman gently asked her questions, then dashed off the first of several stories she would write that night, each a bit longer and more thorough, for transmission by wireless to the *Daily News* offices in New York. On deck, the crew and others still on board held an impromptu celebration—Pop Ederle was seen dancing a jig of joy on deck, ecstatic at both his daughter's victory and his reported haul of $175,000 on his wager. In a matter of moments Captain Corthes turned the *Alsace* to Dover and began to steam away.

Sitting in the pilothouse, the feeling soon began to return to

Trudy's arms and legs as her body slowly warmed. Now the gentle rocking of the boat did what nearly fifteen hours swimming in the sea could not, and Trudy began to feel a little queasy. All the excitement was out on the deck.

The world wasn't waiting for Trudy to start the celebration. It was still early in the afternoon in the Highlands, and there was already a party underway. Gertrude's sister Helen, staked out at the offices of the *New York Daily News*, had called her mother by telephone each time a bulletin came across the wires; now, only a few moments after Trudy reached England, she called again with word of her arrival. A moment later someone raced over from the offices of the *Highland News* with the same information.

There were hundreds of people milling around the cottage— friends, neighbors, and perfect strangers on vacation caught up in the excitement, as well as representatives of the *Daily News* and other papers. Interviewed while sitting in a rocking chair on the porch, Mrs. Ederle said that Trudy had made her "the proudest mother in the world." She described her daughter as "a plain home girl," who did not smoke or drink, and, she added, as if suddenly aware that her daughter was not just hers anymore, but the world's, "she does not go out with young men, except just once in a while. She has no sweetheart that I know of." Trudy's little brother Henry, age six, then proceeded to steal the show. Mrs. Ederle told the press that the day before, as Trudy was preparing for her swim, little Henry and a young playmate, a little girl, had been playing in a boat just offshore. It capsized, and Henry, who could already swim, kept the young girl afloat until Mrs. Ederle had waded in, fully dressed, and hauled both children to shallow water. Then Henry piped up that not only was he, too, going to swim the English Channel one day, but he claimed he could "breathe underwater."

At Ederle Brothers Meats on Amsterdam Avenue, the scene was no less festive. Trudy's uncles, John and Ernest, who managed the business for her father, closed the shop early and gave each of the nearly thirty employees the rest of the day off. Most, however, stayed behind and joined in the fun while John started giving away sausages and frankfurters as the sidewalk and the streets outside the store soon became choked with well-wishers.

In pressrooms all across the country editors barked orders, front pages were scrapped, and headlines were recast as word of Ederle's triumph trumped the other news of the day. Even the hunt for the "Jersey leopard," which had escaped from its crate while being transported to a zoo and was terrorizing the New Jersey countryside—at least according to the papers—was pushed below the fold in New York's late afternoon and evening papers.

As soon as the papers hit the street bearing news of Trudy's triumph, the younger generation had a new catchphrase, as "What for?" rapidly supplanted the impertinent "So's your old man." Reporters from every paper in the city spread out far and wide, tracking down Trudy's friends and teammates in the WSA, Louis Handley, Charlotte Epstein, and anyone else who cared to comment on the young woman's accomplishment.

In England and France there was no less interest in Trudy, although the reportage was a bit more restrained, for not only had the Channel been conquered by an American, rather than a representative of either of the two nations that met at the Strait of Dover, but Trudy was of German extraction, still a source of some disquiet less than a decade after the end of World War I. The European newspapers also had the advantage of time, as it was too late to report the story that evening—their readers would have to wait until the following morning to find out the details of Trudy's triumph.

Aboard the *Alsace*, Trudy stayed in the pilothouse as Burgess, Corthes, and Henry Ederle discussed their next move. Burgess had originally planned to return to Cape Gris-Nez immediately after the swim, and in his heart he probably expected to return many hours earlier with a very disappointed Channel swimmer. But Trudy's success, combined with the weather, which Burgess and Corthes knew might be problematic in mid-Channel, and the late hour, caused a change in plans. The three men decided that they would spend the night in England, and as the *Alsace* steamed back out from shore they decided to set a course for Dover.

Trudy shed the blanket and coat, put on some dry, warm clothes, and spent the next few hours slowly getting warm and recovering from her ordeal. She sat with Meg and Julia Harpman, chatting a bit, but the two women realized that she was exhausted and didn't press her to talk—Harpman had enough for now, and there would be time to talk over the next few days. Now that Trudy had succeeded, her assignment lasted until the young woman returned to the United States.

By the time the *Alsace* steamed into Dover harbor at 11:30 P.M., a large crowd had already gathered along the pier, guessing that she might put in there for the evening. But the tug couldn't dock until a large barge pulled away. Trudy, anxious to come ashore and still a bit queasy, left the pilothouse for the deck, breathing heavily as she tried to quash the touch of seasickness she now felt.

At length, Corthes pulled the boat alongside the dock, and Trudy and everyone else on board gathered their meager possessions— none had thought to bring a change of clothes, except for those provided for Trudy to wear after the swim—and prepared to disembark.

But they were not allowed to leave the boat. About the only people who were not impressed with Trudy's feat were British customs officials. Even as the crowd that had gathered to welcome the world's newest hero grew, minions of the customs office refused to allow the passengers to leave the *Alsace* because none of them—whose citizenship was divided among America, France, Egypt, and England— carried a passport.

Burgess and Corthes pleaded their case, and at length an official with sufficient authority was roused from his slumber to address the situation. He was perhaps not only the only man in England who seemed completely unaware that Trudy Ederle had swum the Channel, but apparently had never even heard of her. The skeptical official boarded the boat and proceeded, while the crowd waiting on the pier booed and hissed, to interview each and every passenger as if he or she were a spy who had been caught laying mines across the Strait of Dover.

The interrogation of Trudy was particularly impudent. When asked her age, Trudy, her tongue swollen, tried to mumble "Nineteen." In truth, she was twenty, but the WSA and her family had long ago decided not to correct an earlier reporting error. The customs officer misheard and jotted down "thirteen" then looked Trudy up and down, evidently concluding she was older and had tried to deceive him for some nefarious purpose, leading to an ever more aggressive interrogation concerning her background.

The questions came fast, one right after the other, and Trudy, exhausted and increasingly frustrated, struggled to hear and stammered out her answers in a near panic. She was just starting to come to terms with what had just happened—and now this. So far swimming the English Channel had been nothing but a huge bother, what with all the questions and people and strangers. She just wanted to go to bed.

At length—but not until Trudy was subjected to a cursory search to make sure wasn't smuggling anything into the country—the official reluctantly agreed to allow everyone to come ashore but insisted that each person report to the customs office the following day for more grilling.

The raucous crowd barely parted as Trudy's party left the pier, and Trudy, almost staggering with fatigue, grasped every hand again as she half walked, half stumbled, her father's arm around her shoulders and Meg beside her. It took nearly a half mile before the crowd thinned, and, finally, they found a car willing to take them to the hotel.

Trudy made her way to her room in a fog, and Meg prepared a warm soda bath to soothe her muscles and erase the chill she still felt deep inside. As Trudy slipped beneath the water she felt warm for the first time since—well, for the first time since she had arrived in Cape Gris-Nez. Not only was there no hot water at the Hotel du Phare, but Burgess, afraid that warm water might make the Channel feel even colder to Trudy, had ordered Trudy to take cold baths exclusively, and she had followed his instructions religiously. Now as the warm water covered her entire body, save for her face, she thought she might never take another cold bath for the rest of her life.

She was hungry, finally, her store of energy depleted from her swim, and ordered four ham sandwiches and some tomatoes from the kitchen, eating them one right after the other. Warmed by her bath and with her belly full of food, sometime between 1:00 and 2:00 A.M., after being awake for almost twenty-four hours, swimming for fourteen hours and thirty-one minutes, covering some twenty-one miles as the crow flies by swimming more than thirty miles along her jagged course, and making an estimated twenty-two thousand arm strokes, Trudy Ederle, at last, blessedly, pulled down the covers to her bed and lay down. Earlier in the summer she had bought a doll, which she dubbed "the Channel Sheik" and took with her everywhere. Now she held the doll close in her arms, closed her eyes, and tried to go to sleep.

It was almost impossible. Deep inside, her body, although exhausted, still buzzed and vibrated as if not quite ready to turn off after so much sustained activity, and her muscles were on the edge of cramping. When she closed her eyes she still felt the lift and fall of the sea, and almost felt as if she were about to roll out of the bed. When her body did relax, her mind did not, as a thousand thoughts raced through her head as the swim played itself out again like a newsreel, only nothing was in the right order as she went from the sea to Gris-Nez to the boat and then the beach and back again. The images and the thoughts in her mind swirled back and forth like the Channel waters, taking her first one way and then the other, until, late at night, at last, she finally found the slack water of her dreams and drifted off, fitfully, afloat in an uncertain and somewhat frightening future. To Trudy, now that she was out of the sea, the question was now not "What for?" but "What next?"

BULLETIN
Dover, England, Aug 7.—(By the Associated Press)—
Gertrude Ederle bounced out of bed this morning declaring she was ready for another swim.

She showed no traces of the terrible strain of Friday's ordeal . . .

As Trudy slept, the world was waking to the realization of just how revolutionary her swim had been. Trudy hadn't just conquered the Channel, a remarkable achievement in itself for a woman, but she had beaten—make that *shattered*—the men's record, and by such an enormous margin that it caused a complete recasting of perceptions. Even those who had been indifferent to the whole notion of swimming the Channel and thought it was just another stunt akin to marathon ballroom dancing couldn't help but pay attention. This was different—hers was not just an individual success, or just another example of American superiority, but a triumph that recast the way women were viewed everywhere. The phrase "weaker sex" suddenly sounded old-fashioned.

The *Washington Post* viewed her performance as a triumph both for her as an individual and for her gender. In an editorial the paper offered that "the English Channel . . . is no longer the supreme test of feminine swimming endurance, while it remains the great test for males," but it also heralded Trudy with nationalistic fervor, concluding that "much benefit to American womanhood will result . . . The American girl is alright!" In the *New York Herald-Tribune* the next day, sports editor W. O. "Bill" McGeehan was effusive in his praise of Ederle, writing, "Let the men athletes be good sportsmen and admit that the test of the Channel swim is the sternest of all tests of human endurance and strength. Gertrude Ederle has made the achievements of the five men swimmers look puny . . . The daughters of the younger age are a different breed and, to my mind, a better breed. You cannot class Gertrude Ederle as a freak and an exception . . . After this, the odds against women in any line of endeavor will shorten."

McGeehan's sentiments were echoed in columns and editorials all over the world. In Berlin the sports editor of the *Zeitung am Mittag* hailed her achievement as "new and conclusive proofs of the athletic emancipation of the once 'weaker sex,' . . . Miss Ederle's triumph is also the triumph of the modern woman athlete." The French newspaper *Le Figaro* heralded her as "the most glorious of the nymphs," while the *London Star* offered that by "knocking the men's record for the Channel swim sky high," Ederle had "given the lords of creation cause to think furiously," and other London papers heralded Trudy as "Gertrude of America." They gave her plenty of ink, but many British journalists, understandably perhaps, chose to lather their most effusive praise upon Burgess. They overlooked his French residency and embraced him as English once again. Alec Rutherford touted him for his discovery of what he termed "the Ederle course," a winning route across the Channel waters, giving nearly as much credit to his skills as navigator as to Ederle's swimming prowess.

But in the United States, in particular, politicians, pundits, and fellow athletes fell all over themselves offering praise for Trudy. Louis Handley said, "Gertrude's swim overjoyed us all, but it surprised none in the Women's Swimming Association . . . The swim was a vindication of women's capability as athletes." The acting mayor of New York, Joseph McKee, praised her for "bringing honor to the city of New York." Even New York Yankees owner Jacob Ruppert felt the need to weigh in, calling her feat "a great American accomplishment!"

The emphasis on the "American" portion of her accomplishment by such a well-known German-American as Jacob Ruppert was no accident, for in the wake of her victory German-American groups were already claiming Trudy as their own—both the United German Societies, representing 2,500 German-American groups in the United States just beginning to reemerge after the war, and the Manhattan Council of the Steuben Society extended public congratulations to Trudy, hoping that her triumph would help their groups regain acceptance and legitimacy. They were slapped down immediately, and the *New York Times* criticized such "vicarious glorification of German stock." America was not going to share its hero.

But the swim had an immediate impact that went farther than mere words of praise, both practically and philosophically. Women's rights advocates such as Carrie Catt, a colleague of Susan B. Anthony and founder and president of the League of Women Voters, recalled the days when "it was thought that women could not throw a ball or even walk very far down the street without feeling faint." She believed that equal rights for women went "hand in hand with bodily strength," something Trudy Ederle had proven beyond all possible doubt.

Ironically enough, as Trudy had battled the Channel, the IOC, with great reluctance and under a great deal of pressure from women's advocates around the world, had been debating whether to allow women to compete in track and field events for the first time, as arguments that touted women's strength and athleticism had been countered by those who believed that, by their very nature, women were just not cut out for sport, and that competition by women in track events was positively dangerous to a woman's delicate constitution. But just as Trudy had asked "What for?" the measure had reluctantly been approved and the IOC sanctioned competition in the 100-meter and 800-meter run as well as the 4-by-100-meter relay at the 1928 Olympics. Now that Trudy had swum the Channel, the decision that had seemed so controversial suddenly seemed conservative. Similarly, just a few days earlier, on August 3, the French tennis champion Suzanne Lenglen had become the first female tennis player to turn professional, a decision widely derided in the sporting press and elsewhere as unbecoming of a woman. But now, following Trudy's triumph, that attitude suddenly seemed quaint—if a woman could beat a man's record in sports, why should she not also enjoy the same financial benefits as a professional male athlete?

The change did not escape notice by the French champion, perhaps the world's best-known female athlete before Trudy's triumph. Tracked down by reporters in Paris, where she was trying on gowns in anticipation of her first professional tour of America, Lenglen called Ederle "a super woman," and said, "Her exploit definitely enthrones woman in the field of sport. Contests requiring deftness, skill and adroitness, such as archery, golf and tennis, have long been recognized as woman's province, but Gertrude has definitely proved that woman is man's equal in contests requiring endurance, strength and grit." In the future, it would become ever more difficult to argue otherwise, and that was perhaps the greatest impact of all—Trudy's swim provided dramatic evidence that women were not limited by their physical differences from men, and that in fact, it was quite possible that at least in some areas they were actually *better* than men, a concept that just a day earlier would have been considered heresy. Tom Robinson, a well-respected swimming coach at Northwestern University and close colleague of Louis Handley, told the Associated Press that the psychological impact Trudy's swim would have on women was incalculable. "The complete conquest of fear will do more to bring about the development of the woman athlete as much as anything else," he declared. "As far as physical strength is concerned, women . . . have shown a prowess equal to men. Physical education has brought about an evolution of common sense that has wrought a complete turnover not only in women's physical condition but in her whole mental attitude . . . It has taught her to think freely and it has helped her to enjoy life as she never had a chance to before. As a result it has brought a new race of women athletes."

Trudy, of course, was suddenly the de facto leader of this new race, and young girls on both continents suddenly imagined themselves to be Trudy Ederle. Yet, like so many revolutionaries, Trudy herself would not experience the full benefit of the emancipation she inspired. Instead, as the woman who spearheaded those changes, she would soon find herself caught up in the rough currents of social change.

As yet she was still all but oblivious to the hubbub her swim had caused all around the world. But she would soon find evidence of just how much had changed.

The night passed slowly for Trudy as she awoke a dozen times to find her tongue still swollen and feeling strange in her mouth, and her muscles still unable to settle down. She climbed out of bed at nine o'clock, and Bill Burgess came to her room after she had dressed and gave her a quick invigorating massage. She then took another hot bath and found that the longer she was awake the better she felt, as the swelling of her tongue finally began to subside. Julia Harpman dropped by, and now Trudy gave a lengthier, more circumspect interview so Harpman could begin work on a more detailed account of Trudy's own story of the swim.

She still couldn't quite comprehend precisely what had happened, telling Harpman she felt as if she were "back at our starting point." Although she had never felt melancholy or down during the swim itself, now that it was over she was strangely unaffected. Something big had happened, she knew that, but *she* hadn't changed at all—yet, somehow, everything else had.

She knew this from the scene at the beach and at the dock the night before, but Trudy hadn't seen anything yet. When she parted the curtains to check on the weather she discovered that there were hundreds, if not thousands, of people gathered around the hotel. Overnight, a rumor had swept Dover that because of her trouble with customs, Trudy would leave for France first thing in the morning, and everyone in Dover hoped to get a glimpse of her before she left.

Trudy wasn't in control of much of anything anymore. Harpman and Trudy's father were savvy enough to ask Trudy to don a swimsuit for her first public appearance. They wanted her to go back down to the water and take a swim. That was all right with Trudy—she tried to swim every day—but this would be no relaxing dip in the ocean, rather an arranged event for the press and the cameras.

When Trudy came down from her room into the hotel lobby at about 10:00 A.M., reality hit her in the face like a rogue wave. The front desk was swamped with telegrams and bouquets of flowers, and the lobby itself was packed with well-wishers, journalists, cameramen, local governmental officials, and English bobbies trying to maintain order. Hundreds more were gathered outside the hotel, pressing for admittance, all just hoping for a glimpse of the young woman who only a few short months before could have walked down the street in almost any city in the world and not drawn a second glance. That was no longer possible. The world wanted her—*now*—and it was not going to wait.

Trudy lasted only a few moments in the tumult before she asked to be taken away. She was hustled into the hotel dining room to catch her breath and then to the pavilion at nearby Granville Gardens, where an impromptu press conference of a sort was held. As she sat at a small table before piles of telegrams, flanked by her father, her sister, Burgess, and Helmi, who was acting as something of a security guard, Trudy took a few questions from the handful of reporters lucky enough to be allowed inside. Wearing her WSA swimsuit, Trudy looked alert and healthy, if a bit wide-eyed, as the newsreel cameras whirled in her face—but she was clearly less than comfortable, laughing nervously, glancing about anxiously, unaccustomed to being the focus of such sustained attention from so many strangers. Physically, she felt fine, with little residual soreness, although she was still a bit tired and her face was puffy from the relentless slap of the waves and the salt water. Her only problem was a sore right hand— she had already shaken so many hands it was sore to the touch. When someone approached her and grabbed her hand, she cringed and actually called out in pain, then shook and flexed her fingers.

Nothing had prepared her for such attention. She had trained to swim the Channel, not so much to be the first woman who swam the Channel, and she kept saying that it all felt "unreal . . . like a dream."

She opened a few telegrams, including one from Jabez Wolffe, who suddenly found it advantageous to be magnanimous, causing Trudy to laugh out loud. But most of the messages were from people she had never met before, all of whom wanted something. It was embarrassing and bewildering. There were invitations to banquets and dinners, requests for her to give swimming demonstrations and speeches, and the thousand other mostly innocuous requests that come with being a celebrity. There were—she couldn't believe it!—even marriage proposals from men all over the world, people she had never met.

There were also dozens and hundreds of offers that dripped money, and Pop Ederle separated them from the other telegrams. Vaudeville producers, book publishers, magazine editors, toothpaste and tobacco companies, everyone and anyone suddenly wanted the name Trudy Ederle on a masthead, a marquee, a byline, or a cut line.

Trudy had known that if she swam the Channel she would reap some financial benefit—that red roadster had to be paid for somehow—but there was no precedent that allowed her to foresee what was ahead. This had never happened before—to anyone.

Dudley Field Malone's wildest dream seemed about to come true. The attorney had been savvy enough to figure out that Trudy's triumph could be parlayed into cash, and he had thoroughly won over Henry Ederle. That was important. Trudy was still a minor, and Malone's contract, technically, was with her guardian—Henry Ederle—and not Trudy herself. In fact, Trudy deferred to her father and paid little attention to the financial side of her swim and evinced little interest in any part of it. As an athlete, Trudy was the equal of a man, but in almost every other area she was still being treated not even as a woman, but as a girl.

Trudy's success kicked in the remainder of her contract with the *Tribune-News*—more than enough to pay back the money Malone advanced to her and leaving $2,500 to spare. But that, in the parlance of the day, was mere "peanuts." Malone saw dollar signs floating on the Channel and knew that if he played his hand correctly his five-thousand-dollar advance to Trudy would pay off at odds even better than those Henry Ederle received from the oddsmakers of Lloyd's of London.

There was just one problem—well, two actually. Dudley Field Malone wasn't in Dover. He had been in France, managing his divorce office in Paris, but left on August 4 for the United States on the French liner *France* and was halfway across the Atlantic when Trudy completed her swim. While he was still able to receive offers by cable while aboard the vessel, he couldn't really consult with Henry or Trudy or participate in any substantive talks concerning her post-Channel career.

That would have to wait until Trudy was back in the United States, where the clamor for her services was already at a fever pitch. There seemed little question that Trudy—and everyone around her—would soon become very wealthy. Suzanne Lenglen's agent, the promoter C. C. Pyle, had already negotiated a fifty-thousand-dollar fee for the French star's first professional tour of America, and Trudy was now many, many times more popular. If Lenglen was worth fifty thousand dollars, Trudy was worth at least a half million dollars, if not more.

But with Trudy's name on everyone's lips all over the world, her picture on the cover of virtually every newspaper in the country, her achievement still fresh and with her popularity and fame at its absolute zenith, and an entire country breathlessly waiting for more, Trudy wasn't going to America. Although any ship sailing for the United States would have welcomed her aboard as their guest just for the publicity, her father had booked passage to return to America on the *Berengaria*—on August 21. In the meantime he decided to take Trudy to Germany to visit with her grandmother and other relatives.

Trudy didn't really care—although she was anxious to get home and see her mother, she had Meg with her and looked forward to seeing her grandmother and cousins—but the decision to go to Germany was the first of a number of poor decisions made by her father and by Malone that would hasten Trudy back to anonymity. The most famous woman in the world was hardly dry, yet her renown was already about to fade.

But in Dover, she was still a hero. After the press conference Helmi and Louis Timson delivered her back to the hotel atop their shoulders to keep the crowd off her, and for the rest of the afternoon Trudy was ushered all over town to meet this person, greet that one, and have her picture taken here and there, including before a bust of Captain Webb in front of the Hotel Burlington. She even managed to check in with the customs office, where her reception was much more pleasant—and briefer—than the previous evening's.

Before sailing for Boulogne, Trudy went back home, down to the water, and with hundreds of onlookers gathered on the beach, she dove back into the sea. For a moment she forgot the last fifteen or sixteen hours, and as she swam she felt the stiffness leave her body and her anxiety begin to fade. Had it been up to her, she would have kept swimming, but it would be a long time before she could just swim for herself again. The real purpose of the swim was to provide the newsreel cameramen some footage of Trudy stepping onshore and reenacting her arrival less than twenty-four hours earlier. They had complained that due to the fact that she had reached Kingsdown at night, there were no photographs or film of Trudy walking out of the water, and after all, that was what was important.

Trudy dutifully did her duty, reenacting her arrival, only this time in broad daylight and being enveloped by the crowd. Within a week the staged shot would be foisted off to the world as genuine. In fact, most newsreel accounts of her achievement not only utilized such staged footage, but film of her from her failed swim the previous summer, which had been taken under better weather conditions and was far superior. Audiences were so eager to see Trudy that they seemed not to notice the changing boats, weather conditions, coaches, or, most notably, the swimsuit and the goggles Trudy wore while swimming.

Later that afternoon Trudy and her entourage reboarded the *Alsace*, crossed the Channel once more, landed at Boulogne to a raucous reception, and then returned to Cape Gris-Nez, where Pop Ederle was still in a celebratory mood and held a party at the hotel. Trudy turned in early and finally received a little rest, but the next day Trudy, her father and sister, Julia Harpman, and Arthur Sorenson left for Germany, where she was looking forward, at last, to the opportunity to get some extended rest away from the crowds. Bill Burgess was left behind, his job done, and was disappointed that Henry Ederle didn't even see fit to give him a bonus, but after all, had it been up to him, Trudy never would have finished. He sought out Lillian Cannon and began training her again.

Yet before she left Cape Gris-Nez, Trudy was able to do something she had been trying to do ever since she walked onto the beach. She had been so busy and so tired, that apart from a brief telegram, she had never had a chance to write a letter to her own mother. Julia had offered to do it for her, but Trudy wanted to write this one herself.

My Dearest Loving Mother:

We did it, Mother, we did it! The trick is turned and aren't you just so proud? We are all so happy. England and France are rejoicing in the glory. Oh, the crowds that follow us here and there. The paper people are just impossible, but grand.

Mom, I had the feeling of sure success—just wouldn't give up. Not once was I on the point of abandoning the swim. The good God led me on safely. It all went so quick . . . Get there or die, that was my motto . . . Really Mom, I can't dope it all out yet . . . [Margaret] was just lovely, did everything in her power to get me over. Didn't I say I need people like her? Pop, too, was helping me on, only he felt bad, I mean sorry for me. He just had to cry and, Mommie, he wants to say that you are too soft! . . .

Coming back from England yesterday they buried me in flowers.

How happy everyone is.

Last night pop gave a party. We did it. No more worrying!

Love and kisses galore for you, dear Mother. I am only your "Trudy."

25

Swept Away

THERE WAS NO end to it.

As Trudy traveled from Cape Gris-Nez to Calais and then to Germany, stopping first in Stuttgart before finally making her way to Bissingen, where she hoped to spend some time relaxing with her family, she was swarmed over by the crowds, feted by government officials, and otherwise swept along in a frenzy of adoration for which she still wasn't prepared. Thirty thousand people greeted her in Stuttgart, packing the streets around the train station, forcing her to participate in an impromptu parade just to leave town. And when she arrived in Bissingen, it was utterly unrecognizable. The quiet little village was flooded with visitors.

Trudy tried to stay out of public view and hardly left her grandmother's home and business, the Lambs' Inn, the center of the family's substantial farm holdings. Yet there was still no escape from her fans. An unending stream of telegrams, letters, bouquets of flowers, and other gifts piled up and spilled over. The local postman, the sole employee of the office, was reported to be near a nervous breakdown just trying to keep up.

She gave few interviews, as Julia Harpman was still protective of her story and eager to keep other reporters away, but at the same time it was becoming ever clearer that while Trudy might have conquered the Channel, her nerves were proving to be an ever greater challenge. Everywhere she went there was always someone who wanted to ask something of her, and, increasingly, Trudy's first response was to recoil and back away.

The European press viewed her reticence with suspicion—what

was she hiding? Back in Cape Gris-Nez there were still newspaper reporters assigned to cover those swimmers waiting to swim the Channel, and those swimmers, particularly the females, were disappointed that Trudy had stolen their thunder and more than a little jealous. They resented not only her accomplishment, but all the attention that had subsequently been foisted upon her. Clarabelle Barrett, Lillian Cannon, Mercedes Gleitze, and Mille Gade Corson had all hoped to reap the financial windfall that being the first woman to swim the Channel promised—a windfall that now seemed certain to be Trudy's alone. Gade Corson had been absolutely blunt about that, telling the press she intended to swim the Channel "for the kiddies," to provide for the financial well-being of her two young children, and both Barrett and Cannon, like Trudy, had financial backers who hoped to see a return on their investment.

Despite Trudy's achievement, all four women were still determined to duplicate Trudy's effort. If one of these other swimmers could better Trudy's time or if Trudy's accomplishment were somehow called into question, the next woman to swim the English Channel would still be famous and could still cash in. There was a long tradition of false claimants when it came to swimming the Channel, and while Trudy was in Germany, rumors that called her swim into question found their way into print.

After the initial wash of good publicity, a backlash soon began to appear in newspapers on both sides of the Channel as reporters were denied access to Trudy. Will Rogers, America's leading humorist, took note of the jealousy and joked that "England is trying to get credit for it [Ederle's crossing]. They claim they furnished the land for her to land on, otherwise she never would have made it. France can't get any ad out of it at all, outside of being a good place to start somewhere from." While the European press certainly understood the nature of Trudy's agreement with the *Tribune-News* syndicate, they had to sell newspapers, too, and a controversy with Trudy at its center was the next best thing to Trudy herself. Her first lesson in the life of a celebrity was about to come.

The newspaper *Phare du Calais* (*Lighthouse of Calais*) got right to the point and asked whether proper neutral witnesses had been present during Trudy's swim. Simply by asking the question the paper left the impression that they had not. Newspapers in Dover and Kent followed up and wondered aloud why so few details of her swim had been released, ignoring Harpman's stories entirely, but that wasn't the point. Their intention was to raise questions surrounding Trudy's swim, and in that they succeeded. The *Westminster Gazette* interviewed a Folkestone boat captain who believed the tugboats provided Trudy with unfair assistance and asked "whether a swim assisted by adventurous aid, such as the shelter of a boat, is comparable with the unaided effort of the other swimmers who have succeeded." The paper speculated that Trudy had somehow been able to take advantage of the "suction" of the tug plowing through the water and had, in effect, been towed across the Channel, drafting in the wake of the tug.

Such questions gave new life to the efforts of swimmers like Cannon and Gade Corson. If Trudy were discredited, the next woman to swim the Channel might nab at least a share of the glory and renown that was now Trudy's alone.

When these reports made their way to the Lambs' Inn, the reaction was instantaneous. Trudy, understandably, was upset. She knew what she had done, and to have that called into question hurt her deeply.

It was a manufactured controversy—Trudy accurately called it a "made up story." Most of those who had tried to swim the Channel in recent years had been accompanied by a tug, and the presence of a second tug on Trudy's swim had been entirely out of her control and had hardly been of any help. "The wash was absolutely fearful," said Trudy in reference to the rough water created by the boat, which, since it is mixed with turbulent air, actually provides less buoyancy; "It almost took me down." But within twenty-four hours the charges that Trudy had somehow received unfair aid while swimming the Channel swept the globe.

Julia Harpman stepped to the fore, protecting not only her story, but both her own reputation and Trudy's, not to mention the financial offers now piling up on Dudley Field Malone's desk in New York. Harpman gathered witnesses and drafted an affidavit that stated, "We, the undersigned witnesses of the Channel swim of Miss Gertrude Ederle, hereby certify in the presence of American Consul M. Gaston Smith, that on the morning of Friday Aug. 6, Miss Ederle walked into the water at Cape Gris Nez and swam to Kingsdown, England, where she arrived 14 and a half hours later and that she received no aid in her swimming and that she abided faithfully by all rules of Channel swimming and international sportsmanship." Of course there were no "official" rules or governing authority overseeing Channel swims, apart from the long-standing custom that swimmers could not be touched or receive direct assistance, but the affidavit served its purpose. It was then signed not only by Harpman and Trudy's father and sister, but by several others on board both the *Alsace* and *La Morinie*, including Arthur Sorenson, Minott Saunders, Alec Rutherford, and Frederick Abbot, the French correspondent of the International News Service, who expressly had been invited aboard the *Alsace* to serve as an impartial observer.

The affidavit stopped the controversy in its tracks, but the attacks taught Trudy a lesson. Even as she set world records and won Olympic medals, she always had been able to remain "one of the girls." As if she needed any more evidence, swimming the Channel set her apart. She wasn't just herself anymore, but a symbol—and to some, a target. Her departure for America on August 21 aboard the *Berengaria* could not come soon enough.

Aboard the boat Trudy finally, finally had some time to relax. Although the passenger list included the best-known socialites of the era, Trudy topped the list. She enjoyed a first-class suite as the captain and crew of the vessel did everything in their power to ensure that she had a pleasant and relaxing journey. Apart from giving a few swimming demonstrations in the ship's Pompeian-inspired pool, she was, by and large, segregated from the bulk of the ship's passengers by her status in first class. She enjoyed the privacy and found she enjoyed meeting people on a smaller scale in the restaurants and lounges dedicated to the ship's wealthier passengers. Some of the richest and most important people in the world were asking her, Trudy Ederle, for her autograph. She signed for everyone, using the same salutation she would for the remainder of her life, "Swimmingly Yours."

Mostly, however, she had just slept and rested, not so much from her ordeal in the Channel, but from everything that had come after. In the last three weeks she'd hardly had any time to think. Then came New York.

As Trudy stood on the promenade of the *Berengaria* as it steamed into New York Harbor in midmorning of August 27, she once again found herself completely taken aback. Since swimming the English Channel only three short weeks before, that was becoming something of a pattern.

She'd never seen anything like it. No one on board the ship had ever seen anything like it. No one in *New York* had ever seen anything like it. As the Manhattan skyline came into focus and began to grow tall, the boat was greeted from all directions as vessels of every size and shape came out to meet it—fireboats spraying water high into the air, tugboats, cutters, motorboats, private launches, and yachts, all with their sirens tied down wide open, creating the loudest din anyone on the water ever recalled hearing before.

At first Trudy didn't understand, but as the *Berengaria* drew closer and Trudy saw banners flying on the boats that said, "Welcome home Trudy," and "Queen of the Seas," she began to realize it was all for her, every bit of it. A few moments earlier, she'd been asked to go to the upper deck. Once she arrived two biplanes circling the ship dropped flowers overhead, their petals falling like rain all around her, the sky raining flowers.

It was all for her.

The greeting was organized by a man known as "Mr. New York," Grover Whalen, the city's official greeter, who liked to refer to himself as the "doorman to the western hemisphere." In 1919, when Whalen was put in charge of the city's reception for the Prince and Princess of Wales, he came up with the notion of the ticker-tape parade. Although the first few such parades were relatively modest, since then Whalen's efforts had become ever grander. They culminated in the reception afforded Trudy and, a year later, Charles Lindbergh. The scene Trudy was watching unfold in New York Harbor was just the beginning.

New York came to a stop. Nothing else mattered. America's foremost film star, Rudolph Valentino, had died of peritonitis on August 23, and ever since his body had lain in state at Campbell's Funeral Parlor under twenty-four-hour guard by a phalanx of New York City police officers. But on the day of Trudy's arrival, the bulk of the guard was transferred to Trudy's home, and the crowd that had gathered around the funeral home for days suddenly disappeared. Trudy was bigger than any motion picture star.

New York was gaga for Trudy, and in the days prior to her arrival Whalen and the New York press, particularly the *Daily News*, had whipped the city into a frenzy. Now that the day arrived, Whalen rounded up Trudy's entire family—forty-two strong including aunts, uncles, and cousins—and divvied them up aboard two tugs owned by the city, the *Riverside* and the official VIP vessel, the *Macom*. As the *Berengaria* approached, the *Macom* made its way alongside the gigantic vessel.

From aboard the *Macom*, Mrs. Ederle spotted her daughters first, standing in an open window on the promenade deck, and began waving her arms back and forth, trying to get their attention. She did, and Trudy nearly jumped out of the window to reach her. "Mamma," she cried, "Mamma!" Even amid the din in the harbor, everyone aboard the *Macom* could hear Trudy's voice above the tumult.

Trudy wouldn't have to wait for the big ship to dock. A few minutes later the *Macom* pulled alongside the *Berengaria*, and Trudy and her entourage came aboard the *Macom* to be ferried ashore, reunited, at last, with her mother. She left in such a rush that she left all her bags behind and nearly knocked her mother to the ground as they met and hugged, tears streaming down both of their faces, Trudy wearing a blue serge coat and a lavender felt hat, clutching her doll, her hair bronze from the summer sun, and her face tanned and healthy.

After the *Macom* docked at Pier A in the Battery on the southern tip of Manhattan, the same place Trudy's swim for Sandy Hook had begun in virtual anonymity only a few months before, Trudy was hustled through a crowd numbering in the thousands, then into an open car for a procession to City Hall Plaza, but the crowds were so immense the car barely moved as everyone pressed forward to get a glimpse at Trudy. At City Hall Plaza the scene was even wilder, as ten thousand people crowded into the plaza and the surging crowd threatened to turn into a dangerous crush. Trudy and her family were pushed inside by a phalanx of police, and the big iron doors of the city hall closed and locked to prevent hundreds of onlookers from crashing the reception.

Trudy, her family, and other VIPs were escorted to the mayor's reception room, where New York mayor Jimmy Walker paid tribute to

Trudy. "When history records the greatest crossings, they will speak of Moses crossing the Red Sea, Caesar the Rubicon, and Washington the Delaware, and frankly, your crossing of the English Channel will take place alongside these."

Trudy hardly had the time to take a breath before she was taken back outside onto the steps for a photo op. The flash of the cameras had barely gone off when the crowd surged, sending people tumbling up the steps, swamping over Trudy. A bulky policeman grabbed Trudy with both arms and lifted her in the air and carried her back inside the building as Mayor Walker called for reinforcements.

At 2:30 P.M. with a gauntlet of police protecting her, Trudy, with Dudley Field Malone at her side, was put into another open car in the midst of a motorcade. As the entourage made the turn from Ninth Street to Fifth Avenue, torrents of paper fell from the sky as New York witnessed its first, gigantic, no-holds-barred ticker-tape parade. This was no modest celebration that lasted only a few blocks, like that which greeted the Prince of Wales. This celebration lasted all the way uptown, before crowds unlike any the city had ever seen, as hundreds and hundreds of thousands of New Yorkers lined the streets. At times onlookers rushed the car, stopping it in its tracks, grabbed at Trudy and knocked her from her feet, backward into the seat of the car, desperate for souvenirs. The crowd even tore a bracelet from her wrist and grabbed at her coat and hat, before police, mounted and armed with billy clubs, managed to free her.

Trudy stood in the car, her face tilted upward and spinning back and forth as if her eyes alone were not sufficient to see the entire scene, waving a flag, dizzy from the adulation, absolutely, totally, and completely overwhelmed. Trudy waved and laughed and cried and looked up in wonder, almost drowning in the attention, knowing that the crowds, later estimated as at least a quarter of a million strong, were cheering for her, but barely able to hear them herself.

The motorcade finally made its way to its destination, Trudy's home on Amsterdam Avenue, where four thousand people crammed the single block that contained the Ederles' home and butcher shop. Trudy's family had decorated the tenement in bunting and American flags, and a huge banner that said WELCOME HOME TRUDY hung from the sills. In the front window of the shop was a sort of diorama, an imitation of the English Channel cut from green cardboard, complete with cutout waves powered by an electric motor that lifted and fell, and a cutout of Trudy, an automaton bobbing though the "water," her arms fixed in the crawl stroke, a smile frozen on her lips. Along the side was a copy of a poem that read, "Pop Ederle by cutting meat made for himself a name, / His daughter Trudy by cutting waves won victory and fame. / You see her now she fights the seas, and how she puts it over. / Hurrah for her, first of her sex to swim from France to Dover."

Finally, at last, Trudy's car pulled up before the house, and the police cleared the crowd so she could get out, but before she did a young girl selected by the neighborhood stepped forward, climbed aboard the car, and tried to place a gold and white satin crown on Trudy's head. Trudy didn't want it, and pleaded, "I'm tired," but when the little girl looked heartbroken, she finally agreed, and, as the cameras of news photographers flashed over and over again, turning Trudy nearly blind as well as deaf, someone draped a blue sash over her shoulders that read "Queen Gertrude the First." Almost as quickly as the crown went on, Trudy took it off, as the crowd of friends and acquaintances of a lifetime chanted, "Trudy, Trudy, Trudy!" over and over and over, suddenly starstruck at seeing the girl next door.

Police made a corridor through the crowd, and Trudy was hustled inside, Dudley Field Malone pushing her from behind, then Trudy climbed upstairs to her family's apartment. There, the scene was only somewhat less frenetic, as dozens of people were crammed into an apartment that comfortably held only eight or ten, but now, for the first time in three months, at least she was finally surrounded by people she knew. When the crowd outside failed to disperse, the police asked her to stand before the window for a while and wave to see if that would satisfy them. For the next hour and a half she periodically pulled the curtains back and gave a short wave, but no one on the streets below budged.

Almost lost in the frenzy was the red roadster, the promise of which had helped Trudy across the Channel. It had actually been waiting for her at the pier in the Battery, gleaming in the sun, but the crowds had been so large that Trudy had not seen it. It was a Buick, precisely the one she wanted, painted fire engine red, with a big comfortable rumble seat in back. In exchange for a testimonial from Trudy, Dudley Field Malone had asked the automaker not only for the car, but for fifty thousand dollars. Buick found the price too steep and offered Malone the car plus only one thousand dollars, which he turned down. For a time it appeared that the roadster would have to wait for Pop Ederle to open his own wallet, but at the last minute the *Daily News* stepped in and bought the car for Trudy.

As the crowd finally began to thin out as New York's finest urged everyone to move along, the roadster seemed to magically appear, parked along the curb on Amsterdam Avenue in front of the Ederles' building. Dudley Field Malone had to remind Trudy it was there, asking her, "Do you really want that car?"

The question startled Trudy—that's how crazy things were—she had nearly forgotten the only thing she had hoped for when she swam the Channel. "Yeah," she responded, sounding far more weary than excited. She went downstairs for a few moments, climbed in the car and sat back, spinning the steering wheel and fiddling with the dashboard, but there were still too many people on the street for her to take the car for a drive, and the crowd made her feel claustrophobic and she fled back upstairs.

For Trudy, it was all running together—the crowds, the parades, the gifts, and the autographs and hand shaking, everything—but it still wasn't over. She was placed in another motorcade and ushered to a dinner sponsored by the mayor at the Roosevelt Hotel and made her first and only public statement of the day, speaking for all of twenty seconds. "My dear friends," she said, "after all that has been said I must be polite and thank the Mayor and Grover Whalen for the wonderful reception that has been given to me. It will be remembered during my whole life. All the kind things that have been done and said have shown such a delightful appreciation of my efforts to make the Channel crossing for the sake of my country's flag. I love you for it." After the crowd watched the British Pathe newsreel footage of her swim, Trudy was then whisked off to a show at the Globe Theater featuring the Ziegfeld Follies, and finally to the Club Lido where she danced with the mayor before more cameras. At every stop she had to run a gauntlet, as New York came to a standstill wherever she appeared.

Dudley Field Malone was suddenly everywhere now, always at Trudy's side, telling her when to pose for pictures and when not to, what to say and what to hold in her hands—when he got a look at

Trudy's doll, the Channel Sheik, he pulled it from her arms, disapproving of the impression it gave onlookers that Trudy was still a child, and besides, no one had paid her to hold it. He was sitting on a pile of commercial offers worth nearly one million dollars and was in no hurry, planning to play the offers off one another and up the ante. Various vaudeville producers had already offered her as much as six thousand dollars a week to go on tour, plus expenses, fronting an indoor water show, swimming in a portable tank, speaking to the crowds, and showing films of her swim. There were also piles of endorsements as makers of everything from swimming suits to cisterns wanted Trudy's name attached to their product, overtures from the motion picture industry, more requests to appear at banquets, and more marriage proposals than she could count.

Based on the events of the day, Malone seemed like a genius. Just a few days before, Westbrook Pegler, who was already casting a cynical eye on the commercialization of Trudy, sensing that the real needs of the young woman were being overlooked, had interviewed C. C. Pyle. The manager of Red Grange and Suzanne Lenglen had been hypercritical of Malone. Pyle, whose critics referred to him as "Cash and Carry," derided Malone as a promotional novice and told Pegler that Trudy's delay in returning to the United States had already cost her hundreds of thousands of dollars. Pyle clearly lusted after Trudy as client himself and spoke to Pegler knowing full well that his words would carry weight in the Ederle camp, where Julia Harpman was still a trusted confidante. "I would have had Trudy write her grandmother a nice souvenir postcard," he said. "Altogether Trudy and I would have cleaned up about $200,000 if she had not been under contract to Malone."

But the reception that day seemed to absolve Malone. By waiting things out, interest in Trudy only seemed to be increasing, and now when he entered into negotiations, Malone could cite the tremendous crowds that had turned out to see Trudy's return as a measure of the public's interest in her. There were, in fact, still hundreds of fans gathered on the street outside the Ederles' tenement when Trudy and her entourage finally made it home at about 1:30 A.M., fourteen and a half hours after the *Berengaria* arrived in New York, precisely the same amount of time it had taken Trudy to swim the English Channel.

She would have rather spent the time in the water, battling the waves and jellyfish. For as she exited the limousine that delivered her back home, she passed her beloved roadster, still parked along the curb. The windshield was broken and the car was covered with hundreds of scratches as overzealous fans peeled off the paint as a souvenir. Before Trudy even had a chance to start the engine the car had already been wrecked and needed repair.

Trudy collapsed in her own bed, but when she awoke the next morning it was as if she opened her eyes to a new world. The phone rang nonstop in the Ederle apartment, and the crowd on the street outside began to grow and swell again in numbers only slightly smaller than the day before. As Trudy, her father, and Dudley Field Malone finally sat down and began sorting out the dozens and dozens of telegrams and contracts and offers of various kinds that had been sent their way, a policeman knocked at the door and delivered a request from the press gathered outside on the street. Just a few minutes before, reports had come streaming across the wires from Dover. Mille Gade Corson had swum the Channel, completing the task in fifteen hours and twenty-nine minutes, only an hour slower than Trudy. Trudy was still the first, and still the fastest, but she was not the only woman to have swum the Channel anymore.

The air started coming out of the balloon. Gade Corson wasn't even dry yet, and her backer, Walter Lissberger, claimed he had won one hundred thousand dollars in wagers on her swim and had already given twenty-five thousand dollars to Gade Corson, exactly twenty-five thousand dollars more than anyone had yet given Trudy.

Trudy could scarcely believe it. She didn't think much of Gade Corson as a swimmer, but she was smart enough to say the right things in public, and soon she and Malone released a statement congratulating Gade Corson and sent her a personal cable. In a way, it had been inevitable that another woman would swim the Channel, and it was confirmation of the great changes Trudy's swim had inspired. Her success had not only shown the correct route across the Channel, for Gade Corson's path was eerily similar to hers, but Trudy had broken whatever psychological barriers that had existed and had contributed to preventing a woman from ever swimming the Chan-

304 • YOUNG WOMAN AND THE SEA

nel before. The old view was gone now, but it was still a surprise that the change happened so quickly.

As the day went on, it all caught up with her, all of it. By swimming the Channel Trudy had done something no woman had ever done before, but she had never expected that once she had done so she would find the veracity of her accomplishment attacked, or that once she returned home she'd have to continue to be a trailblazer and face the sudden onslaught of fame in a way no one, man or woman, had ever had to do before. And now, just as it seemed that everything was about to quiet down, Gade Corson had crossed the Channel, and everyone wanted to know what Trudy thought, what she would do, if she would swim the Channel again, and could she swim it even faster than before—or another dozen or two dozen or a hundred questions, it didn't matter because no matter how many times she answered or what she said, everyone still wanted more from her.

Later that day, in the early evening, as the phone kept ringing, Malone and her father kept discussing money, and Trudy was told to get ready to see this person tomorrow morning and that person in the afternoon and go here and say this and stand here and smile, Trudy reached her breaking point. What half a day in the English Channel could not do, twenty-four hours as the most famous woman in the world could. Moaning, she wrapped her arms around her head and curled up like a baby with her hands over her ears and tears streaming down her cheeks.

Trudy was put to bed, and the family physician was called as everyone waited breathless outside her room. After a thorough examination he pronounced Trudy physically fine but utterly exhausted and ordered her to stay in bed for the next twenty-four hours and not do anything or go anywhere. Trudy, Conqueror of the Channel and Queen of the Waves, needed rest. More than anything else she needed to be just plain old Trudy again.

Yet after only one day of rest Trudy resumed her rigorous schedule—there were luncheons and block parties and meetings with the rich and famous that couldn't be rescheduled. Not that anyone asked her if that's what she wanted, but she was caught in a current stronger than any the Channel had ever offered. The world still wanted her after Gade Corson's crossing—not quite as badly or for quite as much money—but still badly enough to sweep her along as if she'd lost her feet in the middle of the rapids.

C. C. Pyle had been right after all. The three-week delay had proven costly. Unlike Trudy, Gade Corson didn't hang around Europe visiting her relatives but left almost immediately for the United States, anxious to get her piece of the pie. Although Gade Corson was not the first woman to swim the Channel, she marketed herself as the first *mother* to swim the Channel, the next best thing and in some ways better. While Trudy attended a luncheon in her honor at Wanamaker's restaurant the following day, a representative of Gade Corson's handed a letter to Malone, challenging Trudy to a race around Manhattan for a purse of twenty-five thousand dollars, a publicity stunt, but an effective one. Malone probably should have milked the offer for all it was worth—Trudy was twice the swimmer Gade Corson was and would have beaten her easily—but his defensive response made it seem as if Trudy were somehow afraid of the competition, making Gade Corson's recent accomplishment seem even greater. "The air is full of challenges," wrote Malone. "They will all be considered according to time, place and importance.

"It is not necessary for Miss Ederle to swim around Manhattan Island with anybody to prove that she is the champion woman swimmer of the world. Her established record proves that. Mrs. Corson, favored by good weather in the daytime and the moon at night, made the crossing in slower time by an hour than Miss Ederle's record. This means that if Miss Ederle had swum across the Channel with Mrs. Corson on the same day with the same weather she would have bettered Mrs. Corson by about two hours.

"As soon as any woman equals or breaks Miss Ederle's record it will then be time enough to discuss a match race to decide who is the better woman.

"The champion in any line of athletic endeavors always has the say as to the time, place and circumstances of a meeting. Miss Ederle, the champion, will therefore have the say as to where, when and under what conditions the race will take place.

"Gertrude Ederle intends to be a swimming champion, not a talking champion."

He could say that again. Since Trudy returned to New York she had done very little talking on her own. Virtually all of it had been done through the mouthpiece that was Malone, and he'd done all her thinking as well.

Then it happened again. On August 30 Ernst Vierkoetter, a twenty-six-year-old German baker, took advantage of extraordinary weather conditions and, using the crawl just as Trudy had, swam the Channel in only twelve hours and forty minutes, breaking Trudy's record by nearly two hours. In three days she'd lost her place as both the only woman to swim the Channel and the fastest person to ever swim the Channel.

With every passing minute Trudy's monetary value dropped. Most of the reported nine hundred thousand dollars in offers began to dry up. Of those that did not, Malone ignored those that required little of Trudy, such as endorsements, rejecting out of hand contracts that promised only a few thousand dollars, even if all that was required of Trudy was a signature and a few photographs. Gade Corson and her representatives wisely scooped them up. Malone also failed to realize that the real gold was probably in Trudy's revolutionary single-view goggles and two-piece swim swimsuit, either of which could have made her millions of dollars with very little effort. Instead he signed a deal with the William Morris Agency to send Trudy barnstorming across the nation headlining an indoor water show. It wasn't a bad deal on the surface—Morris promised six thousand dollars a week—but the agency took ten percent off the top, Malone and Henry Ederle each received a twenty percent commission, and now Trudy had to pay all expenses—salaries for both Aileen Riggin and Helen Wainwright, who would also appear, room and board, transportation, and the cost of setting up and tearing down the portable water tank the three women would use in their swimming demonstration. It was good for the Ederle family—they bought a house in Pelham for eighteen thousand dollars soon after the papers were signed—but not good at all for Trudy.

It was the last thing she needed to do, or should have done, but Trudy wasn't in control. She deferred to her father and Malone in almost everything. Just before the tour started in late September with an engagement in New York, Trudy was finally allowed to take a brief vacation, but by then interest in her had waned even more. The 1926 World Series between Babe Ruth's New York Yankees and the St. Louis Cardinals was about to get underway.

The nationwide tour wasn't a complete disaster, but such small-scale shows were becoming a little old-fashioned. Using the same tank that had been built for Annette Kellerman and used by Thelda Bleibtrey, and accompanied by a local band hired to play the same songs Trudy had listened to while swimming the Channel, the show began with a swimming and diving exhibition by Riggin and Wainwright. Then Trudy came out and swam the crawl back and forth in the little tank, then took the stage, told the story of her swim, and showed the same newsreel footage that had already appeared in local theaters weeks before. That was it.

The show had little of the appeal such shows had a decade or so earlier when the chance to see scantily clad women in the water, like Annette Kellerman, had been titillating enough to guarantee a full house. Women didn't often still wear stockings while swimming anymore, and much of the public saw no need to pay for ticket to see in a theater what could already be seen for free at the beach.

By the time the tour finally got underway—Trudy's sister Helen accompanying her—even swimming the Channel had lost much of its luster and almost appeared anachronistic as yet another swimmer, Georges Michel of France, swam the Channel. He claimed to accomplish the feat on September 10, swimming even faster than Vierkoetter. Even though Michel was later discredited, the fact that others swam the Channel in such close proximity to Trudy made swimming the Channel seem less difficult than it was. In fact, it was still extremely difficult—by World War II only another eighteen people would swim the Channel—but impression was everything. In one more year swimming the Channel would not even be worthy of a front-page story in the newspaper, much less a banner headline

All Trudy had ever really wanted to do was swim the Channel and then drive off happily ever after in her new car, but now she found herself on the road playing to half-empty theaters in places she'd never heard of with hardly any time at all to herself. While Riggin and Wainwright could perform and then enjoy whatever charms each city offered, Trudy was stuck looking after the show and giving interviews. Wherever she went, the questions—and the requests—were numbingly the same.

What was particularly difficult for Trudy was that in nearly every town she appeared, if someone had recently drowned, Trudy, because of her swimming prowess, was often called upon to help search for the body. It was a gruesome duty she didn't want but one that was impossible to refuse.

By November, only one month into her tour, Harry Carr, well-known columnist for the *Los Angeles Times*, was driven to write, "The glowing fame of Trudie [*sic*] Ederle, who swam the English Channel, went out into the blackness the quickest of any athletic hero I can ever remember."

Nothing was going well. While she was on the road a cousin was shot and nearly killed in a mail robbery back in New Jersey, and her uncle John died in a car wreck that also injured several other family members. Meanwhile Trudy soldiered on before dwindling crowds. In the summer of 1927 she received a brief respite when she was offered a small part in a film, *Swim, Girl, Swim*, starring Bebe Daniels, and while she enjoyed the experience and received second billing to the Hollywood star, the end product, which has since been lost, did not launch Trudy into stardom. Yet while she was at the beach in Los Angeles, posing for publicity pictures, she dashed into the surf and rescued Mary Ashcroft, a Ziegfeld girl who had gone under and was drowning.

By the end of the summer in 1927, the tour finally petered out, and the grind had worn Trudy down. "It was just too much for me," she later admitted. "It was appear here, attend a tea, greet city officials, talk at luncheons, and good-hearted Trudy couldn't refuse. I finally got the shakes. I was a bundle of nerves," later saying she "broke down," and "having achieved fame upsets your life." Plans to take the show to Europe collapsed, and Trudy returned to New York. Instead of earning nine hundred thousand dollars, she had earned far less than that, later saying her total take, excluding the expenses she was forced to pay, ended up being something around fifty thousand dollars. That was still no small sum of money, but it hardly set up Trudy for life.

Apart from appearing in her act, she hardly had the chance to swim anymore, and although she was invited to participate in potentially lucrative, competitive swims to Catalina Island and elsewhere, she knew she was in no shape to do so. Besides, since swimming the Channel, her hearing had begun to deteriorate badly. Day after day of being immersed in water while training for the Channel and then on tour had taken its toll, causing additional ear infections and exacerbating her original condition caused by the measles. By 1928, the woman who had been in the papers nearly every day only a few years before had drifted almost out of sight, back, in her own way, to that special place Julia Harpman had written about only a few years before, secure in the womb of her own family in Pelham, virtually forgotten by everyone else. For a time, it appeared as if she would marry, as she was, as she described it, "practically engaged" to a family friend, a handball player she later identified only as "Charlie." But one day in conversation Trudy mentioned to him, "With my poor hearing, it might be hard on a man," expecting him to disagree. He did not, saying instead, "I guess you are right," and broke off their romance. "I never got over it," she admitted years later. "There never was anyone else. I felt too hurt . . . I've often wondered, though, that maybe I didn't hear him right."

She briefly emerged in 1930, when Lorena Hopkins, star reporter for the Associated Press and later known as a confidante and possible romantic partner of Eleanor Roosevelt, discovered Trudy teaching swimming at a public pool in Rye, New York.

Apart from her bathing suit, which had her last name stenciled across the back, Trudy was utterly anonymous. Hopkins described her as a "bronzed young woman with a determined grin," but "unless you raise your voice she can not hear you, and looks at you with an expression that has in it embarrassment, bewilderment and fear." When she asked Trudy about her Channel experience, Trudy was brutally frank.

"I'm not sorry I did it. Only—if I'd known how it was going to be, that I'd lose my hearing—I don't think I'd have done it.

"It wasn't worth it."

She was twenty-four years old.

Although Trudy tried to back away from those comments when they appeared in the press, they left the impression that her story was, in the end, a tragedy, a perception that only a few years later nearly became true. In 1933 after moving out of her house and into her own apartment, Trudy fell on some broken tile while walking down the stairs, twisting her spine, leaving her in a cast, periodically bedridden, hobbling around on a cane or with crutches, her legs all but paralyzed, unable to work, and hardly able to stand. No less than nineteen doctors pronounced that she would never swim again or walk with anything approaching normalcy.

But it was swimming, which had both given her everything and taken it away, that ultimately saved her. In 1938 while visiting with her old family doctor, he suggested that she shouldn't just try to walk so she could walk, but walk so she could swim again. She didn't think she could, walking was hard enough, but if she could walk, then she could swim again, so she tried.

At first she could take only a few steps, but over time those few steps became a few yards, then a few dozen, and finally a few blocks and even more. Then, as she later recalled, "I risked a dip in the pool. I told my legs to kick and my arms to beat, and they did . . . It was something like swimming the Channel, only harder." Eighteen months later she was swimming well enough to appear in impresario Billy Rose's water show at the 1939 New York World's Fair. The crowd remembered her, and for the first time in more than a decade she could hear them, albeit faintly, cheering for her again.

After swimming the English Channel, Trudy Ederle should have taken her place as one of the foremost athletes of the twentieth century, on par with such luminaries as Jim Thorpe, Babe Didrickson, and other pioneers, the female equivalent of Hillary and Norgay, or Jackie Robinson, yet through no fault of her own—except, perhaps, her own innate shyness and reticence—she was forgotten almost immediately. If there is any continuing tragedy to her story, it is that.

For even as Trudy was fading from memory, due in large part to her effort, women athletes were becoming ever more commonplace and accepted. Just as no one dared question whether Black athletes could compete on an equal footing with white ballplayers after Jackie Robinson broke the color line in Major League Baseball in 1947, after Trudy swam the Channel no one dared legitimately question whether a woman should swim, or whether it was somehow "proper" anymore for a woman to be an athlete. Of course, that didn't mean that female athletes would find their way easily. Prejudice would prove to be a foe nearly as challenging as the Channel, and the ensuing journey was never an easy undertaking, yet year after year the cause of women's athletics and equality would make slow but steady progress.

Less than two years after Trudy swam the Channel, in the 1928 Olympics in Amsterdam, American women again dominated the swimming competition, but the rest of the world was rapidly catching up—by then Trudy's mastery of the American crawl had inspired imitators everywhere. Women also competed in track and field for the first time, participating in the 100-meter, 200-meter, and 400-meter runs, the high jump, discus, and 4-by-100-meter relay. There was no turning back. Over time, participation by women in the Olympics only increased, thereby providing an impetus for women to compete elsewhere, until today women can and do compete in every sport imaginable, from baseball to boxing, wrestling, and hockey. And while that undoubtedly would have happened without the efforts of Trudy Ederle, it would not have happened as quickly, nor as confidently, without her. And as a swimmer, she was, truly, extraordinary. She retained the women's record for fastest time across the Channel until 1950, when Florence Chadwick swam the distance in thirteen hours and twenty-three minutes.

And despite what happened in the years immediately following her crossing of the Channel, Trudy Ederle's own life did not end as a tragedy. After she recovered from her back injury she continued to live quietly, eventually sharing a home with two other women in Flushing, Queens, enjoying her nieces and nephews, spending much of her time teaching deaf children to swim, and continuing to swim herself. She made some money endorsing a swimming pool, patented an Ederle doll, and occasionally spoke about telling her story in a book, but she seemed satisfied to be just plain old Aunt Gertrude. She rarely gave interviews, preferred to stay out of the limelight—she'd had enough of that—and was still sensitive about her hearing around strangers, even though modern hearing aids made it possible for her to hear much better than when she was younger. Still, every few years someone would seek her out, and she would reluctantly agree to revisit the past for a while, perhaps even sing a bit of "Let Me Call You Sweetheart" or "Yes, We Have No Bananas," or the song called "Trudy" that was written about her shortly after she swam the Channel, which asked, "Tell me, Trudy, who is going to be the lucky one?" But she would always tell the reporters not to write a sob story, never mentioned being poisoned in 1925, and never complained about how others made more money off her achievement than she did, once saying, "I never cared about the commercial part. I was just a young girl."

She was not bitter about her fate but in many ways seemed glad to be forgotten. She was well aware of her role as a pioneer and followed women's swimming and other sports closely, secure in the knowledge that as a young woman—swimming the Channel because others didn't think she could, because they'd tried to stop her once before, to make her family and her country proud, and to get that red roadster—that she had done far, far more than swim the Channel. She knew that in all the girls sweating in a gym or doing laps on a track or swimming intervals in a pool, there was at least a bit of Trudy Ederle in each and every one.

Halfway across the Channel, when told to stop and get out of the water, she had asked, "What for?" Over the remainder of her life, before she passed away on November 20, 2003, at the age of ninety-eight, that question was answered each and every day in the achievements of every woman and girl who followed in her wake. One of the reasons Trudy was so quickly forgotten and overlooked is that the changes she inspired took such a strong hold and became so pervasive so quickly. Her achievement was so stunning, so profound, and so unexpected that the momentum of her accomplishment kept shattering stereotypes for decades. Trudy didn't need to be there for that to happen, at the front of the line, breaking down the doors herself time and time again, because she had already blown them away. All other women needed to do was force their way through the opening, to follow Trudy into the water or onto the track, and when told they should stop, ask "What for?" themselves.

In one of her final interviews, Trudy spoke of the feeling that came over her in the water, the feeling she first felt that day in the Highlands off the pier, the feeling that drew her to the Channel and drew her to the seas over and over again.

"Sometimes," she said, "after I've been swimming a few hours, I can feel myself lifting in the water as I come into stride . . . At that instant, when I bring myself on top of the water, the memories of what I did, and who I was, start coming back."

Trudy Ederle is still there today, in every woman and in every girl who has ever competed or who has ever wanted to, aiming toward a distant shore, testing herself, a young woman in the sea.

Afterword

When I began to research Trudy Ederle's life and her norm-shattering swim twenty years ago, my daughter was only about five years old. I wanted to write a book for her, and other young girls, so she would never have to wonder, like I did when I first encountered Trudy's name, who this woman was and why her accomplishments made such a difference in the lives of so many.

Young Woman and the Sea was published in the summer of 2009, the first full biography of Trudy Ederle in book form. Before that time, since she first conquered the English Channel, Trudy's story had only been told intermittently and incompletely, either in brief, almost encyclopedic profiles, or as a smaller part of larger stories about either the Roaring Twenties or the history of women's sports. Trudy, unfortunately, never told her own story, abandoning several attempts at an autobiography.

Similarly, just as Trudy had been overlooked, swimming the English Channel, once one of the great achievements in sports, was no longer newsworthy. Since Trudy became the sixth person and first woman to swim the Channel, her exploit had faded from the front pages. By the summer of 2009 fewer swimmers had duplicated her once-solitary triumph than the number of people who had climbed Mount Everest, most with little fanfare and even less adoration and respect. Even though Trudy's women's record lasted until 1950, when it was broken by Florence Chadwick, familiarity with swimming the Channel had stripped the feat of much of its cachet by then. To most people swimming the Channel was almost quaint, a once nearly impossible feat that over time had become, if not commonplace, almost conventional, an obscure stunt that appealed to only a very few.

How that has changed.

Today, due in some measure to the publication of *Young Woman and the Sea*, Trudy's story is much better known, the central subject of several subsequent books for adults and children. It has become part of a radio drama, at least one stage production, and, in truncated form, several documentaries. On YouTube one can find videos of schoolgirls reenacting her story for class projects. Teachers have added Trudy to the curriculum, and on March 8, International Women's Day, Trudy's face now lights up the internet. Moreover, it seems that *Young Woman and the Sea* has also played a part in something of a resurgence in Channel swimming itself. About as many solo crossings have been made since this book was first published as in all the years before. And while, through 2009, the majority of Channel swimmers were overwhelmingly male, since that time more and more women have chosen to test themselves in the waters of the Channel, and in recent years their annual number has nearly equaled that of men.

Since *Young Woman and the Sea* was first published, I have heard from a number of Channel swimmers—all women, interestingly enough—who have told me how important this book was in their pursuit of that distant shore. For many, Trudy's story provided both inspiration and, in a practical sense, helped demystify the process. Several have told me that they found the actual physical description of swimming the Channel as portrayed in this book to be uncannily accurate, akin to their own experience in the cold and choppy waters of the Channel. And these women don't just swim the Channel hoping to survive; they race across in times that would have amazed even Trudy. The fastest female swimmers now cross in less than eight hours, almost twice as fast as Trudy and within minutes of the existing men's record. Chloë McCardel has swum the Channel an incredible forty-four times, more than any person on the planet. And in 2019 Sarah Thomas, a breast cancer survivor, became the first person ever to swim across the Channel four times consecutively, nonstop, spending an astounding fifty-four hours in the water.

Of course one need not be a Channel swimmer, or even a swimmer at all, to take motivation from *Young Woman and the Sea*. Trudy provided irrefutable evidence that women could compete in all kinds of sports, blowing out of the water the now thoroughly discredited belief that women were too delicate for strenuous activities. Some people, mostly men, continued to adhere to that notion, but after

Trudy the logic of their arguments, well, simply didn't hold water. To some degree, every female athlete today is riding in Trudy's wake. The ripples from her achievement even extend beyond the realm of sports, providing inspiration to anyone, anywhere, who seeks to achieve something others say is impossible.

And now the visions of producer Jerry Bruckheimer, director Joachim Rønning, screenwriter Jeff Nathanson, actor Daisy Ridley, and others have translated Trudy's story onto the screen. As Disney+ streams the motion picture adaptation of *Young Women and the Sea* into homes and classrooms in every corner of the globe, the film version of this book will share Trudy's story with millions of viewers all over the world, for the universal lessons of her life transcend language and culture.

One of my favorite moments in the book is when Trudy, in mid-Channel, is admonished to get out of the water and give up. She famously responds, "What for?" I have a granddaughter now, and it is my hope that this book and this movie help provide an answer to that question, one that speaks not only to the present, but also to a future based in equity, equality, and opportunity for all, regardless of gender or any other division.

As Trudy Ederle proved most eloquently, barriers are not meant to be accepted, but to be crossed.

Glenn Stout
May 25, 2022

Acknowledgments

I would like to thank the following individuals and institutions for their assistance with this project: editor Susan Canavan, Elizabeth Lee, Beth Burleigh Fuller, Meg Hannah, Patrick Barry, and Brian Moore with Houghton Mifflin Harcourt Publishing, agent John Taylor Williams and Hope Denekamp of Kneerim and Williams at Fish Richardson, researcher Denise Bousquet, John Dorsey and Aaron Schmidt at the Boston Public Library, David Dewyea, Richard Johnson, Howard Bryant, Joe Farara, the New-York Historical Society, and the International Swimming Hall of Fame.

Notes and Sources

I first encountered the story of Trudy Ederle in 2000 while researching another project and finding myself distracted by accounts of her
attempt to swim the English Channel. Despite the fact that I have been
writing sports history for more than two decades and have written
about notable female athletes such as Eleanora Sears, Louise Stokes,
Mia Hamm, Tara Lipinski, and others, I was unfamiliar with Ederle
and somewhat mystified by the fact that she was so little known and
apparently had been forgotten so easily. In an era in which female athletes from Billie Jean King to Annika Sorenstam and Danica Patrick
have tested themselves against men, I found the fact that she had swum
the English Channel faster than any man absolutely fascinating, and I
filed a few clips away for future reference as I worked to complete other
projects. One year later I was further intrigued when I read a brief interview with Gertrude Ederle written by Elliott Denman in the *New
York Times* and was surprised to learn that Gertrude Ederle was still
alive. At this point I began to consider Ederle and her quest to swim the
Channel as a subject for a book—no one to date had ever taken on the
subject—but contractual commitments to other projects prevented me
from doing so at that time.

Shortly after Gertrude Ederle's death in 2003, as my other commitments came to an end, I began the research that has resulted in this
book. I spent much of the next three years accumulating every clipping
and article on Miss Ederle that I could find, not only in newspapers,
microfilm, and online, but in magazines and serial publications. Once
again, my background as a librarian was extremely helpful in ferreting
out the most remote sources.

The foundation for this book is the daily newspaper, most notably
the *New York Times, New York Herald-Tribune, New York Daily News,*
and *Chicago Tribune.* The *Tribune-News* syndicate financed Ederle's
second attempt to swim the Channel, and detailed accounts, nearly

identical to one another, appeared in both newspapers. Alec Rutherford's sober accounts in the *New York Times* were particularly helpful. Wire reports, which appeared in newspapers on both sides of the Atlantic, were also valuable, particularly those including reports by the Associated Press, United Press, and International News Service. Such accounts were gleaned from literally hundreds of different newspaper titles, many accessed through www.newsarchives.com, which contains no fewer than eight thousand references to either Gertrude or Trudy Ederle. Unless otherwise indicated, these clippings—which number more than six thousand separate stories and reports—served as my primary source material for the writing of *Young Woman and the Sea.*

Trudy Ederle belongs to another time, when newspaper and sports journalism were far different from what they are today, when the never-ending twenty-four-hour news cycle makes celebrities of athletes who have yet to accomplish much of anything. When Trudy Ederle was swimming competitively, from about 1920 through 1926, swimming, particularly women's swimming, was still something of a fringe sport. Most swim meets in which she participated were covered in cursory fashion, as newspapers rarely did more than list the results. Even as Trudy became one of the most accomplished swimmers in history, setting record after record, she was never really the subject of in-depth, personality-based profiles. The *New York Times*, for instance, despite publishing more than seven hundred articles that mention Trudy, published no more than a handful of stories that one might reasonably term a feature about her. Such portraits simply weren't done then. Even the few magazine stories written about her at the time were hardly comprehensive, and although she was the subject of numerous such stories later in her life, Ederle herself shied away from the spotlight. Shy by nature and made even more so by her hearing trouble, she rarely gave lengthy interviews and tended to tell the same few anecdotes over and over again. As a result most previous accounts of her career are little more than thumbnail reports, few of which provided much detailed information and many of which inadvertently repeat factual errors.

The task of any biographer is to create a three-dimensional, nuanced, and accurate portrait of a subject, and I have been fortunate that it was still possible to accomplish this through the close reading of so many disparate pieces of information. Trudy's story is told from the accumulation of data, from facts gleaned from an enormous variety of sources, including not only the thousands of newspaper and magazine stories discussed above, but the oral histories of fellow swimmers and residents of the Highlands, official Olympic reports, a wide variety of reference works available both in print and online, accounts of Channel swims by other swimmers, period swimming manuals, photographs, films, official weather reports, and other sources. It is for this reason that I chose not to provide detailed notes required by an academic study. In many instances, the information contained in a single sentence was gleaned from a half-dozen sources—detailed footnoting would not only be unwieldy but, I fear, prove to be confusing and to obscure as much as it revealed. Instead I have opted to create a brief bibliography of those sources that were most significant to this account, and provide a chapter-by-chapter discussion of those individual sources I found most valuable.

One cannot write about Trudy Ederle without confronting the water. Although I can swim, no one would mistake me for anything but a novice. Although I had hoped to add to this skill set during the writing of this book, several minor health issues prevented me from doing so. Yet the water still managed to inform this process. I am fortunate enough to live on Lake Champlain in northern Vermont, a body of water more than 120 miles in length and, at its widest point, 11 miles wide. To assist me with this book—and for my own enjoyment—over the last two years I have spent hours and hours on Lake Champlain, traveling several hundred miles by kayak in a wide variety of weather conditions to gain some insight into the challenge and conditions Trudy Ederle faced when she attempted to swim the Channel. I have made trips as long as fifteen miles that have lasted half a day or more, both in calm water and in storms that caused waves and swells of several feet, in water temperatures ranging from the upper middle forties to the low seventies, in the sun, the rain, and the fog, against and with winds of upward of fifteen knots—Beaufort force four—at dawn and dusk, at night, and in other conditions that sometimes skirted the edge of common sense and more than tested my own abilities and endurance. When one is already exhausted and alone several miles from shore in deteriorating weather and solely dependent on one's own physical effort to make it to shore, one becomes acutely aware of the challenges and dangers posed by the water.

And while I am not much of a swimmer, I still managed to spend as much time as possible in the water itself, including one chilled hour paddling about in the shallows in water of only sixty degrees. As a longtime runner I also have some experience with the solitude of athletic competition. Although all these experiences do not compare with those Trudy Ederle faced in the English Channel, they still provided me with some valuable insight into not only the physical challenge of her quest, but the mental and psychological challenges as well. These experiences were invaluable in the writing of this book.

Formal interviews played little role in this volume. All of Trudy Ederle's contemporaries are deceased, as are her siblings, although she was survived by nieces, nephews, and other relatives who helped take care of her in her final years. At the beginning of this project I contacted her nephew, informed him about this project, and inquired as to whether he or anyone else in the family would either care to share any material they might have in their possession or agree to interviews. He indicated that the family intended to pursue its own project and declined to become involved in mine. That was certainly the family's right and I respected that decision. In the end, in fact, it was probably best that this project proceeded independently, unfettered by the constraints that families sometimes impose upon a subject. Over two decades of writing sports history I have found that families are rarely the best resource in regard to a subject. Their judgment is too often clouded by sentiment and compromised by personal relationships with the subject. Family myths, passed down generation by generation, often get in the way of the truth and are can sometimes be at odds with objective reporting.

I was able to locate a substantial amount of newsreel footage of Trudy Ederle both in training and swimming the Channel in both 1925 and 1926, as well as motion pictures that detailed her reception in New York, much of it produced by the British Pathe film company. While the narration and/or captioning of such newsreels was often incorrect, and the film itself sometimes misleading (despite what the newsreels infer, there is no film of Trudy arriving at Kingsdown—it is a re-creation made during daylight the following afternoon), often combining footage of both swims into a single account, they were nevertheless quite useful for the details the images revealed. British Pathe films consulted include *Girl Conquers the Channel* (1926), *"Trudy's" Welcome Home* (1926), *For Channel Swim* (1925), and *"Trudie" Turns Teacher* (nd). Bud Greenspan's *The Barrier Breakers* includes not only much of the same newsreel footage, but footage of Trudy Ederle in her later years and interviews with Ederle's niece and nephew. Unfortunately no copies are known to exist of the silent film *Swim, Girl, Swim* in which Trudy appeared with Bebe Daniels, playing a swimmer. Although minor health issues prevented me from traveling to the English Channel, I was fortunate to survey hundreds, if not thousands, of photographs not only of Trudy Ederle and other principals in this book, but also of the settings in which her story took place. These sources include Corbis, Getty, Brown Brothers, the Library of Congress, the Boston Public Library, the *New York Times*, the Associated Press, the New-York Historical Society, Topfoto, and photographs that have been preserved in newspapers both in microfilm and online. No physical description of any person or place in this book has been made that was not informed by facts.

Similarly, all dialogue used in this book is taken directly from a previously published source. Anything that appears in quotation marks is from a written document. No dialogue has been created, although in a few instances in which different sources reproduced dialogue about a specific event or occurrence that was not identical, I have used my own judgment or created a composite statement.

The greatest challenge of this undertaking was to animate my subject, to give her life and reveal her personality, a task that is never easy in any instance, but one that is particularly difficult when the events took place so long ago. For this reason I have chosen to refer to her as "Trudy" throughout this book rather than her given name "Gertrude." Although she herself used "Gertrude" throughout her adult life, as a girl and young woman her family and friends, by all accounts, referred to her as "Trudy," and I have chosen to do the same. Again, I have used the accumulation of detail in an attempt to provide genuine insight into her experience in swimming the Channel. But all impressions, events, and experiences I assign to her during her time in the water are factually based on statements later made by Trudy Ederle herself or by others.

SELECTED BOOKS

Cleveland, Marcia. *Dover Solo: Swimming the English Channel.* Canada: MMJ Press, 1999.
An account of the preparations necessary to swim the Channel today.

Cox, Lynne. *Swimming to Antarctica.* New York: Knopf, 2004.
The most accomplished open-water swimmer of the modern age, Cox's acute observations about long-distance swimming and her colorful accounts of her various swims, including her swim of the Channel, should be required reading for anyone contemplating swimming the Channel or writing about it.

Danzig, Alison, and Peter Brandwein, eds. *Sport's Golden Age: A Close-up of the Fabulous Twenties.* New York: Harper and Brothers, 1948.
Louis de Breda Handley authored the chapter on American swimming.

Dawson, Buck. *Mermaids on Parade: America's Love Affair with Its First Olympic Women Swimmers.* Huntington, NY: Kroshka Books, 2000.
Dawson, the executive director of the International Swimming Hall of Fame, profiled more than thirty women swimmers, including Trudy Ederle and other Women's Swimming Association stars such as Aileen Riggin, Ethelda "Thelda" Bleibtrey, Helen Wainwright, and others. His 1994 interview with Ederle is the most thorough ever published. Although Dawson incorrectly states that it was her first interview in more than fifty years, it was certainly her most revealing. She had politely turned down interview requests for years before Dawson surprised her the day after her eighty-eighth birthday and spoke with her for two hours.
Ederle was surprisingly frank. In addition to her remarks about herself, she offered that she did not believe that many who claim to swim the Channel actually accomplish the feat. She stated bluntly that Louis de Breda Handley told her that "the next one," Mille Gade Corson, "didn't do it honestly."

Gipe, George. *The Great American Sports Book.* New York: Doubleday and Company, 1978.
Contains a surprisingly accurate account of her swim and a valuable overview and background on the development of women's athletics.

Handley, Louis de Breda. *Swimming for Women.* New York: American Sports Publishing Company, 1925.
Handley was widely considered the greatest swimming teacher and coach of the era. This book was endorsed by the Women's Swimming Association and includes valuable background on the organization.

Johnson, Captain Tim. *History of Open Water Marathon Swimming.* Buzzard's Bay, MA: Captain's Engineering Services, 2005.
An overview of the history of swimming, focusing on long-distance swims in open water.

Johnston, Charles H. L. *Famous American Athletes of Today.* Essay Index Reprint Series. Freeport, NY: Books for Libraries Press, 1971.
A reprint of a book first published in 1928, it includes a lengthy, if somewhat overwrought, profile of Ederle's career.

Mortimer, Gavin. *The Great Swim.* New York: Walker and Company, 2008.
Although I was initially distressed to learn that another author was writing about

Trudy, Mortimer's thorough account focuses not on Trudy Ederle alone, but on the events of the summer of 1926, when more than a dozen swimmers were planning to swim the Channel. Although I disagree with his thesis, which I believe much overstates the competition between the four swimmers he chooses to focus upon, it is nonetheless a worthy addition to the literature of the sport.

O'Donnell, Edward T. *Ship Ablaze*. New York: Broadway Books, 2003.
    A superb account of the Slocum *disaster.*

Unwin, Peter. *The Narrow Sea*. London: Review, 2003.
    A thorough survey history of the English Channel.

Watson, Kathy. *The Crossing*. New York: Jeremy P. Tarcher/Putnam, 2000.
    A fine biography of Matthew Webb, the first person to swim the English Channel.

Wennerberg, Conrad. *Wind, Waves, and Sunburn: A Brief History of Marathon Swimming*. New York: Breakaway Books, 1974.
    Contains a lengthy chapter on swimming the Channel.

Whelan, Grover. *Mr. New York*. New York: G. P. Putnam's Sons, 1955.
    Whelan provides a detailed account of Ederle's reception in New York.

NOTES

Prologue

My account of Trudy's time in the water during her successful swim is gleaned from a number of sources, but the extensive interview she gave to Buck Dawson of the International Swimming Hall of Fame, which appeared in his book *Mermaids on Parade*, was among the most valuable, as were the accounts of her swim by her ghostwriter, Julia Harpman, for the *Tribune-News* syndicate, Alec Rutherford's reporting for the *New York Times*, and wire reports. As previously stated, all impressions, events, and experiences I assign to her during her time in the water are based on facts and on statements later made by Trudy Ederle herself or by others. Background on the history of Channel swimmers was provided by three Web sites: www .channelswimmingassociation.com, the governing body overseeing Channel swims today; www.channelswimming.net, the site of the Channel Swimming and Piloting Federation; and www.doversolo.com, Marcia Cleveland's Web site promoting her book of the same name.

1. Overboard

The role that the sinking of the *General Slocum* played in the dissemination of swimming, particularly in regard to women, was inspired by an online exhibit maintained by the International Swimming Hall of Fame (ISHOF). Edward T. O'Donnell's account of the disaster, cited above, was invaluable. Anna Weber's story was one of many first-person accounts made by survivors of the disaster and appears on www .garemaritime.com/features/general-slocum/. Sadly, her tragic experience was typical. The online exhibit at the International Swimming Hall of Fame, From Bloomer's to Bikini's: How the Sport of Swimming Changed Western Culture in the 20th Century (www.ishof.org/pdf/history_swimwear.pdf), first alerted me to the connection between women's swimming and the *Slocum* disaster.

2. The Challenge
I found no single comprehensive history of swimming to be entirely satisfying, but the online resources of the International Swimming Hall of Fame were useful, as was ISHOF's "The Development of the Modern Stroke," as reprinted by the *Washington Post* online during the 2004 Olympics (nd). See also Charles Sprawson's *The Swimmer as Hero* and Johnson's *History of Open Water Marathon Swimming*. Unwin's *The Narrow Sea* provides a comprehensive history of human interaction with the English Channel.

3. Highlands
Background and history of the Ederle family was acquired through *New York Passenger List* records, *Petition for Naturalization Records, World War I Draft Registration Cards, Social Security Death Index,* and *U.S. Census Records* for both 1910 and 1920. Background on the Highlands came from a variety of standard reference sources. Flora T. Higgins's *Remembering the 20th Century: An Oral History of Monmouth County*, Interview with Mae Schwind Bahrs (Monmouth County Library, Monmouth, NJ, 2002), and "Still Making Splash" (*Star-Ledger*, October 3, 2003) were particularly useful to provide detailed background.

4. The Painter
George Catlin's *Letters and Notes on the Manners, Customs, and Conditions of North American Indians*, Vol. I and II (Willis P. Hazard, Philadelphia, 1857), first published in London in 1844, was invaluable, as was the online biography of Catlin maintained by the National Gallery of Art that appears at www.ibiblio.org/nga/catlin.html. Profiles of John Trudgen and other swimming pioneers can be found on the Web site of the International Swimming Hall of Fame.

5. The Women's Swimming Association
The pioneering role of the WSA in women's athletics is unquestioned and well documented. Of particular use was "The Cradle of American Champions, Women Champions . . . Swim Champions: Charlotte Epstein, Gender, and Jewish Identity and the Physical Emancipation of Women in Aquatic Sports" by Linda Borish (*International Journal of the History of Sport* 21, no. 2, March 2004, 197–235), and *The Women's Swimming Association of New York: The Golden Years 1920–1940* by Harold Lerch and Paula Welch, Educational Resources Informational Center, ERIC #: ED174591.

Oral histories of several swimmers (see chapter 16) and profiles from Dawson's *Mermaids on Parade* were also of great help in charting the course of the WSA and the role of Charlotte Epstein, as was Handley's *Swimming for Women*. See also "An Olympian's Oral History: Aileen Riggin," an interview by Dr. Margaret Costa (Los Angeles: Amateur Athletic Foundation of Los Angeles, 2000), and Kari Lydeson's "An Olympic Life" from *Swimming World and Junior Swimmer* (April 2000).

6. The Crossing
Kathy Watson's *The Crossing* is the most thorough published account of Matthew Webb's life.

7. The Teacher
For background on Handley, see Cecil Colwin's article "The Gentleman Jim of Swimming," which appeared in *Swim Canada* 22, no. 7 (1995): 16–19. Handley's own

work provides the best description of the development of the American crawl and his teaching methods, as do interviews with Ederle and Aileen Riggin.

8. The Channel
Sanjeev Gupta and Jenny Collier at the Imperial College, London, were the first to prove definitively that the Channel was created by two megafloods; their work appears in *Nature* 448 (2007): 342. See also *New Scientist* 195.2613 (July 21, 2007): 11. John McPhee's article "Season on the Chalk" in *The New Yorker* (March 12, 2007) includes a description of the creation of the chalk beds that underlie the Channel. The best information available on the impact of the tides on a Channel swimmer can be found at www.chan nelswimmingassociation.com. For a clear and concise discussion of the creation of the island of Britain, see www.nhm.ac.uk/discover/the-making-of-an-island.html.

9. The Best Girl
The description of the Day Cup swim is based on newspaper reports from the *New York Times, Herald-Tribune*, and others. Trudy's achievement was carried by the Associated Press and widely reported all over the country, the first time she came to the attention of the general public. For the next four years she was easily the most famous woman in America.

10. The Next Man
Somewhat surprisingly, the stories of Jabez Wolffe and Bill Burgess have only been told in pieces. Newspaper accounts were most valuable, in particular "The Forgotten Man of the Channel" from the *Sheffield Star* (1961), "Man Has Flown the English Channel, But Can He Swim It?" which appeared in the *Chicago Tribune* (September 5, 1909), and "Other Channel Swimmers," from the *New York Times* (August 15, 1926). The number of times each man attempted to swim the Channel varies widely according to the source. Suffice to say that each man likely made more attempts than any other swimmer before succeeding, and Wolffe surely holds the record for the most attempts without success.

11. Goals
Marguerite Mooers Marshall's profile of Trudy Ederle not only appeared in the *New York World Telegram* and *Herald-Tribune* but was widely reprinted all over the country in late August and September 1922.

12. Rivals
Accounts of aspiring Channel swimmers and their attempts appeared regularly in American and European newspapers in the years after World War I. See also Wennerberg's *Wind, Waves, and Sunburn* and Johnson's *History of Open Water Marathon Swimming.*

13. Records
Hardly a week passed from the fall of 1922 through 1923 without an account appearing in a newspaper somewhere of Trudy Ederle swimming, and often setting a new record.

14. Girl in the Water
Annette Kellerman's life and career is well documented, most notably in Emily Gibson and Barbara Firths's *The Original Million Dollar Mermaid* (East Melbourne, New

South Wales, Australia: Allen and Unwin, 2006) and Annette Kellerman's own unpublished biography, *My Story*, portions of which appear on www.annettekellerman.com.

15. Trials
Primarily newspaper accounts, as previously cited above. See also Weissmuller's own book, *Swimming the American Crawl* (Boston: Houghton Mifflin, 1930), in which he discusses Ederle.

16. Agony
Trudy Ederle expressed her reaction to her performance in the Olympics in Dawson's *Mermaids on Parade* and also spoke of her problem with cramps due to transportation issues. Her larger Olympic experience and the experience of the women's swim team were derived primarily from the following sources:

American Olympic Committee. *Report on the VII Olympic Games, Paris, France, 1924*. New York: American Olympic Committee, 1924.
    Louis de Breda Handley's report on the women's swimming team was particularly useful.
"American Youth Vindicated at Colombe," *Literary Digest* (August 9, 1924).
Costa, Margaret, interviewer. "An Olympian's Oral History: Aileen Riggin." Amateur Athletic Foundation of Los Angeles, 2000. Available at www.la84foundation.org.
DeFrantz, Anita, interviewer. "An Olympian's Oral History: Claritta Hunsberger Heher." *Amateur Athletic Foundation of Los Angeles*, July 1987. Available at www.la84foundation.org.
Dyreson, Mark L. "Scripting the American Olympic Story-Telling Formula: The 1924 Paris Olympics and the American Media." *Olympika* 5 (1996): 45–80.
Hodak, George A., interviewer. "An Olympian's Oral History: Doris O'Mara Murphy." *Amateur Athletic Foundation of Los Angeles*, July 1987. Available at www.la84foundation.org.
———. "An Olympian's Oral History: Samuel Clarence Hauser." *Amateur Athletic Foundation of Los Angeles*, 1988. Available at www.la84foundation.org.
———. "An Olympian's Oral History: William Neufeld." *Amateur Athletic Foundation of Los Angeles*, 1988. Available at www.la84foundation.org.
Mitchell, Sheila. "Women's Participation in the Olympic Games 1900–1926." *Journal of Sport History* 4, no.2 (1977): 208–28.
Strayer, Martha. "Warsaw Woman Was 1924 Olympics Star." Available at www.yesteryear.clunette.com/olympic.html.

17. Comeback
Ederle mentions in many, many different accounts the role her sister Margaret played in her Sandy Hook swim, in her decision to swim the Channel, and in her swimming career, but the most complete retelling of the scene that led her to swim the Channel appears in Dawson's *Mermaids on Parade*.

18. Wolffe
Unlike for her 1926 attempt, Trudy Ederle was not ghostwriting accounts of her swim for a syndicate in 1925. However, due to her fame as a swimming champion, her summer at the Channel received more press coverage than that of any previous

Channel aspirant. The Associated Press provided regular accounts as did the British swimming expert Alec Rutherford in the *New York Times*. Many of these accounts focused on the problems between Ederle and Jabez Wolffe.

19. Touched

My account of Trudy's first attempt to swim the Channel is gleaned primarily from a wide variety of newspaper reports and newsreel films that document portions of her preparation and the swim itself, as well as still photographs from the same day. Trudy's story remained consistent throughout her adult life—she felt that if she had not been touched she could have continued her swim and possibly succeeded.

20. Poison

In an interview with the student newspaper of Harvard University, the *Harvard Crimson*, on October 24, 1926, Trudy Ederle told a reporter:

> I am sure that Harvard will just trample on Princeton and the other football teams after beating Dartmouth . . . You know I won a bet from Helen Wainwright on the Dartmouth game. I felt that Harvard was bound to win, just because it wasn't the newspaper favorite.
>
> The members of the team must have felt the same way I did when I was going to swim the channel. No one thought I had a chance of getting across. The newspapers were all sympathetic, but skeptical just the same. It made me awfully determined to succeed.
>
> The first attempt I made, I nearly went to sleep in the water. Some one had put drugs in the beef tea I drank before starting. My trainer proved this beyond any doubt. Well, before my second attempt, all my food was prepared by my sister. I was more confident than ever of making the swim, though no one else thought I would.

The story appeared the next day and was then picked up by the Associated Press and reprinted in newspapers throughout the country.

Although Ederle had never publicly mentioned the poisoning incident before or after, intimations that something was amiss during the swim—by Trudy, Elsie Viets, and Charlotte Epstein—give credence to the notion, as does the WSA's attempt to muzzle Trudy on her return. By 1926, when she did speak of it, the focus was not on her failure of the year before but her recent success. The story quickly disappeared, and in subsequent years no interviewer knew enough to ask Ederle to provide more details concerning her suspicions. The "trainer" she refers to is probably Burgess.

21. Cape Gris-Nez

The presence of both Julia Harpman and her husband, Westbrook Pegler, on the trip across the Atlantic and during Trudy's time training in Cape Gris-Nez was extremely helpful. Harpman was a precise reporter, and Pegler's observations are acute, particularly in regard to the hotel and the cast of characters assembled there. Harpman's work, both under Trudy's byline and her own, appeared in both the *Chicago Tribune* and the *New York Daily News*. Pegler's work appeared only in the *Tribune*. The Meteorological Office daily weather report for southeast England on August 6, 1926, was provided by the Meteorological Office, National Meteorological Archive, the British Weather Service.

22. What For?

The specific story of Trudy's crossing is created from her own statements both at the time and in later interviews, the stories of Julia Harpman, and accounts by other observers, including Alec Rutherford, Minott Saunders, Sydney Williams, and other wire service reporters. In some instances these reports are conflicting—only Harpman was aboard Trudy's vessel and had access to her—and I have tended to give her reports a bit more credence, all the while keeping in mind that they were ghostwritten and designed to present Trudy Ederle in the best possible light. Plotting her specific route across the Channel proved to be a particular challenge, as various bulletins and reports do not always coincide with one another, various observers were themselves not always well versed in the language of the sea, and many were seasick at the time.

Contemporary reports time Trudy's crossing as fourteen hours and thirty-one minutes. Subsequently, and for no reason I could determine, her "official" time as maintained by the Channel Swimming Association has since been adjusted to fourteen hours thirty-nine minutes. I have chosen to use the earlier figure throughout.

23. Kingsdown

Although newsreel footage and photographs exist that purport to show Trudy reaching the beach at Kingsdown, no such documentations exists—most assuredly, Trudy Ederle reached shore at night.

24. Shore

Julia Harpman's reporting about the events of the first few days following Trudy's success and her return to America aboard the *Berengaria* were invaluable. The impromptu press conference at the hotel the morning after Trudy reached Kingsdown exists in the film *Girl Conquers the Channel*, as does her return to the water later that afternoon.

25. Swept Away

Whelan's biography, *Mr. New York*, cited above, provides a detailed, inside account of her reception in New York, supplementing the already detailed coverage that appeared in New York newspapers at the time.

Although Trudy shied away from the spotlight in her later years, she still gave the occasional interview or was the subject of a feature profile. The most valuable of these, as well as other notable articles that were particularly useful, are listed below:

Anderson, Kelli. "Young Woman and the Sea." *Sports Illustrated*, November 29, 1999.

Benjamin, Philip. "Then and Now," *New York Times Magazine*, August 6, 1961.

"Channel Swimmer Is 42 and Plump Now." *Winnipeg Free Press*, August 4, 1940.

"Channel Swimmer Outdid Men and Won Hearts." *International Herald Tribune*, December 2, 2003.

"Cohn-ing Tower." *Oakland Tribune*, May 12, 1940.

Cooper, Cynthia L. "Laughing with the First Woman to Swim the Channel." *Women's eNews*, December 5, 2003. Available at www.womensenews.org/article.cfm/dyn /aid/1628/context/ourdailylives%3E.

Deford, Frank. "America's Best Girl." *Sports Illustrated*, December 3, 2003. Available at http://sportsillustrated.cnn.com/2003/writers/frank_deford/12/03/viewpoint/index.html.

Denman, Elliot. "Gertrude Ederle, Pioneer Swimmer, Looks Back at Her Unforgettable Feat." *New York Times*, April 30, 2001.

Ederle, Gertrude. "The Swim of My Life." *Lenten Guideposts*, March 18, 1960.

"Ederle Celebrates Anniversary of Swim." *CNN/SI*, August 3, 2001. Available at http://sportsillustrated.cnn.com/more/news/2001/08/03/ederle_anniversary_ap/.

"Ederle Fan Meets Heroine." *New York Times*, August 4, 1976.

"Ederle, Now Near Deafness, Says It Wasn't Worthwhile." Associated Press, July 29, 1930.

"Ederle Swam the Long Course." *Investor's Business Daily*, September 22, 2003.

"Gertrude Ederle Dedicates Ederle Park." *New York Times*, August 15, 1975.

"Golden People: Gertrude Ederle." *Washington Post*, January 26, 1964.

"Greased Lightening." *Guardian*, October 16, 2006.

"Hard Moments for the Frailer Sex." *Independent*, January 8, 1927.

"How a Girl Beat Leander at the Hero Game." *Literary Digest*, August 21, 1926.

Kornheiser, Tony. "Gertrude Ederle Has Channeled Her Life toward Helping Others." *Chicago Tribune*, May 4, 1976.

Markey, Morris. "Presto! Fame!" *The New Yorker*, September 4, 1926.

"Miss Ederle Upsets Male Supremacy." *Chicago Tribune*, September 1, 1925.

Reddy, John. "The Girls Who Swam the Channel." *Reader's Digest*, September, 1958.

"The Roar of the Crowd." *New York Daily News*, March 24, 2000.

"She Was the Wave of the Future." *Bergen Record*, January 25, 2000.

Smith, Red. "Trudy Relives Channel Swim." *New York Herald-Tribune*, November 14, 1958.

"Swim It or Drown: Gertrude of America." *New York Daily News*, April 26, 1998.

Talese, Gay. "Memories Are Still Golden for Gertrude Ederle." *New York Times*, August 6, 1958.

"Trudy Ederle, First Girl to Swim Channel." Associated Press, September 7, 1958.

"Trudy Has Swum a Sea of Troubles." *Washington Post*, October 1, 1966.

"Trudy Remains Strong Swimming Fan." Associated Press, September 11, 1958.

Trumbull, Walter. "Queen of the Waters." *St. Nicholas* 53 (October 1926).

"Valiant Trudy Teaches Deaf to Swim." Associated Press, July 8, 1958.

Index